The Raft of Odysseus

# The Raft of Odysseus

The Ethnographic Imagination of Homer's *Odyssey*

CAROL DOUGHERTY

OXFORD

UNIVERSITY PRESS

2001

# OXFORD
UNIVERSITY PRESS

Oxford   New York
Athens   Auckland   Bangkok   Bogotá   Buenos Aires   Calcutta
Cape Town   Chennai   Dar es Salaam   Delhi   Florence   Hong Kong   Istanbul
Karachi   Kuala Lumpur   Madrid   Melbourne   Mexico City   Mumbai
Nairobi   Paris   São Paulo   Shanghai   Singapore   Taipei   Tokyo   Toronto   Warsaw

and associated companies in
Berlin   Ibadan

Library of Congress Cataloging-in-Publication Data
Dougherty, Carol.
The raft of Odysseus : the ethnographic imagination of Homer's Odyssey /
Carol Dougherty.
  p.   cm.
Includes bibliographical references and index.
ISBN 0-19-513036-7
1. Homer. Odyssey.   2. Homer—Knowledge—Ethnology.   3. Homer—
Knowledge—Geography.   4. Epic poetry, Greek—History and criticism.
5. Odysseus (Greek mythology) in literature.   6. Trojan War—
Literature and the war.   7. Geography, Ancient, in literature.   8. Ethnic groups in literature.
9. Ocean travel in literature.   10. Ethnology in literature.   11. Commerce in literature.
I. Title.
PA4167 .D68   2001
883'.01—dc21       00-039207

9 8 7 6 5 4 3 2 1

Printed in the United States of America
on acid-free paper

*For my family,*

Joel, Nathan, *and* Megan

# Acknowledgments

Although it has not taken me as long to finish this book as it did Odysseus to get back home again, it has been a lengthy journey, and I would like to thank the people who helped me avoid the many distractions and pitfalls involved in writing a book. Above all, I owe a huge debt of gratitude to my friend and collaborator Leslie Kurke, for all her support, both intellectual, bibliographical, and moral. As always, Leslie knew which sentences I had left out and, most important, when the book was done.

The book got its start as papers given at the Center for Literary and Cultural Studies at Harvard and to the Classics Department at Boston College, and I thank Gregory Nagy and Ken Rothwell for giving me the opportunity to launch a new project in such hospitable company. I am grateful to Greg as well for encouraging me to stick with the book in those early days when I was having my doubts. Thanks, too, go to Richard Martin and Helene Foley for their support at the early stages of the project and for their comments and suggestions at the eleventh hour. Karen Bassi, as always, provided invaluable encouragement throughout the entire process, and Carla Antonaccio was a great help in sorting out matters of archeological details.

Part of this book was written during my stay as Visiting Fellow at Clare Hall, Cambridge University, and I owe a special debt of thanks to Paul Cartledge for helping arrange my visit. Clare Hall proved to be a particularly productive place to work, and members of the Classics and History faculties at Cambridge, especially Paul Cartledge, Patricia Easterling, Simon Goldhill, and Anthony Snodgrass, provided a very stimulating and collegial environment. In particular, Paul Cartledge and Anthony Snodgrass helped me think through some of the historical and archeological arguments of the book. In addition, I owe thanks to Oliver Taplin for inviting me to speak at Oxford University, as well as to those in attendance for their comments and suggestions about the relationship between ships and song.

Thanks, too, go to those colleagues at Wellesley College who have listened to me talk about this project over the years and who have read parts of the book in manuscript form, especially Roxanne Euben, Alison McIntyre, Brendon Reay, and Marilyn Sides. Caroline Bicks was helpful on Shakespearean bibliography, and as always, I thank Pat Bois, without whom nothing would get done in the Classical Studies Department. I would also like to acknowledge Elizabeth Chapman, who helped me track down some of the illustrations that appear here. Work on this book was supported both by Wellesley College's generous academic leave policy and by a stipend from the American Council of Learned Societies. The editors at Oxford University Press, Susan Chang and Elissa Morris, have been tremendously helpful and supportive over the course of the project. Thanks, too, to the press's anonymous readers.

Finally, I dedicate this book to my family—to my husband, Joel Krieger, whose like-minded partnership has sustained me on this journey, as always. And to my two children, Nathan and Megan, whose recent arrival gave new meaning to the sense of a deadline. They both have turned my own world upside down.

A few words about abbreviations, translations, and transliterations. Abbreviations for ancient works follow the *Oxford Classical Dictionary* (3rd ed.). All the translations that appear here are my own. They aim more for clarity and an accurate portrayal of the Greek than for elegance and style. Again, in the interests of clarity, I have used the conventional and more familiar latinized transliteration of names (Achilles, not Akhilleos) rather than a literal transliteration of the Greek spelling.

*Jamaica Plain, Massachusetts*                                    C. D.
*April 2000*

# Contents

The Raft of Odysseus

# Introduction: The Ethnographic Imagination of Homer's *Odyssey*

## Travel and Knowledge

ὡς δ᾽ ὅτ᾽ ἂν ἀίξῃ νόος ἀνέρος, ὅς τ᾽ ἐπὶ πολλὴν
γαῖαν ἐληλουθὼς φρεσὶ πευκαλίμῃσι νοήσῃ,
"ἔνθ᾽ εἴην, ἢ ἔνθα," μενοινήῃσί τε πολλά,
ὣς κραιπνῶς μεμαυῖα διέπτατο πότνια Ἥρη·

As when the mind leaps, the mind of a man who has traveled across much territory and thinks with shrewd intelligence, "If only I were there or there" and wishes many things, so quickly did the eager Hera, a goddess, fly.

*Iliad,* Book 15

The Greeks have always been fascinated with travel and its connection to knowledge or wisdom. The figure of Solon, the sixth-century B.C.E. Athenian lawgiver and one of the Seven Sages, typifies this association for the early historical period. According to Herodotus, Solon traveled widely after establishing his new set of laws in Athens, in part for the purpose of sightseeing (*theoria*) and in part to avoid having to repeal any of the laws he had laid down. As Herodotus tells it, during these travels he comes to visit the Lydian dynast Croesus, who captures the importance of Solon's travel in his opening address to the sage:

Ξεῖνε Ἀθηναῖε, παρ᾽ ἡμέας γὰρ περὶ σέο λόγος ἀπῖκται πολλὸς καὶ σοφίης εἵνεκεν τῆς σῆς καὶ πλάνης, ὡς φιλοσοφέων γῆν πολλὴν θεωρίης εἵνεκεν ἐπελήλυθας·

Athenian guest-friend, a great deal of news about you has arrived in our court, both about your wisdom and about your travels—how you have come as a philosopher (φιλοσοφέων) across a great deal of land for the sake of sightseeing. (Hdt. 1.30.2)

3

The word order in this passage underscores the important connection between Solon's travels and his role as sage. First, Herodotus links Solon's wisdom (σοφίης) to his travels (πλάνης): both have been the subject of much talk about Solon. But, even more interesting, in the passage that glosses this intersection of wisdom and travel, Croesus again connects Solon's activities as philosopher to his mobility. The words for a great deal of land (γῆν πολλὴν) occupy a middle position between the verbal activity of philosophizing (φιλοσοφέων) and that of movement or travel (ἐπελήλυθας). Grammatically they could function as the direct object of either—or both. In addition, in this passage we find one of the earliest uses of the term *theoria*, from which we derive our words "theory" and "theorize." In its use here, *theoria* designates the process of traveling to see something, to sightsee, but we can see how its later meaning of "speculate" or "think about" evolves through this connection between the processes of traveling and looking and that of intellectual effort. To quote James Clifford, a contemporary cultural critic, "Theory is a product of displacement, comparison, a certain distance. To theorize, one leaves home."[1]

Later, in Book 3 of the *Histories*, Herodotus implies that there are three reasons to travel: commerce, war, and sightseeing. This definition sends us back to the Homeric hero Odysseus, who serves as the prototype of the traveler-observer figure, like Solon, which becomes so important to Greek thought.[2] Odysseus' travels are prompted by his role in the Trojan War, and as we will see, he engages in commercial transactions around the world. But, most important, as the opening lines of the *Odyssey* tell us, the poem's hero is "a man who has traveled a great deal; he has seen the cities of men and learned their minds."[3] The myth of Odysseus, the timeless story of one man's travel and return, is one that continues to spark the imagination, to incite wanderlust, and to prompt exploration. We still use the word "odyssey" to capture the exotic or protracted nature of a trip, and the name Odysseus continues to conjure up images of discovery and adventure. Not just in personal terms but on a broader level as well, the myth of Odysseus remains productive for what we might call cultural self-exploration. His story, or the story of his travels, helps to conceptualize a culture's experience with travel and new worlds. In the book that follows, I have set out to explore the ways in which the Homeric Odysseus comes to represent this nexus of travel and knowledge so central not just to the world of ancient Greece but to many other cultures as well.[4] Part of what explains the continued cultural relevance of the Odysseus story is both its association of travel with knowledge and the role that travel plays in generating responses to innovation and transformation. One way to address change at home is to displace it—to say that it comes from far away ("To theorize, one leaves home").

Many modern cultural critics have fastened onto the notion of travel as intricately linked with the production and circulation of knowledge. "Travel," according to Clifford, "denotes a range of material, spatial practices that produce knowledges, stories, traditions, comportments, musics, books, diaries, and other cultural expressions."[5] In particular, spatial and travel metaphors are especially useful for describing and negotiating periods of transformation and transition both personal and cultural.[6] On the personal level, we talk of death as a "passing," life as a "journey," initiations as "rites of passage," and in discussions of societal or cultural breaks or moments of transition, this same imagery appears as well. Fredric Jameson argues that in the postmodern age, new ways are needed to grasp our social structures and processes, and "mapping" provides a useful theoretical framework: "A model of political culture appropriate to our own situation will necessarily have to raise spatial issues as its fundamental organizing concern. I will therefore provisionally define the aesthetic of such new (and hypothetical) cultural form as an aesthetic of cognitive mapping."[7] I would argue that the cultural, political, and economic changes that beset the archaic period in Greece (eighth to sixth centuries B.C.E.)—a time that saw increased population, the transformation of major economic institutions, overseas expansion, and the development of the polis—were as threatening, as destabilizing, and as truly revolutionary as those that mark the postmodern world.

In particular, the eighth century B.C.E. was a time of remarkable movement for the Greeks.[8] Technological innovations in shipping produced faster, safer ships that could carry more cargo, and as a result, Greeks were sailing from one end of the Mediterranean to the other, transporting people, goods, and information with increased speed and reliability.[9] Commercial contacts with the east were thriving, and colonial prospects drew many Greeks westward as well. At the same time that some Greeks were traveling widely and exploring the possibilities of new worlds abroad, however, some argue that within the old Greek world at home, there was a contrasting trend toward localism—a clearer definition of land boundaries, a decline in the mobility of settlements, and an overall contracting sense of place.[10] The disjunction between the expansive experience of trans-Mediterranean travel and the contraction of life at home in Greece produced what Ian Morris (invoking the human geographer David Harvey) calls "space-time compression," that is, "processes that so revolutionize the objective qualities of space and time that we are forced to alter, sometimes in quite radical ways, how we represent the world to ourselves."[11] These changes can be both exciting and destabilizing; either way, they generate a diversity of political, social, and cultural responses. The myth of Odysseus, especially as told in the *Odyssey*, I propose, offered the Greeks of the early archaic period one particularly fruitful context for such a cultural refashioning. Or, to return to Jameson's terms, the themes of mapping and travel that dominate the narrative of Odysseus' travels help the Greeks (and us) make sense of the spatial, temporal, social, and representational crises of early archaic Greece.

Following very much in this tradition of thinking about travel in the context of cultural self-scrutiny, François Hartog, in his book *Mémoire d'Ulysse*, looks at traveling figures, beginning with Odysseus and concluding with the neo-Pythagorean Apollonius of Tyana, as guides to a cultural history or an anthropological exploration of ancient Greece and its sense of identity.[12] Are these travelers ambassadors of certainty or of doubt? Do they confirm or destabilize notions of cultural identity? Do they make room for the "other," or do they put it in its place? Hartog focuses on the rhythm or regular movement created by these men of travel between notions of the same and the other within Greek culture. In this respect, Hartog emphasizes that he is interested not in the details or itineraries of real travel, but rather in travel as what he calls a "discursive operator" or narrative scheme—in particular, insofar as the notion of travel functions as the resolution or response to a problem.[13] In this respect, travel operates as a prominent figure for the process of gaining knowledge both about others and about the self.

Hartog is interested in travelers and what he calls "men of boundaries" ("hommes-frontières").[14] By the latter he means men who take themselves to the borders, who embody the boundary mark and yet remain mobile. He attempts to look at the ways in which these travelers are intermediary figures, operating on both sides of a border, for, he argues, in traversing the boundaries, they come to represent the very point of demarcation. The goal of his book, he explains, is not to provide a monolithic map of ancient culture, but rather "to choose some travelers and follow them a bit."[15] Setting aside issues of topography or geography, he focuses on the combined notions of movement and vision, topology and itinerance ("le mouvement et le regard, la topologie et l'itinérance"), interrogating the ways in which the route of these travelers through space provides an itinerary of their own cultures. Thus Odysseus, in his wanderings, traces the contours of Greek identity; he marks its boundaries. He travels to the extreme limits of the Greek experience, right to the point of no return—to the Underworld, the land of the Lotus-Eaters, the island of Circe.

Within this framework, Hartog reads the *Odyssey* as what he calls a "poetic anthropology," an account of the place and the destiny of mortals on earth.[16] While Hesiod, in the *Theogony* and the *Works and Days*, uses the myth of Prometheus as a model for explaining and justifying the definitive roles of humans, gods, and animals, the *Odyssey*, according to Hartog, addresses these anthropological categories in a fundamentally different register; it locates them in an account of Odysseus' travels. Whereas Hesiod's anthropology is static and normative, Hartog suggests that Homer's is dynamic and narrative. The categories are put in motion, illustrated by Odysseus' adventures in new surroundings, in different categories of space: divine (Calypso, Circe), animal (Laestrygonians, Cyclopes), and human (Phaeacians). Thus Hartog argues that the *Odyssey* is at the heart of the vision that the Greeks have of themselves and of others; it has provided a long-term paradigm for seeing and talking about the world, for traveling it and representing it, a model for living in the world and for making it human, that is to say, Greek.[17]

Hartog's reading of the *Odyssey* as a poetic anthropology is extremely helpful, especially in its focus on the journey as a discursive element, its close attention to the association between travel and knowledge, and its questions about the role and place of the other. Following in the tradition of Pierre Vidal-Naquet's influential essay, "Land and Sacrifice in the *Odyssey*," Hartog shows how productive it can be to bring an anthropological approach to a literary text in an effort to uncover the *mentalité* of those who produced and consumed the text. I am very much indebted to both of these works. Where I differ, however, stems from working at the intersection(s) of myth and history, literature and politics, past and present. Far too often, structuralist, anthropological readings like those of Hartog (and less so of Vidal-Naquet) run the risk of focusing on basic synchronic categories, both mythic and social, to the exclusion of the specific historical circumstances of any one time and place.[18] This kind of analyis, as a result, runs the risk of being too abstract or without context. What I set out to do in this book is to historicize this kind of approach. If the travels of Odysseus trace the contours of Greek identity (and I think they do), and, in particular, if the *Odyssey* mobilizes Hesiod's anthropological categories and locates them in Odysseus' travels, how do issues of foreign contact and commerce complicate the construction of Greek identity as not divine or animal? The expansion of the Greek world through both trade and overseas settlement has an important impact on the ways in which Greek identity is reevaluated and reconfigured in the early archaic period. What are the different kinds of responses to the changes and innovations of this fairly volatile time? How do the issues and dynamics at play at the time of the *Odyssey*'s production and circulation—increased mobility, trade, the east-west dynamic, notions of the foreign, and so on—come to articulate and contest notions of Greekness?[19] What do we make of Odysseus' travels and contacts beyond the comfortable world of fellow Greeks and into the territory of Phoenicians, Libyans, and Egyptians—not to mention that of man-eating Cyclopes and Laestrygonians? In other words, how does this poetic vision of Odysseus, the man of many ways, a man of travel and vision, relate to, capture, represent, and imagine the experience of its contemporary audience, both at home and abroad?

## Doing Ethnography

> Doing ethnography is like trying to read (in the sense of "construct a reading of") a manuscript—foreign, faded, full of ellipses, incoherencies, suspicious emendations, and tendentious commentaries, but written not in conventionalized graphs of sound but in transient examples of shaped behavior.
>
> Clifford Geertz, *The Interpretation of Cultures*

Perhaps one way to characterize the difference between my approach and that of Hartog is to focus on our different choices of metaphor, on the distinctions between an anthropology—the study of mankind in general—and an ethnography, the study of a particular people in a particular place at a particular time. In this book, I set out to explore what I call the "ethnographic imagination" of early archaic Greece—the vision, as articulated in the *Odyssey*, of a fabulous world long ago and far away and the ways in which that vision helps accommodate and articulate particular issues pertaining to the early archaic Greek world. In the passage just quoted, Clifford Geertz compares the process of "doing ethnography" to that of constructing a reading of a manuscript, "foreign, faded, full of ellipses"—that is, the process of creating meaning from an incomplete or fragmentary text. What I propose here is that we turn Geertz's analogy on its head to suggest that constructing a reading of an ancient text is a little like doing ethnography.[20]

First, in the more obvious sense, I mean that my reading of the *Odyssey*, certainly a foreign and faded text encumbered by more than its fair share of tendentious commentaries, is a kind of ethnographic exercise. I am engaged in the practice of producing what Geertz would call a "thick description" of the text—a term that Geertz borrows from the Oxford philosopher Gilbert Ryle to explain the kind of intellectual effort that defines the practice of ethnography. Geertz elaborates on his choice of term by recounting Ryle's illustrative anecdote about the differences between a wink and a twitch:

> Consider, he says, two boys rapidly contracting the eyelids of their right eyes. In one, this is an involuntary twitch; in the other, a conspiratorial signal to a friend. The two movements are, as movements, identical; from an I-am-a-camera, "phenomenalistic" observation of them alone, one could not tell which was twitch and which was wink, or indeed whether both or either was twitch or wink. Yet the difference, however unphotographable, between a twitch and a wink is vast; as anyone unfortunate enough to have had the first taken for the second knows.[21]

Ryle points out that the winker has done two things—contracted his eyelid and communicated something to someone—while the boy with the twitch has merely contracted his eyelid. He then goes on to add a third possibility (a boy who is pretending to wink, attempting not to communicate surreptitiously with anyone but rather to parody) and then a fourth (the would-be satirist who practices his fake winks at home before the mirror). The point of Geertz's use of this story is to suggest that between the "thin" description of this last possibility (rapidly contracting his right eyelid) and the "thick" description of what is going on (practicing a parody of a wink intending to deceive someone into thinking a conspiracy is afoot) lies the object of ethnography,

> a stratified hierarchy of meaningful structures in terms of which twitches, winks, fake-winks, parodies, rehearsals of parodies are produced, perceived, and interpreted, and without which they would not

(not even the zero-form twitches, which as a cultural category, are as much nonwinks as winks are nontwitches) in fact exist, no matter what anyone did or didn't do with his eyelids.[22]

This is my goal here as well—to read the *Odyssey* in such a way as to appreciate and describe the "stratified hierarchy of meaningful structures" in terms of which the stories, characters, and themes of the poem are produced, perceived, and interpreted. A literary text, like any culture, has its own sets of rules and conventions that need to be taken into account in order to construct a meaningful reading of it. While it may not be as hazardous to one's status at a social gathering as mistaking twitches for winks, I would suggest that it can be equally misleading to mistake, say, the literary construction of a Phoenician in a text such as the *Odyssey* for a real one. The *Odyssey*, like any other work of literature, is a site for the deployment of many different systems of meaning (myth, metaphor, allusion, just to name a few), and in order to read it in all its richness, we need to try to sort out the winks from the twitches.

And so in this respect, my reading of the *Odyssey* aims to be ethnographic—to provide modern scholars and readers with a rich or "thick" account of the poem and all its "meaningful structures," steeped as they are in the culture that produced them. By this I do not mean specific factual information about trade routes or exchange practices, but rather a more nuanced understanding of the broad social and economic issues that confronted the ancient audience of the *Odyssey*.[23] But in addition to an ethnographic reading of the *Odyssey*, I want to propose something perhaps slightly less obvious and more provocative—namely, that we read the *Odyssey* itself as an ethnographic text, the product of a culture, late eighth-century B.C.E. Greece, that was trying to construct a reading of the worlds and peoples of its own mythic past in order to make sense of a tumultuous and volatile present.

Although there has been much discussion recently about the nature and goals of ethnography, one theme that continues to emerge is the recognition that one studies the habits, customs, and rules of another culture as a way to understand better what lies at home.[24] As Paul Rabinow puts it in his *Reflections on Fieldwork in Morocco*, ethnography is a kind of hermeneutics, or "the comprehension of self by the detour of the comprehension of the other."[25] As Michel de Certeau remarks about Jean de Léry's (1578) account of his journey to Brazil, "The story effects his return to himself through the mediation of the other."[26] Traditionally, ethnographers have traveled, often overseas, to study foreign cultures firsthand—to observe as an eyewitness the different ways and practices of a people so that they could report their findings accurately, intelligently, and persuasively upon returning back home.[27] The culture studied, the "ethnos" in "ethnography," was understood to be foreign, far away, and fantastic: Herodotus' cannibalistic Scythians, Tacitus' savage Britons. E. E. Evans-Pritchard traveled to Africa to study the Azande, and Claude Lévi-Strauss sailed overseas to capture the tribes of Brazil in his ethnographic masterpiece, *Tristes tropiques*. Thus the practice of ethnography has always been located at the margins of two worlds or systems of meaning; it decodes one culture and then recodes it for another.[28]

Ethnographic writing depends on the structural difference between "over there" and "over here," but then the narrative plays on the relationship between the structure that establishes the separation and the operation that overcomes it in an attempt to create meaning for the audience at home. The effort to translate "over there" to "over here"—the search for analogy, metaphor, and so on—inevitably compromises the difference that prompted the attempt in the first place. Ethnography thus serves to make the strange familiar and, by so doing, to make the familiar strange—the better to understand them both. In this respect it is not just the traveling to encounter the other that is important to the project of ethnography; equally, if not more significant, is the journey home, the return to the self.

In several ways, then, we might say that both the plot and the orientation of the *Odyssey* are ethnographic. First, its protagonist travels (he "sees the cities of men and learns their minds"), and above all, he returns home from his travels to tell the story of his adventures.[29] The *Odyssey* is a tale of worlds as foreign, far away, and fantastic as that of any ethnographer: cannibal Cyclopes, women who turn men into swine, gold and silver palaces guarded by magic dogs, and so on. And Odysseus sees all these wonders with his own eyes; like the ideal ethnographer, he is the eyewitness to his own story. Second, and perhaps even more signficant, the *Odyssey* is equally a story of return. The poem divides structurally, after all, into twelve books of travel and twelve books devoted to Odysseus' return. Thus the narrative impulse for Odysseus to return home after his travels coincides with the ethnographic preoccupation with a similar return to self. In this respect, Odysseus, the hero of both travel and return, the eyewitness narrator, comes to take on an ethnographic function in the poem, to embody its ethnographic imagination—the discovery of the self by detour of the other.[30]

In claiming that the structure and orientation of the *Odyssey* are "ethnographic," I do not mean to suggest that Homer's *Odyssey* is the functional equivalent of ethnographic treatises along the lines of Evans-Pritchard's study *The Nuer* or Malinowski's classic treatment of the Trobriand Islanders in *Argonauts of the Western Pacific*. The *Odyssey* is, of course, a highly polished literary text, an epic poem that tells the well-known story of the Greek hero Odysseus' belated return home to Ithaca. Nevertheless, embedded within this familiar mythic story pattern of a time and people long ago are details and themes that belong to the real contemporary world of its audience. In this respect, contemporary experience with worlds overseas is projected into the distant Mycenean past, and it is the relationship between myth and history, between past and present, and especially between foreign and Greek, that is revealed by an ethnographic logic.[31] In other words, by telling a story that articulates a better understanding of what it means to be Greek by means of accounts of far-off worlds (both temporal and spatial), the *Odyssey* reveals a glimpse of what I call the "ethnographic imagination" of the early archaic period. To return to Geertz's formulation, the poem "constructs a reading" of the exotic worlds of the mythic past and the far away, and it does so with an eye always on the return. Many scholars have shown that on the thematic level what Odysseus sees and learns in his travels enables him to return home. On a broader, cultural level as well, the knowledge and experience gained in the first half of the story are brought home to the audience in the poem's second half.

And so, by suggesting that the *Odyssey* embodies the "ethnographic imagination" of early archaic Greece (rather than offering a more general or abstract "poetic anthropology"), I aim to be culturally and historically specific about the ways in which Odysseus charts the contours of Greek identity. In addition to confirming the Hesiodic categories that define Greek identity as being neither animal nor divine, the poem articulates the complexities of cross-cultural identity and contact at a time of particular upheaval and change, that is, the early archaic period (more on the poem's date in the following section). James Redfield has remarked that ethnography reflects a hunger for expressing a cultural system: "It is no accident that we became theoretically interested in these cultures just as we began, practically, to appropriate and destroy them."[32] While Redfield is talking about modernism as an unprecedented historical experience where "for the first time one cultural system is taking over the world," much the same argument could be made for the coincidence of the *Odyssey*'s production and the archaic Greek colonial movement.[33] Is it an accident that the *Odyssey* is especially interested in the worlds beyond Greek shores, interested in exploring the nature of relationships (commercial and colonial) between Greeks and peoples overseas, at exactly the moment when its audience is settling those shores and establishing trade contacts throughout the Mediterranean?

Homer's *Odyssey* is a poem about travel, cross-cultural contact, and narrative, and in it, New World accounts of trade and overseas exploration intersect with familiar tales of epic poetry to produce a rich and complex picture of a world in transition. Homer's fabulous tales of savage lands and magical palaces are more than folktale or fantasy; they are also steeped in the social, political, and cultural transformations taking place in the early archaic Greek world. The poem embodies the ethnographic imagination of the period; it contains a "stratified hierarchy of meaningful structures" by means of which its audience makes sense of its own world. Like many European accounts of the New World, the *Odyssey* reveals glimpses of a culture attempting to represent and accommodate new worlds both abroad and at home.

### History and Literature

We should rather think of the epics themselves as artifacts—arguably the most important, for modern classicists as for ancient Greeks—generated in the great upheavals of the eighth century.

The poems and the archaeological record can only be properly understood when read alongside each other and woven together, as remnants of competing eighth-century efforts at self-fashioning, out of which classical Greek civilization was created.

Ian Morris, "Homer and the Iron Age"

But which "worlds at home and abroad" are we talking about? What is the setting, both historical and chronological, of the *Odyssey*? The historicity of the Homeric poems is a topic that has provoked a fair amount of scholarly debate, and I would like to take some time here to be clear about what I mean by offering a "historicizing" rather than what some might call a strictly historical reading of the poem.[34] There are (at least) two issues involved. The first concerns the specific dating of the poem, and the second the relationship between literature and history more generally. As for the first, I agree with the majority of scholars who date the *Odyssey* to the second half of the eighth century B.C.E.[35] In other words, this is the time frame in which the poem was composed, performed, and circulated in a form very similar, although certainly not identical, to what we now read.[36] The *Odyssey* is the product of an oral tradition rather than the pen of a single poet, and for this reason it enjoyed a public, collective status that is unfamiliar to literature since the age of printing.[37] The immediacy of its composition/performance context ensures that the *Odyssey* is responsive to its immediate audience above all else.[38] And so we can assume that the "world of the *Odyssey*" (by which I mean the world that is constructed through the characters, plots, and landscapes of the poem) is very much a part of the tremendous flux and upheaval of the early archaic period.[39]

But let me be clear. By locating the "world of the *Odyssey*" toward the end of the eighth century, I do not mean to suggest that we read the poem as an objective source of historical information about the archaic period. This leads me to the slightly more problematic issue of the relationship of literary texts to the worlds from which they emerge.[40] Poetic texts, like the *Odyssey*, both represent (rather than objectively reflect) what happens outside the realm of textual production and actively participate in those events in a variety of ways. They may challenge or reinforce them, they may contain the traces of competing interpretations of them, and any or all of the above. And for this reason, while it may be a misleading source of information about "how life really was," the *Odyssey* offers a unique glimpse into the workings of a culture which it also conditions. The poem provides valuable insight into the areas of ideological contention, sources of conflict, and issues of strife at work in a culture experiencing a time of transition and upheaval. And so we must learn to read this text for the kinds of information it can provide, remembering that to whatever extent the *Odyssey* offers an analyis of the early archaic period, its social perspective is itself poetic, that is, it cannot be separated from the duplicitous capacity of language both to inform and to deceive. Odysseus, after all, like Hesiod's Muses, knows how to say many false things that sound like the truth.[41] (And so we come back to the difference between winks and twitches.)

Thus, with respect to the *Odyssey*, I agree with Ian Morris, who argues that material and poetic culture are two different ways in which the eighth-century Greeks constructed their world for themselves. Neither is a passive reflection of the other; both must be read together to provide a picture of the world in which they participate.[42] And it is in this spirit that, from time to time, I look to historical and archeological practices to sustain and supplement my reading of the poem—not to posit the material record as an unproblematic background for the literary text. Instead, my use of historical and archeological evidence is an attempt, to borrow William Thalmann's formulation, "to understand the system (or cultural *langue*) of which the practices depicted in the poem are instantiations (or *parole*)."[43] I am not engaged in the strict historian's endeavor to read the *Odyssey* for information about the archaic period. Rather, I aim to offer a reading of the poem that is embedded in its larger cultural and historical context, and in this respect, I would characterize my treatment as a historicizing, rather than a historical, reading of the *Odyssey*.[44]

## A Brief Overview

Gentle breath of yours my sails
must fill, or else my project fails,
which was to please.

Shakespeare, *The Tempest* V.i

Ships and overseas travel play a significant role in both the *Odyssey*'s narrative and its ethnographic imagination, and so I begin with an investigation into the literary and cultural associations of ships and song in Greek poetry. From the Iliadic Catalogue of Ships to Derek Walcott's *Omeros*, nautical imagery has often helped the poet characterize the process of making poetry and locate himself within the larger poetic tradition. Walcott exploits the similarities of terminology—the poetic craft and literary passages—while the Catalogue of Ships invokes a lengthy and elaborate overseas voyage to represent the vastness and complexity of the poetic enterprise. In addition, in the case of the early Greek poets, the coincidence between two ancient techniques for shipbuilding (sewing planks together or fitting them together with pegs) with prominent metaphors for oral poetic composition (sewing and carpentry) helps ground this common figurative alliance of ships and song within the culturally specific metaphors of poetic production in early archaic Greece.

But ships are not just literary tropes in the *Odyssey*. They also carry real cargo and travel far and wide. The second and third chapters explore the cultural implications of the literary association of ships and songs. Odysseus' raft is said to be as big as a cargo ship; this choice of metaphor suggests that in addition to techniques of production, the potential for profit plays a key role in the poetics of the *Odyssey*. Various figures in the poem employ the language of commerce—especially the polarized terms of profit and theft—to evaluate good and bad poetry, and Odysseus himself trades his songs for goods to take home. In this respect, the figure of Odysseus' raft embodies the potential of both commerce and song and addresses issues of economic and poetic value.

Finally, Odysseus' raft travels the open seas. In chapter 3 I argue that sea travel operates metaphorically in the *Odyssey* to articulate a notion of narrative that is mobile and flexible. The poem is itself a travel narrative, and it accommodates two competing ways of thinking about the relationship between travel and narrative. One view, represented by the court poets Phemius and Demodocus, associates travel with the potential for deception and prefers to link narrative truth with a fixed, well-ordered song. The other, represented by Odysseus, associates movement and travel with all the flexibility and mobility of oral poetry, and celebrates the contingency rather than the absoluteness of narrative truth. The latter approach, symbolized by the mobility of Odysseus' raft, suggests that the truth of a story lies precisely in its ability to travel and contributes further to the rich and complicated poetics of the *Odyssey* in a world of flux.

The second part of the book then turns from the literary and cultural image of sailing to representations of the new worlds that Odysseus travels to and sings about over the course of the poem. Chapter 4 focuses on Phaeacia as the gateway to the ethnographic imagination of the *Odyssey*. It explores the choice of Phaeacia as the site for Odysseus' fabulous tales as well as their ethnographic structure. The combined force of the New World and Golden Age associations of Alcinous' island provides Odysseus with an ideally productive setting for his travel tales. At the same time, the heterological nature of the ethnographic narrative—the us versus them structure—establishes a framework for connecting the world of Odysseus' travels overseas with the more familiar one he returns to at home in Ithaca.

The Phaeacians themselves are a complicated and contradictory people, and in chapters 5 and 6 I look further at the issues that form the basis for these contradictions. The Phaeacians occupy a pivotal position within two sets of oppositions that articulate the important ethnographic themes of the *Odyssey*: overseas trade and settlement. Chapter 5 examines the ways in which the carefully schematic representations of the Phaeacians and the Phoenicians address the potential and the problems presented by overseas trade. The stereotype of the Phoenicians in the poem presents an unmitigatedly negative view of trade, associating it with the dangers of piracy and theft. The idealized Phaeacians, by contrast, dwell in an isolationist fantasy world in which ships sail, but without cargo, and where a kind of one-sided gift exchange, not trade, is the primary mode of circulating goods. Thus the Phoenicians and the Phaeacians operate together to

articulate the broad spectrum of Greek aspirations and anxieties about participating in a world of travel and trade.

Chapter 6 then looks at the ways in which the Phaeacians operate, together
with their overbearing relatives the Cyclopes, to address the costs and benefits
of overseas conquest and settlement. Again, the Phaeacians represent the idealized picture, a magical, prosperous world in which the native inhabitants welcome strangers into their midst with generous hospitality and offers of marriage.
Their cannibalistic relatives, however, provide a quite different picture of overseas settlement. The savage and lawless Cyclopes embody the colonists' worst
fears—either that they will be eaten or that, in the process of subduing the native peoples, they will regress to a primitive, savage state themselves. In this way,
the opposition between the Phaeacians and the Cyclopes explores the tensions
between utopian representations of the New World and more alarmist visions of
a dangerous and primitive landscape.

Part II culminates in a look back at the Phaeacians and their role in accommodating and articulating the ethnographic imagination of the *Odyssey*, both as
a productive setting for the telling of Odysseus' travel tales and as the pivotal
point in two key sets of oppositions at work in the poem. Chapter 7 further examines the heterological structure that dominates the world of the Phaeacians—
neither Phoenician traders nor Cyclopean cannibals—and allows us first to think
about what this structure says about the relationship between overseas settlement and trade and, second, to extend the structure outside the boundaries of
the poem itself and into the world of its audience. How can the Phaeacians help
archaic Greeks think about themselves as traders and colonists?

The logic of the ethnographic narrative travels to worlds far away in order
to bring knowledge and experience of these new worlds back home again. The
final part of the book focuses on the nature and consequences of Odysseus' return to Ithaca. Chapter 8 explores Odysseus' skill at linking representations of
the world abroad to his experiences at home. Odysseus' role as an epic hero is a
new one. As trader, colonist, traveler, and poet, Odysseus explores new territory
and breaks new ground; his job is not to protect the old world, but rather to survive the dangerous seas of change and innovation to make a successful transition to the new world, both at home and abroad. In particular, the colonial
themes that dominate his encounters with the Phaeacians and the Cyclopes reappear in the second half of the poem to describe Odysseus' return to Ithaca as a
kind of refoundation. In killing the hungry and greedy suitors and in remarrying the queen, Penelope, Odysseus transforms prewar Ithaca and resettles it in
the new world of early archaic Greece.

The concluding chapter returns to Odysseus' raft and to the themes of travel,
ships, and song with which the book begins. Odysseus, poet of the *Odyssey*, literally tied to the mast of his ship, personifies the metaphorical connection between ships and poetry with all its rich associations, and the Sirens episode connects this image with Odysseus' role as the hero of a culture in transition. It is

the mobility of Odysseus and his ship that allows him and his ethnographic vision to move forward and to avoid foundering on the rocks of the past. As the
poem draws to its conclusion, however, Odysseus' raft, which had crashed upon
the shores of Scheria, is resurrected and reconstructed in the form of the marriage
bed that enables the recognition of Odysseus and his reunion with Penelope. In
other words, the raft, the symbol of the mobility of narrative, is significantly
transformed instead into a figure of the steadfastness of marriage and a signal
that the story is drawing to an end. This image of Odysseus and Penelope's bed,
constructed by Odysseus' shipbuilding skill and yet rooted in Ithacan soil, thus
provides a framework for imagining the transition from travel to home. It
grounds the ethnographic vision of Odysseus' overseas travels in the future of
his home in Ithaca.

# 1    Setting Sail

# 1

## Ships and Song

> I said Omeros
>
> and *O* was the conch-shell's invocation, *mer* was
> both mother and sea in our Antillean patois,
> *os*, a grey bone, and the white surf as it crashes
> and spreads its sibilant collar on a lace shore.
>
> Derek Walcott, *Omeros*

Throughout much of his poetry, but particularly in his epic poem *Omeros*, the contemporary Caribbean poet Derek Walcott invokes images of the sea and navigation as metaphors for the poetic process. He places the sea right at the heart of Omeros' name—"*mer* was / both mother and sea in our Antillean patois"—and at the center of his poetics. There are two journeys in Walcott's *Omeros*, one that the hero makes as he travels from town to town, and the other that the poet embarks upon as he recounts his hero's adventures:

> For both, the 'I' is a mast; a desk is a raft
> for one, foaming with paper, and dipping the beak
>
> of a pen in its foam, while an actual craft
> carries the other to cities where people speak
> a different language, or look at him differently . . . (p. 291)

Walcott's hero travels on an actual seagoing craft, while the poet conducts his own odyssey from his desk, a metaphorical raft, and Walcott anchors this navigational imagery firmly in the language of poetry by linking raft and craft here in the alternating scheme of his terza rima.[1] Obviously, there is something about ships and the sea that powerfully captures the essence of making poetry for Walcott, and, as so often, the modern Caribbean poet sends us back to Homer with fresh eyes to discover a similar metaphorical system already at work in early Greek poetry as well.[2]

Starting with the *Iliad*, allusions to ships and their construction take on a metaphorical force in Greek poetry, creating a framework for talking about po-

etic authority and tradition. Hesiod, Ibycus, Pindar, and many other Greek poets take up this figurative use of sailing imagery within their own work.[3] But it
is with Homer's *Odyssey* that the full potential of this imagery is explored: the
poem's hero is, after all, both a consummate singer of tales and an experienced
sailor. In Book 5 Odysseus builds a raft to continue his journey home to Ithaca,
and this scene sets out the metaphorical association of poetry and sailing that is
key to the poetics of the *Odyssey*. Odysseus' raft—the process of its construction, its capacity for carrying large-scale cargo, and its success in putting Odysseus
back on the road home—comes to embody many of the ways in which overseas
trade and travel combine to structure both the poetics and the ethnographic
imagination of the poem. While, as Walcott's *Omeros* suggests, the collocation
of ships and song is prevalent among many poetic traditions, the figurative association between poetry and sailing in Greek poetry is grounded in culturally
specific metaphors of poetic production and, in this respect, reflects something
about the ways in which the Greeks conceptualized and articulated the nature
of poetic composition in the archaic period.

## Ships and Song

A passage from Hesiod's *Works and Days* sets out some of the issues that support this metaphorical alliance of ship and song. In the midst of a discussion of
the difficulties and strategies of sailing and merchant trading (618–45, 663–94),
Hesiod includes a passage that appears at first glance to be a momentary departure from this subject, a brief reminiscence about the time he won a poetic contest and dedicated his prize to the Muses. Upon closer inspection, however, this
apparent digression fits closely within its outer framing section on sailing to provide a commentary on Hesiod's poetic expertise and to locate his own poetic skill
within the preexisting tradition.[4]

Following on his discussion of the seasonal demands of agriculture and his
advice about how to be a successful farmer, Hesiod turns to the topics of seafaring and trade in a section of the *Works and Days* often referred to as the
Nautilia. He offers tips about the best seasons for sailing, the appropriate
amount of cargo to carry, and the proper care and maintenance of ships. He then
promises to show his brother Perses "the measures of the loud-roaring sea"
though he has no experience of sailing. In this way, what begins as advice about
sailing turns quickly into a poetic manifesto of sorts:

Εὖτ᾽ ἂν ἐπ᾽ ἐμπορίην τρέψας ἀεσίφρονα θυμόν
βούληαι χρέα τε προφυγεῖν καὶ λιμὸν ἀτερπέα,
δείξω δή τοι μέτρα πολυφλοίσβοιο θαλάσσης,
οὔτέ τι ναυτιλίης σεσοφισμένος οὔτέ τι νηῶν·
οὐ γάρ πώ ποτε νηΐ γ᾽ ἐπέπλων εὐρέα πόντον,

εἰ μὴ ἐς Εὔβοιαν ἐξ Αὐλίδος, ᾗ ποτ᾽ Ἀχαιοὶ
μείναντες χειμῶνα πολὺν σὺν λαὸν ἄγειραν
Ἑλλάδος ἐξ ἱερῆς Τροίην ἐς καλλιγύναικα.

But if you turn your ever-mindful heart toward trade and wish to escape necessity and unpleasant hunger, I will show you the measures of
the loud-roaring sea, although I have no professional skills neither in
sailing nor in ships. For I have never yet sailed across the wide sea, at
least not in a ship, except to Euboea from Aulis, where the Achaeans
once waited out the storm and gathered their large host to go from sacred Greece to Troy, land of beautiful women. (WD 646–53)

Hesiod first mentions sailing in the context of overseas trade: the practice of carrying cargo across the sea can provide an escape from the poverty of the land
and the vicissitudes of farming. He then offers to introduce Perses to the measures of the sea, all the while disclaiming any personal nautical experience. At
first the logic of this sentence appears puzzling, but the use of σεσοφισμένος following the reference to the "measures [μέτρα] of the loud-roaring sea" suggests
that we read this skill as a poetic rather than a strictly nautical one—or both.[5]
For while the terms *metra* and *sophia* can designate the rules and expertise required to master the sea, their semantic scope includes the world of poetic skill
as well. In early Greek poetry, *sophia* often refers to the technical skill or expertise possessed by the poet or musician.[6] Moreover, *metra* is generally used to designate the rules and formulas known to the expert, again often within a poetic
context. A passage from Solon brings together these two terms in the description of a poet "who has been taught the gifts of the Olympian Muses, knowing
the measure of delightful skill" (Ὀλυμπιάδεων Μουσέων πάρα δῶρα διδαχθείς
διδαχθείς/ ἱμερτῆς σοφίης μέτρον ἐπιστάμενος, 13.51–52).[7] The broad semantic
scope of these terms emphasizes professional training and skill—whether in shipbuilding or song-making—and Hesiod's careful word choice emphasizes potential similarities between the two professions and suggests a figurative alliance
between them. What began as a discussion of the rules of sailing has drifted into
a poetic commentary with a particular focus on Hesiod's authority as singer.

After sketching out these points of convergence between nautical and poetic
discourse, Hesiod proceeds to compare sea journeys. He claims that although he
has not sailed the whole sea, he has made a short trip from Aulis to Euboea. As
others have already shown, Hesiod contrasts his own modest trip with the longer
and more elaborate sea voyage from Aulis to Troy, the famous expedition that
produced both the Trojan War and the epic poems that celebrate it. This nautical competition thus signals a poetic contest in which the Homeric epic is contrasted with Hesiodic song.[8] The heroic range and scope of the *Iliad*, a poem that
tackles the monumental clash between east and west, is here captured by the size
and daring of a whole fleet of ships sailing across the broad sea from sacred
Greece to the land of Troy, full of beautiful women. Hesiod's more modest po-

etic endeavor, by contrast, whether it be the *Theogony* or another poem, is the equivalent of a mere sixty-five-meter jaunt from Aulis to Euboea. Thus Hesiod's mention of poetic/nautical skill sets the stage for the metaphorical use of overseas journeys to designate poetic endeavors. He has not sailed the wide sea—"not in a ship, at any rate"—but as Walcott writes in *Omeros*, "there are two journeys in every odyssey," and Hesiod's voyage, I will suggest, is a poetic one.[9]

Once he has made the transition from sailing to poetry, Hesiod speaks explicitly of song: the reason for his brief journey was to compete in the games honoring Amphidamas. He was victorious in a poetic contest there and won a tripod with his song:

> ἔνθα δ᾽ ἐγὼν ἐπ᾽ ἄεθλα δαΐφρονος Ἀμφιδάμαντος
> Χαλκίδα τ᾽ εἰς ἐπέρησα· τὰ δὲ προπεφραδμένα πολλὰ
> ἆεθλ᾽ ἔθεσαν παῖδες μεγαλήτορος· ἔνθά μέ φημι
> ὕμνῳ νικήσαντα φέρειν τρίποδ᾽ ὠτώεντα.
> τὸν μὲν ἐγὼ Μούσῃς Ἑλικωνιάδεσσ᾽ ἀνέθηκα,
> ἔνθά με τὸ πρῶτον λιγυρῆς ἐπέβησαν ἀοιδῆς.

> There, for the contests of wise Amphidamas, I crossed to Chalcis, many contests which his great-hearted sons had proclaimed and established. And there I say that, victorious in song, I carried off the winged tripod, which I dedicated to the Heliconian Muses where they first launched my sweet song. (*WD* 654–59)

The agonistic undertone of the nautical competition with Homer thus comes to the surface here with the mention of the games of Amphidamas. Hesiod says that he dedicated his prize to the Muses of Helicon in the place where they first launched his poetic career—he uses ἐπέβησαν here, a term that can describe embarking on a ship[10]—and this nautical image provides Hesiod with the transition back to his discussion of sailing:

> τόσσόν τοι νηῶν γε πεπείρημαι πολυγόμφων·
> ἀλλὰ καὶ ὣς ἐρέω Ζηνὸς νόον αἰγιόχοιο·
> Μοῦσαι γάρ μ᾽ ἐδίδαξαν ἀθέσφατον ὕμνον ἀείδειν.

> That is the extent of my experience with many-pegged ships, but I speak the mind of aegis-holding Zeus, for the Muses taught me to sing their divine song. (*WD* 660–62)

In this concluding section, Hesiod once again conflates nautical and poetic skill. He offers his success at the poetic competition in Chalcis as proof of the extent of his experience with ships. Hesiod's nautical expertise (or lack thereof) is supported by his claim to have been taught to sing by the Muses.

The key to charting the logic of Hesiod's movement from advice about sailing and trade to an account of his own poetic competition at Chalcis and then back again to a discussion of the best seasons for sailing is precisely this intersection of language about poetic and nautical skill. Taking a slightly different approach from that of Walcott, whose "desk is a raft," Hesiod represents his poetic endeavor in terms of a sea journey—a short trip across the straits rather than an epic-length voyage. The figurative association between sailing and poetry here is nevertheless quite clear. Hesiod uses terms for professional knowledge and expertise (μέτρα, σεσοφισμένος, πεπείρημαι) to make the transitions from sailing to poetry and back again. He then takes this linguistic ambiguity as a point of departure from which to launch a metaphorical system whereby nautical experience and ship travel set the framework for locating Hesiod's own accomplishments within the larger poetic tradition, exemplified, as always, by Homer.[11]

For Hesiod's metaphor in the Nautilia section of the *Works and Days* (and perhaps all subsequent use of sailing as a figure for poetry) points back to the Iliadic Catalogue of Ships, the locus classicus for the figurative intersection of ships and songs. The famous catalogue appears in Book 2 of the *Iliad* right after Agamemnon's dream and the Greeks' near-retreat to their ships and home. Although the *Iliad* opens in the midst of the tenth year of the war between the Greeks and Trojans, the catalogue provides the poem's audience with a brief return to the beginning of the story, reprising its geographic movement from Greece to Troy. It captures a shift from ships to battle and celebrates the Greeks' renewed commitment to the war before them. The Greeks' decison not to flee to their ships to return home but rather to stay and fight leads the audience to expect, perhaps, a quick transition to the battlefield. Yet Homer offers instead a lengthy poetic tribute to the sea voyage ten years earlier that brought so many Greeks from the beloved land of their fathers to battle at Troy. Faced with the daunting task of representing this vast Greek army at Troy, the poet of the *Iliad* begs the Muses for help:

Ἔσπετε νῦν μοι, Μοῦσαι Ὀλύμπια δώματ᾽ ἔχουσαι—
ὑμεῖς γὰρ θεαί ἐστε, πάρεστέ τε, ἴστέ τε πάντα,
ἡμεῖς δὲ κλέος οἶον ἀκούομεν οὐδέ τι ἴδμεν—
οἵ τινες ἡγεμόνες Δαναῶν καὶ κοίρανοι ἦσαν·
πληθὺν δ᾽ οὐκ ἂν ἐγὼ μυθήσομαι οὐδ᾽ ὀνομήνω,
οὐδ᾽ εἴ μοι δέκα μὲν γλῶσσαι, δέκα δὲ στόματ᾽ εἶεν,
φωνὴ δ᾽ ἄρρηκτος, χάλκεον δέ μοι ἦτορ ἐνείη,
εἰ μὴ Ὀλυμπιάδες Μοῦσαι, Διὸς αἰγιόχοιο
θυγατέρες, μνησαίαθ᾽ ὅσοι ὑπὸ Ἴλιον ἦλθον·
ἀρχοὺς αὖ νηῶν ἐρέω νῆάς τε προπάσας.

Tell me now, Muses who hold Olympian houses, for you are goddesses, and you are present and you know everything. But we only hear the report and know nothing. The leaders and chiefs of the Danaans—I could not list them nor could I name them, not if I had ten tongues and ten mouths, or an unbreakable voice and a bronze heart in me unless the

>Olympian Muses, daughters of aegis-holding Zeus, remembered how
>many went to Troy. And so I will tell of the leaders of the ships and all
>the ships. (*Il.* 2.484–93)

The sheer length of the catalogue that follows this plea to the Muses delays the
battle action still more. Eagerly anticipating bloody, dusty accounts of hand-to-
hand combat between the Greek and Trojan heroes, the listener finds instead a
detailed and meticulous accounting of ships and sea captains.

On one level the catalogue operates as the functional equivalent of the three
similes that preceed it, each one emphasizing incalculable numbers or quantity:
multitudinous flocks of birds (459–63), ever replenishable numbers of leaves
and flowers (468), and great hordes of insects (469–71). Similes drawn from nature are a common Homeric technique—one poetic solution to the challenge of
representing vast numbers of warriors. Here, the poet claims to be unable to
name all the men who sailed from Greece to Troy—not even if he had ten mouths
and a bronze heart—and he offers the Catalogue of Ships as an alternative,
metonymic solution to the poetic challenge of listing all those men who fought
at Troy.

The catalogue not only conveys the vast numbers of Greeks who sailed to
Ilium, but also captures by its very length a sense of the distance and magnitude
of the journey itself. The catalogue displaces the duration of the journey to Troy
onto the number of ships that sailed. In nearly four hundred lines, divided into
twenty-nine entries, Homer counts up 1,186 ships. The repeated refrain of numbers of ships marks the end of each entry with the regular rhythm of a captain's
daily ship log or the measured beat of oars. In addition to conveying a sense of
the monumentality of the Greek expedition against Troy, the catalogue is full of
topographical detail; it begins with the Boeotians just as the expedition itself
started from the Boeotian city of Aulis. Although the catalogue is full of place
names, this litany of geographic detail does not, as we might first expect, trace
the actual steps of the journey itself.[12] Instead, it superimposes onto the sea
journey to Troy a topographical map of the Greek lands that the heroes have
left behind. Organized in three geographic tours of Greece, the catalogue conveys a sense of the range and breadth of the Greek lands and peoples involved
at Troy.[13]

The *Iliad*'s Catalogue of Ships is a poetic tour de force, completed only with
the help of the Muses. The lengthy catalogue, rich with proper names and places,
helps the audience imagine the length and extent of a ten-year war. Marked as it
is by the poet's articulate and impassioned appeal to the Muses, the catalogue
assumes a metapoetic status. The poet respectfully identifies himself as merely
mortal in comparison with the Muses—they know all; he knows nothing—and
then proceeds to produce poetry that sets the standard against which all future
poets will measure themselves. Thus the Catalogue of Ships, I propose, comes to
catalogue poetic skill as well as battleships; it establishes a metaphorical frame-

work for representing not just the heroic deeds on the battlefield but the excellence of poetic composition as well.

And so when Hesiod boasts in the *Works and Days* that he has "no professional skills neither in sailing nor in ships," he follows in the wake of the Iliadic poet, who "only hear(s) the report and know(s) nothing" of the Greeks who sailed to Troy. Both poets depend on their special relationship with the Muses for their poetic skill and professional status. Furthermore, Hesiod alludes specifically to the Catalogue of Ships as a monumental poetic expedition (from Aulis to Troy) against which he locates his own, more modest voyage from Aulis to Chalcis. Hesiod's journey, like the Iliadic catalogue, takes Boeotia as its point of departure; his itinerary, however, takes him only a short distance. Hesiod thus offers his own more diminutive efforts in the *Works and Days* in contrast to the monolithic Homeric Catalogue of Ships. Like the poet of the *Iliad*, however, he uses the language of ships and sailing metaphorically to represent the art of poetry, focusing in particular on locating his own role as poet within that ongoing tradition.

In a poem in praise of the beautiful Polycrates, the sixth-century poet Ibycus positions a similar association between poetry and sailing within a poetic disclaimer (Fr. S151 *Poetarum Melicorum Graecorum Fragmenta*). The beginning of the poem is lost; our fragment starts by mentioning the sack of Priam's Troy, the strife over Helen's beauty, and golden-haired Aphrodite. Ibycus soon disavows any interest in singing epic themes, however, in favor of conferring undying fame on the beautiful Polycrates. His use of the *praeteritio* evokes both Hesiod and the Catalogue of Ships as sources for his figurative association of ships and songs within the poetic tradition. Ibycus has no wish to sing of Paris or the capture of Troy, nor could he attempt to list the great number of ships that went from Aulis to Troy. Only a Muse could embark on such a story:

οὐδεπ[

ἡρ]ωῶν ἀρετὰν
ὑπ]ερἀφανον οὕς τε κοίλα[ι
———
νᾶες] πολυγόμφοι ἐλεύσα[ν
Τροί]αι κακόν, ἥρωας ἐσθ[λούς·
τῶν] μὲν κρείων Ἀγαμέ[μνων
ἆ]ρχε Πλεισθ[ενί]δας βασιλ[εὺ]ς ἀγὸς ἀνδρῶν
Ἀτρέος ἐσ[θλοῦ π]άις ἔκγ[ο]νος.

———
———
καὶ τὰ μὲ[ν ἂν] Μοῖσαι σεσοφι[σ]μέναι
εὖ Ἑλικωνίδ[ες] ἐμβαίεν † λόγω[ι,
θνατ[ὸ]ς † δ' οὔ κ[ε]ν ἀνὴρ
διερὸς τὰ ἕκαστα εἴποι,
———

ναῶν ὅ[σσος ἀρι]θμὸς ἀπ᾽ Αὐλίδος
Αἰγαῖον διὰ [πό]ντον ἀπ᾽ Ἄργεος
ἠλύθο[ν ἐς Τροία]ν
ἱπποτρόφο[ν,

... nor [shall I recount] the proud virtue of the heroes whom the hollow, many-pegged ships brought as an evil to Troy, good heroes, over whom lord Agamemnon Pleisthenid ruled, king, leader of men and son of noble Atreus. On these things the skilled Heliconian Muses could well embark in story, but no mortal man alive could tell each thing: what number of ships came from Aulis across the Aegean Sea from Argos to Troy, nourisher of horses ... (15–30)[14]

The poem then goes on to mention individual Homeric warriors, ending with a promise to confer epic fame (κλέος ἄφθιτον, 47) on Polycrates precisely because his beauty rivals that of the great Homeric heroes.

The verbal echoes of both Hesiod's Nautilia and the Iliadic catalogue ring loud and clear.[15] First, Ibycus alludes to the Catalogue of Ships by identifying the Homeric heroes in terms of the "hollow, many-pegged ships" (νᾶες πολυγόμφοι, 17–18) that brought them to Troy. Second, like the Iliadic poet, who claimed to be physically and poetically unable to list all the Greeks who had come to Troy, Ibycus announces that it would take a skilled Muse (23); no mortal man like himself could detail the number of ships that sailed from Argos to Troy.[16] Although Ibycus' poetic disclaimer takes a different turn from that of the Iliadic catalogue—his inability to list the number of ships that sailed to Troy enables him to shift focus to the beautiful heroes who fought there and thus to ennoble his addressee, Polycrates—both poets nevertheless adopt a humble pose vis-à-vis the Muses in order to highlight their own poetic expertise. Ibycus alludes to the Catalogue of Ships in this poem as a gesture of poetic bravado—to locate himself within the tradition of professional and skilled poets ranging back to Homer and Hesiod—and it is the metaphorical connection between ships and poetry that makes this gesture work.

For in addition to these Iliadic echoes, Ibycus makes several specific verbal allusions to Hesiod's Nautilia and to his juxtaposition there of poetry and seafaring. When distinguishing the Muses' far superior skill from his own mortal poetic limitations, Ibycus first identifies them as Heliconian (rather than the Olympian Muses of Homer), alluding to Hesiod's programmatic encounter with the Muses on Mount Helicon. He then describes these Heliconian Muses as thoroughly skilled (Μοῖσαι σεσοφ[ισμ]έναι, 23), and the perfect form of the verb immediately recalls Hesiod's similar use of the term (σεσοφισμένος, WD 649) in a context that designated professional skill in the realms of both poetry and sailing. Moreover, Ibycus' skilled Muses are able to "embark" on a story (ἐμβαίεν λόγω[ι, 24), and his use of the nautical term here echoes their role in launching Hesiod upon his poetic career (λιγυρῆς ἐπέβησαν ἀοιδῆς, WD 659). Finally,

Ibycus describes the Homeric ships as "many-pegged"—"nor [shall I recount] the proud virtue of the heroes whom the hollow, many-pegged ships" (νᾶες] πολυγόμφοι) "brought as an evil to Troy" (15–19)—choosing exactly the adjective that Hesiod used to mark the point where poetics and nautical expertise intersect: "That is the extent of my experience with many-pegged ships [νηῶν . . . πολυγόμφων] . . . for the Muses taught me" (WD 660).

In the Polycrates poem, Ibycus locates his own poetic strategy, his wish to avoid epic themes in favor of erotic praise, within a preexisting poetic discourse—a metaphorical association of poetry and sailing that goes back to the great early poets Homer and Hesiod. Two general themes emerge from this programmatic dialogue. First, both Ibycus and Hesiod evoke the ambitious scale of the Iliadic Catalogue of Ships—its self-conscious programmatic appeal to the Muses already calls attention to the making of poetry—to represent the heroic nature and vast scope of epic poetry. By contrast, Hesiod's smaller-scale poetic venture is the equivalent of a very short sea journey from Aulis to Euboea. Read figuratively, his explicit denial of sailing knowledge thus echoes the Iliadic poet's claim to know nothing about the Trojan War. Ibycus takes a slightly different tack, but one that depends equally on comparison with the Homeric catalogue. Instead of comparing length of sea journeys, Ibycus goes back to the catalogue directly and claims that he could not even list the number of ships that sailed to Troy. Instead of honoring the host of Homeric heroes, he prefers to sing the praises of just one boy, the beautiful Polycrates. Both Hesiod and Ibycus allude in some way to seafaring and the Catalogue of Ships as a poetic benchmark against which they distinguish and position their own work. A second strategy is to highlight the construction of ships themselves to represent the professional craft of poets and the process of poetic composition. Both Hesiod and Ibycus refer to Homeric ships as "many-pegged" (πολυγόμγοι) in their metapoetic sailing passages. An important key to unlocking the puzzle of sailing and ships as a metaphorical system lies in the similarities between the techniques used for constructing Homeric ships and those of song-making.[17]

### Early Greek Shipbuilding

The type of boat that was probably most prevalent in Mycenean times is known as the sewn boat. The sides and bottom of the ship were made of long planks laid flush side by side, and holes were drilled into the planks, which were then sewn together with cords of hemp or papyrus. This particular method of ship construction has been in wide use all over the world, and is still found in some places. Marco Polo describes the sewn boats he saw at the entrance of the Persian Gulf:

> [They were] wretched affairs and many get lost; for they have no iron
> fastenings and are only stitched together with twine made from the husk

of the Indian nut. They beat this husk until it becomes like horse-hair and from this they spin twine and with it stitch the planks of the ships together. It keeps well and is not corroded by sea-water but it will not stand well in a storm.[18]

The earliest example of this type of boat to survive was found beside the great pyramid at Giza, but the technique apparently dates back to primitive times and was in common use throughout the ancient Mediterranean.[19]

It is surely this system of planks and cordage that Agamemnon refers to in the *Iliad* when he complains about the damage to their ships that the Greeks have sustained during their nine-year stay at Troy: the planks of the ships have rotted and the cords have worked loose (καὶ δὴ δοῦρα σέσηπε νεῶν καὶ σπάρτα λέλυνται, *Il.* 2.135). In the *Suppliants* of Aeschylus, the chorus speaks metaphorically of a ship as a "linen-sewn home of wood that keeps out the sea" (λινορραφής τε / δόμος ἅλα στέγων δορός), and the scholiast outlines the shipbuilding technique in order to explain the metaphor: "They used to drill ships and sew them together with cords, and the phrase in Homer 'mending ships' indicates the sewing them together."[20] While the sewn boat was eventually replaced by a more sophisticated technique, nevertheless the memory of sewn boats and their association with the early times of epic poetry remains strong in classical literature. In Virgil's *Aeneid*, Aeneas crosses the river Styx in a *cumba sutilis*.[21] In his second-century B.C.E. play based on the *Odyssey*, Pacuvius has the hero make a raft of sewn planks in order to sail off Calypso's island.[22]

A new technique of shipbuilding, however, appears to have been adopted by the Greeks during the eighth century B.C.E.[23] Evidence brought to the surface by underwater archeologists has shown that the Greeks also used a mortise and tenon system, a technique that Lionel Casson has characterized as more like cabinetwork than carpentry.[24] The planks were joined together by carving broad (two-inch) tenons, or wooden tabs, to be inserted into corresponding mortises, or slots, carved and drilled into the neighboring plank. These joints were then fixed externally with dowels or pegs.[25] This technique, as Casson has argued, is the same one that Odysseus uses to build a raft or ship on Calypso's island.[26] Calypso gives Odysseus an axe, an adze, and a drill and then leads him to the wooded part of the island so he can fell trees to make the planks for the boat. Once he has cut the planks, sanded them well, and made them straight and true, he then drills them and hammers them together snugly with pegs and cords:

τέτρηνεν δ' ἄρα πάντα καὶ ἥρμοσεν ἀλλήλοισι,
γόμφοισιν δ' ἄρα τήν γε καὶ ἁρμονίῃσιν ἄρασσεν.

He drilled them all and fitted them to one another, and with pegs and cords he hammered it together. (*Od.* 5.247–48)

Reference to this mortise and tenon technique appears in a simile in *Odyssey* Book 9 as well, where the act of sharpening the stick to blind the Cyclops is

Ship with oars. Fragment of a clay plaque. Proto-Attic, ca. 700 B.C.E. No.14935. Photo courtesy of the National Archeological Museum, Athens.

likened to a shipbuilder's drilling a ship's plank by twisting his auger or drill back and forth with a leather strap.[27]

A shipwright works with raw, unfinished planks of wood; his job is to sand and plane those planks and then to fasten them together into a seaworthy vehicle. The emphasis, understandably, is on a good fit—when making his raft, Odysseus fits the planks next to one another and then hammers them together with pegs and joints—since a loosely jointed ship will surely sink once it has left shore. What is significant for our argument is that the pegs (γόμφοισιν) that hold together Odysseus' raft are the very same pegs that hold together the metapoetic ships of Hesiod and Ibycus (πολυγόμφοι). Indeed, many of the skills and tools of the shipwright are important to poetic construction as well: a song, like a ship, must be well fitted or sewn together.

### Early Greek Song-Making

Both of the techniques used to construct ships in the archaic period—either stitching planks together with cord or the pegging and joinery of cabinetmaking—overlap with a metaphorical network of sewing and woodworking images used in Greek poetry to represent the skills of an oral poet. Songs, like ships, are stitched together, and this particular metaphor appears most prominently, of course, in the etymology of the term *rhapsode*, "the one who sews the songs."[28] At the beginning of Nemean 2, for example, Pindar refers to the "sewn songs" (ῥαπτῶν ἐπέων, 3) of the Homeridae. Some have understood this etymology to distinguish the oral poet who composes songs himself from the later performer who merely sings songs of others, stitching together previous material into a new performance.[29] Gregory Nagy has shown, however, that this is a false distinction.[30] Within an oral tradition each poet composes anew in performance, as Hesiod boasts in the following fragment:

ἐν Δήλῳ τότε πρῶτον ἐγὼ καὶ Ὅμηρος ἀοιδοὶ
μέλπομεν, ἐν νεαροῖς ὕμνοις ῥάψαντες ἀοιδήν,
Φοῖβον Ἀπόλλωνα χρυσάορον, ὃν τέκε Λητώ

Then first at Delos, I and Homer, poets, sang, having sewn our song into new hymns, for Phoebus Apollo of the golden sword, whom Leto bore (Fr. 357 Merkelbach and West)

Here the great early poets Hesiod and Homer themselves are identified as rhapsodes; the passage literally etymologizes the term *rhapsode* in such a way as to suggest that their skill as poets lies in their ability to stitch together preexisting poetic traditions into a new song, one that fits this new occasion. This sewing metaphor is related to the Indo-European image of weaving songs: both capture the skills involved in creating new songs within a preexisting oral tradition.[31] Songs, like some early "sewn" ships, are thus composed by stitching together, in a seamless fashion, the materials of production—poetic themes.

The second type of shipbuilding, one that employs cabinetry skills to fit the planks together, also corresponds to a set of imagery that emerges from another metaphor of poetic production, that of the craftsman. Metalworkers or woodworkers, like poets, work with their raw materials to fashion a work of art. Pindar uses this image of fitting materials together when he invokes the figure of poet as craftsman, the skilled *tekton* of words, in Pythian 3:

Νέστορα καὶ Λύκιον Σαρπηδόν᾽, ἀνθρώπων φάτις
ἐξ ἐπέων κελαδεννῶν, τέκτονες οἷα σοφοὶ
ἅρμοσαν, γινώσκομεν.

We know of Nestor and Lykian Sarpedon, the report of men from resounding songs, the kind that skilled craftsmen have fitted together. (Pyth. 3.112–14)

Pindar here brings the familiar terminology of craftsmanship—skill and a focus on good fit—to bear on the techniques of poetry. In Book 10 of the *Republic*, Plato uses the analogy of the craftsman, especially the woodworker, in his discussion of poetry and its imitative nature.

The craft of song-making is thus conceptualized metaphorically as working with metals or wood or stitching cloth. These skilled craftsmen use raw materials to compose, or fit together, something new and beautiful.[32] The shipbuilder, too, whether he stitches or hammers together the planks of his boat, creates an oceangoing vessel out of wood and pegs or twine. It comes as no surprise, then, that Daedalus, the famous Cretan craftsman, is credited with the invention of sails and other nautical innovations.[33] Shipwrights, woodworkers, stitchers, poets: these professional craftsmen use *sophia* and *techne* to fashion skilled products out of raw materials; they aim for harmony in their work—a good fit.[34]

In addition, nautical terminology overlaps in some suggestive ways with that of song-making. The space in which the oar fits, for example, is called the *metron*, the term used to measure or regulate the rhythm of a line of poetry; in Aeschylus' *Persians*, the association is made explicit when the strict rhythm of the oars provides the measures for song.[35] Hesiod, we remember, boasts that he will show Perses "the measures of the loud-roaring sea" in a phrase that refers both to the realm of overseas travel and to poetic skill (*WD* 648). Like a line of poetry, the sails of a ship convey meaning, and in his account of the battle of Salamis, Herodotus emphasizes this communicative power. In the heat of battle, men must read and interpret the signs conveyed by the sails of a ship to determine who is an ally or an enemy.[36] In much the same way, the sail of Theseus' ship, its black or white color, telegraphs the story of his success or failure in Crete to his father anxiously awaiting news in Athens. A ship's sails convey meaning no less than they help carry men and cargo across the sea, and a pair of Homeric metaphors suggests that the oars of ships move in much the same way. Oars, says Teiresias, are the wings of ships (ἐρετρά, τά τε πτερὰ νηυσὶ πέλονται, *Od.* 11.125), and this image calls to mind the famous winged words of epic poetry (ἔπεα πτερόεντα).[37] Richard Martin has argued quite persuasively that the metaphor of winged words appears specifically in contexts of directed speech; the image of flight represents the focused direction of the speech and highlights its intended audience.[38] Although not conclusive, the metaphorical intersection of ships and songs is highly suggestive: equipped with wings, oars, or sails, they keep to their charted course and deliver their cargo whether it be men, merchandise, or meaning.

While poetic production shares some actual terminology with shipbuilding, an even more interesting connection between poetics and seafaring is not articulated directly but rather triangulated with the process of textile production. As we have seen, stitching and weaving are common metaphors for making poetry, and some of the equipment necessary for sailing also belongs to the realm of textile production.[39] The sails of a ship, like the planks of some types of ships, are stitched together. Calypso brings cloth (φᾶρος), the product of her loom, for Odysseus to use to make sails for his new ship, and one word (σπεῖρον) is used in the *Odyssey* to designate both the sails of a ship and clothing.[40] For example, during the storm that arises after Odysseus leaves Calypso's island, the mast breaks up and the sail (σπεῖρον, 5.318) is thrown together with the upper deck into the water. When Odysseus washes ashore naked on the island of Phaeacia after the wreck of his raft, he asks Nausicaa if she has a piece of cloth (εἴλυμα σπείρων, 6.179) for him. While his immediate request is for clothing, his need for sails and a ship is no less pressing. This intersection of weaving and sailing is a particularly rich one in the *Odyssey* and is structurally reinforced by the very architecture of ship and loom; one word (ἱστός) designates both the mast from which a ship's sails hang and the upright of a woman's loom.[41] In fact, the gender roles of the magical Phaeacians reinforce this inherent connection between sailing and weaving. The poet says that the skill the Phaeacian men show at sailing swift ships is directly matched by the knowledge and proficiency of Phaeacian women at their looms:

> ὅσσον Φαίηκες περὶ πάντων ἴδριες ἀνδρῶν
> νῆα θοὴν ἐνὶ πόντῳ ἐλαυνέμεν, ὡς δὲ γυναῖκες
> ἱστῶν τεχνῆσσαι· πέρι γάρ σφισι δῶκεν Ἀθήνη
> ἔργα τ᾽ ἐπίστασθαι περικαλλέα καὶ φρένας ἐσθλάς.

To the extent that the Phaeacians excel all men in their skill at driving a swift ship upon the sea, so the women are skilled at the loom; for Athena taught them to produce very fine crafts and gave them good intelligence. (*Od.* 7.107–11)

In fact, this gendered opposition of sailing and weaving reflects the overarching structure of the whole poem: as Odysseus sails across the wide seas in an attempt to return home, Penelope manages to keep this home intact through her skills and wiles at the loom.

Similarities in technique, exemplified by the metaphors of production, help explain the nexus of overlapping vocabulary belonging to the worlds of textiles, ships, and songs at work in the *Odyssey*. Both ships and songs are stitched, woven, or hammered together by craftsmen skilled in fitting together disparate materials to create a harmonious product. The figurative association between sailing and poetry that first appears in the Catalogue of Ships and continues to thrive in later Greek (and other) poetic traditions is thus rooted in Greek metaphors of production as well as in early literary traditions of poetic expertise. And now, turning to the *Odyssey*, we will see that when both Hesiod and Ibycus phrase their poetic programs with nautical imagery, they look back not just to the Catalogue of Ships but also to the *Odyssey* and especially to the raft of Odysseus. For this raft is secured with these very same pegs—γόμφοι—and his success, both as hero and as poet of the *Odyssey*, depends on his skilled construction of this raft.

## Odysseus' Raft

Book 5 of the *Odyssey* opens with the second council of the gods, where Athena persuades Zeus to send Hermes to Calypso with instructions to let Odysseus return home. Once Calypso agrees to send him on his way, she has no ships to give him. Instead, she helps the stranded hero put together a raft. She gives Odysseus a bronze-headed axe and a well-finished adze; she leads him to the part of her island where tall alder and poplar trees grow, and then she returns to her own house (5.234–42). Next, Homer details how Odysseus goes about trimming the timbers into planks, fitting them together to form the raft, fashioning the mast and upper deck:

εἴκοσι δ' ἔκβαλε πάντα, πελέκκησεν δ' ἄρα χαλκῷ,
ξέσσε δ' ἐπισταμένως καὶ ἐπὶ στάθμην ἴθυνεν.
τόφρα δ' ἔνεικε τέρετρα Καλυψώ, δῖα θεάων·
τέτρηνεν δ' ἄρα πάντα καὶ ἥρμοσεν ἀλλήλοισι,
γόμφοισιν δ' ἄρα τήν γε καὶ ἁρμονίῃσιν ἄρασσεν.
ὅσσον τίς τ' ἔδαφος νηὸς τορνώσεται ἀνὴρ
φορτίδος εὐρείης, εὖ εἰδὼς τεκτοσυνάων,
τόσσον ἔπ' εὐρεῖαν σχεδίην ποιήσατ' Ὀδυσσεύς.
ἴκρια δὲ στήσας, ἀραρὼν θαμέσι σταμίνεσσι,
ποίει· ἀτὰρ μακρῇσιν ἐπηγκενίδεσσι τελεύτα.
ἐν δ' ἱστὸν ποίει καὶ ἐπίκριον ἄρμενον αὐτῷ·
πρὸς δ' ἄρα πηδάλιον ποιήσατο, ὄφρ' ἰθύνοι.
φράξε δέ μιν ῥίπεσσι διαμπερὲς οἰσυΐνῃσι
κύματος εἶλαρ ἔμεν· πολλὴν δ' ἐπεχεύατο ὕλην.

He threw down twenty [trees] in all and trimmed them with his bronze axe; he planed them expertly, and made them straight to a chalk line. Then Calypso, the shining goddess, brought him an auger. He drilled them all and fitted them to one another, and with pegs and cords he hammered it together. And as great as the hull of a broad cargo-carrying ship when a man well skilled in carpentry fashions it, such was the size of the broad raft that Odysseus made for himself. Next, setting up the platforms and fitting them to close uprights he worked, and finished them with broad boards on top. Then he made the mast, finished with an upper deck, and, in addition, he made a rudder so that he could steer; he fenced it completely with wattled wicker to be a defense against waves, and he piled on a great deal of lumber. (*Od.* 5.244–57)

Odysseus' work on the raft is knowledgeable (ἐπισταμένως, 245); like the poets of Pythian 3, he works with the skill of a professional craftsman (εὖ εἰδὼς τεκτοσυνάων, 250). The description of Odysseus' construction of this raft emphasizes the cabinetry or carpentry skills typical of both shipbuilding and song-making (ἥρμοσεν, 247; ἁρμονίῃσιν, 248; ἀραρὼν, 252). In addition, forms of the verb ποιέω appear four times in five lines (251–55), recalling the similar use of ποιέω and other verbs of making in the Iliadic metapoetic scene describing the making of Achilles' shield. The raft-building passage thus brings together the terminology of skill and harmony that, as we have seen, belongs equally within the worlds of shipbuilding and poetry, especially oral poetry.

Calypso then reappears with the material to make a sail, but it is Odysseus alone who carefully works the cloth into sails, attaching straps and halyards:

τόφρα δὲ φάρε᾽ ἔνεικε Καλυψώ, δῖα θεάων,
ἱστία ποιήσασθαι· ὁ δ᾽ εὖ τεχνήσατο καὶ τά.
ἐν δ᾽ ὑπέρας τε κάλους τε πόδας τ᾽ ἐνέδησεν ἐν αὐτῇ.
μοχλοῖσιν δ᾽ ἄρα τήν γε κατείρυσεν εἰς ἅλα δῖαν.

Next Calypso, the shining goddess, brought out the sailcloth to make
sails, and he worked these well also; he tied the straps and halyards and
ropes upon the raft, and then with levers dragged it down to the shining salt water. (*Od.* 5.258–61)

Calypso provides the raw material (φάρε᾽), but it is Odysseus' skill (εὖ τεχνήσατο)
that transforms the cloth into sails, just as he created a raft out of timber and
tools. Then, when the raft is finally completed, the goddess gives him clothes,
water, and wine for the trip; she even sends a favorable wind at his back (οὖρον
δὲ προέηκεν ἀπήμονά τε λιαρόν τε, 268). In other words, the divine nymph provides Odysseus with the tools and raw material necessary to build the raft, but
she leaves him to fashion them into an oceangoing vessel all on his own. The
word for "raft" here is σχεδίη, etymologically related to the adverb σχεδόν,
something that is close by or near at hand. This same root produces the compound αὐτοσχεδιάζω, meaning "to improvise."[42] One improvises from things
that are close at hand, and an improvised ship is thus a raft. And so, in addition
to its manner of construction, the two components—divine intervention and improvisation—that build Odysseus' raft coincide with the complementary aspects
of oral poetic composition: familiarity with the poetic tradition often represented
by the Muses and an ability to innovate within that tradition.

Oral poetry is composed in the moment of performance, and a successful
poet skillfully combines traditional legends and story patterns with a strategy for
improvisation, incorporating what is new seamlessly into the old.[43] This twofold
technique is perhaps best articulated by Phemius in his death-averting speech in
Book 22 of the *Odyssey*, when he asks Odysseus not to kill him precisely because he is a poet:

αὐτοδίδακτος δ᾽ εἰμί, θεὸς δέ μοι ἐν φρεσὶν οἴμας
παντοίας ἐνέφυσεν·

I am self-taught, and the god inspires me with all kinds of songs. (*Od.*
22.347–48)

The god inspires him with songs, he says, but his skill is his own. The mention
of divine inspiration represents the poetic tradition, most often personified in the
role of the Muses, and the concept of being self-taught (αὐτοδίδακτος) is in fact
expressed by a newly coined adjective, invented on the spot to characterize the
improvisational component of oral poetry. A poet depends on the larger poetic
tradition to provide him with the raw material necessary to produce his songs,
and yet, like Odysseus building his raft, he brings his own skill and professional

expertise, his ability to improvise within the tradition, to produce the kind of song necessary and appropriate for each particular occasion.[44]

In other words, we might say that the goddess Calypso represents the divine or traditional component of raft-building; she provides the raw materials that all rafts are made of and even a favoring breeze, but Odysseus himself must figure out how to build and steer the raft in order to get home, drawing on his skills, knowledge, and familiarity with tools. That Odysseus' raft breaks up before he arrives onshore captures the contingent nature of oral poetry, in which bits of songs are put together in interesting and useful ways to fit a specific occasion. No oral composition is likely to remain intact to be sung in exactly the same way twice. Instead, oral performances get taken apart and reassembled in a different order, just as parts (or planks) of the stories that Odysseus tells to the Phaeacians (Books 9–12) reappear in different forms, in different contexts, incorporated into the many tales he tells to Eumaeus, Telemachus, and Penelope after his return to Ithaca.

The construction of Odysseus' raft, then, corresponds to the techniques of producing oral poetry. He builds his raft to sail home from Ogygia, hammering together planks and pegs, just as an oral poet fashions his poetic craft and plies it upon the metaphorical sea of the Greek epic tradition. The ways in which sewing and cabinetry, figures of both nautical and poetic production, emphasize skill and close-fitting construction help us recognize and appreciate exactly how Odysseus' raft represents the poetic process and, equally important, what it can tell us about the ways in which the Greeks conceptualized the process of making poetry.

The metapoetic status of Odysseus' raft, together with the poetic manifesto of the Iliadic Catalogue of Ships, lays the foundation for the figurative association between ships and songs that poets such as Hesiod and Ibycus tap into more explicitly. In addition to the ways in which the techniques of shipbuilding articulate the process of poetic composition, the sea journey itself, its length or direction, comes to represent the greater poetic tradition and one poet's place in it. When Hesiod says he knows nothing of ships since he has sailed only a short journey from Aulis to Euboea, he alludes directly to the Catalogue of Ships; his mention of "many-pegged ships" recalls Odysseus' metapoetic shipbuilding technique. He thus locates himself squarely within this Homeric tradition of equating nautical experience and skill with poetic status. Ibycus specifically brings together the peg and plank technique of Odysseus' raft with the Iliadic catalogue when he claims to be unable to list the number of many-pegged ships that sailed to Troy. Both poets import the language and terminology of ships and sailing from the Homeric poems and then set off in new directions.

Odysseus' raft-building is thus motivated by much more than the plot—the need to get Odysseus home. In addition, like Walcott's poetic craft, Odysseus' raft functions as a vehicle whose construction echoes the process of making poetry, especially oral poetry. The scene on Calypso's island thus establishes a more

*Calypso's Island*. Bryson Burroughs. Painting, 1928. Photo courtesy of Hirschl & Adler Galleries, Inc., New York.

complicated framework for interpreting the poem's fascination with sailing and ships. The detailed account of Odysseus' raft-building not only prepares the audience for the renewal of the hero's nautical adventures, but also lays the groundwork for the significance of his role as singer and master storyteller in the poem as well. Both Odysseus' arrival and departure from Phaeacia are marked by unusual modes of sea transport—he arrives on a self-made raft but leaves on the ship of another, one of the magical ships of the Phaeacians—thus circumscribing his role as primary poet of the poem within a conspicuously nautical frame.[45]

The audience's first direct encounter with Odysseus does not happen, after all, until Book 5. Up to this point, others have spoken of him; they have told stories of his heroism and lamented his absence, but Odysseus himself has not yet spoken; he has been hidden away on Calypso's island for seven years. As Athena complains to Zeus at the beginning of the book (really the second prologue of the poem), Odysseus has no ships. In other words, I want to suggest, he has no poetic voice.[46] If he cannot sail successfully to Phaeacia, his story, the story of his adventures, will not be told, and his heroic journey will remain forever un-sung.[47] Odysseus first appears in the *Odyssey* precisely at the point of building the raft to set sail off Calypso's island, and what he gains from successfully con-structing the raft is both the ability to sail to Phaeacia, where he will acquire much wealth and ultimately safe passage home, and the opportunity to sing the song of his travels. In other words, the construction of Odysseus' raft not only enables but also prefigures the composition of the tales he sings at Alcinous' court.

Many, many years later, Derek Walcott puts himself in the same boat. He, too, invokes Homer and joins in this dialogue, jockeying for position with his poetic predecessors. Much more explicitly than Hesiod and Ibycus, he draws on the language and imagery of sea travel to explore the analogy between the poet motionless at his desk and the hero traveling the high seas: "there are two jour-neys in every odyssey." A poet needs a hero's adventures to sing, and the hero depends on the poet to sing them. In much the same way, the construction of Odysseus' raft also enables both heroic travel and poetic celebration.

The *Odyssey* is all about travel and about poetry, and the metaphorical as-sociation of sailing and song helps elaborate the mutual implication of these two thematic aspects of the poem. But more important, it helps structure the ethno-graphic imagination of the poem. The world of the *Odyssey* is, after all, a world of amazing new developments in matters of trade and commerce; it is also a time of increased overseas travel and exploration, and the poem's fascination with ships and sailing is linked to this brave new world as much as it reflects methods of poetic construction. The implications of this metaphorical connection are rich—both in terms of how the association of poetry and ships operates within the *Odyssey* and in light of developments and innovations for poetry, commerce, and travel in archaic Greece.[48]

# 2

# Poetic Profit

διὰ ταῦτά τοι καὶ Θεόφραστος αὐτὸν [Democritus of Abdera]
ἐπήνει, ὅτι περήει κρείττονα ἀγερμὸν ἀγείρων Μενελάου καὶ
Ὀδυσσέως. ἐκεῖνοι μὲν γὰρ ἠλῶντο, αὐτόχρημα Φοινίκων ἐμ-
πόρων μηδὲν διαφέροντες· χρήματα γὰρ ἤθροιζεν, καὶ τῆς περι-
όδου καὶ τοῦ περίπλου ταύτην εἶχον τὴν πρόφασιν.

And for these reasons, Theophrastus too praised him [Democri-
tus of Abdera], because he gathered a greater collection of goods
than Menelaus and Odysseus. For those men wandered and
were not at all different from Phoenician merchants. They gathered goods and offered this as their excuse for traveling and sailing around.

Aelian, *Miscellany*

At the end of Book 5, Odysseus builds a raft to sail away from Calypso's island
and return home to Ithaca. In addition to enabling Odysseus to continue his
homeward journey, this raft helps articulate the figurative association of ships
and seafaring with poetic activity in the *Odyssey*. On many occasions, ships—
the manner of their construction and their ability to sail—represent the poetic
process in Greek poetry, and the raft-building scene in Book 5 elaborates the
terms and structure of this metaphor at work in the *Odyssey*. Read metaphorically, then, Odysseus' ability to set sail once again prefigures his emergence as
poet of the *Odyssey* once he arrives safely at Phaeacia.

In building his raft, Odysseus proves that he has the necessary skills of a
professional shipbuilder or poet, but also, and somewhat surprisingly, this
hastily cobbled together raft is said to have the capacity to carry substantial
cargo:

ὅσσον τίς τ᾽ ἔδαφος νηὸς τορνώσεται ἀνὴρ,
φορτίδος εὐρείης, εὖ εἰδὼς τεκτοσυνάων,
τόσσον ἐπ᾽ εὐρεῖαν σχεδίην ποιήσατ᾽ Ὀδυσσεύς.

And as great as the hull of a broad cargo-carrying ship when a man well skilled in carpentry fashions it, such was the size of the broad raft that Odysseus made for himself. (*Od.* 5.249–51)[1]

Odysseus' raft is as big as a commercial ship, and mention of the cargo capacity of this vessel adds a new dimension to the metaphorical connection between ships and songs: it brings the profits of overseas trade to bear on the poetics of the *Odyssey*. Merchant ships, like Odysseus' raft, have the potential to carry valuable goods. This image, linked as it is to the practice of commercial trade in archaic Greece, enriches the metaphor of ships and song. It helps articulate the traffic in goods and song at work in a brave new world of economic and poetic innovation.

### Poetic Cargo

Hesiod, we remember, embeds his own discussion of sailing and poetry within a larger section in the *Works and Days* devoted to the advantages and disadvantages of overseas trade as an alternative to farming. A closer look, then, at the entire sailing section will be of help in sorting out some of the issues underlying Homer's own allusion to Odysseus' raft as a large-hulled cargo boat and the implications of this comparison for the poetics of the *Odyssey*. Hesiod opens the Nautilia with a discussion of weather and seasons, warning his brother Perses against setting sail during the stormy season. Sailing, he continues, is most profitable in the right season:

αὐτὸς δ᾽ ὡραῖον μίμνειν πλόον, εἰσόκεν ἔλθῃ·
καὶ τότε νῆα θοὴν ἅλαδ᾽ ἑλκέμεν, ἐν δέ τε φόρτον
ἄρμενον ἐντύνασθαι, ἵν᾽ οἴκαδε κέρδος ἄρηαι . . .

You, yourself, wait until the sailing season, whenever it comes, and then drag your swift ship down to the sea, and place an appropriate cargo in it so that you may bring home a profit . . . (*WD* 630–32)

Seafaring, he says, is uncomfortable (ναυτιλίης δυσπεμφέλου, 618), but overseas trade is a good way to bring home profit (κέρδος), provided you wait until the right time of year and stow an appropriate cargo (φόρτον ἄρμενον). Setting sail in good weather is an important consideration, but the size of the ship is equally significant:

νῆ᾽ ὀλίγην αἰνεῖν, μεγάλῃ δ᾽ ἐνὶ φορτία θέσθαι.
μείζων μὲν φόρτος, μεῖζον δ᾽ ἐπὶ κέρδει κέρδος
ἔσσεται, εἴ κ᾽ ἄνεμοί γε κακὰς ἀπέχωσιν ἀήτας.

Praise a small ship, but put your cargo in a big one. The greater the
cargo, the greater profit there will be upon profit so long as the winds
hold off the destructive blasts. (*WD* 643–45)

The ability to make significant profit is thus directly linked to the size of the ship.
Bigger ships can carry more cargo to trade, and Hesiod's advice about how to
maximize profit from trading cargo overseas leads directly into his metapoetic
discussion of sailing and poetry. Poetry must be a profitable enterprise as well.
It is at precisely this point that he tells Perses that he will show him the measures
of the sea if he ever decides to look to trade (ἐμπορίη), as a way to avoid poverty
and starvation (646–48). After the metapoetic section, Hesiod returns to the
theme of weather and the best time for sailing, and then concludes the Nautilia
with one more piece of advice about cargo and profit:

μηδ᾽ ἐν νηυσὶν ἅπαντα βίον κοίλῃσι τίθεσθαι·
ἀλλὰ πλέω λείπειν, τὰ δὲ μείονα φορτίζεσθαι.
δεινὸν γὰρ πόντου μετὰ κύμασι πήματι κύρσαι.
δεινὸν δ᾽, εἴ κ᾽ ἐπ᾽ ἄμαξαν ὑπέρβιον ἄχθος ἀείρας
ἄξονα καυάξαις καὶ φορτία μαυρωθείη.
μέτρα φυλάσσεσθαι· καιρὸς δ᾽ ἐπὶ πᾶσιν ἄριστος.

Do not put all your livelihood in your hollow ships, but leave the majority behind, and stow the lesser part as cargo. For it is a terrible thing
to encounter disaster among the waves of the sea, just as if you should
pile an excessive load upon your wagon, you would break the axle, so
your cargo would be wiped out. Observe the guidelines; the right
amount is best in all things. (*WD* 689–94)

A sense of proportion is instrumental in matters of trade as in all endeavors. If
you lose all your cargo in a storm, there is no profit to be made from the expedition. Hesiod thus embeds his programmatic discussion of sailing and song
within a larger description of overseas trade, emphasizing ways to stow cargo in
order to bring home profit: not everything you own, not too much for the ship.
Most important, a big ship is best if you want to gain big profits. Hesiod's use
of *metra* at the end of the section recalls his earlier reference to measures of the
sea (μέτρα θαλάσσης, *WD* 648) to designate both nautical experience and modes
of regulating poetic composition.[2] Hesiod thus articulates poetic value and exchange in terms of cargo and ships. But how does this work? What kind of cargo
does a metapoetic boat carry?

Pindar takes up Hesiod's image of merchant ships and song in Nemean 5,
and a brief look at how this theme operates in a fifth-century context will shed
some light on how the notion of profit may be applied to the business of poetry
in early archaic times as well.[3] In Nemean 5, Pindar draws on both the notion
of a merchant ship itself as metaphor for the value of poetry and the potential

of cargo ships to bring profit to himself as poet and to the victor celebrated by his song. In the opening lines of the poem, Pindar sends his song forth on every cargo freighter and ship to spread the news of Pytheas' victory:

Οὐκ ἀνδριαντοποιός εἰμ', ὥστ' ἐλινύσοντα ἐργά-
   ζεσθαι ἀγάλματ' ἐπ' αὐτᾶς βαθμίδος
ἑσταότ' · ἀλλ' ἐπὶ πάσας
   ὁλκάδος ἔν τ' ἀκάτῳ, γλυκεῖ' ἀοιδά,
στεῖχ' ἀπ' Αἰγίνας διαγγέλλοισ'. . .

I am not a sculptor, who turns out statues that stand idle on their own bases, but, sweet song, go out in every cargo freighter and in oared galleys, setting out from Aegina, announcing . . . (N.5.1–3)

Not stationary like the statue permanently fixed on its base, Pindar's sweet song sails away from Aegina across the sea. Pindar compares his poem to merchandise that travels on two kinds of cargo boats. A *holkas* is strictly a sailing vessel (its name derived from the occasional necessity to tow it in and out of harbors in the absence of favorable winds) capable of stowing surprisingly large amounts of cargo. The smallest such boats built for overseas shipping could carry 70 to 80 tons, and from the fifth century on, boats carrying 100 to 150 tons of cargo were common. An *akatos*, by contrast, is an oared galley, somewhat smaller than a trireme, that could carry dispatches, passengers, or cargo.[4] The force of Pindar's choice of cargo ships here emphasizes the potential value of Pindar's sweet song; it locates the ode on very big boats within a worldwide system of profit and exchange. Merchant expeditions are never one-way trips; one loads a ship full of cargo with the firm expectation that the return trip will bring even more valuable goods back home. Thus Pindar's song leaves Aegina, the home of the victor Pytheas, carrying news of his victory, in order that it might bring back something even more valuable than local fame: a worldwide reputation.[5]

Pindar's poetic cargo travels abroad; it reaches many audiences, like a commercial freighter that carries valuable goods from one port to another. Both the mobility of travel and the potential for profit stored in a ship's hull are at work here to represent Pindar's poem as an object of trade. The image of treasure (*agalmata*) and the vehicles of trade are in turn linked to the corresponding contrast of fixity (statue) and mobility (ships) to bring competing notions of value and exchange into focus. First Pindar introduces a system in which an *agalma* (a source of talismanic power) remains fixed on its base; its value is correspondingly constant, firmly located within the aristocratic system of gift exchange.[6] He then opposes this fixed statue to his own poetry, which moves across the sea like cargo in a commercial freighter. He has put his poetry on the open market, so to speak, trusting that this ship will bring him and his client back great profit in return. As others have already noted, Pindar thus represents his own poem as an object of value.[7] What is even more interesting about this particular passage, however, is the contrast between the image of a stable aristocratic system of exchange and a more volatile, yet potentially more profitable, system of trade. Pindar appropriates the vocabulary of these competing systems of exchange to replace cultural status and talismanic power with real economic profit as his metaphor for the value of his own poetry.

Pindar returns to the association of ships and songs at the end of Nemean 5, appealing to others who would join in his praise of Themistius, the victor's great-uncle, to give voice and unfurl their sails. At this point, he emphasizes the metapoetic nature of the sailing image:

> εἰ δὲ Θεμίστιον ἵκεις
>    ὥστ᾽ ἀείδειν, μηκέτι ῥίγει· δίδοι
> φωνάν, ἀνὰ δ᾽ ἱστία τεῖνον
>    πρὸς ζυγὸν καρχασίου
> πύκταν τέ νιν καὶ παγκρατίου
>    φθέγξαι ἑλεῖν Ἐπιδαύρῳ διπλόαν
> νικῶντ᾽ ἀρετάν . . .

If you have come to sing of Themistius, no longer hold back, but give voice, unfurl the sails toward the masthead. Announce that he is a boxer and that he took a second victory, winning in the *pankration* in Epidaurus . . . (N. 5.50–53)

Pindar addresses those who would sing of Themistius as fellow crew members on his metaphorical cargo freighter. To sing is to let loose the sails, to fill them with the collective breath of song that will launch this figurative ship and set it on its way.[8] The ease with which Pindar here moves between poetic and nautical imagery—between songs that set sail and sails that sing songs—depends on the analogy between the construction of boats and of poetry, as we saw in chapter 1. His choice of cargo-carrying boats, however, emphasizes the potential for profit as an essential part of this nautical metaphor.[9] Pindar draws on the world of commerce and trade to represent his song as a kind of product, open for trade, and this commodification of song is a common theme in archaic lyric and elegiac poetry.[10] Two centuries earlier, in his programmatic association of poetry and sailing in the *Works and Days*, Hesiod, too, introduces the notion of profit from overseas trade within a context of poetic value. With these two models in mind, we can now return to the *Odyssey*. Homer makes Odysseus' raft unusually large—the size of a cargo-carrying ship—and his choice of imagery suggests that a similar link between the potential profits of trade and those of poetry is already at work in the *Odyssey* as well.

In fact, several figures in the *Odyssey* borrow from the language of trade and commerce, especially the polarized terms of profit and theft, to evaluate the songs that Odysseus sings.[11] Good poetry brings profit, evoking the positive images and potential of legitimate trade, but bad poets are compared to deceptive, thievish traders, linking poetry with the illegitimate gains associated with commercial enterprise. In Book 11, for example, when Alcinous praises Odysseus for telling such good stories, he implies that a bad poet is like a thief:

ὦ Ὀδυσεῦ, τὸ μὲν οὔ τί σ᾽ ἐίσκομεν εἰσορόωντες
ἠπεροπῆά τ᾽ ἔμεν καὶ ἐπίκλοπον, οἷά τε πολλοὺς
βόσκει γαῖα μέλαινα πολυσπερέας ἀνθρώπους
ψεύδεά τ᾽ ἀρτύνοντας, ὅθεν κέ τις οὐδὲ ἴδοιτο·
σοὶ δ᾽ ἔπι μὲν μορφὴ ἐπέων, ἔνι δὲ φρένες ἐσθλαί·
μῦθον δ᾽ ὡς ὅτ᾽ ἀοιδὸς ἐπισταμένως κατέλεξας,
πάντων Ἀργείων σέο τ᾽ αὐτοῦ κήδεα λυγρά.

O Odysseus, looking upon you, we do not at all liken you to a deceptive man or a thief, such as the dark earth nourishes—many, who wander widely and tell lies, from whom one could learn nothing. Yet there is a beauty to your words, and there is sense in them, and expertly as a singer you have told the story of your own sorrows and those of all the Argives. (*Od.* 11.363–69)

In praising Odysseus' song, Alcinous draws from the aristocratic notion of poetry, which demands that songs be pleasing, well suited, and instructive to their audience. Odysseus told his story "expertly," just like a professional poet (ὅτ᾽ ἀοιδὸς ἐπισταμένως); his song had beauty (μορφὴ) and intelligence (φρένες ἐσθλαί). In characterizing a bad poet, by contrast, Alcinous alludes to the world of traders—those who travel widely and tell lies. What is going on here? How do we explain Alcinous' choice of imagery? Is it connected to the cargo-carrying capacity of Odysseus' raft?

## Exchange in the World of the *Odyssey*

The *Odyssey* portrays a world very much concerned with modes of exchange; it is one in which a broad spectrum of social and commercial transactions takes place, ranging from the highly controlled, mutual reciprocity of gift exchange among aristocratic peers to the random, one-sided profit-taking of pirates who sail the high seas, trafficking in all kinds of goods. In between these two extreme modes of exchange is the more problematic arena of commodity exchange and trade. In this respect, the range of exchange possibilities present in the world of the *Odyssey* conforms broadly to the anthropologist Marshall Sahlins's formal typology of reciprocities. As part of his discussion of "the interplay in primitive communities between forms, material conditions, and social relations of exchange," he suggests a spectrum ranging from what he calls "generalized reciprocity" or putatively altruistic transactions to "negative reciprocity" or the attempt to get something for nothing with impunity. At the midpoint of this spectrum is the direct exchange of "balanced reciprocity."[12] Sahlins explains this typology with reference to "social distance": the more closely related the parties involved in the exchange, the more generous the means of exchange. Generalized reciprocity takes place among friends and kin, while negative reciprocity occurs between strangers or enemies. Sahlins's analysis emphasizes the fluidity and range of exchange possibilities as well as the close relationship of material transactions to social categories and helps provide a framework for thinking about the entire range of exchange possibilities at work in the literary world of the *Odyssey* as well.[13] A closer look at exchange in the *Odyssey* reveals some interesting and significant areas of contestation, especially with respect to notions of value and the role of profit in exchange.[14]

On the one hand, the poem presents a world in which kings like Menelaus and Nestor belong to well-established networks of gift exchange, circulating precious goods to maintain social and political relationships within a closed aristocratic community. As many have shown, the world of Homeric epic includes landed aristocrats who establish and maintain social, political, and economic ties with one another through the highly ritualized process of gift exchange rooted in the reciprocal hospitality or *xenia*, extended by host to guest.[15] When Athena arrives in Ithaca, for example, she claims to be Mentes, a guest-friend of Odysseus, and Telemachus responds appropriately by offering hospitality and gifts:

> ἀλλ᾽ ἄγε νῦν ἐπίμεινον, ἐπειγόμενός περ ὁδοῖο,
> ὄφρα λοεσσάμενός τε τεταρπόμενός τε φίλον κῆρ,
> δῶρον ἔχων ἐπὶ νῆα κίῃς, χαίρων ἐνὶ θυμῷ
> τιμῆεν, μάλα καλόν, ὅ τοι κειμήλιον ἔσται
> ἐξ ἐμεῦ, οἷα φίλοι ξείνοισι διδοῦσι.

> But come now, stay, although you are eager for your journey, so that you may first bathe and take pleasure in your heart, then go back to your ship with a gift, rejoicing in your spirit, something prized, very beautiful, which will be your treasure from me, the kinds of things dear guests and hosts give each other. (*Od.* 1.309–13)

According to Gabriel Herman, "in Homeric society, gift-exchange was the chief method of organising the supply of goods and structuring social relations. Gifts flew in all directions, but of particular importance were gifts exchanged between the heads of different noble households."[16] Not only does this mechanism enable the circulation of wealth across households and introduce goods, especially metals, from the outside world into the closed world of the *oikos*, but also the reciprocal action of gift exchange functions as a means for maintaining social status and political power.[17] M. I. Finley has argued that the primary value of treasure (that is, metals and clothing) is symbolic and derives not from "using" it but from storing it and then giving it away.[18] Gifts demand counter-gifts, and so these exchanges cement long-term relationships. One gives gifts to repay past services, to incur new obligations, and to reinforce the validity of the relationship.[19] The *Odyssey* abounds with tales of such hospitality, articulating the nature of Odysseus' relationships with the inhabitants of the variety of foreign worlds that he encounters in his voyages. Aeolus sends him off with a bag of winds; Polyphemus offers to eat him last as his guest gift; the Phaeacians send him home with more gifts than he would have brought home as booty from Troy.

On the other hand, at the very opposite end of the exchange spectrum in the *Odyssey*, we find pirates. They are unconcerned with giving on any level; instead, their primary aim is the unfettered acquisition of wealth.[20] Pirates frequently travel across the seas to find their booty, as we can see from scenes such as the one in which Telemachus arrives at the court of Nestor at Pylos. Nestor asks who he is and why he has come, listing pirates as one of the two categories of men most likely to travel the seas:

> ὦ ξεῖνοι, τίνες ἐστέ: πόθεν πλεῖθ᾽ ὑγρὰ κέλευθα:
> ἤ τι κατὰ πρῆξιν ἢ μαψιδίως ἀλάλησθε
> οἷά τε ληιστῆρες ὑπεὶρ ἅλα, τοί τ᾽ ἀλόωνται
> ψυχὰς παρθέμενοι, κακὸν ἀλλοδαποῖσι φέροντες;

> Strangers, who are you? From where do you come sailing over the
> watery ways? On business? Or do you idly wander like pirates do
> when they sail on the salt sea and endanger their lives as they wander,
> bringing evil to alien peoples? (*Od.* 3.71–74)[21]

Unlike merchants who travel overseas for a purpose (κατὰ πρῆξιν), pirates travel at random (μαψιδίως), putting their own lives at risk and bringing trouble to others far away. They take as much as they can, giving nothing in return. In Book 14, Odysseus compares the insatiable greed of Penelope's suitors to that of pirates; Zeus will punish both in the end:

> καὶ μὲν δυσμενέες καὶ ἀνάρσιοι, οἵ τ᾽ ἐπὶ γαίης
> ἀλλοτρίης βῶσιν, καί σφι Ζεὺς ληίδα δώῃ,
> πλησάμενοι δέ τε νῆας ἔβαν οἶκόνδε νέεσθαι

> And they are unfriendly and hostile, those who go to the lands of others—and Zeus will give them punishment—and after filling up their ships, return home. (*Od.* 14.85–87)

In the Homeric world, pirates are reckless and violent, and they take booty by force from strangers. Obviously, there is no real exchange here—just one-sided theft—although occasionally, as we learn from Eumaeus' story, pirates sell their booty to maximize their gain. The Phoenician serving woman in Eumaeus' father's house recounts that she was taken from her home by pirates and then sold for a good price:

ἐκ μὲν Σιδῶνος πολυχάλκου εὔχομαι εἶναι
κούρη δ᾽ εἴμ᾽ Ἀρύβαντος ἐγὼ ῥυδὸν ἀφνειοῖο·
ἀλλά μ᾽ ἀνήρπαξαν Τάφιοι ληΐστορες ἄνδρες
ἀγρόθεν ἐρχομένην, πέρασαν δέ τε δεῦρ᾽ ἀγαγόντες
τοῦδ᾽ ἀνδρὸς πρὸς δώμαθ᾽· ὁ δ᾽ ἄξιον ὦνον ἔδωκε.

I boast to be from Sidon, rich in bronze; I am the daughter of Arybas,
for whom riches flow. But Taphian pirates snatched me as I was working in the fields, and bringing me here, to this man's house, they sold
me, and he paid a worthy price for me. (Od. 15.425–29)

These Taphian pirates are thus participants in the slave trade as well: they kid-
napped the woman and sold her into slavery, negotiating a good price for her. In
sum, piracy emphasizes greed and unilateral gain—the goal is to take as much
as possible without giving in return—and is best practiced on strangers overseas.

In between the reciprocal generosity of gift exchange and the unilateral theft
of piracy in the world of the Odyssey is a third, more complicated category of
exchange: commercial trade. As the stories that Odysseus and Eumaeus exchange in the swineherd's hut show, the world of the Odyssey is also one in which
traders operate, ferrying goods from one port to another, exchanging metals,
clothing, and even human cargo outside the bounds of either the personal, ongoing host-guest relationship or the dangers of piracy.[22] Eumaeus' life story, for
example, includes a richly detailed account of Phoenician merchants doing business on the island of Syrie. He calls them "gnawers" (τρῶκται) because of their
insatiable hunger for profits:

Ἔνθα δὲ Φοίνικες ναυσίκλυτοι ἤλυθον ἄνδρες,
τρῶκται, μυρί᾽ ἄγοντες ἀθύρματα νηὶ μελαίνῃ.

There, Phoenician men arrived, famous for their ships, gnawers, bringing thousands of trinkets in their black ship. (Od. 15.415–16)

In other stories told in the Odyssey, the Phoenicians sail the high seas, always
eager for profit, trading in all kinds of commodities, especially slaves, textiles,
and metalwork.[23]

Phoenician traders are known to be deceptive or tricky in the world of the
Odyssey. Eumaeus tells Odysseus that there was a Phoenician servant woman
working in his father's household, and that these merchants beguiled her (ἠπερο-
πεύον, 15.419), offering to take her back to Phoenicia with them.[24] She readily
agrees and then outlines a plan to get aboard their ship safely—a plan that includes a great deal of detail about the mechanics of trade negotiations. She tells
the Phoenician traders to go about securing their return cargo (ὦνον ὁδαίων,
15.445), and when the ship is full of goods, she asks them to send a message
swiftly to the house so she can join them. She promises to bring some gold, too,
whatever is at hand, and something else to add to the cargo:

παῖδα γὰρ ἀνδρὸς ἑῆος ἐνὶ μεγάροις ἀτιτάλλω,
κερδαλέον δὴ τοῖον, ἅμα τροχοώντα θύραζε·
τόν κεν ἄγοιμ᾽ ἐπὶ νηός, ὁ δ᾽ ὑμῖν μυρίον ὦνον
ἄλφοι, ὅπῃ περάσητε κατ᾽ ἀλλοθρόους ἀνθρώπους.

I take care of the master's son in the house, such a profitable child, as
he runs outside. I could bring him aboard and he would bring you a
handsome price, wherever you sold him among foreign peoples. (*Od.*
15.450–53)

Young Eumaeus would (and does) fetch a good price since he is a source of profit
(κερδαλέον).[25] Eumaeus then continues his story, recounting how the Phoenicians
stayed in town for a whole year, trading, to get a substantial cargo to take away
with them (βίοτον πολὺν ἐμπολόωντο, 15.456).

Eumaeus presents a realistic picture of the mechanics of trade, showing that
the world of the *Odyssey* is also engaged in commodity exchange as a way to
circulate people and goods throughout the Mediterranean.[26] Traders, unlike gift
exchange partners, exchange commodities (items that can be exchanged for one
another) outside long-term social and political relationships. In Eumaeus' story
we find a range of things open to exchange—from gold cups and other trinkets
to human beings like Eumaeus himself—and the traders must negotiate the terms
of exchange on the spot. Unlike piracy, trade is bilateral; one thing is exchanged
for another. The value of a given commodity, however, is not absolute, since any
commodity can be exchanged for a wide array of things, and in a traditional
economy such as that of the Homeric poems, it is at the moment of exchange
that their value is determined.[27] As we can see from the serving girl's attention
to Eumaeus, the goal of commercial exchange is obviously profit—Eumaeus
would be a great source of profit (κερδαλέον) for the Phoenician traders—and
the greed associated with Phoenician traders (they are τρῶκται) is a clear indica-
tion of their love of gain and success at making a profit from trade.

On the spectrum of modes of exchange in the world of the *Odyssey*, it is
overseas trade—a bilateral mode of exchange that seeks profit—which occupies
the problematic and shifting middle position between gift exchange and piracy.
Sometimes, for example, trade is attracted into the world of aristocratic gift exchange. When Mentes arrives at Ithaca, for example, he establishes himself as a
guest-friend of Odysseus, and for that reason receives generous hospitality from
Telemachus. Yet he also announces that he is currently traveling on a trade expedition:

Μέντης Ἀγχιάλοιο δαΐφρονος εὔχομαι εἶναι
υἱός, ἀτὰρ Ταφίοισι φιληρέτμοισιν ἀνάσσω.
νῦν δ᾽ ὧδε ξὺν νηὶ κατήλυθον ἠδ᾽ ἑτάροισι
πλέων ἐπὶ οἴνοπα πόντον ἐπ᾽ ἀλλοθρόους ἀνθρώπους,
ἐς Τεμέσην μετὰ χαλκόν, ἄγω δ᾽ αἴθωνα σίδηρον.

I boast to be Mentes, son of the wise Anchialos, and I rule the Taphians who love oars. But now I have come with my ship and companions having sailed across the wine-dark sea to foreign peoples. I am going to Temesa after bronze; I bring gleaming iron. (*Od.* 1.180–84)[28]

Mentes, king of the Taphians and guest-friend of Odysseus, is also a trading partner with Temesa, but the passage does not present these two identities as conflicting or problematic. There is no mention of greed or profit here. Instead, the passsage emphasizes the reciprocity of the trading mission: Mentes brings iron and is looking to acquire bronze in exchange—he hopes to make a good trade.

Similarly in the *Odyssey*, Menelaus, king of Sparta, also appears to have engaged in commercial trade on his way home from Troy. As Nestor tells Telemachus, Menelaus sailed home from his travels abroad "bringing back many possessions, as much a burden as his ships could carry" (πολλὰ κτήματ᾽ ἄγων, ὅσα οἱ νέες ἄχθος ἄειραν, *Od.* 3.312).[29] Menelaus himself explains to Telemachus where he got the wealth that conspicuously decorates his home and palace:

ἦ γὰρ πολλὰ παθὼν καὶ πόλλ᾽ ἐπαληθεὶς
ἠγαγόμην ἐν νηυσὶ καὶ ὀγδοάτῳ ἔτει ἦλθον,
Κύπρον Φοινίκην τε καὶ Αἰγυπτίους ἐπαληθεὶς,
Αἰθίοπάς θ᾽ ἱκόμην καὶ Σιδονίους καὶ Ἐρεμβοὺς
καὶ Λιβύην, ἵνα τ᾽ ἄρνες ἄφαρ κεραοὶ τελέθουσι.

Having suffered a great deal and traveled a great deal, I brought this back in my ships in the eighth year. I wandered to Cyprus and Phoenicia, to the Egyptians, I reached the Aethiopians, the Sidonians, the Eremboi, and Libya, where the rams grow their horns quickly. (*Od.* 4.81–85)[30]

Although he does not mention trade partners or commodities specifically as Mentes does, Menelaus does mention some details that characterize this as a commercial expedition. Menelaus relates that he brought his wealth—gold, silver, bronze, ivory—back from Cyprus, Phoenicia, Egypt, and Libya, an itinerary that includes the primary stops on the Greek trade route. Phoenicia, as we have already seen, is famous for its prestige goods and its deceptive traders. Egypt, too, is well known as a rich source of gold, silver, and other wealth—a site known for profitable trading prospects.[31] Menelaus thus proudly represents himself as a participant in an overseas trade market that links Greece with the Near East and North Africa, and his success at trade is well known and celebrated by later writers.[32] Again, no mention of profit or gain is made in this passage, although it seems clear that Menelaus' elaborately decorated palace owes as much to the profits he earned trading as it does to gifts and treasures from other kings.[33]

Thus at some points in the *Odyssey* the categories of gift exchange and trade converge peacefully to describe trade as a productive, reciprocal mode of moving people and goods around the Mediterranean. The attraction of trade into the world of aristocratic gift exchange downplays the significance of profit and instead emphasizes the reciprocity of commercial exchange conducted among peers.

At the same time, however, the poem takes great pains to distinguish trade from aristocratic gift exchange, and in so doing, it attributes to trade the worst qualities of piracy. In Book 8, for example, Euryalus, one of the Phaeacian nobles, taunts Odysseus for his lack of athletic abilities. He suggests that Odysseus does not belong within the aristocratic world of games and gifts by characterizing him as one of those traders who travels the seas, concerned only with the profits of his cargo:

οὐ γάρ σ᾿ οὐδέ, ξεῖνε, δαήμονι φωτὶ εἴσκω
ἄθλων, οἷά τε πολλὰ μετ᾿ ἀνθρώποισι πέλονται,
ἀλλὰ τῷ ὅς θ᾿ ἅμα νηὶ πολυκλήϊδι θαμίζων,
ἀρχὸς ναυτάων οἵ τε πρηκτῆρες ἔασι,
φόρτου τε μνήμων καὶ ἐπίσκοπος ᾖσιν ὁδαίων
κερδέων θ᾿ ἁρπαλέων· οὐδ᾿ ἀθλητῆρι ἔοικας.

No stranger, for I do not liken you to a man of contests, such as now are practiced among men, but rather to one who plies his ways in his many-locked vessel, master over sailors, who are also traders, a man who is mindful of his cargo and ever on the lookout for greedy profits for his return cargo. You are not like an athlete. (Od. 8.159–64)

Whereas a truly aristocratic warrior-athlete would be concerned with his future reputation (κλέα ἀνδρῶν), Odysseus here, like merchants and pirates, is interested only in potential profits (φόρτου τε μνήμων).

Unlike Mentes or Menelaus, Euryalus emphatically contrasts aristocratic behavior (i.e., competition for prestige and honor within a system of prizes and gifts) with that of merchant traders, who are ever attentive to their cargo and to the potential for economic gain. For Euryalus these are mutually exclusive categories representing competing worldviews and systems of exchange; aristocrats do not engage in trade. He identifies the love of profit, seized at all costs, as the defining characteristic of traders and compares this greed unfavorably with the ideology of equality and reciprocity inherent in aristocratic sites for circulating goods, such as athletic competition or gift exchange.[34] More specifically, the phrase κερδέων θ᾿ ἁρπαλέων associates commercial profit with the asymmetry of the ill-gotten gain of pirates and thieves: both traders and pirates try to get more than they give. Euryalus thus distinguishes trade sharply from gift exchange and likens it instead to piracy. It is profit and greed that are the points of contention. The pure profit, achieved through theft, of piracy represents the furthest extreme of the potential for gain that resides in a commercial transaction as well as the possibility of deception. Euryalus raises the specter of piracy to emphasize the negative potential of commercial trade, the dangers that stem primarily from the pursuit of profit above all else and from dealing with strangers.[35]

In the *Works and Days*, Hesiod identifies generosity and theft as two extreme positions in a discussion of reciprocity and the dangers of negative profits: "Giving is good; taking is bad" (δὼς ἀγαθή, ἅρπαξ δὲ κακή, *WD* 356). We might use this formulation, together with Sahlins's typology, to mark out the extreme poles of the exchange spectrum presented in the *Odyssey* as well. Gift exchange as an example of using the reciprocity of exchange to achieve and maintain status among peers occupies one end of the spectrum; piracy, with its unilateral notion of economic gain, occupies the other. In between is the more complicated and problematic system of trade or commodity exchange. At times, trade is attracted into the prestige economy of aristocratic guest-friends; at other times, it is associated with the greed and profits typical of pirates who sail the seas and bring trouble to strangers. What seems to be at stake is both the context of exchange—Is it enacted between friends or between strangers? Is it bilateral or one-sided?—and the potential for economic profit instead of (or in addition to) cultural status as the goal of the exchange. In this respect, the different associations of trade articulated by Mentes (= gift exchange) and Euryalus (= piracy) problematize the notions of value and profit in the world of the *Odyssey* and raise questions about what constitutes a fair exchange.

Returning to the metaphor of poetic cargo implicit in the description of Odysseus' broad-hulled raft, I want to suggest that it is the raft's potential for big profits, together with its emphasis on construction, that locates the poetics of the *Odyssey*—the production, consumption, and circulation of poetry—within this same contested framework of exchange and value that is at work in the poem. The unexpected reference to commercial trade (in all its rich ambiguity) suggests first that the *Odyssey*, like the works of Hesiod and Pindar, appropriates commercial imagery to represent the poetic exchange, and second, that the notion of poetic exchange, like that of economic exchange, is equally contested in the world of the *Odyssey*.

## Poetics in the World of the *Odyssey*

In addition to presenting a complicated picture of economic exchange, the *Odyssey* accommodates two rather different kinds of poets within its world. First, Demodocus and Phemius exemplify the poet permanently attached to an aristocratic court. As part of the hospitality that Alcinous offers to Odysseus, for example, the king asks Demodocus to sing for the court. The passage that introduces the poet's first song captures a sense of his important role within this aristocratic community:

Κῆρυξ δ' ἐγγύθεν ἦλθεν ἄγων ἐρίηρον ἀοιδόν,
τὸν πέρι Μοῦσ' ἐφίλησε, δίδου δ' ἀγαθόν τε κακόν τε·
ὀφθαλμῶν μὲν ἄμερσε, δίδου δ' ἡδεῖαν ἀοιδήν,

τῷ δ᾽ ἄρα Ποντόνοος θῆκε θρόνον ἀργυρόηλον
μέσσῳ δαιτυμόνων, πρὸς κίονα μακρὸν ἐρείσας.
κὰδ δ᾽ ἐκ πασσαλόφι κρέμασεν φόρμιγγα λίγειαν
αὐτοῦ ὑπὲρ κεφαλῆς καὶ ἐπέφραδε χερσὶν ἐλέσθαι
κῆρυξ· πὰρ δ᾽ ἐτίθει κάνεον καλήν τε τράπεζαν,
πὰρ δὲ δέπας οἴνοιο, πιεῖν ὅτε θυμὸς ἀνώγοι.
οἱ δ᾽ ἐπ᾽ ὀνείαθ᾽ ἑτοῖμα προκείμενα χεῖρας ἴαλλον.
αὐτὰρ ἐπεὶ πόσιος καὶ ἐδητύος ἐξ ἔρον ἕντο,
Μοῦσ᾽ ἄρ᾽ ἀοιδὸν ἀνῆκεν ἀειδέμεναι κλέα ἀνδρῶν,
οἴμης τῆς τότ᾽ ἄρα κλέος οὐρανὸν εὐρὺν ἵκανε,
νεῖκος Ὀδυσσῆος καὶ Πηλείδεω Ἀχιλῆος ...

The herald came from nearby leading the beloved poet, whom the Muse loved most, and to whom she gave both good and bad: she deprived him of his sight, but she gave him sweet song, and for this man, Pontonous placed a silver-studded chair in the middle of the feasters, leaning it against the tall pillar. And he hung his clear-sounding lyre on a peg above his head and the herald showed him how to get it with his hands. He placed a beautiful basket and a table beside him, and a glass of wine to drink whenever his spirit moved him. And they all threw their hands upon the meat ready before them, and when they cast out desire for food and drink, the Muse bid the poet sing the famous deeds of men; the fame of the song reached the broad heavens—the quarrel between Odysseus and Achilles, son of Peleus. (*Od.* 8.62–75)

This passage paints a picture of the poet as an important and fully integrated member of Alcinous' court. Demodocus lives at the court and receives food, drink, and a place of honor at the center of the feasters whom he is to entertain with song.[36] His skill and his poetic authority come directly from the Muse. In fact, Demodocus' poetic expertise is here characterized as the goddess's gift, and his debt to the Muse represents a notion of poetry as a kind of social control—the control exerted by the audience upon the poet.[37] His songs—he sings here the quarrel between Odysseus and Achilles—respond to the tastes and interests of his audience, and his job is to entertain and charm the court of Alcinous.[38] Demodocus' very name, etymologized later in Book 8 as one who is "honored by the people," reflects his success and the extent to which the poet's status and function are linked to the social context in which he sings.[39] Phemius, too, the bard at Odysseus' palace in Ithaca, must accommodate the needs and poetic taste of his audience. As Telemachus tells his mother, the poet must sing the most recent songs—the songs of the heroes' return from Troy—if he wants to keep the suitors satisfied.[40]

Within the world of the *Odyssey*, Demodocus and Phemius occupy the role of the bard embedded within a homogeneous, aristocratic setting; their job is to sing songs that symbolize the values of the group and that help define and maintain its worldview.[41] The mechanism for evaluating songs in this context is immediate and unproblematic: if his songs please and respond to the needs of the community, the poet is rewarded at once with food and drink, and his status as poet of the community is confirmed. Living at the court, the poet enjoys a long-term, mutually beneficial relationship with his audience. He receives food, lodging, and a place of honor in the community; the audience, in turn, gains a flexible poetic tradition that celebrates and validates its way of life. In this respect, the economic status of poets like Demodocus, together with the value of his songs, is thoroughly embedded within this social setting. Songs are produced and consumed within the framework of a long-standing homogeneous community; they form part of an ongoing set of relations between audience and poet.[42]

But with Odysseus, the *Odyssey* makes room for quite a different model of poet as well—one not permanently attached to a court, but who travels from place to place singing songs and collecting goods in return. That Odysseus is a poet in the *Odyssey* should be quite clear; not only does the hero tell stories and sing songs once he arrives home at Ithaca, but also Odysseus' poetic voice is indistinguishable from that of Homer for Books 9–12, the most famous and fantastic books of the poem.[43] Odysseus' identity as poet, however, is not linked to a specific place or community; he has no long-term relationship with a single audience on which his livelihood depends. Instead, as an outsider traveling from place to place, Odysseus offers his songs in exchange for goods.[44] In this respect, poets like Odysseus have much in common with other craftsmen, who travel around the world. As Eumaeus reminds Antinous, who else travels to visit strangers:

εἰ μὴ τῶν οἳ δημιοεργοὶ ἔασι,
μάντιν ἢ ἰητῆρα κακῶν ἢ τέκτονα δούρων
ἢ καὶ θέσπιν ἀοιδόν, ὅ κεν τέρπῃσιν ἀείδων;
οὗτοι γὰρ κλητοί γε βροτῶν ἐπ' ἀπείρονα γαῖαν.

...unless he is a craftsmen, a seer, a healer of evils, a shipmaker or a divine singer who sings with pleasure? For these men are invited across the boundless earth. (*Od.* 17.383–86)

Thus, like other craftsmen, as a traveling poet Odysseus creates a product that he can then exchange all over the world for other goods or services; in other words, we might say that he trades in songs as commodities. His poetic exchanges are the short-term transactions, enacted between strangers, that characterize commodity rather than gift exchange.[45] As a result, Odysseus' status as poet and the evaluation of his songs are not embedded in social relationships; they are negotiated on the open market, and as we will see, this alternative model for conceptualizing the exchange of songs brings with it new ways of evaluating poetry.

Economic and Poetic Exchange

If we return now to Alcinous' response to Odysseus' song in Book 11, we can better understand what he means when he compares a bad poet to a wandering thief or cheat:

ὦ Ὀδυσεῦ, τὸ μὲν οὔ τί σ᾽ ἐΐσκομεν εἰσορόωντες
ἠπεροπῆά τ᾽ ἔμεν καὶ ἐπίκλοπον, οἷά τε πολλοὺς
βόσκει γαῖα μέλαινα πολυσπερέας ἀνθρώπους
ψεύδεά τ᾽ ἀρτύνοντας, ὅθεν κέ τις οὐδὲ ἴδοιτο·
σοὶ δ᾽ ἔπι μὲν μορφὴ ἐπέων, ἔνι δὲ φρένες ἐσθλαί·
μῦθον δ᾽ ὡς ὅτ᾽ ἀοιδὸς ἐπισταμένως κατέλεξας,
πάντων Ἀργείων σέο τ᾽ αὐτοῦ κήδεα λυγρά.

O Odysseus, looking upon you, we do not at all liken you to a deceptive man or a thief, such as the dark earth nourishes—many, who wander widely and tell lies, from whom one could learn nothing. Yet there is a beauty to your words, and there is sense in them, and expertly as a singer you have told the story of your own sorrows and those of all the Argives. (*Od.* 11.363–69)

Instead of claiming that a bad poet would produce a badly shaped poem or one that does not resonate with the audience, Alcinous implies that he would feel "deceived" or "cheated" by Odysseus' stories if they were no good. His use of ἠπεροπῆά to refer to the potential for deception or cheating in Odysseus' song evokes the image of the Phoenician traders who come to Eumaeus' father's house with their ship full of trinkets and best the locals in trade.[46] The adjective ἐπίκλοπον, moreover, attributes to the poet the ability to steal something from the listener just as a clever, profit-hungry merchant might steal from less savvy trading partners. In other words, the language of commerce helps frame Alcinous' critique of bad poets in familiar terms: they are like pirates or the kind of traveling merchants who deceive their clients and cheat them in trade. From Odysseus, however, he feels that he got good poetic value for his hospitality since Odysseus' songs pleased and satisfied him, and he expresses his approval in terms familiar to an aristocratic audience. We are now in a better position to appreciate what is striking about Alcinous' response. He draws on the competing characterizations of trade at work in the *Odyssey* to frame his assessment of Odysseus' song. He praises him as poet with the language of aristocratic guest-friendship, but he looks to the world of piracy and theft to characterize a bad poet.[47]

Athena also uses the language of theft and deception to chide Odysseus in Book 13 when he tells her a story about being a murderer in exile from Crete. Moreover, she links the image of theft mentioned by Alcinous specifically with the potential for profit:

κερδαλέος κ' εἴη καὶ ἐπίκλοπος ὅς σε παρέλθοι
ἐν πάντεσσι δόλοισι, καὶ εἰ θεὸς ἀντιάσειε.
σχέτλιε, ποικιλομῆτα, δόλων ἆτ', οὐκ ἄρ' ἔμελλες,
οὐδ' ἐν σῇ περ ἐὼν γαίῃ, λήξειν ἀπατάων
μύθων τε κλοπίων, οἵ τοι πεδόθεν φίλοι εἰσίν.
ἀλλ' ἄγε, μηκέτι ταῦτα λεγώμεθα, εἰδότες ἄμφω
κέρδε', ἐπεὶ σὺ μέν ἐσσι βροτῶν ὄχ' ἄριστος ἁπάντων
βουλῇ καὶ μύθοισιν, ἐγὼ δ' ἐν πᾶσι θεοῖσι
μήτι τε κλέομαι καὶ κέρδεσιν·

It would be an enterprising man, a stealthy one, who would ever get
past you in any deceits; even if it were a god against you. You wretch,
so devious, never weary of tricks, not even in your own country would
you leave off your deceiving ways and thievish tales. They are dear to
you. But come, let us talk no more of this, for you and I both know profitable skills, since you are by far the best of all mortal men for counsel
and stories, and I among all the divinities am famous for my profitable
skills. (*Od.* 13.291–99)

Athena links the thievish quality of narrative with its potential for deception, as
Alcinous did, but she brings the notion of profit that belongs to the world of
commercial trade into the picture as well. It would take a really enterprising man
(κερδαλέος) to outdo Odysseus in storytelling since he, like Athena, excels all
others in profitable skills (κέρδε'). The semantic field of *kerdos* and its related
words spans the range between the kind of cunning associated with *metis* and a
sense of profit or advantage understood in a real economic sense, and the poetic
skill of cleverness is assessed here in terms of commercial profit or theft.[48] A persuasive speech can be one that literally brings profit, as Homer suggests when
describing the speech with which Odysseus persuades Nausicaa to help him after he arrives naked and alone on the shores of Phaeacia. His speech is both
honey-sweet (μειλίχιον) and designed to reap profit (κερδαλέον, 6.146). As a result, Nausicaa provides him immediately with clothing and subsequently arranges
for him to meet her father, who will give him many gifts and eventually secure
his trip home. But Athena's response to Odysseus suggests that the notion of
profit may be applied more generally to express poetic value as well.

The language of profit and deception, familiar from its association with the
problematics of trade in the poem, is appropriated and applied to poetry as if it,
too, were the object of exchange. This rhetorical strategy suggests that stories
are being treated like commodities and that poets trade them for other valuable
goods. In fact, if we return to the court of Alcinous in Phaeacia, we see that
Odysseus does, in effect, exchange his stories about his travels for enough gifts
and goods to take back home with him, and in this scene we begin to see the extent to which poetic production and consumption operates within the complicated world of exchange in the *Odyssey*. In particular, Odysseus' stay with the

Phaeacians brings the notion of songs as commodities open for profitable exchange into contact and conflict with a world in which poetry is embedded within a system of aristocratic hospitality and gift exchange.

The court of Alcinous certainly exemplifies aristocratic hospitality. From the moment that the naked and bedraggled hero washes ashore and is given food, clothing, and bathing materials by Nausicaa, to the elaborate display of gifts, feasts, and entertainment offered by Alcinous and his queen, Arete, Odysseus is given the royal treatment.[49] And of course, gifts and song play an important role in cementing the guest-host relationship. After honoring Odysseus with feasts, song, and dance, Alcinous appeals to the other lords of Phaeacia to give guest-gifts to the stranger (ἀλλ᾽ ἄγε οἱ δῶμεν ξεινήιον, ὡς ἐπιεικές, 8.389), and each arranges to give him fine textiles and a talent of gold. Demodocus is then asked to sing for the guest. In other words, Alcinous' reception of Odysseus follows the rules of the aristocratic guest-friend relationship with particular emphasis on its role in sponsoring poetry and in circulating goods as two ways of establishing long-term reciprocal relations among leaders of the Greek world.[50]

Once established as Alcinous' guest, Odysseus proceeds to tell the story of his travels. But in the scene that follows the interruption of his tale in Book 11, he introduces another model for the relationship between stories and goods, one that is quite different from Demodocus' role as resident poet at Alcinous' court. In the intermission, by agreeing to tell the rest of his story in exchange for more gifts to take home, Odysseus reconfigures the traditional relationship between songs and hospitality. In other words, within a setting of hospitality or *xenia*, he trades songs for goods.

In the middle of Book 11, Odysseus stops at a suspenseful moment in his tale; his story is not resolved—he has not yet told how he and his men managed to return from Hades. He then asks his hosts to see to his journey home since it is time for sleep.[51] Odysseus brings the audience up short by stopping his tale so abruptly. Arete is the first to recover. She responds by praising Odysseus' good looks and character and reiterates his status as her guest:

Φαίηκες, πῶς ὕμμιν ἀνὴρ ὅδε φαίνεται εἶναι
εἶδός τε μέγαθός τε ἰδὲ φρένας ἔνδον ἐίσας·
ξεῖνος δ᾽ αὖτ᾽ ἐμός ἐστιν, ἕκαστος δ᾽ ἔμμορε τιμῆς·
τῷ μὴ ἐπειγόμενοι ἀποπέμπετε μηδὲ τὰ δῶρα
οὕτω χρηίζοντι κολούετε· πολλὰ γὰρ ὑμῖν
κτήματ᾽ ἐνὶ μεγάροισι θεῶν ἰότητι κέονται.

Phaeacians, does this man not appear to you to be great in appearance and to have equal intelligence within? Moreover, he is my guest, and each of you has a part in honoring him. So do not hurry him off nor stint on gifts since he is in need. For you have plenty of possessions lying in your halls thanks to the gods. (*Od.* 11.336–41)

According to Arete, Odysseus' status as her guest-friend is reinforced by his good looks and intelligence, and for these reasons, she asks the other nobles to give him more gifts. Her husband agrees and asks their guest to stay another day so that they can gather more gifts; he, too, conspicuously invokes the language and institutions of aristocratic hospitality, referring to Odysseus as his *xeinos*. Odysseus immediately acquiesces, saying that he would stay for a year if necessary in order to get more goods to take home to his family:

Ἀλκίνοε κρεῖον, πάντων ἀριδείκετε λαῶν,
εἴ με καὶ εἰς ἐνιαυτὸν ἀνώγοιτ᾽ αὐτόθι μίμνειν
πομπήν τ᾽ ὀτρύνοιτε καὶ ἀγλαὰ δῶρα διδοῖτε,
καί κε τὸ βουλοίμην, καί κεν πολὺ κέρδιον εἴη
πλειοτέρῃ σὺν χειρὶ φίλην ἐς πατρίδ᾽ ἱκέσθαι·

Lord Alcinous, most famous of all the people, if you urged me to stay here even for a year and hastened my return and gave glorious gifts, I would want that—since it would be much more profitable for me to return to my dear fatherland with a more generous hand. (*Od.* 11.355–59)

While Odysseus agrees to Alcinous' request for more songs, acknowledging the king's promise of more gifts offered within a hospitality context, the language of Odysseus' reply reconceptualizes these gifts as commodities to be exchanged for songs. Instead of emphasizing the future longevity of the relationship now established between Alcinous and himself, Odysseus introduces the notion of short-term gain: it would be much more profitable (πολὺ κέρδιον) for him to keep on singing to get more goods.

In other words, this scene brings the worlds of economic and poetic exchange (in all their complications) face to face. Odysseus puts his performance on the market, so to speak; he invokes the rules of commodity exchange while Alcinous and his wife try to observe the conventions of aristocratic hospitality to negotiate an agreement about the production and consumption of song. We might say that in singing the songs that appear in Books 9–11.332, Odysseus calibrates his poetic performance to be the exchange equivalent of the gifts he has already received. When Alcinous and Arete offer him more gifts, he sings more songs (the rest of Book 11 and Book 12) in return. Unlike Demodocus, whose permanent role in the social structure of Phaeacian society depends on his function as singer, Odysseus has no long-term relationship with the Phaeacians.[52] He does not sing songs as part of the social community; rather he sings them in exchange for goods and commodities to take home. Odysseus, as Athena says, is a man who excels in profitable ways.[53]

A poetic performance is thus represented as a commercial transaction embedded within an aristocratic gift exchange relationship, and Alcinous' problematic assessment of Odysseus' song reflects the clash of paradigms at the root of this exchange. The incongruity of his logic highlights the points of conflict or strain between these two systems and their respective notions of value and exchange. On the one hand, Alcinous praises Odysseus as a knowledgeable singer (ἀοιδὸς ἐπισταμένως, 11.368). He attributes to his song the qualities associated with men of noble birth: there is a beauty to the song (μορφὴ ἐπέων, 11.367), and it shows a noble intelligence (φρένες ἐσθλαί, 11.367).[54] This is language appropriate to the Demodocus model of a poet who sings as part of a closed aristocratic social context. On the other hand, however, Alcinous adopts the negative characterization of traders as virtual pirates on the open seas raised earlier by Euryalus and applies it as well to the realm of poetry: Odysseus does not look like the kind of poet who might be cheating him or stealing from him with his deceptive tales and lies—the kind of behavior to be expected from those who professionally engage in trade. Thus not only does Alcinous' response reflect the clash of economic paradigms present in the world of the *Odyssey*, but it also captures the extent to which the realms of poetry and economics intersect in the poem in interesting and provocative ways.

Moving from the palace of Alcinous to the hut of Eumaeus, the swineherd on Odysseus' estate, we find a second scene in which the contested language of trade describes a poetic exchange. When Odysseus returns to Ithaca, he goes directly to the hut of his swineherd to assess the situation in his palace, and they pass the time telling stories. In Book 14 the disguised Odysseus tells Eumaeus a story about the real Odysseus at Troy in which Odysseus tricks another Greek warrior into going off on a wild goose chase so that Odysseus might take his cloak.[55] When he finishes, Eumaeus replies:

> ὦ γέρον, αἶνος μέν τοι ἀμύμων, ὃν κατέλεξας,
> οὐδέ τί πω παρὰ μοῖραν ἔπος *νηκερδὲς* ἔειπες·
> τῷ οὔτ' ἐσθῆτος δευήσεαι οὔτε τευ ἄλλου
> ὧν ἐπέοιχ' ἱκέτην ταλαπείριον ἀντιάσαντα,

> Old man, this is a blameless fable which you have told; neither have you told a profitless story, nor one that is out of proportion. And so you will not lack for clothes or anything due the unhappy suppliant who approaches us. (*Od.* 14.508–11)

After hearing Odysseus' story, Eumaeus praises it and gives Odysseus a coat in return. In his response, the swineherd shows that he is concerned with the rules of proper exchange: the story is not out of proportion (παρὰ μοῖραν), so it will receive its fair recompense; it was not without profit (νηκερδὲς). But while it seems clear that Odysseus trades a story about a cloak for a real cloak, Eumaeus refuses to interpret this transaction as a commodity exchange. Earlier in their conversation he had spelled out his rules more clearly. He tells Odysseus that he will provide him with food and shelter, but not because Odysseus told him a good story; that is, he will not participate in an economy in which goods and stories are freely exchanged. He prefers to obey the rule of Zeus Xenios:

καὶ σύ, γέρον πολυπενθές, ἐπεί σέ μοι ἤγαγε δαίμων,
μήτε τί μοι ψεύδεσσι χαρίζεο μήτε τι θέλγε·
οὐ γὰρ τοὔνεκ᾽ ἐγώ σ᾽ αἰδέσσομαι οὐδὲ φιλήσω,
ἀλλὰ Δία ξένιον δείσας αὐτόν τ᾽ ἐλεαίρων.

And you, much-suffering old man, since some god led you to me, do
not favor me with lies or bewitch me, for I will not honor you or be-
friend you for this reason, but rather because I fear Zeus Xenios and
take pity. (*Od.* 14.386–89)

Eumaeus insists on working within the system of aristocratic hospitality, one that
includes stories and gifts, instead of using an exchange system to evaluate poetry
that trades stories for other commodities, thus raising the specter of the deception, trickery, and misconstruction that may accompany a commercial transaction. He will honor Odysseus and his songs as a guest-friend or as a suppliant—
these are social relationships—but he will not trade cloaks or anything else for
a story.[56]

Eumaeus' anxiety about the exchange of goods for stories stems, I contend,
from the problematic construction of trade in the poem—the contested issues of
profit and value. Like Alcinous, Eumaeus brings to the reception of songs the
same set of concerns that Euryalus raises about merchants: What is the nature
of exchange? How do you determine exchange value? How do you keep from
being cheated by unfamiliar, profit-happy merchants? Who profits from this exchange? Eumaeus prefers the well-established rules and value system of aristocratic hospitality to the notion of profit that emerges from commodity exchange.
Moreover, he is more comfortable with a poet who does not travel from city to
city, but who belongs to a community and who sings songs that reflect its values.

It is impossible to think about ancient Greek poetry outside the realm of the
exchange process. In Greek, even the notion of answering (expressed by the verb
*ameibomai*, "to change with another," "to get in exchange") lies within the semantic scope of giving and taking. Along these lines, both the scenes at Eumaeus'
hut and those at Alcinous' palace demonstrate how the issues of profit and value
raised by the different kinds of exchange at work in the poem frame questions
of poetic assessment in light of competing models of poetic production and consumption. In other words, the poetics of the poem are very much embedded in
its systems of economic exchange, and issues of profit and value that stem from
commoditization are brought face to face with more traditional modes of as-
sessing the worth of poetry. Either poetry can be appreciated within the cultural
framework of hospitality, as Eumaeus and Alcinous would prefer, or it can be
traded for textiles and talents of gold, as Odysseus shows.[57] Eumaeus' insistence
on locating his gift of a cloak to Odysseus within the framework of *xenia* rather
than in commodity exchange reflects, perhaps, his role as servant in the agricultural economy of Ithaca. Alcinous' reluctance to trade goods for song, by contrast, may stem from Phaeacia's role as idealized aristocratic community in the

poem.[58] Most important, however, both scenes draw on the problematic notion of profit that arises from commercial exchange to frame what look like comparable questions about the role and value of poetry once it is disembedded from the closed world of aristocratic hospitality. If a stranger sings a song, how do you know what it is worth? If a poet trades stories for clothes and other commodities, how do you negotiate the exchange? Where does the value lie? Who will profit from the exchange? These, I submit, are the issues of exchange that are opened up—but by no means resolved—by the convergence of economic and poetic notions of profit and value in the world of the *Odyssey*.

In Book 19 the disguised Odysseus tells a story to Penelope designed to reassure her that her husband is alive and will return home soon. He explains that Odysseus would have been home sooner, but he was out collecting goods to bring home:

> καί κεν πάλαι ἐνθάδ᾽ Ὀδυσσεὺς
> ἤην· ἀλλ᾽ ἄρα οἱ τό γε κέρδιον εἴσατο θυμῷ,
> χρήματ᾽ ἀργυρτάζειν πολλὴν ἐπὶ γαῖαν ἰόντι·
> ὡς περὶ κέρδεα πολλὰ καταθνητῶν ἀνθρώπων
> οἶδ᾽ Ὀδυσεύς, οὐδ᾽ ἄν τις ἐρίσσειε βροτὸς ἄλλος.

> So Odysseus would have been home a long time before this, but in his mind he thought it more profitable to go about and visit many lands, collecting possessions. For Odysseus knows profitable ways beyond all other men who are mortal; no other man could rival him at it. (*Od.* 19.282–86)

Odysseus' ability to acquire more profit than any other mortal stems directly from his exceptional skill at singing songs, as we have seen him do both among the Phaeacians and at home in Ithaca. In other words, it is poetic merchandise that is stowed aboard Odysseus' cargo-carrying raft—the potential for singing an unlimited range of songs in exchange for other valuable goods and commodities, a source of great profit. Unlike Demodocus' songs, which are valued and rewarded by a place at Alcinous' court, Odysseus' poetic value is measured by the goods he receives in turn. More like Pindar who sends his songs out on a merchant freighter, Odysseus stows his poetic cargo on his divinely inspired yet humanly improvised raft. The metapoetic force of Odysseus' raft is thus extended beyond representing the nature and modes of oral poetic construction to address questions of poetic value as well—to suggest a poetics of value within a context of poetic and economic innovation in the world of the *Odyssey*.

But, as we will see in the next chapter, something else is going on here as well. The ability of heroes and songs to travel like merchants and the commodities they trade helps reorient the direction of epic poetry. The association of epic poetry with trade and commerce shifts its focus away from martial prowess—

sacking cities and overseas conquest (i.e., the *Iliad* model)—toward the adventures of travel and the potential of *kerdos*, literally in the form of commercial profit and metaphorically in the form of knowledge and experience. As Michael Moerman observes about the late nineteenth- and twentieth-century traveling traders of northern Thailand, although they were delighted with the large profits they made, "a more dominant memory is of the fun they had, of the sights along the way, of opportunity for song and riddle."[59] To judge from Aelian's remarks about Odysseus'and Menelaus' motivation, cited at the beginning of this chapter, it seems likely that trade offered early Greeks a similar excuse "for traveling and sailing around." In other words, within this world of travel, trade, and discovery, Odysseus and his cargo-carrying raft set epic song in motion to see new worlds and learn new things.

# 3

# Travel and Song

Ulysses' journey, like that of Oedipus, is an itinerary. And it is a discourse, the prefix of which I can now understand. It is not at all the discourse (*discours*) of an itinerary (*parcours*) but, radically, the itinerary (*parcours*) of a discourse (*discours*), the course, *cursus*, route, path that passes through the original disjunction, the bridge laid down across the crevices.

Michel Serres, *Hermes*

When, in Nemean 5, Pindar bids his sweet song set sail on every freighter and commercial galley, his allusions to trading vessels compare his victory ode to their valuable cargo, thus locating his own poetry within a larger cultural system of profit and value.[1] This choice of imagery both celebrates the athlete's accomplishments and enhances the poet's status since his songs acquire increased value as the appropriate measure of personal and civic excellence. In addition to celebrating the potential value of his poetry, however, the mobility of these cargo ships, in stark contrast to the statue fixed on its base, expands the metaphorical association between cargo ships and songs even further to highlight the extensive range of Pindar's poetic skill. Pindar's song will sail on every freighter, putting into foreign harbors, recounting the news of victory, spreading the fame of both athlete and poet well beyond Greece and the original site of victory. In this way, the figurative connection between ships and song celebrates the ability of poetry to transcend its immediate occasion, to be transported across vast oceans to unknown international audiences.

Theognis, too, invokes the image of overseas travel to represent the extent to which his song will bring fame and renown to his addressee, Cyrnus. His poetry gives Cyrnus wings to fly across the sea, to range across the mainland and islands of Greece. His name will be known everywhere:

ἰχθυόεντα περῶν πόντον ἐπ᾽ ἀτρύγετον,
οὐχ ἵππων νώτοισιν ἐφήμενος, ἀλλά σε πέμψει
   ἀγλαὰ Μουσαῶν δῶρα ἰοστεφάνων
πᾶσιν ὅσοισι μέμηλε . . .

... crossing the fishy, barren sea, mounted not upon horseback, but the
glorious gifts of the violet-crowned Muses will send you to all those who
care ... (Thgn. 248–51)

It is the poet's skill that creates Cyrnus' worldwide fame, and Theognis' poetry,
thanks to the gifts of the Muses, has the power to travel far and wide.[2] In this
respect, the familiar trope of the immortality of poetic fame takes on a geographical cast. Theognis' skill will ensure Cyrnus' fame both for a long time and
across great distances.

Again, the association between poetry and travel so explicitly articulated in
the work of the late archaic poets Pindar and Theognis, and in particular its role
in representing the broad scope and range of their poetic skill, helps guide our
thinking about the metapoetic significance of Odysseus' raft as well. Poets like
Odysseus, as we have seen, travel themselves, singing new songs for new audiences as they move from city to city.[3] But in addition to characterizing Odysseus
as a traveling poet, the image of Odysseus' raft as a vehicle of song takes some
key issues of poetic production and reception and sends them on the road. Poetry
itself travels in the *Odyssey* just as its hero does, and questions of poetic truth
and authority are very much linked to this mobile image of poetic production—
Odysseus' raft.

In the previous two chapters we have explored how the many-pegged raft
of Odysseus, with its extra large cargo hold, embodies the ways in which poetics and economics intersect in the *Odyssey*, but there is still one more set of associations connected to Odysseus' raft that is worth exploring. Perhaps most important, Odysseus' raft enables the poet-hero to travel. It liberates him from his
seven-year stay on Calypso's island and sets him on his heroic path of song and
return. Travel, particularly overseas travel, does not just provide the means for
commercial profit; it also prompts encounters with extraordinary peoples and
produces stories of new worlds, and in this respect the metapoetic nature of
Odysseus' raft also helps articulate the complicated relationship between travel
and song at work in the *Odyssey*. Sea travel operates at the level of poetics in
the *Odyssey* to constitute a notion of narrative that is about travel and is itself
mobile and flexible. In other words, the *Odyssey* is a travel narrative that also
describes new ways of conceptualizing the relationship between travel and narrative.

### The Truth in Travel

We can best see this connection between travel and song at work by returning to
Eumaeus' hut, to the scene where the swineherd receives the disguised Odysseus
into his home and the two men spend the night exchanging stories of their past.
We have already seen the extent to which the language of economics together

with the competition between exchange systems helps structure both the telling of stories in the *Odyssey* and the terms of their evaluation. In fact, Book 14 both opens and closes with reference to Odysseus' profit-making abilities. When Odysseus first arrives at Eumaeus' hut, his decision to drop his stick and fall to the ground to avoid being attacked by the swineherd's dogs is marked as an example of profitable cunning (κερδοσύνῃ, 14.31). And, as we have already seen, the book closes with Eumaeus' response to Odysseus' story in quest of a cloak: he has told a story that is not unprofitable (οὐδέ . . . νηκερδὲς, 14. 509). Yet, embedded within this frame of profitability is a series of interchanges between Odysseus and Eumaeus that focuses not on the potential value of narrative but on the relationship between narrative truth and travel.

Eumaeus first introduces the concept of travel in his greeting to the disguised Odysseus. He explains that he takes care of the livestock while his unnamed master "wanders among the lands and cities of foreign peoples" (πλάζετ᾽ ἐπ᾽ ἀλλο-θρόων ἀνδρῶν δῆμόν τε πόλιν τε, 14.43). In thus accounting for his master's absence, Eumaeus uncannily echoes the description of Odysseus with which the poem begins—a man who has traveled much and learned the minds and cities of many men. Eumaeus prepares a meal for the stranger, and once they have eaten, Odysseus asks who Eumaeus' absent master is, suggesting that he might have some news of him to report since he, too, has traveled widely:

εἰπέ μοι, αἴ κέ ποθι γνώω τοιοῦτον ἐόντα.
Ζεὺς γάρ που τό γε οἶδε καὶ ἀθάνατοι θεοὶ ἄλλοι,
εἴ κέ μιν ἀγγείλαιμι ἰδών· ἐπὶ πολλὰ δ᾽ ἀλήθην.

Tell me, and perhaps I might know such a man. For Zeus and the other immortal gods know if I might have seen him and have some news. For I have traveled a great deal. (*Od.* 14.118–20)

The swineherd picks up on the mention of travel and responds with a surprising speech that begins to articulate the problematics of travel and narrative in the poem:

ὦ γέρον, οὔτις κεῖνον ἀνὴρ ἀλαλήμενος ἐλθὼν
ἀγγέλλων πείσειε γυναῖκά τε καὶ φίλον υἱόν.
ἀλλ᾽ ἄλλως κομιδῆς κεχρημένοι ἄνδρες ἀλῆται
ψεύδοντ᾽, οὐδ᾽ ἐθέλουσιν ἀληθέα μυθήσασθαι.
ὃς δέ κ᾽ ἀλητεύων Ἰθάκης ἐς δῆμον ἵκηται,
ἐλθὼν ἐς δέσποιναν ἐμὴν ἀπατήλια βάζει·

Old man, no one who has wandered could come with news of that man and persuade his wife and dear son. And yet wandering men in need of sustenance tell lies, they do not wish to tell the truth. Every wanderer who comes to the people of Ithaca goes to my mistress and babbles deceptive tales. (*Od.* 14.122–27)

Wandering men tell lies, and Eumaeus categorically denies that any itinerant stranger arriving in Ithaca could convince Penelope and Telemachus with the truth about the absent Odysseus. Yet, Eumaeus' use of οὖτις (Nohbody) in this response, the punning name that Odysseus adopted to escape death at the hand of the Cyclops, renders the following reading also possible: "Odysseus [= *Outis*], having traveled, could come with news of that man and persuade his wife and dear son." In other words, just at the moment when Eumaeus rejects the old man's travels as a source of true stories about his master, the ambiguity inherent in Odysseus' signature pun makes just the opposite claim, suggesting that it is precisely the act of Odysseus' travels that guarantees his true and persuasive story.

Indeed, there are several things going on in this speech that locate the notion of narrative truth within the framework of travel. First, although Odysseus offers his travels as a source of accurate information about the whereabouts of his master (ἐπὶ πολλὰ δ᾽ ἀλήθην), Eumaeus rejects this notion since wandering men (ἄνδρες ἀλῆται; ὃς . . . ἀλητεύων), in his experience, tell lies (ψεύδοντ᾽); they refuse to tell the truth (ἀληθέα). Instead, they utter tales of deception (ἀπατήλια βάζει). Eumaeus introduces the polarized notions of truth and lies and firmly places the stories of wandering men on the side of falsehood and deception. Alcinous had offered a similar analysis in Book 11 when he sharply distinguished Odysseus' song from the kinds of lies that wandering men usually tell.[4] At the same time, however, the clustering of forms of the verb ἀλάομαι, "to wander," and its related nouns bring the act of travel or wandering into an etymological relationship with the concept of narrative truth. Odysseus' use of the aorist passive form of the verb "to wander" (ἀλήθην) is unwittingly etymologized as the word for "truth" (ἀληθέα) in Eumaeus' response to his offer of news. Travel, according to this model, is a source not of lies but of narrative truth.

At first glance, this passage paradoxically brings travel together with the mutually exclusive notions of truth and lies. The essence of Eumaeus' complaint about the mendacity of travelers is countered by the punning etymology at the heart of his speech that equates truth and travel. If all travelers lie, how can truth emerge from a traveler's tale? Most scholars have approached this passage within the long-standing debate about the ways in which language, especially poetic language, expresses and conceals truth.[5] The punning wordplay of Eumaeus is thus taken to be indicative of the problematic relationship between truth and fiction in the *Odyssey*, revealing the poem's self-conscious interest in matters of self-representation and narrative authority. Lying, like disguise, is part of the larger dynamic between appearance and reality that dominates the thematics of the poem.[6]

But there is much more at stake in this passage than the ironic relationship between truth and lies within poetic discourse. Since Eumaeus explicitly locates the question of true and false stories within the specific context of travelers' tales, I want to shift our focus away from the conflict between truth and lies to bring the notion of travel and its connection to narrative truth to the forefront of the discussion. Rather than simply establishing an equivalent relationship between lying and truth, the implicit etymological connection between *alaomai* and *alethea* expressed in Eumaeus' speech unites the notion of travel and truth, thus laying the groundwork for a richer, more complicated relationship between the truth of stories and travel. Instead of asking only how truth can emerge from a lying tale, we need to recognize that the paradoxical nature of the passage poses a different kind of question as well: What kind of truth can be found in a traveler's tale?

In Homer, the term *alethea* does not refer to aspects of truth or veracity more generally; instead, *alethea* is almost always used as the object of verbs of speaking to refer to a notion of narrative truth.[7] Eumaeus here claims that wandering men do not wish to tell the truth (ἀληθέα μυθήσασθαι, 14.125). Earlier in the poem, Nestor promises to tell Telemachus the whole truth (ἀληθέα πάντ᾽ ἀγορεύσω, 3.254) about his father; Telemachus similarly promises his mother that he will tell her the truth about his travels (ἀληθείην καταλέξω, 17.108).[8] This close association with various verbs of speech thus narrows the scope of *alethea* and focuses it on the truth inherent in narrative, in the stories people tell. The *Odyssey* then complicates this notion of narrative truth by taking it on the road. Travel, especially overseas travel—stories about travels, stories learned while traveling, the very vehicles that enable travel—plays a key role in the *Odyssey*'s construction of narrative truth, and this is part of what underlies the metapoetic nature of Odysseus' raft. In addition to the ways in which the image of the raft both represents the nature of oral poetry and prompts metaphors of poetic value, the ability of Odysseus' raft to travel helps articulate a new, more mobile notion of narrative authority and truth, one in which travel and song are mutually implicated.[9]

## Travel and Song

First, at the most basic level, people tell stories about their travels. The *Odyssey* opens, of course, with a plea to the Muse to sing of a man of many ways (Ἄνδρα μοι ἔννεπε, Μοῦσα, πολύτροπον, 1.1). The use of πολύτροπον alludes to Odysseus' famed cleverness and to his many travels, uniting both elements of Odysseus' unique heroic nature in one compound adjective and establishing a strong connection between the travels and tricks of the poem's hero. The poet wants to sing of Odysseus' travels and the knowledge that he gains from them—knowledge about the minds and cities of many men. But it is not just Odysseus whose overseas adventures provide the material for song. Other people's travels, too, are a key part of the narrative content of the poem. At the beginning of the poem, Athena (disguised as Mentes) tells Telemachus to set sail in search of some news about his father, and so the first four books of the *Odyssey* relate Telemachus' travels to Pylos and to Sparta in search of word of Odysseus.[10] There is an interesting multiplying effect here, underscoring the poem's fascination with travel, knowledge, and narrative, for not only does Telemachus travel to get information about his father's return, but also the knowledge he gains from Nestor and Menelaus is, in fact, a collection of travel tales about Greek heroes returning home from Troy. Furthermore, Telemachus' travels become their own story as well. The "Telemachia," as the first four books are often called, tells the tale of a son's travels and adventures in search of his father.

Curiosity about the world across the sea motivates both travel and the telling of travel stories. Certainly part of the general appeal of travel tales is that they are a rich source of information about the world, and the *Odyssey* is no exception in this regard.[11] Odysseus' accounts of man-eating Cyclopes, witches that turn men into swine, and the magical gold and silver palaces of Phaeacia paint an imaginative and informative picture of the world beyond the familiar shores of Greece. Alcinous' eager request to learn of the lands and men that Odysseus has encountered in his voyages—were they savage or god-fearing?—captures the eager anticipation of the poem's larger audience as well.[12] Insofar as travel narratives are a source of knowledge or truth about the world overseas, we can now begin to understand part of what lies at the root of Eumaeus' etymological connection between travel and truth. Truth or knowledge about the world abroad stems from direct experience in that world. Overseas travel thus leads both to authoritative travel narratives and to identifying travel as the source of narrative authority.

Characters in the *Odyssey* and elsewhere travel to learn the truth about places far away, and they return home to tell the stories of their travels. As in more traditional ethnographic writing, it is the act of having traveled—that is, the fact of having "been there"—that guarantees the authenticity of stories about other places and other peoples.[13] In other words, the narrative authority and credibility of the traveler depend on his being an eyewitness. The story is a good one if the poet can convince the audience of its truth, of accurately recounting events and describing places that he himself has seen and experienced, and so, as we will see, the value of a story overlaps with its authenticity and truth.

### Travel, Truth, Trade, and Song

The association between trade and poetry, elaborated in chapter 2, is related to this discussion of the link between travel and poetic truth, and we might now think futher about the potential intersections between travel, truth, trade, and song. First, Odysseus' extended overseas journey includes a search for both knowledge and real tangible goods—metals, food, clothing, and so on.[14] As a result, he returns home with a boat full of goods and many stories about his trip (and his cargo). In one sense, the cargo that he brings home serves as a guarantee of the authenticity of his stories, as in Book 13, when Odysseus tells Athena that he was abandoned on the island by Phoenicians together with his possessions.[15] His tale of murder, war booty, and Phoenician traders accounts for the piles of cargo surrounding Odysseus, and the cargo in turn authenticates his story. In other words, the actual goods brought back from overseas prove that he was really there, and in this way do not just represent the potential value of the narrative but document its authenticity as well. It might be objected that Odysseus is lying here (as in much of the second half of the *Odyssey*), thus calling this rhetorical strategy into question. That is, the goods piled before him came from the Phaeacians, not the Phoenicians, and are thus not a reliable guarantee of the truth of his story. But even if we do think of this speech as a lie— and I would prefer not to, as I will argue shortly—the rhetorical gesture that unites goods and song remains a persuasive mechanism for guaranteeing the authenticity of his tale to his audience.[16]

In a slight variation on this configuration of the complicated relations among stories, travels, and trade, Odysseus tells Penelope a tale about an object from his travels (instead of offering the object itself) in order to validate and authenticate his story. When, in Book 19, the disguised Odysseus tries to convince Penelope that he has seen the real Odysseus overseas, he explains that he comes from Crete, where he had once entertained her husband. Blown off course by a storm, Odysseus and his men stayed in Crete for twelve days, were well entertained and fed, and on the thirteenth day set off again. Penelope wants proof that he was really there, and so she asks the stranger to describe the clothing that her husband and his men were wearing.[17] The disguised Odysseus passes her test with flying colors. Not only does he recount for Penelope the purple double cloak and the shining tunic that Odysseus was wearing, but also he describes in intricate detail a golden pin, inscribed with an image of hounds hunting a fawn. In other words, he offers her a narrative description of the treasure she gave him in exchange for the original gift itself. At the same time, the original gift and its story serve successfully to authenticate and validate his story about his travels.

The ultimate intersection of narrative, travel, and trade happens, as we have already seen, when the stories that Odysseus tells about his travels enter into free exchange with other valuable commodities such as metals, clothing, or food. In the hut of the swineherd, for example, the disguised Odysseus trades a story about the real Odysseus at Troy and a cloak for a real cloak. Similarly, at the court of Alcinous in Phaeacia, Odysseus exchanges his stories about his travels for enough gifts and goods to take back home with him—more than he would have brought home from Troy. Now we can see that the valuable goods and commodities available for trade from overseas do not just serve as a representation of the potential value of song; they also provide the poet with proof of his narrative authority. The truth of his song lies in his travels, and the goods gained from those travels provide the physical evidence of this truth.

The poetics of the *Odyssey*, especially its notion of narrative truth, are very much tied up with the poem's fascination with overseas travel and encounter. First, the *Odyssey* is, after all, a poem about travel—about the expeditions of Odysseus, Telemachus, and the others who fought at Troy—and these travel stories provide knowledge about the worlds and peoples across the seas. Second, it is the act of sailing to new worlds, often corroborated by actual goods acquired there, that provides the poet with the narrative authority to convince his audience of the truth of his song. For in addition to giving knowledge about the worlds abroad, overseas travel provides valuable goods and commodities from them. Finally, goods and stories brought back home from abroad enter into free exchange with each other, both of which are easily accommodated by the generous cargo hold of Odysseus' metapoetic raft. This raft, with its many-pegged mode of construction, its ability to carry large quantities of commodities, and its potential for movement, comes to embody the nexus of travel, trade, and narrative that dominates the poetics of the *Odyssey*. By untangling the complicated ways in which the metapoetic nature of Odysseus' raft locates the poetics of the poem within a world of travel and trade, we begin to see that the poem is not just about Odysseus' travels, but that it looks to the notion and possibilities of travel to explore the nature, value, and authority of narrative itself. If we return to Book 14, to Eumaeus' response to the disguised Odysseus' offer of news about his absent master, we can see that it is not just poets who travel; the *Odyssey* suggests that poetry itself is a mobile phenomenon.

## Traveling Song

After dismissing the stories of travelers as mere lies, the swineherd challenges Odysseus to sing a song himself, hinting that someone might give him a cloak in return. In particular, he asks Odysseus to build an *epos* (ἔπος παρατεκτήναιο), using the language of carpentry or shipmaking to designate poetic construction.[18] His use of the prefix παρα- suggests, however, that he expects Odysseus to put together a story that is out of order or contrary to reality—the kind of deceptive story to be expected from a traveling man. Odysseus proceeds to tell a tale of travel and adventure that draws extensively on elements of the story the audience has heard in Books 9–12, but which also departs quite significantly from it. Eumaeus' response to this reordered tale of wandering is again articulated in terms of truth and falsehood:

ἆ δειλὲ ξείνων, ἦ μοι μάλα θυμὸν ὄρινας
ταῦτα ἕκαστα λέγων, ὅσα δὴ πάθες ἠδ᾽ ὅσ᾽ ἀλήθης.
ἀλλὰ τά γ᾽ οὐ κατὰ κόσμον ὀΐομαι, οὐδέ με πείσεις
εἰπὼν ἀμφ᾽ Ὀδυσῆι· τί σε χρὴ τοῖον ἐόντα
μαψιδίως ψεύδεσθαι;

O most wretched of strangers, how you have stirred up my heart saying such things, as much as you have suffered and wandered. But I do
not think it is all in order, nor do you persuade me in talking about
Odysseus. Why should such a man as yourself lie to me recklessly? (*Od.*
14.361–65)

Here, too, Eumaeus characterizes Odysseus' wandering and the tales it produces
in terms of truth and falsehood, and the etymology of wandering as truth is again
confirmed precisely by Eumaeus' strong rejection of it in these terms. He suspects
that the story is out of order (οὐ κατὰ κόσμον), and he chastises the beggar for
lying to him idly (μαψιδίως).[19] The phrase οὐ κατὰ κόσμον picks up the sense of
narrative derailment implied by the prefix παρα- used earlier in παρατεκτήναιο,
suggesting that Odysseus' story wanders idly from place to place just as he did.
In addition, Eumaeus' use of μαψιδίως to characterize Odysseus' song evokes images of pirates who sail the seas with equal abandon and lack of purpose or order (μαψιδίως ἀλάλησθε, 3.72), whose unpredictable movement is contrasted
with that of sailors who travel with a fixed plan or agenda (κατὰ πρῆξιν, 3.72).[20]
This opposition between unpredictable mobility and fixed order underlies Eumaeus'
response to Odysseus' tale as well. Odysseus' story was not told in order (οὐ κατὰ
κόσμον); instead, like pirates who wander (μαψιδίως ἀλάλησθε), he lied in a reckless and aimless way (μαψιδίως ψεύδεσθαι).

Eumaeus' reply emphatically articulates a notion of narrative in which a
good song is associated with truth, and where narrative truth, in turn, is linked
with conceptions of stability and order. Accordingly, the swineherd rejects
Odysseus' elaborate tale of travel and adventure because it moves around too
much; it does not follow the familiar and predictable patterns that he has come
to associate with good stories. A stable, well-ordered narrative from which
everyone knows what to expect depends on a fixed notion of audience as well,
a closed poetic community, like that at the court of Alcinous, in which everyone
shares a common set of expectations about what constitutes a good and successful song. Within this kind of poetic community, as we have seen, the poet's
source of authority or skill is identified as the Muses; they know all things, past
and future, and inspire poets with their songs. Eumaeus' conception of a fixed
narrative truth, of songs sung in order, recalls, in fact, the kinds of songs that
Demodocus sings at the court of the Phaeacians. After the bard sings the song
of the destruction of Troy, Odysseus gives him high praise for his well-ordered
song:

Δημόδοκ᾽, ἔξοχα δή σε βροτῶν αἰνίζομ᾽ ἁπάντων·
ἢ σέ γε Μοῦσ᾽ ἐδίδαξε, Διὸς πάις, ἢ σέ γ᾽ Ἀπόλλων.
λίην γὰρ κατὰ κόσμον Ἀχαιῶν οἶτον ἀείδεις,
ὅσσ᾽ ἔρξαν τ᾽ ἔπαθόν τε καὶ ὅσσ᾽ ἐμόγησαν Ἀχαιοί·
ὥς τέ που ἢ αὐτὸς παρεὼν ἢ ἄλλου ἀκούσας.

> Demodocus, I praise you most of all mortals: either the Muse taught
> you, the daughter of Zeus, or Apollo, for you sing the story of the de-
> struction of the Achaeans in very good order—what they did and ex-
> perienced and how much the Achaeans suffered—as if you yourself
> were there or heard it from another. (*Od.* 8.487–91)

Odysseus praises Demodocus' song for its accuracy; it was told in good order
(κατὰ κόσμον), as if the poet himself had been an eyewitness to the events he recounts.[21] The terms of this praise, its allusion to eyewitness authority, evoke the
famous poetic appeal to the Muses that preceeds the Catalogue of Ships in the
*Iliad*. There the poet prays to the Muses for help in singing about the Trojan War,
since "you were there and know all things" (ὑμεῖς γὰρ θεαί ἐστε, πάρεστέ τε,
ἴστέ τε πάντα, *Il.* 2.485). He derives his poetic authority directly from them; they
set the order of songs. The songs of Demodocus are similarly inspired (he was
taught by Apollo or the Muse), and his connection to the Muses provides him
with poetic authority as well as with an endless supply of well-ordered songs.[22]
In the *Odyssey*, this notion of a stable narrative tradition, associated with order
and sponsored by the Muses, is synonymous with stories of the Trojan War and
the grand Iliadic poetry of the past. The well-ordered songs that Eumaeus longs
to hear in his swineherd's hut on the island of Ithaca are, in fact, Demodocus'
songs of the Trojan horse or the conflict between Odysseus and Achilles.[23]

At the same time, however, the tales of Odysseus challenge Eumaeus' association of song with the fixed and familiar stories of the *Iliad* to present a competing view of narrative that is not just about travel but that derives its very nature and authority from travel. Odysseus' poetic authority, after all, comes not
from the Muses; rather, it is located in his own experiences and adventures overseas. He has learned the minds and cities of men directly, and the authenticity of
his songs stems from his personal eyewitness experience as he traveled from land
to land. In addition, the value of his songs, as we have seen, is associated with
the wealth of knowledge and real goods that he brings home from the new world.
Odysseus' songs thus articulate a notion of narrative that is associated on every
level with the potential of travel and the possibilities of movement. His songs are
not fixed or well ordered; rather, they wander as he does, taking unexpected detours, including new details to appease particular audiences or to suit specific occasions.

Again the contrast between Demodocus and Odysseus is instructive. Demodocus sings his well-ordered songs about the Iliadic past as a permanent fixture
at the court of the Phaeacians. Both he and his poetry represent a model of poetry that is stable and fixed, authorized by the Muses. Odysseus, by contrast, is
a poet on the move, singing new songs for new audiences at new places, and his
songs are equally mobile. Never the same twice, his songs represent a flexible
and mercurial notion of poetic truth, one that is authorized not by the Muses but

rather by the actual travels of the poet himself.[24] The *Odyssey* thus also articulates a notion of narrative that is mobile and flexible, in which narrative truth is rooted in travel.[25] Unlike the traditional, well-ordered songs of Demodocus, moreover, this "Odyssean" notion of narrative is not interested in retelling the Iliadic past. Rather, it looks to new worlds and the opportunities of the future and the far away as the sources and inspiration for song.

Odysseus' traveling song intersects with the more traditional view of a fixed and stable narrative tradition most conspicuously at the island of the Sirens. Again the metaphorical associations between ships and song help articulate the tensions between these two models of narrative at work in the poem. Circe first alerts Odysseus to the dangers of these seductive monsters, famous temptresses of ships and song, warning him that whoever listens to their song loses all interest in returning home. The Sirens sing out to those who pass by:

ἀλλά τε Σειρῆνες λιγυρῇ θέλγουσιν ἀοιδῇ,
ἥμεναι ἐν λειμῶνι· πολὺς δ᾽ ἀμφ᾽ ὀστεόφιν θὶς
ἀνδρῶν πυθομένων, περὶ δὲ ῥινοὶ μινύθουσι.

But the Sirens charm with their pure song, sitting in their meadow; the shore is full of bones of rotting men, with the skin shrinking around them. (*Od.* 12.44–46)

The initial enticing image of seductive and charming songstresses gives way quickly to a picture of stagnation and decay, and Circe offers Odysseus advice about how he might listen to their beautiful song without ending up like all the others piled up on the beach. She tells him to fill his men's ears with wax so that they will not hear the song and be tempted to stop rowing. If Odysseus himself wants to hear, he should have his men tie him to the mast of his ship with tight, unbreakable knots.

Odysseus keeps Circe's advice in mind, and when they reach the island of the Sirens, he follows her instructions. All breezes have died down, and a windless calm sets in over the water. Odysseus' men take down the sails and begin to row, with Odysseus tied firmly to the mast of the ship. The Sirens sing their sweet song directly to Odysseus:

"Δεῦρ᾽ ἄγ᾽ ἰών, πολύαιν᾽ Ὀδυσεῦ, μέγα κῦδος Ἀχαιῶν,
νῆα κατάστησον, ἵνα νωιτέρην ὄπ᾽ ἀκούσῃς.
οὐ γάρ πώ τις τῇδε παρήλασε νηὶ μελαίνῃ,
πρίν γ᾽ ἡμέων μελίγηρυν ἀπὸ στομάτων ὄπ᾽ ἀκοῦσαι·
ἀλλ᾽ ὅ γε τερψάμενος νεῖται καὶ πλείονα εἰδώς.
ἴδμεν γάρ τοι πάνθ᾽ ὅσ᾽ ἐνὶ Τροίῃ εὐρείῃ
Ἀργεῖοι Τρῶές τε θεῶν ἰότητι μόγησαν·
ἴδμεν δ᾽ ὅσσα γένηται ἐπὶ χθονὶ πουλυβοτείρῃ."

Odysseus and the sirens. Attic red figure stamnos, ca. 450. E 440. Photo courtesy of British Museum, London.

Come here, much-famed Odysseus, great pride of the Achaeans; stop your ship so that you may hear our song. For no one has ever driven past in his black ship before hearing the honey-sweet song from our mouths. But having been pleased, he returns, knowing more. For we know all that the Argives and Trojans suffered in broad Troy at the hands of the gods; we know all that happened in the very fertile land. (*Od.* 12.184–92)

As others have argued, the Sirens sound here very much like the Muses of the *Iliad*. They enchant, seduce; they know all that happened, especially at Troy.[26] In fact, the song that they offer to sing for Odysseus is essentially the song of the *Iliad*—the sufferings of the Greeks and Trojans. There is a kind of intertextual debate going on here between the *Iliad* and the *Odyssey* in which the Sirens, posing as Iliadic Muses, threaten the poetic success of the *Odyssey*. If Odysseus had given in to their blandishments, his own poem, the song of his travels, would never have been heard. In order for the *Odyssey* to survive as a poem, its hero must avoid shipwreck on the shoals of the Iliadic past; he must keep on sailing.

In other words, the tension or poetic competition between the *Iliad* and the *Odyssey* expressed by the Sirens episode is articulated precisely in the terms of the stasis and movement inherent in sea travel. Within this system, to continue to sing the *Iliad* is to be becalmed, to rot on the windless shores of the Sirens' island, doomed to sing the past over and over again. To stop Odysseus' ship is tantamount to putting an end both to his travels and to his song. Odysseus counters this fate by his ability, and the ability of his song, to keep moving, and the sailing/poetry analogy helps structure the terms of this conflict. Odysseus' ship sails on by the Sirens' island, and the mobility of Odysseus' ship, like that of his raft, associates the potential value and authority of his song with the wealth and knowledge that comes from travel, from experience of the new world. At the same time, Odysseus is literally fused with his ship; he "remains steadfast there straight against the mast" (ἔμπεδον αὐτόθι μίμνων ὀρθὸν ἐν ἱστοπέδῃ, *Od.* 12.161). While the ship's ability to sail signifies the mobile success of Odysseus' song, his own steadfast position (ἔμπεδον) both bears witness to the alternative narrative model—that of a fixed and ordered song—and offers an icon of a poet literally one with his song. Odysseus, hero and poet, has become part of the very architecture of his metapoetic ship.

The image of Odysseus tied to the mast of his ship as it successfully sails by the alluring Sirens thus embodies the tension between these two competing notions of poetic truth and depends on the metaphorical association of ships and song. The song of the Sirens, confined to their island, celebrates a narrative of the past, a story well known and told in order each time. Odysseus, however, literally fused with his ship, represents a new model of narrative, one that travels far and wide just like its hero. Thus, although some may prefer the familiar songs of the past, there also emerges from the world of the *Odyssey* an alternative view of narrative, one that is mobile and mercurial, whereby songs are flexible and ever adaptable to each new narrative context. These two different notions of narrative truth are very much contested in the *Odyssey* (as are questions about narrative value), and it is through careful readings of episodes such as Odysseus' encounter with the Sirens and his conversations with Eumaeus that we can begin to detect the terms and issues raised by these debates.

## Travel Tales, Lying Tales

An important part of the contest over narrative truth and authority in the *Odyssey* hinges on the relationships between travel and truth, on the one hand, and truth and falsity, on the other. Insofar as poetic truth is rooted in the experience and essence of travel, its flexible and mobile nature brings it into uncomfortable proximity to lying tales. And so, in light of my discussion of the problematic nature of narrative truth in the *Odyssey*, especially with respect to its association with travel and lies, I conclude with a brief look at the string of travel tales that Odysseus tells over the course of the poem—both those that are often called the "lying tales" and the grand narrative that Odysseus tells to the court of the Phaeacians in Books 9–12. The narrative voice of Odysseus merges with that of Homer for Books 9–12 as Odysseus enthralls the Phaeacians with the tale of his travels to the mythical lands of Cyclopes and Lotus-Eaters, to the worlds of enchanting nymphs and savage sea monsters. This fusion of Homer's and Odysseus' narrative voices, together with Alcinous' highly positive response to the story, has led centuries of scholars and readers to consider this tale of Odysseus to be a "true" one—what really happened to him once he left Troy. In contrast to this story, then, the tales told by Odysseus over the course of the second half of the poem have always been considered "lying tales" in that they diverge significantly both from one another and, more important, from the accounts told in Books 9–12.[27] Instead of asking which of these tales are true and which are lies, however, I want to focus on what taking all these stories equally seriously as "travel tales" can contribute to our understanding of the notion of narrative truth in the poem.

Upon arriving at Ithaca, Odysseus, disguised as a beggar, tells a different version of his story to Athena, to Eumaeus, to Antinous, and finally to Penelope and to his father, Laertes. Each of these stories is a primarily a travel tale. Odysseus tells Athena, for example, that he was exiled from Crete for murder and then fled to the sea, begging the Phoenicians to take him on as a passenger. They agreed to do so in exchange for some of his plunder from Troy; but a storm drove them off course, and they left Odysseus there (in Ithaca) and sailed back to Sidon.[28] In his story to Eumaeus, Odysseus also claims to be from Crete, but this time he chooses to leave home in search of adventure and wealth. He fought at Troy, he led pirate expeditions, and he traveled to Egypt for commercial interests. There he was enslaved, was rescued by the king of Egypt, and then set sail with Phoenician traders. Again, a storm impeded his travels, and he was shipwrecked in Thesprotia.[29] Odysseus' story to Antinous in Book 17 is much less detailed, but here, too, he claims that he ran off to Egypt with much-wandering pirates; theirs was a long journey (δολιχὴν ὁδόν, 17.426). He was enslaved there and sent to Cyprus, and then traveled from Cyprus to Ithaca.[30] Finally, in his tale to Penelope, Odysseus reprises many of the now familiar themes—he comes from Crete—but in this story the travels he recounts are not those of "the beggar" but rather those of Odysseus who had been driven off course to Crete on his way to Troy. He explains that he heard that Odysseus was now safe but was traveling around, going to many lands, to get lots of goods to bring home with him.[31] Even the story he tells to his father, after the slaughter of the suitors, emphasizes the motif of travel. He claims to be from Alybas (a mythical town with a name that evokes the verb "to wander," ἀλάομαι), and suffered trouble at sea when a god drove him to Ithaca against his will.[32]

In spite of their variations, each of these accounts is a travel tale. Collectively they emphasize the themes of wandering, of being driven off course; they account for Odysseus' movement across the sea and back again. In this respect, the content of Odysseus' tales in the second half of the poem reflects the devious, mendacious nature of the tales as expressed by their audiences. As we have already seen, Eumaeus categorizes Odysseus' story in Book 14 as "out of order." Athena reponds to the account Odysseus tells her by celebrating his powers of deception and cleverness.[33] And at the end of Odysseus' story to Penelope, the Homeric narrator comments quietly that Odysseus knows how to speak many false things that are like the truth (ἴσκε ψεύδεα πολλὰ λέγων ἐτύμοισιν ὁμοῖα, 19.203). In other words, these tales wander just as their narrator did; they deviate from the ordered itinerary of familiar narrative.

Instead of identifying and then rejecting these tales as false, however, we might push the association of travel and song a bit further and join Michel Serres in thinking of the travels of Odysseus, as told over the course of the whole poem, as emblematic of the journeys of narrative itself. Serres invokes the Odysseus cycle as part of a larger discussion of the relationship between language and space, suggesting the *Odyssey* is not at all the story of a journey but rather, radically, the journey of a story.[34] If we think about narrative and travel within the *Odyssey* along these lines, it becomes clear that the complexity of the narrative structure of the poem—partial flashbacks, multiple narrators—takes great pains to undercut the coherence of Odysseus' journey. As a result, the *Odyssey* fails to recount, in a chronological and coherent manner, each stage of Odysseus' travels. The exact itinerary of Odysseus' return home is not at all what the poem is really about. But if we follow Serres and turn the tables, we can see that it is precisely the chaotic confusion of the journey—all the false starts and stops at magical islands, the close encounters with cannibal monsters, the savage storms at sea—that creates the essence of the narrative. In other words, the poetics of the *Odyssey* are firmly embedded within a discourse of travel. It is travel that provides the authority and knowledge for true narratives, and it is travel that provides the image for the mobility and flexibility of narrative itself. Pierre Vidal-Naquet has observed that "Odysseus' travels have nothing to do with geography."[35] Instead, I would add, they have everything to do with narrative. To categorize the stories that Odysseus tells back home as lies, thus relegating them to secondary status in the poem, is to overlook some spectacular storytelling in the second half of the *Odyssey*. But even more important, it means ignoring how travel intersects with the poetics of the *Odyssey* to conceptualize a new way of thinking about narrative truth.

The tales told in Books 9–12 and those told in the second half of the poem refuse to fall neatly into the categories of true and false, real and fantasy. The stories that Odysseus recounts to the Phaeacians are, after all, full of mythical creatures and fabulous places.[36] The Lotus-Eaters are not "real" peoples, nor is the magical Circe, nor Charybdis the sea monster. The allegedly "lying" tales that Odysseus tells to Eumaeus and Penelope, however, are full of historical peoples and places: Phoenicians, Cretans, trading ventures to Egypt and Cyprus. In other words, the "true tales" include mythical, fantastic content, but the "lying tales" draw on realistic, historical information. Another way to look at this dichotomy is to focus on the site of narrative production. Tales told by Odysseus at home, on his native soil of Ithaca, are considered false tales, while the stories he tells on the fantasy island of the Phaeacians are known as the real thing. What does this tell us about the source of truth in narrative? Fantastic, faraway worlds provide the material for the real and true story, while everyday events and places produce nothing more than lies. In other words, the truth of narrative lies somewhere in its ability to travel back home from its distant origins, and questions of narrative truth and falsity are embedded in the potential and possibilities of foreign travel.

The *Odyssey* thus yet again presents and contrasts two competing views of narrative or poetic truth: one associates truth with a fixed, ordered narrative; the other privileges a mobile, flexible text.[37] But instead of making hard and fast distinctions between the true story that Odysseus tells the Phaeacians and the lying tales he tells at home in Ithaca, the *Odyssey* suggests an even more destabilizing notion: the truth of a story lies precisely in its ability to travel. This view represents the truth or knowledge of narrative as contingent rather than absolute and provides the Greeks with another framework for addressing questions about narrative and value in a volatile world. Eumaeus' objections to the traveling tales of Odysseus, based on their lack of fixed and familiar order, are thus quite similar to his refusal to engage in the practice of trading songs for cloaks or other commodities. In both cases, he prefers a world based on fixed and familiar rules of exchange and expectation to the volatile and unstable world of trade and travel that the returned Odysseus represents. While overseas travel and commerce hold out the potential for great wealth, they also threaten perilous danger—and Eumaeus resists locating the production and consumption of song within this brave yet unstable new world.

The mobile poetics of the *Odyssey*, in particular its association of poetic authority with travel and the experience of travel, may have contributed to the ways in which later poets invoke the *Odyssey* itself as a source of poetic authority, especially with respect to the genre of the romance-adventure. Scholars who look to the *Odyssey* for the origin of the romance genre emphasize the way the poem shifts its action from the traditional battlefield setting of epic to the sea, the world of traders and sailors. As David Quint suggests, the enchanted boat is a common topos of chivalric romance and is a "close relative of the wandering ship of Odysseus, whose storm-tossed course maps out the apparently random, deviating structure of the romance plot."[38] At odds with the more teleological orientation of martial epic, the boat's travels describe a romance narrative that is open-ended, in which the digression is the story itself. We can now see that this notion of a digressive, mobile conception of narrative is already at work in the poetics of the *Odyssey*, in its very construction of poetic authority and value. The Sirens episode, perhaps the very origin of this Renaissance opposition of genre, articulates the tension between the poetics of the *Iliad*—a teleological epic of conquest—and those of the *Odyssey*—a song that travels just as its hero does—in terms of the ability of Odysseus to sail, to keep his poem moving toward new adventures and songs.[39]

### The Raft of Odysseus

It is time now to bring together the different themes generated by the metaphorical image of Odysseus' raft and to draw some preliminary conclusions about this symbol of the complex nexus of overseas travel, trade, and poetry in the world of the *Odyssey* before moving on to a more detailed analysis of the "ethnographic imagination" of the poem. The image of Odysseus' raft both articulates the poetic intersection of narrative, trade, and travel and provides a useful vehicle for making the transition from these discussions of metaphor and sea travel to an exploration of the new worlds and peoples that Odysseus travels to visit and sings about on his return.

Odysseus puts together his raft at the end of Book 5. Insofar as the technique of the raft's construction mirrors that of oral poetic composition, the raft prefigures and represents Odysseus' poetic voice precisely at the point in the poem when he is about to take over the narration of the poem at large. The cargo, both poetic and commercial, that this raft can accommodate articulates new ways to conceptualize the value of song, and the ability of the raft to travel underscores the connections between travel and song that emerge from the poetics of the *Odyssey*—both songs about travel and the notion of traveling song.

And so Odysseus' raft—an image that embodies this intersection of poetics, travel, and trade in the world of the *Odyssey*—will now carry us forward, in the following chapters, to explore these new worlds encountered in Odysseus' travels, the worlds and peoples far away and across the seas. In particular, the next section will focus on the modes and mechanisms for imagining the New World, especially the ways in which the "ethnographic imagination" at work in the *Odyssey* interrogates change and innovation at home as much as it addresses the anomalies of new worlds abroad. The travel books of the *Odyssey* not only explore the potential opportunities of the New World, both real and fanciful, but also they appropriate images of the foreign and the magical to question cultural constraints at home. In this respect, the *Odyssey*, like many travel narratives, explores the tensions between the possibilities of the unknown and the limitations of the familiar. Odysseus' travels, his encounters with an entire range of magical islands and monstrous figures, provide the early archaic Greek ethnographic imagination not just with information about new worlds and peoples, but also with ways to reconfigure their sense of their Greek selves. Embedded, for example, within the contrasting ethnographic portraits of the Phoenicians and Phaeacians as two different models of the "other" are precisely the socioeconomic issues about the potential advantages and dangers of trade that are very much alive to the Greek audience of the *Odyssey*. It is the *Odyssey*'s fascination with the world of travels that enables the poem to demystify and renovate the familiar concepts of home.

Sailing thus operates both figuratively and more literally in the *Odyssey* to make possible this ethnographic imagination. As we noted with Derek Walcott at the beginning of this section, "there are two journeys in every odyssey":

> For both, the 'I' is a mast; a desk is a raft
> for one, foaming with paper, and dipping the beak
>
> of a pen in its foam, while an actual craft
> carries the other to cities where people speak
> a different language, or look at him differently . . . [40]

On one level, then, metaphors of sailing make poetry possible. But in addition to creating an image for addressing questions about the nature, the value, and the authority of narrative, Walcott reminds us that it is the actual practice of sailing overseas that makes ethnography possible in the *Odyssey* as well. Ships take Odysseus to "cities where people speak a different language," where he learns "the minds and cities of many men."

# II    Phaeacia, Gateway to the Ethnographic Imagination

# 4

# A Brave New World

O wonder!
How many goodly creatures are there here!
How beauteous mankind is! O brave new world
That has such people in't!

Shakespeare, *The Tempest* V.i

At the end of Book 5, Odysseus makes his preparations to leave Calypso and to return home at long last. Once the raft is built, Calypso brings him clothing and provisions for his trip and stirs up a favorable wind to send him on his way (5.263–68). Odysseus then raises the sails to catch the breeze and settles himself expertly (τεχνηέντως, 5.270) at the rudder of his newly built raft. Initially all goes well, and Odysseus successfully navigates the open sea for seventeen days. On the eighteenth, however, just as he catches sight of the island of the Phaeacians appearing like a shield on the sea, Poseidon spies Odysseus making his way home. Furious, the sea god curses this change of events and stirs up a monumental storm intending to smash Odysseus and his raft to bits:

> Ὣς εἰπὼν σύναγεν νεφέλας, ἐτάραξε δὲ πόντον
> χερσὶ τρίαιναν ἑλών· πάσας δ᾽ ὀρόθυνεν ἀέλλας
> παντοίων ἀνέμων, σὺν δὲ νεφέεσσι κάλυψε
> γαῖαν ὁμοῦ καὶ πόντον· ὀρώρει δ᾽ οὐρανόθεν νύξ.

> So speaking he gathered together the clouds and stirred up the sea, taking his trident in his hands. He roused up all the storms of all kinds of winds, and he hid the land and the sea equally with clouds. And night arose from the sky. (*Od.* 5.291–94)

Odysseus groans in fear at the sounds of the storm and laments his own destiny to die miserably at sea. His companions at Troy were three and four times more blessed to die gloriously on the battlefield. Sure enough, once the storm hits, Odysseus' handmade raft begins to break up:

Ὣς ἄρα μιν εἰπόντ' ἔλασεν μέγα κῦμα κατ' ἄκρης
δεινὸν ἐπεσσύμενον, περὶ δὲ σχεδίην ἐλέλιξε.
τῆλε δ' ἀπὸ σχεδίης αὐτὸς πέσε, πηδάλιον δὲ
ἐκ χειρῶν προέηκε· μέσον δέ οἱ ἱστὸν ἔαξε
δεινὴ μισγομένων ἀνέμων ἐλθοῦσα θύελλα·
τηλοῦ δὲ σπεῖρον καὶ ἐπίκριον ἔμπεσε πόντῳ.

As he spoke a great wave rushed terribly down upon him from up high
and spun the raft around. He himself fell far from the raft and lost the
rudder from his hands. A terrible storm of winds mixing together arrived and broke the mast in the middle, and the sail and the upper deck
fell into the water far away. (*Od.* 5.313–18)

At this point, the sea goddess Leucothea appears and offers Odysseus a magic
scarf that will save him from the storm if he abandons his raft and starts swimming. Initially a bit skeptical, Odysseus vows to stay with his raft as long as it
stays together (ὄφρ' ἂν μέν κεν δούρατ' ἐν ἁρμονίῃσιν ἀρήρῃ, 5.361), but Poseidon
soon sends a wave that scatters the planks of the raft just as a wind blows hard
upon a pile of dry chaff and sends it in every direction (5.365–70). Odysseus
then abandons his raft and finally succeeds in swimming ashore to the island of
the Phaeacians, where he hides himself under an olive bush and falls into an ex-
hausted sleep.

Odysseus' raft—the raft that he constructed with the divine help of Calypso,
the raft that represents the poetic process with all its valuable potential and ability to travel—this raft is shattered to bits in seventeen short days and just a few
lines. Why? If Odysseus' raft is to represent the poetic process within the poem,
why does it break up so soon? What does this tell us about the enduring power
of poetry? One way to think about this apparent contradiction, as I noted in
chapter 1, is to read the temporary, improvisatory nature of the raft's construction as emblematic of the flexible and contingent nature of the poetic process.
The different components and themes of song are arranged to suit a particular
audience and context but need not remain permanently fixed in that order. Like
the planks of Odysseus' raft, the different themes or parts of a song can be taken
apart and rearranged to create new songs for new contexts. And in fact this is
exactly what we find when we compare the songs that Odysseus sings of his adventures to the Phaeacians in Books 9–12 with those that he tells Eumaeus and
Penelope upon arriving at Ithaca.[1]

Another way to think about this question, however, is to focus on the narrative result of Odysseus' shipwreck, namely, the production of his travel tales,
for his wreck selects the ideal site and audience (both Phaeacians and us) for
singing the songs that have come to define the essence of the *Odyssey*—his tales
of adventure and intrigue. The loss of Odysseus' raft, with all its metapoetic associations, is thus compensated within the narrative by the actual stories that he
tells. In this chapter I draw on two Renaissance texts as methodological models

to explore the narrative significance of choosing Phaeacia as the site for Odysseus' storytelling. First, Shakespeare's play *The Tempest* will help us think about the significance of the convergence of New World and Golden Age associations similarly at work in the *Odyssey*. Both Prospero's island and that of the Phaeacians represent ideal landscapes that describe brave new worlds across the seas, all the while negotiating a place for the old world in them. Second, Jean de Léry's account of his trip to Brazil in 1556–58 will provide a model for analyzing the ethnographic structure of the tales Odysseus tells to his Phaeacian audience within the larger narrative context of the poem. In both Renaissance Europe and early archaic Greece, as we will see, the New World and its ethnographic traditions are a particularly productive source of imaginative thinking about the economic, political, and social issues facing the Old World in a time of transition and change.[2]

### Shakespeare's *Tempest*: A Model of New World Discourse

Odysseus' shipwreck on Phaeacia and the stories he tells there share some interesting narrative traits with the great wreck that opens Shakespeare's *Tempest*, and it is worth taking a brief detour here to think about these two texts together for a couple of different reasons: first, as a methodological model for reading literary texts within a historical context, and second, to understand the narrative potential of the New World as a fertile site for literary production.[3]

First, although the plot of *The Tempest* is an original creation of Shakespeare, much of the action of the play is grounded in recent historical events surrounding European settlement of the New World.[4] It is likely that many of the characters in the play take their names from William Thomas's *Historie of Italye*, and Gonzalo's famous speech in praise of the island paraphrases John Florio's (1603) translation of Montaigne's essay *Of the Cannibals*.[5] Most significant, however, is the extent to which Shakespeare appears to have been influenced by the accounts of the shipwreck in 1609 of a fleet of nine ships that left Plymouth for Virginia carrying more than five hundred colonists. A storm separated one ship, the *Sea Venture*, from the rest of the fleet, and while the other ships did eventually arrive at the port of Jamestown over the next few weeks, the *Sea Venture* was given up for lost. Then, nearly a year later, castaways from the lost ship arrived in Jamestown with tales of their experiences. Most interesting, their reports, which Shakespeare may have read, described the islands of the Bermudas, originally thought to be dangerous and hostile, to be like an island paradise:

> Wherefore my opinion sincerely of this island is, that whereas it hath been and is full accounted the most dangerous, unfortunate, and most forlorn place of the world, it is in truth the richest, healthfulest, and

pleasing land (the quantity and bigness thereof considered) and merely natural, as ever man set foot upon.[6]

Among other things, *The Tempest* clearly draws on this contemporary view of the New World as an untapped source of wealth and prosperity.

Much recent scholarship on *The Tempest* highlights the ways in which issues of colonialism and New World settlement help structure and organize the action of the play.[7] The political struggles at home in Italy, the desire for imperial power, and the role of marriage as a way to ensure dynastic continuity are all themes from the play that would clearly resonate with its contemporary audience. Yet at the same time, no one would deny the artistic imagination of *The Tempest*. In fact, the play has long been read as Shakespeare's final farewell to his art as playwright, with Prospero's act of breaking his magic wand foreshadowing Shakespeare's own literary retirement. Yet not even the most historicizing of Renaissance scholars would attempt to read the play as a clear, unmediated reflection of experiences amidst a colonial expedition. In this respect, scholarship on *The Tempest* can provide us with useful methodological models for reading a similar, although certainly not identical, interaction between historical events and the literary imagination within an early archaic Greek text such as the *Odyssey*.[8]

To take just a few examples, like *The Tempest*, the *Odyssey* addresses issues of overseas exploration and cross-cultural contact and settlement. Both poems emerge at a time of simultaneous literary prosperity and New World exploration, and they display, as a result, some thematic similarities. Compare, for example, Odysseus' famous lament (*Od.* 5.306–12) about dying at sea rather than at Troy with a similar wish expressed in *The Tempest* by Gonzalo:

> Now would I give a thousand furlongs of sea for an acre of barren ground—long heath, brown furze, anything. The wills above be done, but I would fain die a dry death. (I.i)

Similarly, Odysseus' encounter with Nausicaa in Book 6, once he washes ashore on her father's island—a passage that resonates with erotic, marriage imagery— is echoed by Ferdinand's arrival and courtship of Miranda in *The Tempest*.[9] In both cases, a shipwrecked foreign male arrives from overseas to displace local suitors for the hand of the young girl and control of the land—a utopian model for foreign settlement or colonial rule.[10] In addition, the action of *The Tempest* is motivated by the rivalry between two brothers, Prospero and Antonio, resulting in Prospero's departure from Milan to live on his island, a theme that appears in the *Odyssey* as well. The emnity between the Cyclopes and their relatives, the Phaeacians, forced the Phaeacians to resettle at Scheria.[11] Finally, as we will see, both the *Odyssey* and *The Tempest* draw on Golden Age, utopian themes to describe the landscape of the New World.

In addition to these thematic parallels, however, the *Odyssey* and *The Tempest* share some similarities of structure, and this brings me to the second, and much more significant, way in which *The Tempest* offers a helpful model for reading Odysseus' shipwreck on the island of the Phaeacians. In *The Tempest*, Prospero contrives the shipwreck of his brother and companions so that he can work out political and family conflicts stemming from the Old World within the New World setting of his magic island paradise. His ability to control the action stems from his books, and through his literary power he contrives a narrative setting in which the struggles between himself and his brother for rule of Milan, as well as those between the rulers of Milan and Naples, can be ideally resolved. Over the course of the play, through Prospero's art, several things become possible. First, the original act of fraternal political usurpation that sent Prospero into exile is reenacted in several different keys and each time is foiled; second, a peaceful union of power between Naples and Milan is forged through the marriage of Ferdinand and Miranda; and third, Prospero negotiaties a return home for himself. The logic of the play insists that these solutions to Old World problems could be found only in the ideal, Golden Age setting of the New World across the seas. Hence the shipwreck. Prospero must orchestrate the shipwreck in order to shift the poetic locale from the Old World as a site of destructive conflict to the New World as a place of productive resolution. This is the brave new world where his literary imagination can help forge new solutions to age-old strife.

Recognizing that a similar poetic logic is at work in the *Odyssey* enriches our understanding of the immediate destruction of Odysseus' raft and his subsequent shipwreck on the island of the Phaeacians. This island, like Prospero's, is a magic combination of Golden Age and New World traditions, and it, too, will provide a productive site for the poem's ethnographic imagination. The creative potential of this choice of locale is further emphasized by the metapoetic nature of the raft. As we have seen, Odysseus' construction of his raft in Book 5 marks the moment in the poem when he first appears with his own poetic voice, and in this respect the building of the raft prefigures Odysseus' role as primary narrator of the poem. Equally important, however, is the way in which the wreck of the raft puts Odysseus ashore at Phaeacia and thus selects this particular magical island as the site for the stories he will tell over the course of Books 9–12. The creation of the raft underscores the nature and process of poetic production; its subsequent and inevitable destruction selects the site and the audience for that poetic production. In other words, Odysseus' raft must be built and then crash so that he can tell his stories at Phaeacia.

New Worlds and the Golden Age

A conflation of New World and Golden Age associations is important to this narrative context. Before turning to the *Odyssey* itself, we can see a productive convergence of the ideals of the past and the potential of the future at work in the second act of *The Tempest*, when the Italian nobles awaken on Prospero's island, happy to have escaped the wreck. Adrian and Antonio remark on the sweetness of the air; Gonzalo praises the "lush and lusty" green grass and then fantasizes about what he would do if he had "plantation of this isle":

> I' th' commonwealth I would by contraries
> Execute all things. For no kind of traffic
> Would I admit; no name of magistrate;
> Letters should not be known; riches, poverty,
> And use of service, none; contract, succession,
> Bourn, bound of land, tilth, vineyard, none;
> No use of metal corn, or wine, or oil;
> No occupation; all men idle, all;
> And women too, but innocent and pure;
> No sovereignty.
> . . . . .
> All things in common nature should produce
> Without sweat or endeavor. Treason, felony,
> Sword, pike, knife, gun, or need of any engine
> Would I not have; but nature should bring forth,
> Of it own kinds, all foison, all abundance
> To feed my innocent people. (II.i)

Gonzalo's vision of this New World that he would like to settle, this island on which they have landed, is characterized in terms of the absence of traditional markers of civilization and corruption: no work, no trade, no sovereignty; no treason, felony, sword, or gun. This negative articulation is common to New World descriptions; the state of nature to be found in the New World overseas is often conceptualized as the very opposite of "civilized" Europe.[12] Gonzalo then goes on to elaborate on this view of the New World by positively expressing his approval of an easy life and ready abundance. In short, he concludes, "I would with perfection govern, sir, / T'excel the Golden Age." Indeed, the abundance and innocence of this island, together with the absence of work, puts it within a well-established tradition of Golden Age landscapes, a tradition that goes back to Hesiod and Near Eastern literature. Hesiod, for example, describes the abundance and fertility of the golden race in the *Works and Days*:

> ἐσθλὰ δὲ πάντα
> τοῖσιν ἔην· καρπὸν δ' ἔφερε ζείδωρος ἄρουρα
> αὐτομάτη πολλόν τε καὶ ἄφθονον· οἳ δ' ἐθελημοὶ
> ἥσυχοι ἔργ' ἐνέμοντο σὺν ἐσθλοῖσιν πολέεσιν.
> ἀφνειοὶ μήλοισι, φίλοι μακάρεσσι θεοῖσιν.

. . . And they had all good things. The fertile field bore fruit of its own free will, a great deal and without stint. And they worked their lands easily and in peace with many good things; they were rich in flocks and dear to the blessed gods. (*WD* 117–20)

As we can see from Hesiod's account, the Golden Age is marked by the abundance of fruit and crops, produced without labor in all seasons, and so the island on which Gonzalo and his friends have landed is a New World marked by the absence of the evils of European life, and, at the same time, it provides them with an opportunity to return to a Golden Age of abundance and commonality, leaving behind the present world of competition and strife. *The Tempest* brings together conventional images of the New World with traditional associations of the Golden Age to create the productive magic of Prospero's island.

A similar convergence of New World and Golden Age themes is at work in the *Odyssey* as well to describe the land of the Phaeacians. First, we recognize echoes of Hesiod's Golden Age. Once the shipwrecked Odysseus is discovered by Nausicaa, she gives him food and clothing, and sets him on his way to see her father to get help in returning home. Odysseus is stunned by the wealth and grandeur of Alcinous' palace with its spectacular mix of gold, silver, bronze, and ivory, flanked by magical gold and silver dogs fashioned by Hephestus and golden boys holding bright lanterns in their hands (7.86–102).[13] The architectural richness of Alcinous' palace is matched by the perpetual fertility of his orchard:

ἔκτοσθεν δ᾽ αὐλῆς μέγας ὄρχατος ἄγχι θυράων
τετράγυος· περὶ δ᾽ ἕρκος ἐλήλαται ἀμφοτέρωθεν.
ἔνθα δὲ δένδρεα μακρὰ πεφύκασι τηλεθόωντα,
ὄγχναι καὶ ῥοιαὶ καὶ μηλέαι ἀγλαόκαρποι
συκέαι τε γλυκεραὶ καὶ ἐλαῖαι τηλεθόωσαι.
τάων οὔ ποτε καρπὸς ἀπόλλυται οὐδ᾽ ἀπολείπει
χείματος οὐδὲ θέρευς, ἐπετήσιος· ἀλλὰ μάλ᾽ αἰεὶ
Ζεφυρίη πνείουσα τὰ μὲν φύει, ἄλλα δὲ πέσσει.
ὄγχνη ἐπ᾽ ὄγχνῃ γηράσκει, μῆλον δ᾽ ἐπὶ μήλῳ,
αὐτὰρ ἐπὶ σταφυλῇ σταφυλή, σῦκον δ᾽ ἐπὶ σύκῳ.

Outside the courtyard there is a great orchard, near the gates, four measures of land, and a fence has been driven all around it. There great blossoming trees are growing, pears and pomegranate and glorious-fruited apple trees and sweet figs and blossoming olive trees. Never does the fruit of these trees rot nor does it ever run out, neither in winter nor summer, but is year-long; and the ever-blowing West Wind starts some growing and ripens others. Pear grows upon pear, apple upon apple, grape upon grape, and fig upon fig. (*Od.* 7.112–21)

Alcinous' orchard is ever productive, his trees bearing fruit in all seasons, and his vineyard is equally prolific:

ἔνθα δέ οἱ πολύκαρπος ἀλωὴ ἐρρίζωται,
τῆς ἕτερον μὲν θειλόπεδον λευρῷ ἐνὶ χώρῳ
τέρσεται ἠελίῳ, ἑτέρας δ' ἄρα τε τρυγόωσιν,
ἄλλας δὲ τραπέουσι· πάροιθε δέ τ' ὄμφακές εἰσιν
ἄνθος ἀφιεῖσαι, ἕτεραι δ' ὑποπερκάζουσιν.
ἔνθα δὲ κοσμηταὶ πρασιαὶ παρὰ νείατον ὄρχον
παντοῖαι πεφύασιν, ἐπηετανὸν γανόωσαι.

There is also planted a very fruitful vineyard, part of it a warm spot on level ground dries in the sun, in other parts they are gathering the grapes and in other parts they are trampling them. In front of these are grapes that have shed their bloom and others are growing dark. There are all kinds of ordered herbs growing below the vineyard, green in all seasons. (Od. 7.122–28)

Here, too, we find an account of vegetation that is magically green and lush all year round. As Anthony Edwards has observed, "The beauty, order, and continuous fertility of the garden, warmed by gentle Zephyr, distinguish Alcinous' garden as an example of the enchanted *locus amoenus* as much as it is a working farm."[14] What is most remarkable, perhaps, is that all this productive fertility is achieved with the conspicuous absence of labor. Edwards points out that the entire passage contains only two verbs of cultivation (τρυγόωσιν, 124, and τραπέουσι, 125), and they are both without an expressed subject.[15] The activity of human work and labor is thus supressed in favor of the bountiful produce. In this respect, the description of the ideal world that Odysseus discovers on the island of the Phaeacians bears a remarkable similarity to Hesiod's account of a Golden Age landscape. Alcinous' orchard and vineyard share this combination of unceasing agricultural abundance—his trees bear fruit in all seasons—and an absence of agricultural cultivation or labor.

Furthermore, the inhabitants of Hesiod's Golden Age are blessed by all good things: they have an easy life and are dear to the blessed gods (φίλοι μακάρεσσι θεοῖσιν, WD 120). A similarly easy life and close relationship to the gods, so Homer tells us, is enjoyed by the Phaeacians. When Alcinous tells his fellow leaders and men of counsel to go home and rest in anticipation of the next day's festivities, he speculates about whether their guest is a mortal in need of their hospitality or a god in disguise, observing that the gods always used to come to them openly:

εἰ δέ τις ἀθανάτων γε κατ' οὐρανοῦ εἰλήλουθεν,
ἄλλο τι δὴ τόδ' ἔπειτα θεοὶ περιμηχανόωνται·
αἰεὶ γὰρ τὸ πάρος γε θεοὶ φαίνονται ἐναργεῖς
ἡμῖν, εὖτ' ἔρδωμεν ἀγακλειτὰς ἑκατόμβας,
δαίνυνταί τε παρ' ἄμμι καθήμενοι ἔνθα περ ἡμεῖς·

εἰ δ᾽ ἄρα τις καὶ μοῦνος ἰὼν ξύμβληται ὁδίτης,
οὔ τι κατακρύπτουσιν, ἐπεί σφισιν ἐγγύθεν εἰμέν,
ὥς περ Κύκλωπές τε καὶ ἄγρια φῦλα Γιγάντων.

But if some one of the immortals has come down from heaven, then the gods are contriving something else; for always before the gods have shown themselves clearly to us, whenever we perform glorious sacrifices, they dine with us and sit beside us. And if one traveling comes alone, then they hide nothing since we are very close to them, as are the Cyclopes and the savage tribes of the Giants. (*Od.* 7.199–206)

Since, as we know, Odysseus is a mortal, the Phaeacians' close relationship with the gods has not been compromised. Their world and their life partake of a Golden Age sensibility of ease, abundance, and closeness to the gods.

At the same time, however, Odysseus travels by sea to this Golden Age world, just as other discoverers sail to the New World, and this narrative detail complicates the significance of ships within this section of the poem. A makeshift raft enables Odysseus' literal transition from Calypso's island to that of the Phaeacians just as it effects the poetic transition from one part of the story to another. At the same time, as we will see, the presence or absence of ships is very much implicated in the connection between Golden Age and New World descriptions. On the one hand, the need for ships has been traditionally associated with the fall from a self-sufficient Golden Age, and yet overseas travel made possible by ships brings the New World, with all its Golden Age qualities, to light.

In the Greek tradition, the advent of ships and sailing conventionally marks the end of the Golden Age. In the *Works and Days*, Hesiod describes the just city in terms that recall many of the characteristics of his Golden Age. The city flourishes (τέθηλε πόλις, 227) as do its people (λαοὶ δ᾽ ἀνθεῦσιν, 227). They work their fields easily (θαλίης δὲ μεμηλότα ἔργα νέμονται, 231), and the earth provides a rich livelihood (τοῖσι φέρει μὲν γαῖα πολὺν βίον, 232). Their fertile fields bear fruit, and it is precisely because of the never-ending fertility of the fields, Hesiod says, that the people of this Golden Age city do not need to travel on ships:

θάλλουσιν δ᾽ ἀγαθοῖσι διαμπερές· οὐδ᾽ ἐπὶ νηῶν
νίσσονται, καρπὸν δὲ φέρει ζείδωρος ἄρουρα.

They flourish continually with good things, nor do they travel on ships, but the grain-giving field bears fruit. (*WD* 236–37)[16]

One sets sail only out of dire necessity, as Odysseus explains to Eumaeus in Book 17 of the *Odyssey*:

γαστέρα δ᾽ οὔ πως ἔστιν ἀποκρύψαι μεμαυῖαν,
οὐλομένην, ἣ πολλὰ κάκ᾽ ἀνθρώποισι δίδωσι,

τῆς ἕνεκεν καὶ νῆες ἐύζυγοι ὁπλίζονται
πόντον ἐπ᾽ ἀτρύγετον, κακὰ δυσμενέεσσι φέρουσαι.

It is not possible to suppress an insistent belly, a terrible thing, that gives
much trouble to mankind, and on account of which well-benched ships
are also fitted out for the barren sea, bringing trouble for their enemies.
(*Od.* 17.286–89)

The necessity for ships, then, is anathema to the Golden Age, or to any context of abundance and fertility, and as a result, the appearance of ships becomes
a marker for the end of the Golden Age. In Olympian 2, Pindar, as part of a fantasy of the afterlife, associates the absence of agriculture and sea travel with a
Golden Age life of easy existence:

ἴσαις δὲ νύκτεσσιν ἀεί
ἴσαις δ᾽ ἁμέραις ἄλιον ἔχοντες, ἀπονέστερον
ἐσλοὶ δέκονται βίοτον, οὐ χθόνα τα-
    ράσσοντες ἐν χερὸς ἀκμᾷ
οὐδὲ πόντιον ὕδωρ
κεινὰν παρὰ δίαιταν . . .

Always having the sun for equal nights and equal days, the nobles enjoy a life without toil, disturbing neither the earth nor the sea's waters
with might of hand for an empty living . . . (Ol. 2.61–65)

Aratus' account of the myth of the ages closely echoes Hesiod's, including a similar detail about the absence of ships from the Golden Age:

χαλεπὴ δ᾽ ἀπέκειτο θάλασσα,
καὶ βίον οὔπω νῆες ἀπόπροθεν ἠγίνεσκον,
ἀλλὰ βόες καὶ ἄροτρα καὶ αὐτή, πότνια λαῶν,
μυρία πάντα παρεῖχε Δίκη, δώτειρα δικαίων.

The difficult sea was far away, and not yet did ships bring their livelihood from far off, but the oxen and ploughs and Justice herself,
queen of the peoples, giver of just things, provided all things in multi-
tudes. (*Phaenomena* 110–13)

The absence of ships, as a commonplace of the Golden Age, underscores the self-
sufficiency and abundance of the time in which men and gods lived peacefully
together.[17] At the same time, however, overseas travel brings to light New Worlds
and new sites of opportunity, and, as we have seen in the cases of Prospero's and
Alcinous' islands, the potential of these New Worlds is often described in terms
of the fertile and prosperous Golden Age. As ships sail between the Golden Age
and the New World, marking the end of the former and the arrival of the latter,

the search for new opportunities overseas is conceptualized as the recovery of a time of wealth and prosperity at home long ago.

The description of Alcinous' orchard and vineyards on Phaeacia shares many qualities with those of Hesiod's Golden Age landscape, especially an emphasis on the fertility and generosity of the earth to provide a never-ending source of livelihood to its inhabitants without the need to work. The rich abundance of Golden Age landscapes would traditionally obviate the need for ships and overseas travel, and so it is all the more interesting that the Phaeacians are famous for seafaring and ships in spite of the magical richness of their land. They are often characterized as both "famed for seafaring" and "men of long oars," and, as we have seen already, their women excel in weaving "as much as Phaeacian men are expert beyond all others for steering a fast ship on the open sea" (7.108–9). Indeed, when Odysseus first arrives in the city of the Phaeacians, he admires their balanced ships and harbors (7.43–45).[18]

Thus the Phaeacians' fame and skill at seafaring take them out of a purely Golden Age context and bring them into a New World of discovery and settlement as well.[19] In this respect, as in the case of *The Tempest*, the island of the Phaeacians participates both in a Golden Age ideology of abundance and ease and in the New World of discovery, settlement, and potential. Whereas *The Tempest* juxtaposes the negative articulation common to New World discourse (no laws, no crime, no work) with the abundance and ease of Golden Age traditions, the *Odyssey* draws on a different marker of the New World—the presence of ships—in conjunction with Golden Age associations to achieve the same effect. The ideal, Golden Age landscape of Phaeacia locates it within traditional mythic patterns like Hesiod's myth of the ages with all of its implications of divine support, equality, and abundance. At the same time, the Phaeacians' affinity with seafaring connects them both with the metapoetic associations with ships in the *Odyssey* and with the connections between seafaring and New World discoveries. Their world represents the great potential for innovation, change, and opportunity that New World settlements offer the ethnographic imagination.

And so, much like Prospero's island, the land of the Phaeacians provides the ideal setting for the production of Odysseus' stories. In *The Tempest*, Prospero contrives the wreck on the island in order to bring his poetic imagination to bear on personal and political issues of dynastic struggle and strife. In the *Odyssey* as well, a poetic landscape is created for Odysseus' tales, and, as we will see, embedded within these exotic and fanciful tales of far-off places are attempts to address important contemporary social and political issues, such as overseas settlement and trade. The metapoetic qualities of the raft underscore the ethnographic imagination that emerges from Odysseus' stories in Books 9–12; the Golden Age and New World aspects of the island of the Phaeacians represent the productive and fertile power of these combined traditions for creatively addressing problems and issues arising from a world in flux. Moreover, the Phaeacians themselves, seafarers dwelling in a Golden Age setting, embody the provocative and potentially productive union of two different narrative traditions: the mythic traditions of the long ago and the New World discourse of the far away.

### Jean de Léry: A Model of Ethnographic Structure

Before we look further at how the Old World/New World dynamic of Phaeacia, a site for telling stories, helps the *Odyssey* address contemporary issues and concerns, it will be helpful to clarify the overall shape and structure of Odysseus' tales and their relationship to the poem as a whole. To this end, another text from the Renaissance, this time an explicitly ethnographic one, will provide a suggestive model for appreciating the narrative structure and organization of the *Odyssey*. Important transformations took place in western Europe from the sixteenth to the eighteenth centuries C.E., many of which are comparable to those taking place in early archaic Greece: the discovery of the New World, the social rifts that accompanied the advent of new political frameworks, the invention of new technologies for writing. Within this world of social and political upheaval, travel writing and ethnographic descriptions of the worlds across the seas played an important role in helping those at home acknowledge and accommodate the changes that emerged from cross-cultural encounters. These were tales about the New World overseas, but their audience was those at home in Europe.

One of the most interesting of these ethnographic treatises is Jean de Léry's *Histoire d'un voyage faict en la terre du Brésil*, the story of his journey at the age of twenty-four into the Bay of Rio from 1556 to 1558. A supporter of the Reformation, Léry first fled his native France for Geneva. Then from Geneva he set out with companions for Brazil to help establish a Calvinist sanctuary there. After becoming disenchanted with the admiral's theological fluctuations, he withdrew from the sanctuary and wandered on his own among the Tupinamba for three months. He then reversed his travels and returned from Brazil to Geneva to France, where he ultimately settled down as a pastor.

Léry's journey and its subsequent narrative account thus form a circle, and through his story of adventures and discovery abroad among the foreign and the savage, he ultimately makes possible a return to himself and to the world of the familiar. Michel de Certeau's analysis of the structure of Léry's account of his expedition to Brazil along these lines, in particular his articulation of its mechanism for moving from "over here" to "over there" and back again, will be very helpful for understanding the complexity of the *Odyssey*'s narrative structure, especially the role of the travel tales.[20]

Let me begin by sketching out briefly de Certeau's analysis of the structure of Léry's tale.[21] The organization of this ethnographic account depends on a structural difference between the world "over there" and that "over here." The

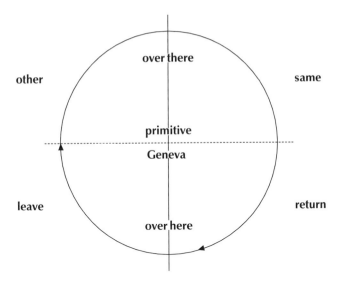

De Certeau's diagram of Lévy's ethnographic narrative.

narrative structure first takes pains to establish this separation, and then the actual telling of the story attempts to transcend that break in order to create meaning from the account. In Léry's tale the separation between "over there" and "over here" manifests itself as the Atlantic Ocean, a physical break between the Old and New Worlds. Thus the opening chapters of the work include accounts of storms, sea monsters, piracy, and the vagaries of ocean travel (chaps. 1–5). The text then begins its movement toward otherness, beginning with tales of cosmological uncanniness and natural wonders (chaps. 7–13), followed by a cultural description of the Tupi (chaps. 14–19), one that emphasizes the theme of dissimilarity. Everything in America is different from Europe, although these anomalies are all conceptualized in terms of the familiar. A previously unseen animal, the *tapiroussou*, for example, is described as being "half-cow" and "half-donkey."[22]

At this point within Léry's account of the Tupi world "over there," a second movement begins, one that starts from the most "other" or primitive elements of this New World (cannibalism, chap. 15) to present an increasingly more social model of the other (laws and police, chap. 18; cult of the dead, chap. 19). The primitive world itself is thus characterized in the opposing terms of nature and culture, and this break within the world "over there" complicates the initial separation between "over there" and "over here." In this respect, the primitive world is no longer entirely synonymous with alterity, but rather the horizontal pole marking the difference between "there" and "here" is supplemented by a vertical axis that delimits alterity from sameness; thus, part of "over there" is brought back "here," shown in de Certeau's diagram of Levy's ethnographic nar-

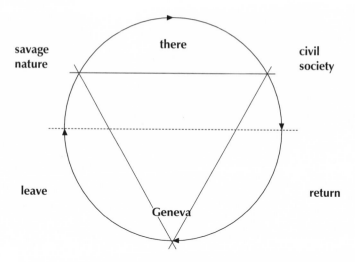

savage
nature

there

civil
society

leave

Geneva

return

De Certeau's "hermeneutics of the other."

rative.[23] The final movement of Léry's account then takes as its point of departure this vision of a more civilized, utopian primitive society, thus reclassifying savage nature as exemplary humanity, and works its way back across the oceanic break (chaps. 21–22) to return home to Geneva.

In this way, the initial bipolar structure of the account—here versus there—is replaced by a circular path built around a triangular framework that articulates a movement from home (Geneva) to the most wild view of nature and the primitive (cannibalism) to an account of an ethical utopian New World (laws, religion) and then back home again to Geneva, as shown here in the second diagram.[24] De Certeau describes this narrative structure as a "hermeneutics of the other," explaining that through it, Léry and his European audience derive meaning about the self from encounters with the other.[25]

The geometrical structure of the tale is central to understanding it. On the one hand, the circular notion of the narrative path from "here" to "there" and back again provides a framework for integrating what is other back into a new, revised notion of the self. The narrative is not fixed in the world "over there"; rather, it maps out the return, the way to bring some of that world to bear on life at home. On the other hand, the triangular scaffolding on which this circular journey depends further bifurcates a simple view of alterity. It supplements the self/other dichotomy with one of nature/culture, locating Geneva somewhere in between the most savage and the most civilized aspects of the primitive world. The combined force of this structure provides the West with an interpretive framework for articulating its identity through a relationship with the other, whether that be with the past or the future, with foreigners or with nature.

### The *Odyssey*'s Ethnographic Structure

Obviously, we cannot impose Michel de Certeau's analysis of Léry's Brazilian account directly on the *Odyssey*, but the general framework of his "hermeneutics of the other," in particular the tripartite narrative movement of the ethnographic narrative, does help illuminate some key structural and thematic themes at work in a poem that is equally concerned with New World discoveries and the process of return as a source of self-knowledge.[26]

If we begin by sketching out Odysseus' journey from the time he left Ithaca for Troy until his return some twenty years later, we find a pattern very similar to that elaborated by de Certeau in his analysis of Léry's account, one that suggests we think about the structure of the *Odyssey* within these ethnographic terms. Any attempt to identify the structure or framework underlying the *Odyssey* is complicated, of course, by the tension between the order or pattern of Odysseus' travels as he experiences them and the order in which he (and Homer) recount them over the course of the poem. For now, however, I want to set aside questions about the narrative order of the poem and outline Odysseus' actual itinerary.

Odysseus first leaves Ithaca to sail to Troy as part of the great Greek expedition to recover Helen. After ten years of battle culminating in victory, Odysseus sets out, with his surviving comrades, to return home to his country and family. As he tells the court of Alcinous at the beginning of Book 9, his voyage home was beset with many troubles, sent by Zeus, as he attempted to make his way home from Troy. Trouble at sea caused his first unscheduled stop among the Ciconians, where he sacked their city and killed their people and lost a few of his own men (9.39–61). Another set of storms, one described in some detail, struck Odysseus and his men upon the open sea:

νηυσὶ δ' ἐπῶρσ' ἄνεμον Βορέην νεφεληγερέτα Ζεὺς
λαίλαπι θεσπεσίῃ, σὺν δὲ νεφέεσσι κάλυψε
γαῖαν ὁμοῦ καὶ πόντον· ὀρώρει δ' οὐρανόθεν νύξ.
αἱ μὲν ἔπειτ' ἐφέροντ' ἐπικάρσιαι, ἱστία δέ σφιν
τριχθά τε καὶ τετραχθὰ διέσχισεν ἲς ἀνέμοιο.

Cloud-gathering Zeus drove the North Wind upon the ships in a divine storm, and hid the land and sea alike with clouds; night arose from the sky. Then the ships were born along, drifting sideways, and the strength of the wind ripped our sails into three and four pieces. (*Od.* 9.67–71)

After surviving this storm and nearly making it back home, once again Odysseus and his men are driven off course by the sea and wind, this time upon the land of the Lotus-Eaters (9.82–86). Their stay among the Lotus-Eaters is a relatively short one (in both duration and narrative), but one that emphasizes the lure of the exotic and underscores the fact that one of the greatest dangers of travel overseas is that one may lose the will to return home. From the Lotus-Eaters, Odysseus sails on to the land of the lawless, cannibalistic Cyclopes.

Up to this point we can see that Odysseus' travels take him farther and farther away from home and the civilized Greek world. He leaves Ithaca for war in Troy, and then, instead of returning home to Ithaca, he is driven farther and farther astray by the powers of the sea. One storm drives him upon the Ciconians and another upon the land of the Lotus-Eaters. As in Léry's account, Odysseus' journey away from the world as he knows it is marked by storms; here the ocean serves as a way to designate a structural break between the familiar world of Greece and the strange new worlds to which he travels. His movement from Ithaca to the land of the Cyclopes can be described as one from home to war (Troy) and warlike peoples (Ciconians) and then, once he is tossed and turned around by the waves, into a unfamiliar primitive world of seductive flora and cannibalistic monsters.

Odysseus' encounter with the Cyclopes is marked in many ways as an especially significant moment in his travel and narrative. We will explore the nature of the Cyclopean episode in further detail in chapter 6. But for now, it is important to note the ways in which the Cyclopes and their land are described in terms that define the primitive aspects of nature in stark contrast to the laws and technology of the civilized world:

Ἔνθεν δὲ προτέρω πλέομεν ἀκαχήμενοι ἦτορ.
Κυκλώπων δ᾽ ἐς γαῖαν ὑπερφιάλων ἀθεμίστων
ἱκόμεθ᾽, οἵ ῥα θεοῖσι πεποιθότες ἀθανάτοισιν
οὔτε φυτεύουσιν χερσὶν φυτὸν οὔτ᾽ ἀρόωσιν,
ἀλλὰ τά γ᾽ ἄσπαρτα καὶ ἀνήροτα πάντα φύονται,
πυροὶ καὶ κριθαὶ ἠδ᾽ ἄμπελοι, αἵ τε φέρουσιν
οἶνον ἐρισράφυλον, καί σφιν Διὸς ὄμβρος ἀέξει.
τοῖσιν δ᾽ οὔτ᾽ ἀγοραὶ βουληφόροι οὔτε θέμιστες,
ἀλλ᾽ οἵ γ᾽ ὑψηλῶν ὀρέων ναίουσι κάρηνα
ἐν σπέσσι γλαφυροῖσι, θεμιστεύει δὲ ἕκαστος
παίδων ἠδ᾽ ἀλόχων, οὐδ᾽ ἀλλήλων ἀλέγουσι.

From there, although grieving at heart, we sailed on further and reached the land of the outrageous, lawless Cyclopes, who, having placed their trust in the immortal gods, neither plant anything with their hands nor plow, but everything grows without being sown or plowed; wheat and barley and grapes, which bear wine, the product of grapes, and the storm of Zeus causes them to grow. They have no marketplaces for taking counsel nor traditional customs, but they live in hollow caves on the peaks of lofty mountains, and each makes law for his children and wives, and they have no concern for one another. (*Od.* 9.105–15)

Circe and Odysseus. Ceramic black figure cup, ca. 560–550 B.C.E., Attica, Athens. Henry Lillie Pierce Fund, 99.158. Courtesy, Museum of Fine Arts, Boston. Reproduced with permission. © 2000 Museum of Fine Arts, Boston. All rights reserved.

The Cyclopes are lacking in all the characteristics of civilized life—no agriculture, no political meetings or institutions, no community laws or customs—and their landscape is correspondingly primitive and wild (9.116–41). They have no ships nor shipmakers, and so they do not engage in commercial or colonial contact with cities of men (9.125–30).[27] Polyphemus lives in a cave and pastures his flock, and when he meets Odysseus, he denies any concern with Zeus or the gods. And before long we learn that he breaks the cardinal rule of all human societies: he eats humans.[28] Much of this episode, in fact, focuses on the ways in which Polyphemus refuses to acknowledge the customs of *xenia* or of suppliant protection, thus setting him and his appetites even further outside the realms of civilized Greek experience. This indeed is a world of savage and primitive nature.

From the land of the Cyclopes, Odysseus continues his journey into the exotic worlds "over there," landing next on the island of Aeolus, king of the winds (10.1–79). From there, another storm (10.46–55) shipwrecks Odysseus and his men upon yet another community of cannibals, the Laestrygonians (10.80–132), in a reprise of the theme of primitive savagery raised first by the Cyclopes. Once escaped from the man-eating Laestrygonians, Odysseus arrives at the island of the magical Circe, and here we find a second meditation on the lure of the exotic and the call of the wild (10.135–574). Circe's magic drugs transform Odysseus' men into swine, representing in this all too graphic manner the fear that too much exposure to the primitive world may cause a Greek traveler to lose his humanity. To go native is thus equated with the most bestial of appetites and desires.

Upon leaving Circe, Odysseus and his men set out for the Underworld, the farthest stage in his journey from "here to there," and the point from which he can begin to make his way back home again. The world of the dead thus represents the ultimate expression of the other and the outer limits of Odysseus' travels. Once he gains the information necessary from Teiresias, he is able to begin to effect his return from the world "over there" back home. Our recognition of the Underworld as the point at which Odysseus' travels end and his return begins is confirmed by Odysseus' need to retrace his steps back to Aiaia and to Circe. He next encounters a series of female monsters—the Sirens, Scylla, Charybdis—who personify the risks of overseas travel. They threaten his seafaring progress as personifications of the dangers posed by the sea (deadening calms, jagged rocks, powerful whirlpools) just as they attempt to forestall his narrative momentum as well.[29] After escaping the maritime threat of Scylla and Charybdis, Odysseus and his remaining crew arrive at an island inhabited by the cattle of the Sun (12.260–402), and from there yet another storm (12.403–50) shipwrecks Odysseus alone upon the island of Calypso.

After a seven-year stay, Odysseus finally builds a raft and leaves Calypso. As we have seen, one final storm shipwrecks him on the island of the Phaeacians, where he is rescued by the young and marriageable Nausicaa, daughter to the king. The world of the Phaeacians could not be more different from that of the Cyclopes. In fact, the Phaeacians moved to get away from the overbearing Cyclopes (6.3–6). Theirs is a hypercivilized, utopian world. The description of the palace and grounds of Alcinous, we remember, evokes a Golden Age vision of endless prosperity rather than emphasizing a lack of cultivation and civilization as in the primitive Cyclopean landscape. Whereas the Cyclopes are unfamiliar with the arts of shipbuilding, the Phaeacians use their magical ships to provide Odysseus with an effortless escort back to Ithaca. The Phaeacians not only respect the gods but are accustomed to receiving them openly as well. Their generous reception of Odysseus reveals their committment to the rules of hospitality in all its manifestations, including many farewell gifts and a safe passage home. In stark contrast to his early storm-tossed voyages away from the Greek world, Odysseus' trip back from the world "over there" to that at home is easy and tempest-free.

This brief outline of Odysseus' journey highlights a basic framework that is quite similar to the geometrical structure of Léry's travel account, as outlined by de Certeau. Certainly, the broad shape of Odysseus' journey articulates a movement from "over here," his familiar world of Ithaca, to "over there," the wild and magical world of his travels, and back again. Furthermore, superimposed on this circular movement of travel and return is a similar tripartite structure that links home with two competing models of abroad.

Odysseus' encounter with Polyphemus sketches out the paradigm that describes the New World across the seas as a place of savage primitivism. This world is characterized by the absence of the traditional markers of civilization—

agriculture, laws, ships—and by the presence of cannibalism, the one practice that most separates humans from animals. In direct contrast to this vision of a savage, primitive New World is the one represented by the third point of the triangle, the land of the Phaeacians. In this episode, Odysseus' final encounter before reaching home, he is confronted with a quite different model for imagining the New World—an idealized, Golden Age utopia. The Phaeacians observe all the rules and customs of the civilized world—hospitality, gift exchange, song and dance—and they live in isolated bliss. These two New World visions, one of primitive savagery and the other of utopian civilization, represent the two most prevalent and persuasive modes of thinking about the relationship between home and abroad. Sandwiched in between are Odysseus' encounters with Circe and Calypso, both representing the erotic lure of travel overseas. Odysseus' initial travels away from the Greek world and those within the New World are marked by the challenges and difficulties of overseas travel—storms, shipwrecks, and sea monsters—and yet his return from Phaeacia to Ithaca is a peaceful one, returning as he does on the magical ship of the Phaeacians.

In other words, with an internal logic quite similar to that of Léry's account of his journey to Brazil, Odysseus' journey, far from being a random collection of adventures, reveals a coherent structure typical of later ethnographic writings. In moving from Ithaca to the land of the Cyclopes to that of the Phaeacians and back home again, Odysseus' travels both move from "over here" to "over there" and, at the same time, articulate a shift from "other" to "same." We might adapt de Certeau's diagram to represent the structure of the *Odyssey* as shown in the following diagram.

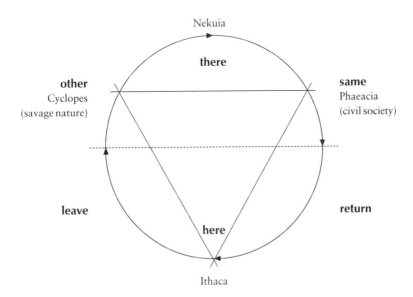

Structure of the *Odyssey* (after de Certeau).

The structure of Odysseus' travels thus brings the familiar nature/culture opposition to bear on the conceptions of worlds overseas.[30] Most important is the way in which the geometry of the journey connects home to the two competing views of the other and provides a blueprint for bringing the experience of the New World back home again.

Now, as I mentioned earlier, this analysis of the *Odyssey*'s structure is complicated by the discrepancies between the order in which Odysseus experiences his travels (as described above) and the order in which he (and Homer) tell the story of his travels over the course of the poem.[31] This complication is further exacerbated by the fact that Odysseus recounts most of his adventures in retrospect and at the court of the Phaeacians, not at home as we might expect. The implications of the time and place of Odysseus' narrative, however, serve to reinforce some of the themes and issues that emerged from our ethnographic analysis of his journey. In particular, the opposition between the Cyclopes and the Phaeacians as two alternative models for conceptualizing the New World is further emphasized through the narrative arrangement of the poem.[32] As Odysseus travels, his encounter with the Cyclopes is one of his first adventures, and his stay with the Phaeacians is his last, the two episodes separated by numerous other encounters both hostile and enticing: the Laestrygonians, Circe, the Underworld, Scylla and Charybdis, the Sirens, and Calypso. As Odysseus tells the story of his adventures at the court of Alcinous, however, he begins with his encounter with Polyphemus, thus juxtaposing his tale of cannibalism and savagery at the hands of the Cyclops with his experience of hospitality and civilization among the Phaeacians.[33]

Furthermore, the choice of Phaeacia as the site for the production of Odysseus' stories makes this magical island, and not Ithaca, the beginning and the end of his narrative journey and, even more significant, the source of his ethnographic vision. The land of the Phaeacians functions narratively as a point of transition from "over there" to "over here," from the New World to the Old. In bringing together Golden Age and New World sensibilities, Phaeacia serves as the gateway to the brave new world of the *Odyssey*'s ethnographic imagination. In reading two important texts from the Renaissance together with the *Odyssey*, we have been able to establish a framework for interpreting the important role that Phaeacia plays in the narrative production of Odysseus' travel tales and their larger significance for the poem overall. *The Tempest* helps us see the significance of Phaeacia as the site of the production of Odysseus' stories. The fertile combination of Golden Age and New World associations provides a productive setting for the poetic imagination. Like Prospero's island, this is the kind of place in which New World solutions to Old World problems can be imagined and tested. While *The Tempest* explains the choice of Phaeacia for the telling of Odysseus' stories, Léry's Brazilian account helps elucidate their ethnographic structure and value. Recognizing the ethnographic qualities of Odysseus' journey reveals the ways in which the *Odyssey*, like Léry's account and many others, addresses and accommodates issues arising from overseas travel and foreign encounter. In particular, the nature and structure of Odysseus' travels highlight the hermeneutic qualities of describing encounters with the "other" as a way to return to and renegotiate a new place for "self" in an ever-changing world. And finally, as we will see in the next two chapters, Odysseus' encounter with the Phaeacians occupies a pivotal position within two sets of oppositions that structure the important ethnographic themes of the *Odyssey*. Chapter 5 explores the ways in which the Phoenicians and the Phaeacians articulate the positive and negative aspects of overseas commerce. Chapter 6 then shows how the Phaeacians and the Cyclopes represent the lures and dangers of New World conquest and settlement.

# 5

# Phaeacians and Phoenicians: Overseas Trade

οὐ γὰρ Φαιήκεσσι μέλει βιὸς οὐδὲ φαρέτρη,
ἀλλ᾽ ἱστοὶ καὶ ἐρετμὰ νεῶν καὶ νῆες ἐῖσαι,
ἧσιν ἀγαλλόμενοι πολιὴν περόωσι θάλασσαν·

For the Phaeacians care nothing for the bow or the quiver, but rather for the masts and oars of ships and for the balanced ships in which they take pleasure as they traverse the hoary sea.

*Odyssey*, Book 6

Ἔνθα δὲ Φοίνικες ναυσικλύτοι ἤλυθον ἄνδρες,
τρῶκται, μυρί᾽ ἄγοντες ἀθύρματα νηὶ μελαίνῃ.

And then Phoenician men, famed for their ships, came, gnawers, bringing thousands of trinkets in their black ship.

*Odyssey*, Book 15

---

With the help of Athena's advice and directions, Odysseus approaches the city of the Phaeacians and the palace of Alcinous at the beginning of Book 7. The general tenor of this initial encounter sets the tone for Odysseus' entire stay among the Phaeacians. Theirs is a world of wonder:

θαύμαζεν δ᾽ Ὀδυσεὺς λιμένας καὶ νῆας ἐῖσας,
αὐτῶν θ᾽ ἡρώων ἀγορὰς καὶ τείχεα μακρὰ
ὑψηλά, σκολόπεσσιν ἀρηρότα, θαῦμα ἰδέσθαι.

And Odysseus marveled at the harbors and balanced ships, at the marketplaces of the heroes themselves and their walls, high and tall and fitted with palisades—a wonder to look at. (*Od.* 7.43–45)

We have already seen how the world of the Phaeacians, especially Alcinous' orchards and vineyard, belongs to a Golden Age tradition of unceasing agricultural productivity, and the emphasis on marvel and wonder here seems to underscore the ideal nature of this land.[1] At the same time, however, this initial description of Phaeacia sounds remarkably familiar—rather like an early Greek city with its harbors, marketplaces, and high walls. The conflicts that stem from this initial description—a source of wonder, yet quite familiar—are but part of the complex double nature of the Phaeacians.[2] Just like the wild and cultivated olive tree under which Odysseus sleeps upon his arrival on Scheria, the land and people of Phaeacia are a bundle of contradictions. The generous hospitality of Alcinous is countered by threats of hostility to strangers; the Phaeacians excel at shipmaking, but they do not like to travel; they live in Golden Age isolation, yet their city is fortified with walls. Instead of trying to smooth out these inconsistencies, as others have, I will suggest that the key to making sense of these and other conflicting aspects of the Phaeacians and their land lies in appreciating their liminal status, their role as the gateway to the ethnographic imagination of the world of the *Odyssey*.[3]

The liminal nature of Phaeacia—its role as a point of transition for Odysseus as he moves from the battlefields at Troy to the postwar world of Ithaca—has long been noted. Charles Segal has argued that Odysseus' stay among the Phaeacians provides him, as hero of the poem, with a restorative framework with which he can integrate the real with the unreal and the familiar with the strange, thus redefining the notion of what it means to be human.[4] Whereas Segal's approach focuses on the psychological aspects of Odysseus' character and development, what I will be doing in the next three chapters is exploring Odysseus' stay among the Phaeacians not in personal terms but in a broader ethnographic sense, as part of a process of cultural self-knowledge and change. Phaeacia serves as the pivot point for two important sets of oppositions that structure the ethnographic imagination of the *Odyssey*. First, a polarized opposition between the Phoenicians and the Phaeacians, both experts in ships and sailing, helps further articulate the problematic notion of overseas trade that I have already discussed in some detail in chapter 2. The Phoenicians embody the worst fears of what trade may bring to a people such as the archaic Greeks, while the Phaeacians represent an isolationist fantasy world in which theft and deception are replaced by magic ships and bountiful goods. Second—and this will be the subject of the next chapter—the Phaeacians, together with their overbearing relatives the Cyclopes, help imagine the world of overseas conquest and settlement. The Phaeacians offer the model of hospitality and the Cyclopes that of cannibalism as two ways that archaic Greeks experience new peoples in the New World. It is this complex role of the Phaeacians, who face discursively, as it were, in two different directions, that helps account for some of the discrepancies and inconsistencies in Books 6–8, and our ethnographic reading of the world of Phaeacia should help explain rather than erase them. At the same time, as we will see in chapter 7, these Janus-like Phaeacians, associated both with trade and with overseas settlement, are a kind of mirror double for the historical Euboeans in the audience, those Greeks who were at the forefront of overseas commerce and colonization in the early archaic period. In other words, the Phaeacians are "good to think with" on several levels, both for the original Greek audience and for ourselves.

## Alcinous' Palace and the Age of Metals

Alcinous' glorious palace is a good place to begin our discussion of the Phaeacian/Phoenician dynamic at work in the *Odyssey*. As I have already noted, important aspects of the Phaeacian world, especially the orchard and vineyards of Alcinous, belong to a tradition of the Golden Age landscape. The trees continuously produce fruit without need of work or agriculture; the people live without toil in easy contact with the gods. But now, as we will see from the detailed account that follows, Alcinous' actual palace belongs to a literal Golden Age as well—an age, that is, in which the precious metals gold, silver, and bronze circulate widely throughout the Mediterranean.

The wealth and splendor of Alcinous' palace nearly blind Odysseus with their brilliance:

χάλκεοι μὲν γὰρ τοῖχοι ἐληλέατ᾽ ἔνθα καὶ ἔνθα,
ἐς μυχὸν ἐξ οὐδοῦ, περὶ δὲ θριγκὸς κυάνοιο·
χρύσειαι δὲ θύραι πυκινὸν δόμον ἐντὸς ἔεργον·
ἀργύρεοι σταθμοὶ δ᾽ ἐν χαλκέῳ ἕστασαν οὐδῷ,
ἀργύρεον δ᾽ ἐφ᾽ ὑπερθύριον, χρυσέη δὲ κορώνη.
χρύσειοι δ᾽ ἑκάτερθε καὶ ἀργύρειοι κύνες ἦσαν,
οὓς Ἥφαιστος τεῦξεν ἰδυίῃσι πραπίδεσσι
δῶμα φυλασσέμεναι μεγαλήτορος Ἀλκινόοιο,
ἀθανάτους ὄντας καὶ ἀγήρως ἤματα πάντα.
ἐν δὲ θρόνοι περὶ τοῖχον ἐρηρέδατ᾽ ἔνθα καὶ ἔνθα,
ἐς μυχὸν ἐξ οὐδοῖο διαμπερές, ἔνθ᾽ ἐνὶ πέπλοι
λεπτοὶ ἐύννητοι βεβλήατο, ἔργα γυναικῶν.
ἔνθα δὲ Φαιήκων ἡγήτορες ἑδριόωντο
πίνοντες καὶ ἔδοντες· ἐπηετανὸν γὰρ ἔχεσκον.
χρύσειοι δ᾽ ἄρα κοῦροι ἐυδμήτων ἐπὶ βωμῶν
ἕστασαν αἰθομένας δαΐδας μετὰ χερσὶν ἔχοντες,
φαίνοντες νύκτας κατὰ δώματα δαιτυμόνεσσι.

For on the one hand bronze walls were laid out here and there, to the center from the foundation, and all around was a frieze made of cobalt. And golden doors enclosed the house closely within, and silver doorposts stood in a bronze threshold with a silver lintel above and a gold door knocker. And on either side were golden and silver dogs, which Hephaestus had fashioned with his clever cunning, to guard the house of great-hearted Alcinous since they are immortal and unaging all their

days. And inside, chairs were placed here and there along the wall, continuously from the threshold into the center, and delicate, fine-spun
fabric was thrown upon them, the work of women. And there the
Phaeacian leaders sat, eating and drinking; for they held this forever.
And golden young boys stood upon well-made bases with burning
torches in their hands, shining light upon the diners day and night. (*Od.*
7.86–102)

Bronze walls with a cobalt frieze, golden doors with silver doorposts standing
on bronze thresholds, silver lintels and golden door knockers: the palace brings
gold, silver, and bronze together in a spectacular metallurgical marvel. The technical skill involved in building such a palace, emphasized by the description of
the magical guard dogs—the work of Hephaestus—as well as the golden lamp-
holding *kouroi*, is matched by the poet's own skill at working with metals. The
description begins with bronze and cobalt before proceeding to the more precious metals, gold and silver. Four lines in a row (88–91) begin with gold and
silver in a chiastic structure in which the more valuable gold encircles the secondary silver metal. Line 89 pairs silver and bronze, while lines 90 and 91 offer
yet another interlocking scheme of silver and gold. In the space of six lines, we
encounter bronze twice and silver and gold three times each.[5] The conspicuous
use of gold, silver, and bronze here in this dramatic description of Alcinous'
palace draws, in part, on the traditional symbolic associations of these precious
metals. As Hesiod's *Works and Days* shows us, gold, silver, and bronze each carries with it a whole set of qualities and attributes, and this symbolic, mythic value
of the different metals is at play in this passage as well.

In Hesiod, each metal—gold, silver, and bronze—characterizes and symbolizes one of a series of ages of mankind.[6] Gold, pure and immutable—the most
precious of metals—is the metal of the gods, and men of the Golden Age thus
enjoy a close relationship with them.[7] Men of the Golden Age are also kingly;
they are concerned with the proper exercise of justice.[8] Gold can be worked in
its natural state, and this feature may help explain the absence of work (metal-
lurgic or agricultural) that comes to define the Age of Gold.[9] Although silver has
no independent set of associations, it is always invoked in the company of gold.[10]
It, too, is a precious metal but inferior in value to gold, and so while men of the
Golden Age are associated with divine rule, men of the Silver Age exhibit hybris
instead and fail to care properly for the gods.[11] Hesiod's bronze and iron ages
are no less symbolic than gold and silver, although they are more connected to
their own spheres of use. The bellicose men of the Bronze Age embody that
metal's association with brute force and the terrors of war, while the never-ending toil and suffering of the Iron Age is linked to its tools of agriculture.[12]

Hesiod thus invokes the metals (gold, silver, bronze, and iron) metaphorically to characterize the different ages of mankind. M. L. West has gathered several possible Near Eastern traditions that may have influenced Hesiod's version

of the myth of the ages.[13] An Iranian tradition has Ahura Mazdah reveal the future to Zoroaster, in which he sees a tree with four branches, one of gold, one of silver, one of steel, and one made of an iron alloy. The god explains that these branches represent the four successive ages predicted for Zoroastrianism.[14] A second tradition is attested in the second-century C.E. Book of Daniel. Here Nebuchadnezzar dreams of a large statue with a head of gold, silver breast and arms, belly and thighs made of brass, legs of iron, and feet of iron mixed with clay. Daniel interprets this dream to signify that the various parts of the statue designate five successive world kingdoms, starting with gold.[15] Obviously, what connects these mythic traditions with the one presented by Hesiod in the *Works and Days* is the articulation of a view of human time that is divided into successive ages, which in turn are designated by a series of different metals. What is more interesting, however, for our reading of the description of Alcinous' palace with its bronze walls, gold doors, and silver door handles, is the way in which these Near Eastern traditions bring the entire spectrum of metallic symbolism into one self-contained image—a tree or a statue.

It is tempting to read the metallic richness and variety of Alcinous' palace in light of this Near Eastern tradition, broadening the notion of the single Golden Age represented by his gardens to embrace the rich symbolic potential of the myth of a series of ages. Like the statue from the Book of Daniel, the gold, silver, and bronze of Alcinous' palace would then represent successive ages of man, each with its own set of associations, all crafted into one coherent image. But there is more going on here. The metallic hyperbole of Alcinous' palace literalizes with a kind of chaotic abandon the symbolic force of the precious metals that appear seriatim in Hesiod's myth of the ages of gold, silver, and bronze. This is not just a wealth of metaphoric imagery; these metals have real value as well.

Indeed, the account of Alcinous' palace—both its marvelous construction and its dazzling effect on visitors—reminds us of another palace in the *Odyssey*, this one in the "real" world of Sparta. When Telemachus goes to Sparta to ask Menelaus if he has any news of his father, he and Nestor's son, Peisistratus, are amazed by the splendor of the palace:

αὐτοὺς δ' εἰσῆγον θεῖον δόμον· οἱ δὲ ἰδόντες
θαύμαζον κατὰ δῶμα διοτρεφέος βασιλῆος.
ὥς τε γὰρ ἠελίου αἴγλη πέλεν ἠὲ σελήνης
δῶμα καθ' ὑψερεφὲς Μενελάου κυδαλίμοιο.

And they led them into the divine house. And they looked and marveled at the house of the god-nourished king. For just as that of the sun or the moon was the brilliance throughout the high-roofed house of glorious Menelaus. (*Od.* 4.43–46)

Telemachus and Peisistratus are dazzled by the palace's brilliance just as Odysseus is when he encounters Alcinous' palace, and the same simile is used in both episodes.[16] Here, Telemachus finds the sight so incredible that his only possible frame of reference is divine: Zeus' palace (that is, nothing from the real world) must look like this:

Φράζεο, Νεστορίδη, τῷ ἐμῷ κεχαρισμένε θυμῷ,
χαλκοῦ τε στεροπὴν κατὰ δώματα ἠχήεντα,
χρυσοῦ τ᾽ ἠλέκτρου τε καὶ ἀργύρου ἠδ᾽ ἐλέφαντος.
Ζηνός που τοιήδε γ᾽ Ὀλυμπίου ἔνδοθεν αὐλή,
ὅσσα τάδ᾽ ἄσπετα πολλά· σέβας μ᾽ ἔχει εἰσορόωντα."

Look, son of Nestor, who delight my heart, at the gleam of bronze and gold and electrum and silver and ivory throughout the echoing house. The inner courtyard of Olympian Zeus must be like this, with as much abundance of things. Wonder holds me as I look upon it. (*Od.* 4.71–75)

Although Menelaus' palace may look to Telemachus like nothing from the real world, it does look quite a bit like the magical palace of Alcinous, for it, too, is made of bronze, gold, silver, ivory, all combined into one marvelous and brilliant construction—a wonder to look at (θαῦμα ἰδέσθαι, 7.45; σέβας μ᾽ ἔχει εἰσορόωντα, 4.75).[17]

But while Telemachus compares Menelaus' palace to that of Zeus, Menelaus explains that his wealth comes not from the gods but rather, as we saw in chapter 2, from his extended travels overseas.[18] Menelaus tells Telemachus that in returning from Troy, he suffered at sea and wandered for eight years, during which time he visited many sites famous for trade (Cyprus, Phoenicia, Egypt, Libya). It is as a result of this traveling and these overseas encounters that he has acquired more goods (κτήμασιν, 4.81) than any other mortal (except Odysseus)—possessions that he brought home in his ships (ἠγαγόμην ἐν νηυσὶ, 4.82).[19]

Menelaus says explicitly that he got his wealth from his travels abroad—travels that include the most prominent trading centers of the Near East and North Africa.[20] If Menelaus' wealth comes from the trading centers of the Near East, and if his marvelous palace foreshadows that of Alcinous, what does this suggest about Alcinous' palace? Are we not meant to recognize, prompted by Telemachus' encounter at Sparta, the Near Eastern origins of Alcinous' wealth as well? In other words, the image of a fantastic, idealized Phaeacia draws on the real historical experience of Greeks visiting, living, and trading in the Near East as well as on mythical Golden Age traditions of prosperity.

It is worth noting that some scholars have seen allusions to the Near East or Egypt in either the topography of the city or the extravagant architecture of Alcinous' palace. In their commentary to the poem, for example, W. W. Merry and J. Riddell find a similarity between the topography of Phaeacia as described in the beginning of Book 6 and that of the Phoenician city of Tyre.[21] H. L. Lorimer suggested an Egyptian origin for some features of Alcinous' palace such as the metal-plated walls, doors, and doorways; the dogs of Hephaestus, accordingly, may have their origin in the sphinxes and rams laid out at Thebes at the Temple of Amenophis III.[22] T. B. L. Webster remarked that the dogs in front of Alcinous' palace echo the lions in front of the Hittite king's palace at Boghazkeuy.[23] More recently, Christopher Faraone has also argued for a Near Eastern origin for Alcinous' magic watchdogs.[24]

Identifying the land of the Phaeacians has, of course, long been a source of fascination for scholars ancient and modern. As early as the fifth century B.C.E., Thucydides linked Phaeacia with the Corinthian colony of Corcyra, emphasizing the expertise with ships enjoyed by both peoples, and many later writers, both ancient and modern, have followed this line of thinking.[25] Others, as we have seen, look to the east for models, and still others reject any historical identification and locate the people and their land in the world of pure fantasy.[26] In calling attention to the Near Easternness of Phaeacia, I do not mean to return to a purely historical reading of the poem; in other words, I do not mean to suggest that Phaeacia really was Phoenicia. Rather, I want to argue for recognizing Phaeacia as a historically informed imaginary site in which our reading of the metallic exuberance of Alcinous' palace is enriched by allusions to a contemporary metals trade between Greece and the Near East.[27] But before considering further what such an understanding of Phaeacia contributes to our reading of the poem, in particular to the dynamic tension between Phaeacia and Phoenicia, we should pause to consider what archeological evidence can tell us about the nature and extent of Greek interaction with Phoenicia and other eastern cities in the archaic period.[28]

## Greeks and the Near East

In the wake of the destruction and disruption attributed to the period around 1200 B.C.E., the beginning of the first millennium marked a time of fruitful contact and interaction between the Aegean and the Levant.[29] Sarah Morris has characterized the history of the intercourse between east and west in the ancient Mediterranean as one of the exchange of natural resources, especially the metals trade, and she emphasizes the continuity of Greek commercial contact with the east from the Bronze Age through the beginning of the Persian Wars.[30] Other scholars, however, argue for a break in Greek trade with the east in the second half of the eleventh century. Ian Morris notes that no Greek objects have been found in the Levant or Cyprus that can be securely dated from the period 1025–925 B.C.E., citing Near Eastern politics as the likely explanation for this decline. By 900 B.C.E., however, he observes that Greek pottery once again appears in the Levant, and there is evidence of Phoenician presence in the Aegean.[31]

Whatever the state of Greco-Phoenician contact in the previous century, by the end of the tenth century B.C.E., both Greeks, mainly Euboeans, and peoples from the Levant, mainly Phoenicians, were traveling and moving goods around the Mediterranean.[32] It seems likely that Phoenicians sailed to Greece in search of copper and iron, bringing luxury goods, especially finished metal goods, in exchange. A bronze foundry in operation near Lefkandi around 900 B.C.E. suggests trade between Euboea and Cyprus, with its abundant supply of copper. Furthermore, the unusual wealth found in this area—more gold was found at Lefkandi during this period than in all the rest of Greece—indicates commercial contacts with the Levant as well. By the mid-ninth century, more rich grave goods suggesting eastern contact are found in Lefkandi.[33] In Athens as well, graves contain fine worked gold jewelry, ivories, and glass. Operations at Thorikos at this time suggest that Athenians may have traded silver, not available in the eastern Mediterranean, for gold and other luxury items.[34] Crete's location and metal resources make it an obvious site for Aegean-Levantine commerce and contact, and this expectation is confirmed by archeological finds.[35]

Assyria's return to power toward the end of the tenth century together with its subsequent aggressive expansion into Syria and Phoenicia both intensified the search for metals in the Aegean—the demands of war and commerce increased the need for iron at this point—and stepped up Phoenicia's commerical and colonial expansion westward.[36] As a result, the eighth and seventh centuries show evidence of increased trade activities between Greece and the Levant—more Greek imports of eastern products and evidence of domestic imitation of eastern techniques, especially in metalworking.

In addition to conducting trade with Phoenicians in Greece, it seems likely that the Greeks, too, set sail to establish commercial contacts and outposts of their own in the Levant. Although the evidence is problematic at best, Greek traders, mostly from Euboea, probably traveled to northern Syria and participated in trading posts like those at Al Mina, Tarsos, and Tell Sukas.[37] From there trading routes opened up to north Syria and on to Mesopotamia. From the tenth to the eighth centuries, a significant corpus of early Greek pottery has been found at Tyre.[38] In the eighth century, Greek cities looked to the west as well, particularly for new sources of metals. Chalcis and Eretria collaborated to establish the trading colony of Pithecoussae on the island of Ischia in the first quarter of the eighth century, and the motivation for this early settlement appears to have been its access to ore—iron from Elba and copper from Etruria.[39]

The Phoenicians came to Cyprus, Crete, and central Greece in search of metals—first copper, then iron. In exchange, the Greeks received luxury items from the east—carved ivory and metalwork. Greeks sailed east as well, establishing trading posts and learning new skills. In addition, long-term contact and cooperation between these two cultures created strong cultural ties and connections. Not only did the Greeks import high-quality metal goods from Phoenicia, but also skilled craftsmen migrated to Greece, especially Crete; they established workshops and trained Greek craftsmen in their skills.[40] Greeks living in the Near East may have trained there as apprentices as well, returning to practice their new trades at home in Greece. While overseas trade, especially in metals, may have initiated the contact between east and west, eastern influence on Greek culture extended far beyond the realm of commerce. The archeological record, myth, and literary traditions combine to create a picture of extensive cultural exchange as well, especially in the areas of religion, letters, and skilled craftsmanship.

As this brief overview shows, a brisk metal trade brought the Greeks in contact with the Near East; moreover, it looks as though the exchanges between the Aegean and the Levant were much more far-reaching than trading gold for bronze. The picture that emerges coincides with that painted by Eumaeus and Odysseus in the second half of the *Odyssey*. Traders, craftsmen, and entrepreneurs from Greece, Phoenicia, and other cities in the Near East and northern Africa must have lived and worked together over extended periods of time in hybrid, bilingual communities across the Mediterranean, linked probably by intermarriage, in order to enable the kinds of exchange of knowledge and skill that took place.[41]

With this picture of contact, cooperation, and competition between Greeks and the Near East in the archaic period in mind, I want to return to Phaeacia, and in particular to Alcinous' palace, to try to read the richness of the episode more concretely. In other words, sources for a Near Eastern influence on the construction, both architectural and literary, of this fabulous palace are not just mythic—Mesopotamian tales of metallic ages—but also commercial. Since the metal trade, in particular, played a key role in establishing and structuring Greco–Near Eastern contact in this period, I propose that we rethink the significance of the hyperbole of metals in Alcinous' palace in this light, to complicate whatever metaphorical, symbolic allusions we find there with recent historical experience.

In his book *Epic and Empire*, David Quint argues for a similar interjection of the historic into a literary tradition in Tasso's Renaissance epic *Gerusalemme liberata*. His analysis can help us imagine how "the real Phoenicia" contributes to the construction of an imaginary Phaeacia. Quint argues not only that literary journeys such as that of Carlo and Ubaldo provided a prototype for Renaissance voyages of exploration and expansion, but also that the Age of Discovery offered real-life adventures that rivaled those of myth and story.[42] This literary-historical convergence becomes even clearer within what Quint calls "the symbolic geography" of the *Liberata*, where the garden paradise of Armida's Fortunate Islands is identified with the potential riches of Columbus's Canaries, a flourishing trading center by the sixteenth century.[43] Shakespeare, too, locates Prospero's fantastic island in *The Tempest* in a real world of overseas discovery that would have been familiar to its audience.[44] In much the same way, I propose, the mythical Golden Age fantasy of Phaeacia is firmly rooted in the contemporary historical experience of the poem's audience—especially trade with Phoenicia and other Near Eastern cities. Not only does this technique have the effect, as Quint points out, of elevating recent voyages of trade and discovery to an epic status, but also it provides a familiar, traditional (epic) framework in which to assimilate and accommodate these new worlds and ways of life.

In other words, Phaeacia belongs not just to a Golden Age (in the mythical sense) but also to an age of metals—gold, silver, bronze, and iron—in the recent historical sense of the archaic period.[45] It is in this light that I propose that we look at the role of the Phaeacians in the poem as part of a polarized opposition with the Phoenicians—as part of a rhetorical strategy that charaterizes these two peoples as antithetical constructions of the best and worst of overseas trade.

### "Phoenicians" in the Odyssey

Irene Winter has shown convincingly that the picture we get of the Phoenicians in the Odyssey is not a historically or ethnographically accurate one; instead, the image of the Phoenicians is a reductive, one-dimensional stereotype of a people who are greedy, duplicitous, and tricky traders. The Phoenicians, she argues, function in the poem as a historically grounded literary trope which can be understood only in light of the larger narrative strategies of the poem.[46] To this end, Winter identifies some interesting similarities between the characteristics associated with the Phoenicians and those attributed to the Phaeacians in the poem. In particular, both love ships. But whereas the Phoenicians are greedy and deceptive, the Phaeacians are just the opposite—generous and sociable (to Odysseus, at least)—and as a result, the Phoenicians operate as foils for the more idealized traits of the Phaeacians. Winter aligns the Greeks and Odysseus with the positive traits represented by the Phaeacians in opposition to the deceptive and greedy Phoenicians, and she links this representational strategy to issues arising from historical contact and competition between Greeks and Phoenicians in the period in which the poems became fixed—the middle of the eighth to the late seventh or early sixth century.[47] In addition to highlighting the potential commercial cooperation and competition that must have taken place as both Greeks and Phoenicians moved goods around the Mediterranean, she suggests that Phoenician cities, already more developed socially and commercially, might have provided models for Greek cities in the process of political, social, and economic developments.[48] Winter thus reads the role of the Phoenicians in Homer as double: they represent both the foreign element, against which the Greeks define themselves, and, at the same time, a projection of the social and economic present, what Winter calls "the becoming 'self.'"[49]

Winter is exactly right in highlighting both the constructed nature of the Phoenicians in the Odyssey and the way in which this image of the Phoenicians is rooted in contemporary issues arising from Greco-Phoenician contact and competition in the archaic period. I am quite sympathetic to her approach to the narrative strategies at work in the poem and her observations about the historical context in which the poem operates. A closer look at the text, however, in particular the ways in which the Phoenician/Phaeacian opposition is articulated, suggests a somewhat more complicated framework for thinking about the relationship between Greeks and Phoenicians at work in the poem with respect to issues of exchange. Instead of aligning the Greeks, represented by Odysseus, with the Phaeacians in opposition to the Phoenicians, as Winter does, we will find that the poem attempts to carve out a position for the Greeks somewhere between the idealized model of gift exchange represented by the Phaeacians and the negative image of trade as a kind of piracy projected by the Phoenicians.[50] Staking out these two extreme positions and identifying them with these two rhetorically constructed peoples thus helps clarify issues raised by commodity exchange and helps find a place for Greek trade somewhere in the middle.[51] So, taking Winter's observations as a point of departure, I return now to the *Odyssey* to look more closely at the relationship between the Phoenicians and the Phaeacians, particularly in light of the Near Eastern associations we have found in the account of Alcinous' palace and the complicated attitudes toward trade discussed in chapter 2. We need to see exactly how this opposition is articulated and how and where Odysseus and the Greeks fit into the picture.

## Phaeacians and Phoenicians: The Best and Worst of Trade

Phoenicia is implicated in the world of the Phaeacians from the moment of Odysseus' first encounter with it. After his raft has broken up in the storm, Odysseus encounters a sea goddess who takes pity on him. She is Leucothea, the daughter of Cadmus, the Phoenician king famous in myth for his founding of Thebes, and it is this Phoenician princess who first points Odysseus in the direction of the land of the Phaeacians.[52] Then, when Odysseus first greets Nausicaa, he compares the awe that holds him with a similar sensation he experienced when he saw a palm shoot (φοίνικος νέον ἔρνος) beside the altar of Delian Apollo, and the choice of wording here again brings the Phoenician element into the Phaeacian picture.[53] In other ways as well, the dynamic tension that contrasts the Phaeacians and the Phoenicians in the poem is countered by several areas in which the two peoples are similar. Both, for example, are associated with great wealth, especially finely worked metal objects. Menelaus gives Telemachus a beautiful gold and silver Phoenician bowl, the finest and most valuable item in his collection.[54] Similarly, among the gifts that Odysseus receives from the Phaeacians is much-worked (πολυδαίδαλος) gold.[55] In addition, both Phoenician and Phaeacian women are known for their fine weaving.[56] But certainly the most interesting and significant sphere of engagement for the Phoenicians and Phaeacians is that of ships and sailing. Both are famous for their ships (ναυσικλύτοι), an epithet that is used of both Phoenicians and Phaeacians and of no one else in the poem.[57]

With just one exception, the Phoenicians are mentioned in the *Odyssey* only in their role as traders, merchants, and overseas sailors.[58] In Odysseus' story to Athena in Book 13, Phoenician merchants from Sidon carried Odysseus from Crete to Ithaca.[59] A deceptive Phoenician man of commerce appears in Odysseus' story to Eumaeus in Book 14; he is a greedy man (τρώκτης); he travels looking for profit, plots lies (ψεύδεα βουλεύσας), and traffics in humans as well as other goods.[60] Eumaeus' tale in Book 15 tells of Phoenician traders who came to Syrie; they, too, are greedy (τρῶκται) and deceptive (πολυπαίπαλοι ἠπερόπευον), and they bring lots of trinkets in their ship to trade. Eumaeus says that they stayed for a year collecting their return cargo and then left with him aboard their swift ship.[61] Phoenicians thus appear in the *Odyssey* as overseas travelers and traders, and a range of epithets is used to describe their ships.[62] With the exception of the Phoenicians in Odysseus' story to Athena (and I will return to this a bit later), Phoenician traders are always presented as greedy, deceptive, and eager for profit.

The Phaeacians, too, are famed for their ships, and a closer look at the picture Homer paints of these mythical people reveals the extent to which ships and sailing are key to their identity, both personal and civic. When we first see the city of the Phaeacians through Odysseus' eyes, we can see that its very layout indicates their nautical orientation:

αὐτὰρ ἐπὴν πόλιος ἐπιβήομεν ἣν πέρι πύργος
ὑψηλός, καλὸς δὲ λιμὴν ἑκάτερθε πόληος,
λεπτὴ εἰσίθμη· νῆες δ᾽ ὁδὸν ἀμφιέλισσαι
εἰρύαται· πᾶσιν γὰρ ἐπίστιόν ἐστιν ἑκάστῳ.
ἔνθα δέ τέ σφ᾽ ἀγορὴ καλὸν Ποσιδήιον ἀμφίς,
ῥυτοῖσιν λάεσσι κατωρυχέεσσ᾽ ἀραρυῖα.
ἔνθα δὲ νηῶν ὅπλα μελαινάων ἀλέγουσι,
πείσματα καὶ σπεῖρα, καὶ ἀποξύνουσιν ἐρετμά.
οὐ γὰρ Φαιήκεσσι μέλει βιὸς οὐδὲ φαρέτρη,
ἀλλ᾽ ἱστοὶ καὶ ἐρετμὰ νεῶν καὶ νῆες ἐῖσαι,
ᾗσιν ἀγαλλόμενοι πολιὴν περόωσι θάλασσαν·

When we reach the city around which is a high wall, there is a beautiful harbor on either side of the city, a narrow isthmus. And easily handled ships are drawn up at the road, for there is a slip for each of them. And there is the marketplace, surrounding the precinct of Poseidon, fitted with quarried stones, sunk in the ground. And there they care for the tackle of their dark ships, the cables and the sails, and they smooth their oars. For the Phaeacians care nothing for the bow or the quiver, but rather for the masts and oars of ships and for the balanced ships in which they take pleasure as they traverse the hoary sea. (*Od.* 6.262–72)

At both the periphery (two beautiful harbors) and the center (the precinct of Poseidon), the city of the Phaeacians is organized to facilitate and celebrate their close relationship with the sea. Instead of allotments of land distributed equally to all citizens, in Phaeacia each ship has its own slip. The marketplace (ἀγορὴ) built around the precinct of Poseidon, is not the focus of political or commercial transactions, as one would expect in a historical Greek city, but rather the center of nautical activity. Here, at the city center, men take care of the tackle of their black ships, the cables and sails, and smooth their oars, suggesting that for the Phaeacians, the business of ships is at the heart of their political life, structuring their sense of civic identity.[63]

In addition, the Phaeacians' devotion to ships and sailing is written into their very names. In Book 8 we find a clever catalogue of Phaeacian names, each one articulating an aspect of nautical skill, terminology, or love of the sea:

> ... ἂν δ᾽ ἵσταντο νέοι πολλοί τε καὶ ἐσθλοί.
> ὦρτο μὲν Ἀκρόνεώς τε καὶ Ὠκύαλος καὶ Ἐλατρεὺς
> Ναυτεύς τε Πρυμνεύς τε καὶ Ἀγχίαλος καὶ Ἐρετμεὺς
> Ποντεύς τε Πρῳρεύς τε, Θόων Ἀναβησίνεώς τε
> Ἀμφίαλος, υἱὸς Πολυνήου Τεκτονίδαο·
> ἂν δὲ καὶ Εὐρύαλος, βροτολοιγῷ ἶσος Ἄρηι,
> Ναυβολίδης, ὃς ἄριστος ἔην εἶδος τε δέμάς τε
> πάντων Φαιήκων μετ᾽ ἀμύμονα Λαοδάμαντα.
> ἂν δ᾽ ἔσταν τρεῖς παῖδες ἀμύμονος Ἀλκινόοιο,
> Λαοδάμας θ᾽ Ἅλιός τε καὶ ἀντίθεος Κλυτόνηος·

... and many excellent young men stood up. Akroneos (Steep-ship) arose and Okyalos (Swift-ship), and Elatreus (Fir-oar), and Nauteus (Ship-y) and Prymneus (Stern-y) and Anchialos (Near-the-sea) and Eretmeus (Oar-y) and Ponteus (Sea-y) and Proreus (Prow-y), and Thoon (Swift), son of Anabesineus (Embarker), and Amphialos (Seagirt), son of Polyneus (Many-ships), the son of Tekton (Shipbuilder). And Euryalus (Broad-sea) stood up, son of Naubolos (Ship-launcher), equal to Ares who brings plague to men, and he is the best of all the Phaeacians in looks and size after the blameless Laodamas. And the three sons of blameless Alcinous stood up: Laodamas, and Halios (Sea-y), and god-like Klytoneos (Famed-for-ships). (Od. 8.110–19)[64]

To this list, of course, must be added the name of Alcinous' father, Nausithous (Swift-ship), city founder.[65] Not just a poetic tour de force, the catalogue embodies the extent to which, for Phaeacians, personal as well as civic identity is associated with the sea. The phrase "Seagirt, son of Many-ships, the son of Shipbuilder," to take just one example, identifies these three Phaeacians with ships and the sea in both genealogical and professional terms.

Finally, the ships of the Phaeacians are not just good, they are the best (ἄρισ-ται); they are endowed with an intelligence of their own:

οὐ γὰρ Φαιήκεσσι κυβερνητῆρες ἔασιν
οὐδέ τι πηδάλι᾽ ἐστί, τά τ᾽ ἄλλαι νῆες ἔχουσιν·
ἀλλ᾽ αὐταὶ ἴσασι νοήματα καὶ φρένας ἀνδρῶν,
καὶ πάντων ἴσασι πόλιας καὶ πίονας ἀγροὺς
ἀνθρώπων, καὶ λαῖτμα τάχισθ᾽ ἁλὸς ἐκπερόωσιν
ἠέρι καὶ νεφέλῃ κεκαλυμμέναι·

For the Phaeacians have no steersmen nor are there any rudders such as other ships have. But the ships themselves know the thoughts and minds of men, and they know all the cities and fertile fields of men, and they traverse the expanse of the sea as swiftly as possible, covered with mist and cloud. (*Od.* 8.557–62)

Like Odysseus, these ships know the minds and cities of men; they need no steering help; they travel swiftly covered with mist. For all their nautical names and civic structure, the activity of sailing and overseas travel among the Phaeacians is displaced from the men themselves onto their magic ships. There is an emphasis on the activity of working with ships—caring for their tackle, building them—but once the ships are at sea, the Phaeacians themselves disappear from view.

And so we begin to see that while seafaring and nautical interests are key to the Phaeacians' way of life, their association with ships and sailing has a very different set of connotations from that of the Phoenicians. With the Phaeacians, the emphasis is on their ships—their ability to travel quickly without trouble, to convey men easily across the sea. The Phaeacians do not actually use these ships to conduct commercial transactions overseas. Instead of being linked to a role as deceptive and greedy traders, as in the case of their rivals, the Phoenicians, the Phaeacians' love of ships is paired with their skill in the rather innocuous areas of running, dance, and song (ὅσσον περιγιγνόμεθ ἄλλων / ναυτιλίῃ καὶ ποσσὶ καὶ ὀρχηστυῖ καὶ ἀοιδῇ, 8.252–53).[66] In fact, as Euryalus' taunt at Odysseus shows, the Phaeacians are quite openly hostile to professional traders. Instead, they use their ships to convey men, and, as is clear from their treatment of Odysseus, they engage in a very generous and one-sided version of gift exchange.

To elaborate on Winter's initial observation, then, the text of the *Odyssey* presents two peoples, the Phoenicians and the Phaeacians, both famed for their ships (ναυσικλύτοι) and nautical skill, and then locates them at opposite ends of the exchange spectrum that I laid out in chapter 2. At one end of the spectrum is the model of ongoing reciprocity embodied in the system of gift exchange; at the other extreme, outright theft or piracy represents the complete absence of exchange in any sense. I noted that in between these two extreme positions—positions that correspond to Hesiod's bipolar statement "giving is good, taking bad"—is a muddy middle ground occupied by commodity exchange and trade, the key issues at stake being ways to establish value and accommodate profit.

My elaboration of the Phoenician/Phaeacian dynamic in this chapter serves to clarify this scheme further. Trade as practiced by the Phoenicians is motivated by greed and conducted by deception, and in this formulation it differs little from outright theft or piracy. When Euryalus accuses Odysseus of being a trader in Book 8, he invokes the Phoenician model of trader, one whose notion of profit is synonymous with greed and theft: κερδέων θ' ἁρπαλέων (8.164). Similarly, Alcinous in Book 11 applies the language of Phoenician trade to the assessment of Odysseus' tale: in telling his story, Odysseus is not like those who cheat (ἠπερο-πῆα), steal (ἐπίκλοπον), and tell lies (ψεύδεά τ' ἀρτύνοντας).[67] Although they never mention the Phoenicians themselves, from their position at the other end of the spectrum, Euryalus and Alcinous help consolidate the negative view of trade that comes to be associated primarily with the Phoenicians in the second half of the poem. The role of the Phoenicians in this system, then, is to elaborate the worst case scenario, the horrors and dangers of trade. They represent what the Greeks most fear about engaging in trade. We recognize in this negative model of trade as deception and theft associated with a foreign people from the east an early example of what Edward Said has termed "Orientalism."[68] The reductive stereotype of the eastern "other" as greedy and manipulative, especially with respect to commerce, serves primarily to articulate the more positive, generous behavior of the Greeks.[69]

At the other end of the spectrum, then, the poem associates an idealized notion of exchange with the Phaeacians, a Golden Age fantasy people who consort with the gods, not men. Their life is very much defined by their magic ships, but they use them only to convey other people and their goods; they do not travel themselves, nor do they convey goods overseas for profit. All the pieces are present—ships, goods, travel—but they do not add up to trade. In fact, we are told that when Nausithous moved the Phaeacians away from their relatives, the Cyclopes, he removed them from the world of profit and trade. He settled them in Scheria "far from profit-hungry men" (ἑκὰς ἀνδρῶν ἀλφηστάων, Od. 6.8). My translation of the adjective used here as "profit-hungry" rather than the more customary "grain-eating" requires a brief digression. In her commentary on the poem, Stephanie West argues that the compound adjective used here—ἀλφησ-τής—is modeled on the form ὠμηστής, "eating raw flesh," with its first element understood as ἄλφι, "grain," and meaning something like "eater of grain." But she also points out that in antiquity, some seem to have associated the first element of the compound instead with ἀλφαίνω, "to bring or yield," to produce a compound meaning "profit-hungry or enterprising."[70] In light of the role that the Phaeacians, together with the Phoenicians, play in sketching out a place for profit within a broad spectrum of exchange possibilities, the latter translation is an attractive one at this point in the poem. In occupying the extreme position of altruistic gift exchange, the Phaeacians live "far from profit-hungry men" and their world of commodity trade. And yet the primacy of this particular meaning here does not rule out the possibility of the simultaneous presence of the "grain-eating" translation in describing the double world of the Phaeacians. The Phaeacians are a two-dimensional people in the *Odyssey*, and, as we will see in the next chapter when we look at the Phaeacians' role in conjuction with the cannibal Cyclopes, there the "grain-eating" definition takes on more resonance. But for now, I want to emphasize that in many respects the Phaeacians live far from the world of profit and gain. Instead, they conduct a kind of one-sided gift exchange with their guests: they give gifts without traveling to receive them in return. To engage in exchange with the Phaeacians, then, is always to come out ahead.

### Odysseus and Athena: Masters of Profit

If the orientalized Phoenicians represent the negative version of trade (theft, deception) and the fantasy Phaeacians embody the other extreme (idealized commodity exchange which is all profit), where are the Greeks in this picture? As always, Odysseus is the key. On the one hand, the character of Odysseus shares significant qualities with the Phoenicians. As Athena says in Book 13, he excels all men in profit (κέρδος), and she exhorts him to leave off his deceptive, thievish songs (ἀπατάων / μύθων τε κλοπίων, 13.294–95).[71] One might debate whether it was greed that led him to visit the Cyclops, but certainly it was his ability to devise tricks and deceptions that allowed him to escape.[72] In other words, like a Phoenician trader, Odysseus travels by sea, practices deception, and brings home a great deal of valuable goods. At the same time, however, Odysseus has much in common with the fictional Phaeacians. Like them, he clearly knows the rules of hospitality. Figures such as Mentes visit his kingdom at Ithaca expecting to be treated well and given gifts, and even before he reveals his heroic identity, he is warmly welcomed within the aristocratic, gift-exchanging world of the Phaeacians.

Thus Odysseus, by virtue of his ambiguous status, sharing qualities with both the Phoenicians and the Phaeacians, straddles these two extremes and helps articulate a middle position with respect to trade. In chapter 2 we looked at the way in which Odysseus brings the model of commodity exchange to bear on a poetic transaction when he negotiates a large number of gifts from Alcinous in exchange for more songs about his adventures in Hades. Alcinous prefers to locate song within a framework of hospitality and gift exchange. In Phaeacia, poetry is integrated into the city's social sphere, exemplified by Demodocus, who sings songs for the people and is welcomed by them. Odysseus, however, represents a different model of poet, one who travels from city to city and offers his song as part of a one-time transaction in exchange for goods. In particular,

Odysseus is eager to make a big profit for himself. He offers to stay and sing songs for a year if necessary so long as the Phaeacians give him glorious gifts (ἀγλαὰ δῶρα, 11.357), since it would be much more profitable (κεν πολὺ κέρδιον εἴη, 11.358) to return home with a more generous hand (πλειοτέρῃ σὺν χειρὶ, 11.359).[73] By virtue of putting his songs on the open market, Odysseus introduces the notion of profit into the world of poetry, suggesting that similar issues of value and exchange operate in both spheres.

Now, however, we can see that there is more going on here than a revolution in the modes of poetic production and consumption. In negotiating his transaction with Alcinous, Odysseus reconceptualizes the practice of gift exchange à la the Phaeacians, with all its emphasis on reciprocity and the maintenance of personal relationships, in terms that look a little more Phoenician—that is, terms that produce profit (not theft) for himself. For Odysseus may arrive at Phaeacia as a poet on a raft, but he leaves, as Polyphemus predicted, on the boat of another and with a great deal of goods. In this respect, Odysseus adopts the role of a merchant who has no ship of his own, but who sails from city to city in the ship of another, trading goods and valuables.[74] As James Redfield has observed, "Odysseus' voyage is not a trading voyage, but it works like one."[75] When Euryalus taunts him in Book 8 for looking more like a profit-hungry merchant than an aristocratic athlete, he highlights one of the chief sources of anxiety about trade: the pursuit of profit. In ridiculing merchants, Euryalus assimilates legitimate gain to the theft and greed of pirates. Odysseus, by contrast, offers a way to incorporate the profits of trade into the aristocratic system of gift exchange. In this respect, he helps imagine (or helps the Greeks imagine for themselves) an intermediary position that describes trade as a comfortable mode of exchange that lies somewhere between theft and gift, and the Phoenician/Phaeacian dialectic helps set the terms for this reconfiguration. These two peoples represent the two ends of the spectrum; in between them lies the way of Odysseus and the Greeks. I do not mean to suggest that the poem offers a clear answer to the question, How can archaic Greeks accommodate trade? Rather, it sets out an interpretive framework for thinking about how to answer that question. The ambiguity and mobility of Odysseus, an aristocratic hero concerned with profit who travels the seas, reflect the complexity and range of these issues.

Another scene that reveals the extent to which the issues presented by overseas trade are elaborated and problematized, not solved, through the Phoenician/Phaeacian scheme is the one in which Athena appears to Telemachus in the guise of Mentes, the aristocratic metal trader:

Μέντης, Ἀγχιάλοιο δαΐφρονος εὔχομαι εἶναι
υἱός, ἀτὰρ Ταφίοισι φιληρέτμοισιν ἀνάσσω.
νῦν δ' ὧδε ξὺν νηὶ κατήλυθον ἠδ' ἑτάροισι
πλέων ἐπὶ οἴνοπα πόντον ἐπ' ἀλλοθρόους ἀνθρώπους,
ἐς Τεμέσην μετὰ χαλκόν, ἄγω αἴθωνα σίδηρον.

I boast of being Mentes, son of the wise Anchialos, and I rule the Taphians who love oars. But now I have come with my ship and companions having sailed across the wine-dark sea to foreign peoples. I am going to Temesa after bronze; I bring gleaming iron. (*Od.* 1.180–84)

Mentes sails from his home among the Taphians across the sea to Temesa, bringing iron to trade for bronze; we need not take this passage literally as real historical evidence for the metals trade to appreciate its role in articulating the *Odyssey*'s problematic world of trade.[76]

In chapter 2 I suggested that Mentes here presents a view of trade that is attracted into the world of gift exchange. There is no mention here of profit; instead the bilateral nature of the exchange is emphasized: he trades iron for bronze. We might now say that Mentes' version of trade is compatible, though not identical, with the idealized notion represented by the Phaeacians in the poem. In particular, neither emphasizes the potential for profit or gain that trade offers. But when we look more closely at this passage, especially in light of the Phaeacian/Phoenician dialectic, there is a slightly jarring detail. Mentes identifies himself as king of the oar-loving Taphians, and the Taphians appear conspicuously in the *Odyssey* as pirates (ληΐστορες)—the kinds of men who travel the seas randomly, putting their lives at risk and bringing trouble to mankind.[77] These are the pirates who kidnap Eumaeus' nursemaid and sell her for a profit (15.425–29).[78] How can we reconcile Mentes' idealized notion of trade with his status as king of the pirates? To further complicate the picture, the adjective "oar-loving" (φιληρέτμοισιν), used here to describe the Taphians, is also used of the Phaeacians, and of no one else in the poem.[79]

Again, what we find here is another expression of the trade problematic that structures the Phoenician/Phaeacian opposition. In this passage Athena's disguise encapsulates the two extreme positions on the exchange spectrum, and this is just what we would expect of the goddess with whom Odyseus shares his cleverness and love of profit. As Athena herself boasts when chiding Odysseus for telling her a lie at the beginning of Book 13, she, too, is skilled in these areas:

ἀλλ᾿ ἄγε, μηκέτι ταῦτα λεγώμεθα, εἰδότες ἄμφω
κέρδ᾿, ἐπεὶ σὺ μέν ἐσσι βροτῶν ὄχ᾿ ἄριστος ἁπάντων
βουλῇ καὶ μύθοισιν, ἐγὼ δ᾿ ἐν πᾶσι θεοῖσι
μήτι τε κλέομαι καὶ κέρδεσιν· . . .

But come, let us no longer speak of these things, for we both know profits, since you are the best of all mortals in planning and speaking, and I excel all the gods in cleverness and profit . . . (*Od.* 13.296–99)

The divine figure of Athena, skilled in cleverness (μήτι) and profit (κέρδεσιν), embodies the range of possibilities raised by the institution of trade—both the potential for profit and the risk of deception—and her identification with Odysseus in the poem reinforces his role in negotiating a middle ground between these two extremes. Winter makes the intriguing suggestion that the Taphians in the *Odyssey* are modeled on the Cypriot Phoenicians and that the place-name may in fact be an invented name drawing on a combination of Tamassos and Paphos.[80] Following this logic, the Taphians, an invented people, function together with the constructed Phoenicians to represent the piratic model of trade, and both peoples are connected to their opposites, the Phaeacians, by shared epithets: they are famed for their ships (ναυσικλύτοι) and lovers of the oar (φιλήρετμοι). This one brief passage, then, uses Odysseus' divine counterpart, Athena, to bring together in a kind of microcosm exactly the same issues that are at work in the larger Phaeacian/Phoenician dynamic.

In conclusion, let us turn to the moment when Odysseus finally arrives on the shores of his native Ithaca.[81] In the story that Odysseus tells to Athena about who he is and how he got there, he explains that in Crete he killed a man who tried to take the booty he had earned at Troy. As a result, he went to sea and begged the Phoenicians to carry him and his booty to Pylos or Elis. They agreed to take him but were knocked off course by a storm, and the Phoenicians left Odysseus and his possessions behind while they sailed off to Sidon. In telling his story, Odysseus goes out of his way to explain to Athena that these traders did not wish to deceive him by leaving him at Ithaca instead of Elis or Pylos, but that a storm drove them off course.

What is puzzling about Odysseus' story is the atypical behavior of the Phoenicians. Instead of being greedy (τρῶκται), they are noble (ἀγαυοί, 13.272)[82]; instead of being deceptive (ἠπεροπεῖς), Odysseus explains, they did not intend to deceive him (οὐδ' ἤθελον ἐξαπατῆσαι, 13.277). Perhaps the way to think about this anomaly is to recognize that these atypical, trustworthy traders are not really Phoenicians at all, but instead they have taken on the attributes of the Phaeacians. Odysseus' arrival back in Ithaca marks the poem's transition from the fantasy world of the Phaeacians to the real world of the Phoenicians, and for a brief moment the poem threatens to collapse the opposition and presents the Phoenicians in terms of their opposite, the idealized, isolationist Phaeacians. And like the Phaeacians, who are famous for transporting men safely, these Phoenicians convey Odysseus and all his loot home without harm.[83] For just a brief moment, then, right before Poseidon puts an end to the idealized world of the Phaeacians and their ships and right before we encounter the negative world of Phoenician trade, we find the two categories momentarily converging— Phaeacians and Phoenicians, both proud transporters of Odysseus and his goods.

The fantasy Phaeacians thus work together with the demonized Phoenicians to articulate the range of possible modes of exchange available in the world of the *Odyssey*. Both peoples function as literary tropes, in Winter's terms—reductive, schematic characterizations of peoples who represent either the dangers or the ideals of trade—and the mobile figure of Odysseus charts a middle course between them, opening up a new world of trade and commerce for the Greek audience. The dynamic tension between the Phaeacians and the Phoenicians at work in the poem is further grounded in the Phoenician elements present in the world of the Phaeacians, especially in Alcinous' palace. His palace is described as a metallurgical wonder ringed by golden walls with silver doorposts standing over bronze thresholds—a description that combines the traditional mythic associations of precious metals best represented in Hesiod's myth of the ages with all the potential wealth of the newly established metal trade. The possibilities of the New World imagination converge here with the familiarity of traditional mythic values and eventually recast symbolic wealth in real terms. No longer are precious metals such as gold and silver the exclusive and defining property of aristocrats, circulated through the closed system of gift exchange. The less restrictive possibilities of trade, especially in metals, open up new worlds of wealth and riches. Thus Alcinous' palace roots the mythical world of the Phaeacians very much in the historical world of the metals trade between the Greeks and the Near East.

And so the Phoenician trope also helps us identify the key elements in the equally carefully constructed picture of the Phaeacians, but not the whole picture. One of the first things we learn about this mythical, magical people is that they are related to the overbearing, man-eating Cyclopes. In the next chapter, we will explore the ways in which the duality of the Phaeacians brings them in contact and contrast with the Cyclopes as well.

# 6

# Phaeacians and Cyclopes: Overseas Settlement

> Peeping through the motif of the Phaeacians' hospitality is the
> image of a Phaeacia comparable to the land of the Cyclopes.
>
> Pierre Vidal-Naquet, "Land and Sacrifice in the *Odyssey*"

---

The world of Phaeacia, with Alcinous' spectacular palace and its wondrous garden, occupies a space in the Greek ethnographic imagination somewhere between the potential wealth of the Near East and the utopian promise of the Golden Age. This is an ideal world, or rather an idealized version of the real world of overseas commerce in metals that implicates the Greeks and Phoenicians in a network of travel and trade. The previous chapter explored the ways in which the world of the Phaeacians works together with that of the Phoenicians to articulate both the positive and negative aspects of overseas commerce in the *Odyssey*. Taken on its own, however, this Phaeacian/Phoenician dichotomy fails to account for some other, still puzzling aspects of the Phaeacians. Although Phaeacia seems to evoke Greek imaginings about Near Eastern cities and palaces, there are other ways in which the layout and founding of the city recall a Greek colonial settlement. In addition, as we have already noticed, in spite of the Phaeacians' famed hospitality—and their treatment of Odysseus is extremely generous—there is an undercurrent of hostility to strangers that runs through Books 6–8. What helps explain these basic inconsistencies in the Phaeacian profile is the recognition that there is a second opposition at work here as well, this time contrasting the Phaeacians with their overbearing relatives, the Cyclopes. In this context, the Phaeacians, together with the Cyclopes, both descendants of Poseidon, represent different pictures of what an overseas settler might find when he lands ashore. Again, as with issues of trade in the *Odyssey*, the institution of hospitality, *xenia*, provides a familiar framework for articulating these extreme possibilities as well as for imagining a more moderate and realistic colonial landscape. In other words, Odysseus' encounter with the Phaeacians occupies a pivotal position within two sets of oppositions that structure the important ethnographic themes of the *Odyssey:* overseas trade and settlement. In this chapter we will look further at the ways in which the Phaeacian/Cyclopes opposition addresses issues of overseas exploration and settlement in the early archaic period.

### Phaeacians and Cyclopes

Odysseus encounters the Cyclopes at the beginning of his travels, and his stay with the Phaeacians marks his last stop before returning home, yet the careful arrangement of the poem sets his experiences with both these peoples side by side. The significant position of these two episodes in both Odysseus' travels and his narrative suggests that we think about them and all their differences together as well. As Segal has observed, the "fullest antithesis to the Phaeacians is the Cyclopes." Scholars have sketched out three general areas of contrast between the two peoples: maritime expertise, social structure, and hospitality.[1]

To begin with, whereas the Phaeacians are famous for their ships and maritime expertise, Polyphemus and the Cyclopes have no experience at all with ships or overseas travel:

> οὐ γὰρ Κυκλώπεσσι νέες πάρα μιλτοπάρῃοι
> οὐδ' ἄνδρες νηῶν ἔνι τέκτονες, οἵ κε κάμοιεν
> νῆας ἐϋσσέλμους, αἵ κεν τελέοιεν ἕκαστα
> ἄστε' ἐπ' ἀλλήλους νηυσὶν περόωσι θάλασσαν·
> οἵ κέ σφιν καὶ νῆσον ἐϋκτιμένην ἐκάμοντο.

> For the Cyclopes have no red-cheeked ships, nor men who are shipwrights, who could build well-benched ships which could accomplish trips to each city [as people do] who cross the sea in their ships; and they could have made the island a good settlement for them. (*Od.* 9.125–30)

The Cyclopes' lack of maritime experience is underscored by the fact that it is the technology of shipbuilding that overcomes Polyphemus.[2] Polyphemus' walking stick, a stick that is as big as the mast of a twenty-oared cargo ship, becomes the instrument of his blinding:

> Κύκλοπος γὰρ ἔκειτο μέγα ῥόπαλον παρὰ σηκῷ
> χλωρὸν ἐλαΐνεον· τὸ μὲν ἔκταμεν, ὄφρα φοροίη
> αὐανθέν· τὸ μὲν ἄμμες ἐΐσκομεν εἰσορόωντες
> ὅσσον θ' ἱστὸν νηὸς ἐεικοσόροιο μελαίνης,
> φορτίδος εὐρείης, ἥ τ' ἐκπεράᾳ μέγα λαῖτμα·
> τόσσον ἔην μῆκος, τόσσον πάχος εἰσοράασθαι.

There lay beside the Cyclops' pen a huge stick of green olive wood; he had cut it so that when it dried out, he could carry it. And looking at it, we likened it in size to the mast of a twenty-oared dark ship, a broad cargo carrier which crosses the broad expanse of the sea—it was so long and so thick to look at. (*Od.* 9.319–24)[3]

Not only does the simile emphasize the sheer size of his walking stick, but also it underscores the Cyclops' lack of familiarity with ships; his only use for such a large piece of timber is as a walking aid. Odysseus, however, knows differently, and he applies the techniques of shipbuilding that will serve him well on Calypso's island to drill the stick into Polyphemus' eye:

ἐγὼ δ' ἐφύπερθεν ἐρεισθεὶς
δίνεον, ὡς ὅτε τις τρυπῷ δόρυ νήιον ἀνὴρ
τρυπάνῳ, οἱ δέ τ' ἔνερθεν ὑποσσείουσιν ἱμάντι
ἁψάμενοι ἑκάτερθε, τὸ δὲ τρέχει ἐμμενὲς αἰεί·
ὡς τοῦ ἐν ὀφθαλμῷ πυριήκεα μοχλὸν ἑλόντες
δινέομεν, τὸν δ' αἷμα περίρεε θερμὸν ἐόντα.

And I, leaning from above, twisted it, just as a man drills a ship's mast with his drill, and [his men] hold on either side and keep it whirling with a strap from beneath, and it turns continuously. Just so, we took the fiery stick and twirled it in his eye, and warm blood rushed out. (*Od.* 9.383–88)

Demonstrating his shipbuilding skills, Odysseus pierces Polyphemus' eye with the sharp augur-like stick. The narrative thus presents maritime expertise as the appropriate and successful response to the threats posed by the Cyclops.[4] Whereas the Phaeacians center their political and private lives on the care and maintenance of their ships, the Cyclopes are completely ignorant of both the potential and the dangers of seafaring.

In addition, both the Cyclopes and the Phaeacians enjoy a rich and productive landscape, but this topographical similarity only serves to heighten the differences between them.[5] While the Golden Age fecundity of the land of the Phaeacians, with its elaborate rows of vineyards and fruit trees, highlights their agricultural skill and the civilized aspect of their social structure, the absence of cultivation necessary for the Cyclopes' land to flourish characterizes it instead as a primitive landscape:

Κυκλώπων δ' ἐς γαῖαν ὑπερφιάλων ἀθεμίστων
ἱκόμεθ' οἵ ρα θεοῖσι πεποιθότες ἀθανάτοισιν
οὔτε φυτεύσουσιν χερσὶν φυτὸν οὔτ' ἀρόωσιν,
ἀλλὰ τά γ' ἄσπαρτα καὶ ἀνήροτα πάντα φύονται,
πυροὶ καὶ κριθαὶ ἠδ' ἄμπελοι, αἵ τε φέρουσιν
οἶνον ἐριστάφυλον, καί σφιν Διὸς ὄμβρος ἀέξει.

The blinding of Polyphemus. Fragment of a clay vase, ca. 650. Photo courtesy of Ecole Française d'Archéologie, Paris.

> We arrived at the land of the reckless, lawless Cyclopes, who, trusting
> in the immortal gods, neither plant crops with their hands nor do they
> plow. But everything grows unsown and unplowed, wheat and barley
> and grapes, which bear full-bodied wine, and the storms of Zeus cause
> them to grow. (*Od.* 9.106–11)

Although Alcinous' garden is conspicuous for the absence of laborers and the process of work, the results of its cultivation are evident: the orchard is fenced (ἔρκος ἐλήλαται, 7.113); the vineyard is planted (ἀλωὴ ἐρρίζωται, 7.122); the grapes gathered (τρυγόωσιν, 7.124) and trampled (τραπέουσι, 7.125).[6] The land of the Cyclopes, by contrast, is entirely without agricultural practice. Instead, this is a pre-agricultural landscape without any contact with the tools of civilization, and the passage emphasizes the lack of cultivation here: the land is unsown (ἄσπαρτα) and unplowed (ἀνήροτα).

This contrast in landscape is mirrored by the differences in social structure between the Cyclopes and the Phaeacians. The world of the Phaeacians is a hypercivilized one that includes rules, customs, and a political structure that is reminiscent of the Greek world.[7] The Cyclopes, however, are conspicuous for their lack of such rules and practices:

τοῖσιν δ᾽ οὔτ᾽ ἀγοραὶ βουληφόροι οὔτε θέμιστες,
ἀλλ᾽ οἵ γ᾽ ὑψηλῶν ὀρέων ναίουσι κάρηνα

ἐν σπέσσι αλαφυροῖσι, θεμιστεύει δὲ ἕκαστος
παίδων ἠδ᾽ ἀλόχων, οὐδ᾽ ἀλλήλων ἀλέγουσι.

They have no marketplaces for deliberation nor bodies of law, but they
dwell upon the tops of high mountains in hollow caves. And each rules
his children and his wife, and they do not care for one another. (*Od.*
9.112–15)

In other words, the world of the Cyclopes is marked by the absence of all the traditional signs of a civilized social structure. This sharp contrast with the well-de-
veloped social institutions of the Phaeacians is perhaps best captured by the comparison of Alcinous' elaborate multi-metaled palace to the rustic cave in which
Polyphemus lives:

ἔνθα δ᾽ ἐπ᾽ ἐσχατιῇ σπέος εἴδομεν ἄγχι θαλάσσης
ὑψηλόν, δάφνῃσι κατηρεφές· ἔνθα δὲ πολλὰ
μῆλ᾽, ὄιές τε καὶ αἶγες, ἰαύσκον· περὶ δ᾽ αὐλὴ
ὑψηλὴ δέδμητο κατωρυχέεσσι λίθοισι
μακρῇσίν τε πίτνυσσιν ἰδὲ δρυσὶν ὑψικόμοισιν.

There we saw a tall cave near the edge of the sea, roofed over with
laurel. And there many flocks, sheep and goats, were sleeping. And a
high courtyard was built all around with large rocks dug into the earth
and pine trees and leafy oaks. (*Od.* 9.182–86)

Alcinous' richly decorated palace is at the center of a bustling city and regularly
filled with feasting noblemen and attendant servants; Polyphemus' cave is isolated on the outskirts (ἐσχατιῇ) of the island, high up, covered by laurel branches.
His companions are the sheep and goats that he tends; there is no extended family or retainers.[8]

But the theme that dominates the poem's contrast between the savage, primitive Cyclopes and their extremely genteel counterparts, the Phaeacians, is that
of hospitality. I will return to this point a bit later in the chapter.[9] For now I want
to emphasize that Odysseus' encounter with each of these peoples is structured
around the presence or absence of hospitality. Among the Phaeacians, Alcinous
welcomes Odysseus into his court and offers him food, clothes, and generous
gifts—all before Alcinous even knows his visitor's name. It is in search of similar hospitable treatment that Odysseus sets out to visit the Cyclopes, but there
he finds a world in which Polyphemus rejects the rules of hospitality and instead
eats his guests.

While, as this brief overview suggests, the contrast between the Cyclopes
and the Phaeacians appears to be broadly structured along the familiar lines of
nature and culture, this opposition is nevertheless complicated by several miti-
gating factors.[10] First, we must remember that these two peoples are related to

each other: both are descended from the god Poseidon.[11] In addition, they used to be neighbors before the hostility and violence of the Cyclopes drove Nausithous to relocate the Phaeacians to Scheria. In fact, both peoples are characterized as excessively reckless (ὑπερφίαλοι, 6.274; 9.106), and the Phaeacians, in spite of all their hospitality, have the potential to treat their guests badly. Both Nausicaa and Athena warn Odysseus that he may encounter some hostility from the local Phaeacians as he approaches the city, and Arete's advice that Odysseus lock up his treasure as he sails home in Phaeacian ships suggests a similar distrust of local hospitality.[12] In other words, the strong set of contrasts between the Phaeacians and the Cyclopes—ships, social structure, *xenia*—is reinforced by some significant similarities between them.

Although the poem suggests that the counterpart to the Golden Age palace of the Phaeacians is the cannibalistic cave of Polyphemus, the point of the contrast is not to oppose nature and culture unequivocally, but rather to stake out the range of the Greek experience somewhere in between these two extreme positions.[13] Although previous scholars have described and discussed the structure of the Phaeacian/Cyclopes opposition in some detail, they have failed to perceive the colonial context in which it operates. In particular, the Phaeacian/Cyclopes contrast focuses on the Greek experience abroad; it establishes a framework for asking and answering questions about the kinds of peoples and places to be found overseas. What kinds of peoples live there? What does the landscape look like? How can Greeks make a life for themselves in these new lands with new peoples? Both episodes open with an explicit reference to colonization, and the focus of this chapter is to historicize the familiar structural opposition of Phaeacians and Cyclopes along these lines: to locate their polarity within the world of Greek overseas settlement.

### The Colonial Context

The archaic Greek colonial movement was a far-reaching one. From the eighth to the sixth centuries B.C.E., the Greeks established an astounding number of colonies as far east as the Black Sea and as far west as the coast of Spain.[14] The Euboeans were particularly important players in the early eighth-century stages of this vast settlement program. In addition to their participation in trade activity in the east (Al Mina, Tell Sukas), some of the earliest colonies were settled by the Euboeans in the west: Pithecoussae (ca. 770) and Cumae (ca. 725) in central Italy; Naxos (ca. 734), Leontini (ca. 728), and Catane (ca. 729) in eastern Sicily; and Zancle (ca. 730), and Rhegium (ca. 720) in the straits.[15] The Euboeans' prominence in early Greek colonial efforts is no doubt related to their leading role in trade with the Near East in the previous century. Perhaps from trade contacts in the Near East they learned about opportunities for both land and metals available in the west.[16]

Debate continues over the motivation for these colonial enterprises—was it a need for land or trade outposts?—but it seems clear that some combination of factors was at work.[17] These early Greek colonies were quickly successful, and although ties were maintained with the metropolis, the colonies functioned as independent cities. Indeed, some of them sent out their own colonial expeditions in turn. The archaic colonial movement meant creating new Greek cities on foreign soil, bringing the colonists into contact and conflict with indigenous populations and forcing them to conceptualize the civic entity from scratch. We can detect some of the issues that arose from these colonial efforts at work in the art and literature of the archaic period, starting with the *Odyssey* and other *nostoi*, or tales of heroes returning home from Troy.[18]

*Nostoi* legends have always provided a fertile ground for mythic traditions encompassing exploration, migration, and colonial settlement.[19] Strabo tells us that Pylians sailing home from Troy with Nestor founded the city of Metapontum.[20] He also recounts how the Neaethus River near the city of Croton got its name from some Greeks who had strayed from the Trojan fleet and settled there. The Greeks had stopped to explore the area, and once the ships were empty, the Trojan women who were sailing with them set fire to the ships. This episode gave the river its name from the Greek νέας ἀέθειν, "to burn ships." The Greeks decided to stay and were immediately joined by others, and many settlements (κατοικίας) arose.[21] Thucydides relates that after the Trojan War, Amphilochus, son of Amphiareus, had returned to his home in Peloponnesian Argos. Unhappy with the state of affairs there, he sailed to the Ambracian Gulf and there founded Amphilocian Argos and colonized the rest of Amphilocia.[22]

Greek heroes returning home from Troy are easily recast as colonial founders: they are already on the road, and their success at Troy links the origins of these new Greek cities with the great epic heroes of the past. The return of Odysseus is also a story well suited to this colonial tradition even though the *Odyssey* is not itself a settlement tale in the literal sense. Rather, by drawing on familiar mythic characters and plots, the poem helps a Greek audience accommodate the challenges of a new world of exploration and settlement within an age-old story of travel and discovery. The *Odyssey*, especially in the opposition between the Cyclopes and the Phaeacians, includes within its narrative scope issues and themes that emerge from the colonial experience and thus participates in the colonial discourse of the early archaic period.[23]

First of all, the colonial theme appears prominently within the Phaeacian and Cyclopes episodes; in fact, it opens both of them. When we are introduced to the city and people of Phaeacia at the beginning of Book 6, the first detail mentioned is their colonial history:

οἳ πρὶν μέν ποτ᾽ ἔναιον ἐν εὐρυχόρῳ Ὑπερείῃ,
ἀγχοῦ Κυκλώπων ἀνδρῶν ὑπερηνορεόντων,
οἵ σφεας σινέσκοντο, βίηφι δὲ φέρτεροι ἦσαν.

ἔνθεν ἀναστήσας ἄγε Ναυσίθοος θεοειδής,
εἷσεν δὲ Σχερίῃ, ἑκὰς ἀνδρῶν ἀλφηστάων,
ἀμφὶ δὲ τεῖχος ἔλασσε πόλει καὶ ἐδείματο οἴκους
καὶ νηοὺς ποίησε θεῶν καὶ ἐδάσσατ᾿ ἀρούρας.

Before, they used to live in wide-plained Hyperia, nearby the Cyclopes, arrogant men who used to harass them, and they were greater in strength. Removing them, godlike Nausithous led them [the Phaeacians] away from there and settled them in Scheria, far from men who eat grain. He drove a wall around the city and built houses; he made temples for the gods and divided up farmland. (*Od.* 6.4–10)

The Phaeacians used to live nearby their relatives, the Cyclopes, but after systematic harassment, Nausithous resettled his people in Scheria, far from men who eat bread (ἀλφηστάων). Here the agricultural aspect of this adjective needs to be emphasized.[24] The description of Nausithous' actions captures the essential activities of a colonial founder: he surrounds the city with a wall, builds houses, erects temples to the gods, and distributes plots of land to the settlers.[25] Scholars, as I have noted, have looked to early Ionian colonial cities as a model for Homer's Phaeacians, and they are right to recognize the explicitly colonial origins of the city and its importance for understanding their portrayal.[26] In spite of all its Golden Age qualities, as Vidal-Naquet has observed, "Phaeacia contains all the characteristic elements of a Greek settlement in the age of colonization."[27]

Our introduction to the Cyclopes in Book 9 is equally implicated in the world of colonization.[28] In his account to Alcinous, Odysseus describes a wooded island that lies opposite the land of the Cyclopes on which wild goats thrive in the absence of human hunters (9.116–21). Empty of men, the island is unpastured and untilled (9.122–24).[29] The island is not at all bad. Rather, it bears fruit in all seasons; it has well-watered meadows, plentiful grapes, easy plowing, and fertile soil (9.131–35). In addition, it offers a good natural harbor and a freshwater spring (9.136–41). In short, this is an island that embodies all the possibilities of the new world of colonization, and Odysseus marks it as such by commenting that this island would make an ideal colonial settlement (νῆσον ἐυκτιμένην, 9.130), if only the Cyclopes had the naval skill to cross the sea (9.125–30). The colonial undertones are further enhanced by Odysseus' mode of arrival. Like the "surprised oikist" of colonial legends, Odysseus and his men arrive at this island unexpectedly and without prior plan or design; instead, in the dark night, a god leads them to it.[30]

And so yet another theme that connects the Phaeacians with Polyphemus and the Cyclopes is the colonial one—or perhaps better, it is the institution of colonization that provides the broader historical context in which the other terms of contrast (ships, social structure, hospitality) operate. The Cyclopes live opposite the ideal colonial site, and their inability to colonize it guarantees and ensures the potentiality and possibilities offered by colonization. The Phaeacians,

by contrast, are successful colonists, and their colonial origins celebrate the newly
settled city in all its actuality. The contrasting landscapes of the Cyclopes and the
Phaeacians, moreover, exemplify two competing visions of the New World that
colonists or explorers find overseas. The utopian productivity of the land of the
Phaeacians corresponds to dreams of rediscovering the Golden Age somewhere
across the seas, and their memory of the ease with which the foundation itself
was accomplished celebrates the ideal colonial experience: no trace of previous
occupants of the land, no evidence of a struggle to take control. The primitive
savagery of the Cyclopes, however, and their landscape—with its lack of agriculture—reminds us of yet another New World scenario in which the fertility of
the land is tempered by a sense of primitivism rather than idealism and where
the native occupants of the land are less than welcoming to newcomers. Indeed,
it is through their very different receptions of Odysseus, presented through the
framework of hospitality, that the opposition between the Cyclopes and the
Phaeacians addresses themes and issues arising from overseas colonization. The
Phaeacians offer marriage and the Cyclopes cannibalism: two very different
models for overseas contact and settlement.

### The Phaeacian Model: Marriage

First, the Phaeacians. Odysseus is made welcome in Phaeacia by Nausicaa and
her father in an extrememly generous display of hospitality. He receives food,
clothing, lodging, and, as gifts, more goods than he would have brought home
as spoils from Troy. Indeed, the ultimate hospitality gift is Alcinous' offer of
Nausicaa's hand in marriage:

> αἲ γάρ, Ζεῦ τε πάτερ καὶ Ἀθηναίη καὶ Ἄπολλον,
> τοῖος ἐὼν οἷός ἐσσι, τά τε φρονέων ἅ τ᾽ ἐγώ περ,
> παῖδά τ᾽ ἐμὴν ἐχέμεν καὶ ἐμὸς γαμβρὸς καλέεσθαι
> αὖθι μένων. οἶκον δέ κ᾽ ἐγὼ καὶ κτήματα δοίην,
> εἴ κ᾽ ἐθέλων γε μένοις· ἀέκοντα δέ σ᾽ οὔ τις ἐρύξει
> Φαιήκων· μὴ τοῦτο φίλον Διὶ πατρὶ γένοιτο.

> If only, Father Zeus and Athena and Apollo, being the kind of man that
> you are and thinking the things that I know you think, if only you would
> take my daughter and remaining here be called my son-in-law. I would
> give you a house and possessions if you would stay willingly. But no one
> of the Phaeacians will force you if you are unwilling. May this not be
> dear to Father Zeus. (Od. 7.311–16)

The theme of marriage runs prominently throughout the Phaeacian episode from
the moment Nausicaa awakens and wants to wash the clothes for her bridal
trousseau to Alcinous' generous offer here of his daughter in marriage to

Odysseus.[31] Since Odysseus is a man of such quality, Alcinous is prepared to make him his son-in-law; along with a bride, a house, and other goods, Odysseus would gain by this act of marriage the role as heir apparent to the Phaeacian kingdom. Indeed, there is more going on in this passage than a romantic subplot. Here, as so often, the ideology and structure of the institution of marriage help articulate an idealized view of colonization as a peaceful and productive process.

Marriage is a common theme in archaic Greek colonial traditions.[32] Within the Greek world the notion of marriage is one of integration and acculturation. The myths and rituals associated with the institution are designed to bring that which is wild and foreign (the female) together with that which is powerful and cultured (the male), thereby transforming the female into something civilized and productive. The theme of acculturation is echoed and reinforced through the agricultural motifs found so often in marriage poetry. The young bride, for example, is compared to a ripe apple to be picked or trampled flowers in the powerful imagery of Sappho's wedding song.[33] In addition, this agricultural or vegetative imagery equates the bride with the actual land to be settled: both will be cultivated to become fertile.[34] Marriage integrates two separate entities (male and female) into one coherent and productive unit (the household). Plutarch, in his *Advice to Bride and Groom*, draws on the image of intertwined ropes to capture the new partnership that is forged.[35] The act of founding a colony overseas is similarly a process of acculturation and integration; it creates one (Greek) city where once there were two different peoples. Colonization necessarily entails the transformation of a local, indigenous culture into a Greek one, and the rhetoric of marriage myths and rituals helps represent this often violent and disruptive act as a familiar and benign process instead; it naturalizes and civilizes what can be an act of harsh brutality.

A good example of how marriage works to represent colonization in this way is the marriage of Aeneas and Lavinia in the *Aeneid*. In many ways, the *Aeneid* provides insight into the narrative potential of Odysseus' story—another way the tale could have been told. Aeneas certainly embodies many of Odysseus' heroic qualities and invokes his mythic memory—Aeneas' first words are an echo of Odysseus' famous lament about dying at sea rather than on the battlefield—but the *Aeneid* makes explicit the colonial themes that operate more subtly in the *Odyssey*.[36] Most obviously, Aeneas' overseas travels culminate in the founding of a new city rather than in a successful return home, but what is significant is the way the eventual founding of Rome is predicated on and conceptualized as the marriage between Aeneas, the newly arrived foreigner, and Lavinia, daughter of the king and representative of the local land and its people.[37] Their marriage represents the unification of two peoples, the newly arrived Trojans and the native Italians, into the city that will one day become Rome. Military conquest and overseas settlement are thus rewritten as marriage.

In addition, the ideological similarities between marriage and colonization acknowledge the signficant role of violence within each endeavor. Not just a celebration of the progression from the wild to the civilized, marriage also contains and expresses the presence of sexual violence. The rape of Persephone by Hades, the god of the Underworld, for example, establishes a model of marriage that unites sexuality and violence.[38] In this respect, the institution of marriage is an ambiguous one, predicated on the fact that the union of male and female is both a civilized and a violent act, and this ambiguity applies to the process of founding a colony as well, especially in situations that displace previous occupants of the land.

In fact, rape is a common motif in colonial legends in which the political and physical violence of founding a colony is represented in erotic terms. One of the clearest examples can be found in Pindar's Pythian 9, in which Apollo's rape of the beautiful nymph Cyrene symbolizes the Greek colonization of the city with the same name:

> τὰν ὁ χαιτάεις ἀνεμοσφαράγων
>     ἐκ Παλίου κόλπων ποτὲ Λατοίδας
> ἅρπασ᾽, ἔνεικέ τε χρυς<έῳ> παρθένον ἀγροτέραν
> δίφρῳ, τόθι νιν πολυμήλου
> καὶ πολυκαρποτάτας θῆκε δέσποιναν χθονός
> ῥίζαν ἀπείρου τρίταν εὐ-
>     ήρατον θάλλοισαν οἰκεῖν.

> . . . whom [Cyrene] the long-haired son of Leto once took from the valleys of Pelion which echo in the wind, and he brought the wild maiden in a golden chariot and made her mistress there and caused her to live in the lovely flourishing third root of the many-flocked and much-fruited land. (Pyth. 9.5–9)

The association of the city with the young girl to be raped is crystallized in the relative pronoun (τὰν) that effects the transition from Cyrene, the city, to its eponymous nymph; both are rendered as female. In addition to the expression of violence (ἅρπασ᾽), the rape transforms a wild girl (παρθένον ἀγροτέραν) into a blossoming (θάλλοισαν) and productive (πολυκαρποτάτας) land.[39]

Later in the poem Pindar offers another view of the same picture—an account of the marriage of Cyrene and Apollo in which Lady Libya gladly receives the Greek god in her house and hands over the land of Cyrene as a wedding present to the bridegroom:

> νῦν δ᾽ εὐρυλείμων πότνιά σοι Λιβύα
> δέξεται εὐκλέα νύμφαν δώμασιν ἐν χρυσέοις
> πρόφρων· ἵνα οἱ χθονὸς αἶσαν
> αὐτίκα συντελέθειν ἔννομον δωρήσεται,
> οὔτε παγκάρπων φυτῶν νά-
>     ποινον οὔτ᾽ ἀγνῶτα θηρῶν.

And now wide-meadowed, reverend Libya will receive the famous
nymph kindly in her golden halls, where at once she will make her a
present of a portion of land to be lawfully hers, land which is neither
lacking in plants of all fruits nor unfamiliar to beasts. (Pyth. 9.56–58)

This picture personifies the rich continent (εὐρυλείμων) of Libya as a genial
mother-in-law who willingly (πρόφρων) welcomes the young girl who represents
this new Greek city. The transfer of ownership of the land (χθονὸς αἶσαν) is represented as the bestowal of a wedding gift (δωρήσεται), and this marriage characterizes the land (and the bride) as fruitful (παγκάρπων). The poem thus combines a story of colonial rape with one of marriage to capture the fundamental
ambiguity inherent in both marriage and colonization: both are acts of civilization predicated on violence.[40]

And so, when, at the beginning of Book 6 of the *Odyssey*, Odysseus awakens to the sound of young girls playing by the water after he washes ashore on
Scheria and goes to confront them, all the signs point at first to a rape narrative.
Like Persephone or Cyrene, Nausicaa, playing by the water's edge with her girl-
friends, is vulnerable to the lust of men who come upon her, especially those who
want her father's land. Indeed, when Odysseus greets Nausicaa by comparing
her to a beautiful palm tree, he draws on the familiar epithalamial rhetoric of
likening the bride to aspects of nature, especially trees, plants, and fruits.[41] But,
in spite of all our expectations, Odysseus does not rape Nausicaa; instead, he
supplicates her kindly, and she takes him home to her father, who then offers her
to Odysseus as his bride. As in the case of Pythian 9, the rape narrative is replaced by that of marriage, and like that of Lady Libya, Alcinous' generous offer of marriage recasts the projected colonial encounter as a marriage. At the moment when Alcinous makes his offer, all the potential of the *Aeneid*-type colonial
narrative with its analogy of marriage and overseas settlement tantalizes the audience. Will Odysseus stay in Scheria? Will he found a Greek city there? Although
the possibility is immediately rejected when he chooses instead to return home,
the idealized model remains as part of the larger ethnographic imagination of the
poem.

In other words, within a context of overseas settlement, the Phaeacians again
represent a utopian model, this time an idealized picture of the nature of the interaction between overseas settlers and the people whose land is settled. The institution of marriage describes a relationship between two peoples that is peaceful and productive. Moreover, the Phaeacian model rejects rape as part of this
picture, thereby further suppressing any hint of the potential violence at the core
of any colonial endeavor. And finally, this marriage model is embedded within
the larger and equally familiar institution of hospitality, and this helps cement
the colonial contrast with the Cyclopes. Odysseus lands on the shore of the
Phaeacians, where he is welcomed with open arms and offered a bride and the
keys to the kingdom. When he arrives at the land of the Cyclopes, however, he

finds a very different kind of welcome—a welcome that offers a sharply contrasting vision of the colonial encounter.

### The Cyclopean Model: Cannibalism

Again, as I noted earlier, the Cyclopes' episode opens within a clear colonial context. After leaving the land of the Lotus-Eaters, Odysseus and his men are driven by a storm onto an island just opposite the land of the Cyclopes, which Odysseus describes as an ideal colonial site (νῆσον ἐυκτιμένην, *Od.* 9.130). Even though this island provides them with plenty of food, Odysseus sees the smoke rising from the Cyclopes' land and wants to learn what these men are like:

> Ἄλλοι μὲν νῦν μίμνετ᾽, ἐμοὶ ἐρίηρες ἑταῖροι·
> αὐτὰρ ἐγὼ σὺν νηί τ᾽ ἐμῇ καὶ ἐμοῖς ἑτάροισιν
> ἐλθὼν τῶνδ᾽ ἀνδρῶν πειρήσομαι, οἵ τινές εἰσιν,
> ἤ ῥ᾽ οἵ γ᾽ ὑβρισταί τε καὶ ἄγριοι οὐδὲ δίκαιοι,
> ἦε φιλόξεινοι καί σφιν νόος ἐστὶ θεουδής.

> The rest of you now remain here, my trusted companions. But I will go with my ship and my companions to find out about these men, to see who they are—whether they are savage and wild and unjust or kind to strangers and respectful of the gods. (*Od.* 9.172–76)

Odysseus imagines that these men will be one of two kinds: either savage (ὑβρισταί τε καὶ ἄγριοι) and unjust (οὐδὲ δίκαιοι) or god-fearing and generous to strangers (φιλόξεινοι καί σφιν νόος ἐστὶ θεουδής). Odysseus posed this same set of questions upon his arrival on the island of Scheria as well, and his choice of categories neatly captures the nature of the differences between the Phaeacians and the Cyclops.[42] While his experiences among the Phaeacians were extremely civilized, what Odysseus finds among the Cyclopes corresponds to the other of his two options: a monster, not a civilized man at all:

> ἔνθα δ᾽ ἀνὴρ ἐνίαυε πελώριος, ὅς ῥά τε μῆλα
> οἶος ποιμαίνεσκεν ἀπόπροθεν· οὐδὲ μετ᾽ ἄλλους
> πωλεῖτ᾽· ἀλλ᾽ ἀπάνευθεν ἐὼν ἀθεμίστια ᾔδη.
> καὶ γὰρ θαῦμ᾽ ἐτέτυκτο πελώριον, οὐδὲ ἐῴκει
> ἀνδρί γε σιτοφάγῳ, ἀλλὰ ῥίῳ ὑλήεντι
> ὑψηλῶν ὀρέων, ὅ τε φαίνεται οἶον ἀπ᾽ ἄλλων.

> There a monstrous man lived, who far away, alone, was pasturing his flocks. He did not go about with others, but apart he knew lawless ways. For he was made a monstrous marvel, not at all like a man who eats bread, but like the shaggy peak of tall mountains, he appeared alone apart from the others. (*Od.* 9.187–92)

Not like a man who eats bread, Polyphemus is more like a mountain peak, and his association with the primitive aspect of nature is thus confirmed in these terms. Already we anticipate that Odysseus' reception here will be less friendly than it was among the Phaeacians.

Indeed, far from being treated to a generous feast, Odysseus's men become the meal itself:

> ἀλλ᾽ ὅ γ᾽ ἀναΐξας ἑτάροις ἐπὶ χεῖρας ἴαλλε,
> σὺν δὲ δύω μάρψας ὥς τε σκύλακας ποτὶ γαίῃ
> κόπτ᾽ · ἐκ δ᾽ ἐγκέφαλος χαμάδις ῥέε, δεῦε δὲ γαῖαν.
> τοὺς δὲ διὰ μελεϊστὶ ταμὼν ὁπλίσσατο δόρπον·
> ἤσθιε δ᾽ ὥς τε λέων ὀρεσίτροφος-- οὐδ᾽ ἀπέλειπεν--
> ἔγκατά τε σάρκας τε καὶ ὀστέα μυελόεντα.

> But he leapt up and threw his hands upon my comrades, and snatching up two of them he smashed them upon the ground like small puppies. Their brains ran onto the ground and moistened the earth. He cut these men limb from limb and prepared his meal. He ate like a mountain-reared lion—he left nothing behind—entrails, skin, and marrow-filled bones. (Od. 9.287–93)

Like a mountain lion, the Cyclops kills and eats Odysseus' men, two by two. Moreover, he eats them raw, washing them down with unmixed milk. Temporarily sated, he then passes out on the floor of the cave; the next morning he eats two more men for breakfast.

Polyphemus' reception of Odysseus and his men, his act of cannibalism, fulfills an overseas traveler or settler's worst fears. In this respect the Cyclopes episode is best understood within the larger framework of colonial discourse as well. The theme of cannibalism figures prominently in later colonial traditions. Although the word "cannibalism" has obvious roots in a more recent historical encounter between European slave traders and indigenous Carib peoples, the term has come to represent a discursive practice that transcends the historical origins of the word. Peter Hulme defines the discourse of cannibalism as "the image of ferocious consumption of human flesh frequently used to mark the boundary between one community and its others."[43] It is in this sense, as a discursive rather than a real practice, that we can make sense of the role and significance of Polyphemus' cannibalism in the Odyssey. Typically, tales of cannibalism operate as an index of savagery within an imperial or colonial context to represent those capable of resisting conquest as themselves violent and voracious. The savagery of conquest is thus displaced onto those who are able to fight back. They are the ones who are truly transgressive since they eat human flesh and are therefore in need of being conquered. Among other things, the discourse of cannibalism addresses both the fear of hostile indigenous peoples and anxieties about subduing them.[44]

But does this discourse of cannibalism have any currency within the archaic Greek world, and if so, how?[45] The ferocious consumption of human flesh is, in fact, a topos that appears frequently in Greek myth and literature. In the *Iliad*, for example, the eating of raw flesh is the mark of savagery—it is what animals do. Although Homeric warriors do not actually eat their enemies, the threat of cannibalism hovers over the action of the *Iliad*. As if too horrible for words, the potential for such savagery expresses itself through similes or the optative mood. Grisly and graphic similes liken Greek and Trojan warriors to bloodthirsty dogs, lions, and wolves devouring the raw flesh of those killed in battle.[46] Hera, Achilles, and Hecuba all wish to eat the raw flesh of their enemy, but do not actually carry out their threats.[47] In each of these three cases, the hypothetical act of eating human flesh is connected with extreme anger and the desire for vengeance. In addition, these passages locate this vengeance beyond the pale of civilized behavior and within the realm of the savage, both animal and foreign.[48]

The act of cannibalism as the quintessential division between civilized human behavior and the savage world of beasts is articulated most clearly in Hesiod's *Works and Days*. In a passage that separates a sense of justice (δίκη) from the threat of violence (βίη), Hesiod explains why animals eat one another but humans do not:

τόνδε γὰρ ἀνθρώποισι νόμον διέταξε Κρονίων
ἰχθύσι μὲν καὶ θηρσὶ καὶ οἰωνοῖς πετεηνοῖς
ἐσθέμεν ἀλλήλους, ἐπεὶ οὐ δίκη ἐστὶ μετ' αὐτοῖς·
ἀνθρώποισι δ' ἔδωκε δίκην, ἣ πολλὸν ἀρίστη γίγνεται.

For Kronion Zeus established this custom for mankind—for fish, on the one hand, beasts, and winged birds to eat one another since there is no justice among them; but to mankind he gave justice, which is by far the best. (*WD* 276–80)

Not only is it a sign of the absence of justice for one species to eat its own kind, but also Hesiod implies that the human refusal to do so is one of the markers of progress away from the animal state.[49] The repression of the cannibal appetite functions as the defining moment in the narrative of mankind's evolution from savage to civilized behavior.

The presence and absence of cannibalism articulates the boundaries between the civilized and savage worlds of Greeks and barbarians as well as between humans and animals. Starting perhaps with Odysseus' encounter with the Cyclopes, Greeks have consistently located cannibals at the edges of the earth, and so it is with the *Odyssey* that we first see the convergence of the cannibal and the colonial.[50] Savage tribes that devour human flesh become a conventional motif in ethnographic traditions that map out the world and the place for Greeks within it. The Greeks are marked as more civilized than foreign races and wild animals in that they no longer eat their own kind, and in a colonial context this motif helps justify the appropriation of the foreigners' land.

In other words, in the early archaic Greek world as well, cannibals are an expression of the anxieties of overseas settlement.[51] First, the discourse of cannibalism addresses the potential violence of a colonial encounter. In the archaic period, founding a new city on foreign soil could be a violent and dangerous process. Among other things, the Greeks often settled territory previously occupied by native populations. Thucydides, for example, tells us that entire Sicel populations were driven out to make room for the Euboean colonists in Sicily.[52] In Nicias' speech to the Athenians prior to the Sicilian expedition, Thucydides compares the military force needed to launch the all-out effort to that required to found a new colony, and this comparison begins to give us a sense of the violence involved in colonial efforts:

πόλιν τε νομίσαι χρὴ ἐν ἀλλοφύλλοις καὶ πολεμίοις οἰκιοῦντας ἰέναι, οὓς πρέπει τῇ πρώτῃ ἡμέρᾳ ᾗ ἂν κατάσχωσιν εὐθὺς κρατεῖν τῆς γῆς ἢ εἰδέναι ὅτι, ἢν σφάλλωνται, πάντα πολέμια ἕξουσιν.

We must consider [that we are like] those going to settle a city among foreign and enemy peoples for whom it is necessary, on the very first day when they land, straightaway to conquer the land or know that if they fail, they will encounter complete hostility. (Thuc. 6.23)

Thucydides' analogy here shows us how dangerous and violent colonial expeditions could be. Like a military expedition, colonization means a dangerous confrontation with hostile peoples and requires a large demonstration of force.[53] Jan-Paul Crielaard has made the intriguing suggestion that part of the attraction of colonization for the aristocratic elite, in addition to the possibility of acquiring large landholdings, was precisely the fact that the territory had to be conquered. In this respect, the violence of colonial settlement is assimilated into the aristocratic warrior ethos.[54] Settling new territory overseas, then, can be a violent process, and within the discourse of colonization, the hybristic act of cannibalism serves to redirect the violence and the transgression involved in settling overseas territory, especially if the colonists kill or displace the previous occupants, away from those taking the land and onto those who previously occupied it.

Second, not only does the discourse of cannibalism relocate the violence from colonizer to colonized, but also it helps justify the aggression of overseas settlement. The act of colonization is thus represented as the act of ridding the land of a dangerous and violent threat. In its place a new Greek city is established—civilized culture where once there was only wild and dangerous nature.[55] And so the clear colonial context of *Odyssey* 9 suggests that we read Odysseus' experience with Polyphemus in this light. Odysseus' encounter with the Cyclops conjures up the nightmare scenario of overseas settlement—the dangers and difficulties of subduing hostile native populations. In this way, Polyphemus' act of cannibalism and Odysseus' triumph over him belong to the larger framework of colonial discourse that first demonizes native populations and then celebrates their conquest as the victory of civilization over the forces of nature.[56]

Moreover, as in the case of the Phaeacians, the colonial reading of Poly-phemus' hostile reception of Odysseus and his men is articulated in the familiar terms of Greek hospitality (or lack thereof)—yet one more way in which the colonial action is made familiar and inevitable. In spite of his uncivilized de-meanor, Odysseus' encounter with the Cyclops is pointedly structured by the rules of *xenia*, or rather by their conspicuous absence.[57] Early on in the story, Odysseus reflects on his decision to visit the Cyclops and wishes that he had fol-lowed his companions' suggestion that they load up the ships with goats and sail away:

> ἀλλ᾿ ἐγὼ οὐ πιθόμην—ἦ τ᾿ ἂν πολὺ κέρδιον ἦεν—
> ὄφρ᾿ αὐτόν τε ἴδοιμι, καὶ εἴ μοι ξείνια δοίη.

> But I did not obey—it would have been much more profitable to do so—so that I could see him and see if he would give me guest gifts. (*Od.* 9.228–29)

If only Odysseus had agreed; but he wanted to see this man and to see if he would give him guest gifts (ξείνια). Similarly, Polyphemus uses the language of hospi-tality to greet Odysseus and his men (῏Ω ξεῖνοι, 9.252) and ask who they are and where they have come from. Encouraged, perhaps, by this greeting, Odysseus proceeds to tell the Cyclops that they are Greeks returning from Troy:

> ἡμεῖς δ᾿ αὖτε κιχανόμενοι τὰ σὰ γοῦνα
> ἱκόμεθ᾿, εἴ τι πόροις ξεινήιον ἠὲ καὶ ἄλλως
> δοίης δωτίνην, ἥ τε ξείνων θέμις ἐστίν·
> ἀλλ᾿ αἰδεῖο, φέριστε, θεούς· ἱκέται δέ τοί εἰμεν.
> Ζεὺς δ᾿ ἐπιτιμήτωρ ἱκετάων τε ξείνων τε
> ξείνιος, ὃς ξείνοισιν ἅμ᾿ αἰδοίοισιν ὀπηδεῖ.

> Moreover, we have come supplicating your knees, to see if you would give us a guest gift or some other gift, which is the custom among guests and hosts. Respect the gods, my fine friend, for we are suppliants. Zeus Xeinios oversees both suppliants and guest-friends, Zeus who also protects deserving strangers. (*Od.* 9.266–71)

Odysseus here invokes the language of both supplication and hospitality and re-minds Polyphemus that Zeus is the protector of both the guest and the suppliant.

Polyphemus responds, however, first by scoffing at Odysseus' request that he respect the gods and second by eating two of his men. His notion of hospi-tality turns the customary rules on their heads. Instead of preparing a meal for

Odysseus and his men, he makes a meal of them. After Odysseus tempts the Cyclops with the potent Thracian wine, Polyphemus promises him a guest gift (ξείνιον, 9.356) if he will tell him his name. When Odysseus says that his name is "*Outis*," or "Nohbody," Polyphemus offers his "gift":

Οὖτιν ἐγὼ πύματον ἔδομαι μετὰ οἷς ἑτάροισι,
τοὺς δ᾽ ἄλλους πρόσθεν· τὸ δέ τοι ξεινήιον ἔσται.

I will eat *Outis* last after his companions, I will eat the others first. This will be my guest gift. (*Od.* 9.369–70)[58]

Again, as in the Phaeacian episode, the rules and customs of *xenia* provide a familiar interpretive framework for imagining something new and different. Here, the risks and dangers of overseas settlement are depicted in terms of a huge, savage monster who traps Odysseus in his cave and eats his men for dinner in blatant disregard of the proper behavior due to guests. Cannibalism in the place of proper hospitality thus emphasizes the dangers of colonization and anxiety about its violence. Among the Phaeacians, by contrast, Odysseus is welcomed by the ideal host who entertains him lavishly, treats him well, and offers his daughter's hand in marriage, and in this model the institution of hospitality conjures up the ideal dream of colonization as a peaceful and productive marriage. The discrepancy between the reputation that the Phaeacians have for being unfriendly and Odysseus' personal experience of generous hospitality makes sense now in light of the problematic issue of native inhabitants in a colonial context. Odysseus spells out the big question facing potential colonists in the New World when he lands across from the Cyclopes' land and asks, "Are these men just and god-fearing or are they savage and wild?" Odysseus' experience of generosity and warm welcome among the Phaeacians imagines the ideal colonial encounter, all the while preserving at the edges of his story the potential for a very different kind of reception. The latter is just what he receives, of course, among the Cyclopes. Within this context, the institution of hospitality provides familiar terms for imagining the possible receptions, friendly or hostile, of Greek colonists by native populations. In addition, our understanding of the opposition between nature and culture that scholars have found at work in the Cyclopes episode is deepened and enriched by locating it within this larger framework of overseas settlement.[59] Odysseus' encounters with the Phaeacians and the Cyclopes sketch out the extreme poles of possible colonial scenarios: a peaceful and productive union of Greeks and natives or a bloody cannibal feast.

In my discussion of the Phoenician/Phaeacian opposition in the previous chapter, we saw that Odysseus represented the Greek attempt to negotiate a more realistic and productive notion of overseas trade somewhere between the two extreme positions occupied by the Phoenicians and Phaeacians. In the case of the Phaeacian/Cyclopes dynamic and issues of colonization, the two extreme positions—marriage or cannibalism—are also mediated in the poem, but in a slightly more complicated way. First of all, elements of both possible colonial models overlap in yet another one of Odysseus' encounters. A brief look at his visit to the Laestrygonians in Book 10 helps confirm our reading of the Phaeacian/ Cyclopes dynamic.[60]

### The Laestrygonians: A Negative Synthesis

After Odysseus and his men arrive ashore at the city of Lamos, Odysseus sends three men to find out who lives there. On their way into town, they meet a girl:

> οἱ δ᾽ ἴσαν ἐκβάντες λείην ὁδόν, ᾗ περ ἄμαξαι
> ἄστυδ᾽ ἀφ᾽ ὑψηλῶν ὀρέων καταγίνεον ὕλην.
> κούρῃ δὲ ξύμβληντο πρὸ ἄστεος ὑδρευούσῃ,
> θυγατέρ᾽ ἰφθίμῃ Λαιστρυγόνος Ἀντιφάταο.
> ἡ μὲν ἄρ᾽ ἐς κρήνην κατεβήσετο καλλιρέεθρον
> Ἀρτακίην· ἔνθεν γὰρ ὕδωρ προτὶ ἄστυ φέρεσκον.
> οἱ δὲ παριστάμενοι προσεφώνεον, ἔκ τ᾽ ἐρέοντο
> ὅς τις τῶνδ᾽ εἴη βασιλεὺς καὶ οἷσιν ἀνάσσοι.

> They debarked and went along an easy road on which wagons carry wood from the tall mountains into the city. They came upon a young girl getting water in front of the city, the powerful daughter of Anti-phates, the Laestrygonian. She had gone down to the sweet-watered Atracian spring, for they used to carry water from there to the city, and they stood beside her and spoke to her, asking who was the king of these people who ruled them. (*Od.* 10.103–10)

The scene bears a certain resemblance to Odysseus' encounter with Nausicaa in Book 6. Here, Odysseus' men come across the daughter of the king as she is getting water, and again, the possibilities of rape are not far from the surface of the narrative. Instead, the men ask her who rules this city, and in response, the young girl points to her father's house. So far this seems all too familiar; but instead of receiving a warm Phaeacian welcome from the local king and queen and an offer of marriage, Odysseus' men come upon a quite different but equally familiar scene:

> οἱ δ᾽ ἐπεὶ εἰσῆλθον κλυτὰ δώματα, τὴν δὲ γυναῖκα
> εὗρον ὅσην τ᾽ ὄρεος κορυφήν, κατὰ δ᾽ ἔστυγον αὐτήν.

> When they entered the glorious house, they discovered a woman as big as a mountain peak and they shrank from the sight of her. (*Od.* 10.112–13)

This particular choice of image recalls all too clearly the description of Polyphemus' similarly monstrous size: he was not like men who eat bread, but like the wooded ridge of a tall mountain (ῥίῳ ὑλήεντι / ὑψηλῶν ὀρέων, 9.191–92).[61] All expectations of a Phaeacian welcome are further shattered when she sends for her husband. With his arrival, the scene loses all of its utopian Phaeacian undertones and takes on instead the grim characteristics of a Cyclopean welcome:

ἡ δ᾽ αἶψ ἐξ ἀγορῆς ἐκάλει κλυτὸν Ἀντιφατῆα,
ὃν πόσιν, ὃς δὴ τοῖσιν ἐμήσατο λυγρὸν ὄλεθρον.
αὐτίχ᾽ ἕνα μάρψας ἑτάρων ὁπλίσσατο δεῖπνον·

At once she called famous Antiphates, her husband, from the market-place, who devised terrible destruction for them. On the spot, he snatched up one of my companions and made his dinner of him. (*Od.* 10.114–16)

This is not the generous hospitality of Alcinous, but rather the gruesome cannibalism of Polyphemus. Antiphates then calls out for help from the other Laestrygonians, who are like Giants, and (unlike Polyphemus' companions) they run from their cliffs to his aid. The reference to the similarity between the Laestrygonians and the Giants reminds us that both the Phaeacians and the Cyclopes are related to the Giants, again prompting a comparison between Odysseus' experience among the Laestrygonians and that among the Cyclopes and the Phaeacians.[62] Finally, the Laestrygonians pelt Odysseus' men with rocks and spear them like fish for their unpleasant feast (ἀτερπέα δαῖτα, 10.124) in an escape scene that sounds all too familiar after Odysseus' recent flight from a rock-wielding Cyclops at the end of Book 9.

And so Odysseus' encounter with the Laestrygonians offers a negative synthesis of the Phaeacian/Cyclopean opposition. Odysseus' men meet up with a young girl, but instead of taking them home to her father, the king, who will offer marriage and a permanent home there, she leads them to a monstrous mother and a man-eating father. What started out with all the promise of a Phaeacian utopia has turned suddenly into a Cyclopean landscape of savage violence. In this respect, the Laestrygonian compromise confirms our analysis of the Phaeacian/Cyclopes colonial dynamic. Here Phaeacian marriage and Cyclopean cannibalism converge in a terrifying perversion of these colonial options.

But if the poem looks to another one of Odysseus' fabulous encounters to imagine the worst possible settlement scene, it postpones any thoughts about a more positive colonial scenario until the second half of the poem and Odysseus' return home to Ithaca. Again, as in the case of overseas trade, it is Odysseus who helps imagine a positive and productive colonial scenario somewhere in between the idealized marriage scene of the Phaeacians and the hostile cannibalism of the Cyclops. The imagery and themes of colonization, as articulated through his experiences with the Phaeacians and the Cyclopes (and as perverted in the Laestrygonian episode), inform Odysseus' return home to Ithaca and what we might call his resettlement there.

In other words, Odysseus' encounter with both the Phaeacians and the Cyclopes sets up the terms for a positive model for colonial settlement that is finally realized only when Odysseus returns home to Ithaca. Alcinous offers him Nausicaa's hand in marriage, yet in spite of the epithalamial imagery that dominates Odysseus' meeting with Nausicaa, he does not marry her. Similarly, when Odysseus confronts the man-eating monster of a colonial nightmare in the cave of the Cyclops, he does not kill him nor does he take his land. He exercises only the violence necessary to escape the cave. It is not until Odysseus reaches Ithaca that these two scenarios converge and are finally and fully enacted. By Odysseus' killing the monstrous men who currently occupy his land and remarrying the princess, his return home is thus represented as a colonial foundation.

# 7

# Phaeacians and Euboeans: Greeks Overseas

οὐ γὰρ Φαιήκεσσι κυβερνητῆρες ἔασιν
οὐδέ τι πηδάλι᾽ ἐστί, τά τ᾽ ἄλλαι νῆες ἔχουσιν·
ἀλλ᾽ αὐταὶ ἴσασι νοήματα καὶ φρένας ἀνδρῶν,
καὶ πάντων ἴσασι πόλιας καὶ πίονας ἀγροὺς
ἀνθρώπων, καὶ λαῖτμα τάχισθ᾽ ἁλὸς ἐκπερόωσιν
ἠέρι καὶ νεφέλῃ κεκαλυμμέναι·

For the Phaeacians have no steersmen, nor any rudders, as other
ships have. But the ships themselves know the thoughts and minds
of men, and they know the cities and fertile fields of all mankind,
and they cross the expanse of the sea swiftly, covered with mist
and cloud.

Odyssey, Book 8

The invention of the ship traditionally marks with pessimism, or at least some trepidation, the fall of the Golden Age and the beginning of New World voyages of exploration. The Phaeacians, however, famous for their nautical expertise, seem able to occupy a place where these two worldviews converge. It is now time to look back at my discussion of the Phaeacians and their role in accommodating and articulating the ethnographic imagination of the *Odyssey*. In this section, we turn from thinking about Odysseus' raft and sailing as a literary and cultural metaphor in the *Odyssey* to look at the representations of the brave new worlds that Odysseus encounters on his overseas voyages. I began, in chapter 4, by asking why Phaeacia and the court of Alcinous are chosen as the narrative setting for Odysseus' famous travel tales. Why should Odysseus recount his travels at this point, at the site of his final adventure, rather than, as we might expect, after he has returned home? Perhaps more important, what does it mean for the poem's audience—both the Greeks and us—to be seated next to the king and queen of Phaeacia rather than beside Penelope and Telemachus in Ithaca as we listen to Odysseus' tales of bloodthirsty cannibals, seductive nymphs, and perilous dangers at sea? In the subsequent chapters I took up the pivotal role the Phaeacians play in two sets of oppositions that emerge from these tales. Together with the Phoenicians, the Phaeacians help sketch out the range of exchange possibilities operating in the world of the *Odyssey*. Paired with the Cyclopes, they articulate the hopes and fears of overseas settlement.

Now I want to take stock of the Phaeacians, themselves, to focus on their key role in defining what de Certeau has called the "hermeneutics of the other" at work in the *Odyssey*. How do we make sense of their pivotal role here as neither Phoenician traders nor Cyclopean cannibals? What does the complexity of the Phaeacian profile suggest about the relationship between trade and settlement? But even more important, what if we take the heterological logic that structures the world of the Phaeacians and extend it outside the poem? How do the Phaeacians help the Greek audience think about themselves as traders and colonists? When Odysseus crashes his metapoetic raft off the shores of Phaeacia, he enters a landscape that is both the product of a poet's imagination and one with poetic force of its own. The potential and promise of this Golden Age New World provides him with a magical setting for conjuring up tales of exotic travels and brave new worlds—tales that inevitably locate issues and concerns of the here-and-now in a world long ago and far away.

## The Double Phaeacians

In chapter 4 I used de Certeau's analysis of Jean de Léry's *Histoire d'un voyage faict en la terre du Brésil* as a model for thinking about the ethnographic structure of Odysseus' travels. Like that of Léry, the broad shape of Odysseus' journey is circular, starting from "over here," the familiar world of Ithaca, traveling to the exotic worlds of Lotus-Eaters, Cyclopes, Sirens, and Phaeacians "over there," and then returning back home again. Superimposed over this circular journey, however, is a triangular framework that first separates the world "over there" into two competing vistas (savage nature/Cyclopes and civil society/Phaeacians) and then connects both of them to Ithaca back home. The horizontal break that delimits the world at home from that abroad thus shifts to mark a distinction between nature and culture and to enable Odysseus' return from the world "over there" back to the one "over here." In this way, the division of alterity into a dangerous "nature" and an idealized "culture" provides a framework for renegotiating these aspects of the self at home, in Ithaca. At first glance this analysis may seem overly schematic or abstract. What do the *Odyssey* and a sixteenth-century ethnographic text have in common? What can Léry's approach tell us about a people living two millennia earlier? But now we can see that this ethnographic structure coincides with and reinforces one of the two significant oppositions at work in the *Odyssey*: that of the Phaeacians and the Cyclopes. In this respect we can begin to appreciate how the structure of the poem reveals the ethnographic imagination of early archaic Greece—how it articulates a sense of Greek identity through its relation with the other, whether that be with the past, the foreign, or the primitive.

With respect to overseas settlement, Odysseus' experience among the Phaeacians imagines the ideal colonial experience in every way: a successful expedition, a productive landscape, and peaceful relationships with native populations. The familiar institution of marriage is called on to conceptualize and naturalize something that is new and unfamiliar—the colonial encounter—and the story it tells is one in which the current inhabitants welcome the newly arrived colonists with generous hospitality into their city and their families. According to this view, there is no violent confrontation, no danger, no risk involved in overseas settlement, only an image of a generous and welcoming landscape. Their violent relatives, the Cyclopes, however, provide an alternative colonial scenario, one that draws on a very different cultural institution: cannibalism. In stark contrast to his promising stay among the Phaeacians, Odysseus' encounter with the Cyclopes embodies the typical fears of overseas exploration: encounters with hostile native populations as well as the potentially uncivilizing effect that colonization may have on the Greek colonists. In addition, the familiar institutions of sea travel and hospitality operate as the focal points for this dynamic. Whereas the Phaeacians, famous for their magic ships and extravagant gifts, welcome Odysseus into a Golden Age world, the Cyclopean landscape remains hostile to strangers, its occupants ignorant of the tools and institutions of civilized life.

Read in a colonial context, then, the *Odyssey*'s well-known opposition between the world of the Phaeacians and that of the Cyclopes becomes richer and more substantive. The more thematically oriented analysis of other Homeric scholars now takes on the specificity and particularity of the Greek colonial encounter. Odysseus' experiences among the Phaeacians and the Cyclopes, juxtaposed as they are in the arrangement of the poem, combine to explore the tensions between utopian representations of the New World and those of a more primitive and violent landscape. Which best describes the Greek colonial experience? What kinds of peoples will Greeks encounter overseas? What kind of a reception can they expect?

At the same time, the Phaeacians and their ships occupy an equally optimistic position within yet another opposition—this time one that extends outside the world of Odysseus' travels and into the second half of the poem. The Phaeacians are a mythical people, the last people Odysseus encounters before returning home to the real world of Ithaca. The Phoenicians, by contrast, are a historical people who primarily appear in the second half of the *Odyssey* in the tales that Odysseus and Eumaeus tell each other after Odysseus returns. Nevertheless, these two peoples are clearly connected within the ethnographic imagination of the poem, and their oppositional dynamic maps out one way to link the "poetic" realm of Odysseus' travels with the "historical" setting of the second half of the poem. The magical world of Odysseus' travels helps imagine a productive response to the challenges posed by the historical world both within and outside the poem.

Taken together, the representations of the Phaeacians and the Phoenicians articulate a vision of the best and the worst of overseas trade, and the heterological logic that links these two peoples further clarifies the poem's interest in issues of value and exchange. The Phaeacians, on the one hand, represent an idealized model of exchange, a kind of one-sided version of gift exchange in which they give gifts without traveling to receive them in return. The Phoenicians, on the other hand, appear in the *Odyssey* as stererotypical examples of the greedy, profit-hungry traders whom the Phaeacians despise, and in this respect they occupy the other end of the exchange spectrum. They look only to profits and deceive their trading partners, moving from city to city, from port to port, embodying what the Greeks fear most about engaging in trade. Taken together, the Phaeacians and the Phoenicians sketch out the entire range of exchange possibilities in the *Odyssey*—from one-sided gift exchange to outright theft or piracy—leaving open for debate the contested status of commodity exchange. Particularly problematic are the context and goals of exchange. What does it mean for strangers to trade goods with one another instead of circulating goods within a closed aristocratic circle? What happens when profit is thrown into the picture? Most important, how does this system construe value? How much are things worth?

And so the Phaeacians, by virtue of their status as neither Phoenicians nor Cyclopes, help establish the range of possibilities available in the brave new worlds of overseas settlement and exchange. It is this heterological structure, de Certeau's "hermeneutics of the other," that helps define the outer limits, the extreme positions between which the Greeks must locate a productive future for themselves. The bimodal nature of the Phaeacians and their world provides an interpretive framework through which the Greek experience can be negotiatied, interpreted, imagined. Phaeacia is a fantasy world, a "poetic landscape" that serves as a productive site for the ethnographic imagination of early archaic Greece. But above all, it is the ideal place for telling stories. The fabulous palace of Alcinous, with its huge, well-lit hall, provides the perfect setting for song. This is the place where Demodocus entertains the Phaeacians night after night with his tales of the Trojan War, and of course this is the setting for Odysseus' own fabulous and ferocious tales. And finally, I want to suggest, Alcinous' palace is the site for another story as well, the story that the archaic Greeks tell themselves about themselves—a tale of overseas trade and settlement.[1]

## The Phaeacians: "Good to Think With"

This story starts from the Janus-like position of the Phaeacians, facing, as it were, in two different directions. One door opens west, into a contest with the Cyclopes for the definitive tale of New World settlement and exploration; the other opens east and, together with the Phoenicians, reveals a world of overseas trade and exchange. In both cases, the heterological logic of the Phaeacian discourse charts out the extreme positions, with Odysseus negotiating a productive path for the Greeks somewhere between the utopian vision of Phaeacia and the dangerous image of colonization and trade represented by the Cyclopes and the Phoenicians. But now I want to look further at Phaeacia itself and the ways in which de Certeau's "hermeneutics of the other" is at work in the poem, structuring its ethnographic imagination. The Phaeacians stand as the point of contrast for a series of oppositions, starting within the world "over there" (Cyclopes) and extending, first, into the "real world" of the second half of the poem (Phoenicians), and finally, I want to suggest, reaching beyond the boundaries of the poem itself into the audience.

My analysis of the Phaeacians shows that it is best to "think with" that which is different or far away, to seek meaning from a relationship with "the other," whether that be the Cyclopes or the Phoenicians.[2] And in Book 7, when Alcinous boasts to Odysseus about his excellent ships, we learn that there is nowhere farther from Phaeacia than Euboea:

" . . . οἱ δ᾽ ἑλόωσι γαλήνην, ὄφρ᾽ ἄν ἵκηαι
πατρίδα σὴν καὶ δῶμα, καὶ εἴ πού τοι φίλον ἐστίν,
εἴ περ καὶ μάλα πολλὸν ἑκαστέρω ἔστ᾽ Εὐβοίης,
τήν περ τηλοτάτω φάσ᾽ ἔμμεναι οἵ μιν ἴδοντο
λαῶν ἡμετέρων, ὅτε τε ξανθὸν Ῥαδάμανθυν
ἦγον ἐποψόμενον Τιτυόν, Γαιήιον υἱόν.
καὶ μὲν οἱ ἔνθ᾽ ἦλθον, καὶ ἄτερ καμάτοιο τέλεσσαν
ἤματι τῷ αὐτῷ καὶ ἀπήνυσαν οἴκαδ᾽ ὀπίσσω.
εἰδήσεις δὲ καὶ αὐτὸς ἐνὶ φρεσὶν ὅσσον ἄρισται
νῆες ἐμαὶ καὶ κοῦροι ἀναρρίπτειν ἅλα πηδῷ."

... and they will travel the calm sea so that you will arrive at your fatherland and your home, and if there is anything else dear to you, even if it is much farther than Euboea, which they say is the farthest place from here, those of our people who have seen it, when they led golden Radamanthys to see Tityus, son of Gaia. And they went there and they accomplished the journey without toil and returned home again on the very same day. You, yourself, will see (and know) in your own mind how my ships are the best as are the men who stir up the sea with their oars. (Od. 7.319–28)

As far as Alcinous knows, the farthest distance from Phaeacia is Euboea, and he promises Odysseus safe passage home even if he lives still farther away, since his ships and their crew are the best. Alcinous' remark about the geographic distance between the Phaeacians and the Euboeans points provocatively outside the boundaries of the poem and into the world of a people at the forefront of matters of trade, settlement, and poetry in the early archaic world. And in so doing, it suggests an important connection between the Phaeacians who live within the borders of the *Odyssey* and the Euboeans who inhabit the world outside the poem.

## The Euboeans

Archeological evidence suggests that a broadly based, well-connected society was thriving in Euboea at the dawn of the first millennium and continued through to the end of the eighth century.[3] The settlement at Lefkandi prospered from 1000 to about 850 or 825 B.C.E., with the cities of Chalcis and Eretria rising to prominence in the eighth century. Burial grounds at Lefkandi from the tenth to the ninth centuries, including the famous warrior's tomb at Toumba, are exceptionally rich, especially in imports from Egypt, Cyprus, the Levant, Thessaly, and Attica.[4] Moreover, the Euboeans were a people skilled and knowledgeable in matters of shipbuilding and sailing. Although a well-built ship decorating a mid-ninth-century local pyxis that was found in the prosperous Euboean town of Lefkandi does not prove nautical expertise, it does suggest, perhaps, a culture familiar with overseas travel.[5] The Euboean reputation for seafaring appears in myth and literature as well. Several family members of the Euboean hero Palamedes have nautical names that recall those in the catalogue of Phaeacian proper names in *Odyssey* 8: Palamedes' brother is called Οἴαξ (Tiller); his father is Ναύπλιος (Shipman), son of Κλυτόνηος (Famed-for-ships), grandson of Ναύβολος (Ship-launcher).[6] In addition, the Homeric Hymn to Apollo characterizes the land of Euboea as "famed for its ships" (ναυσικλειτῆς Εὐβοίης, 219).

Their maritime skill put the Euboeans in the company of Phoenicians, who were also sailing, settling, and trading throughout the Mediterranean at this time. Euboeans visited eastern ports, such as Tyre, perhaps carrying iron or oil, and returned with manufactured goods. Merchants from the Levant sailed west bringing luxury goods, such as ivory and gold, and craftsmen who eventually settled and worked in Greece.[7] It was these same Euboeans who led Greek colonial activity in the west in the eighth century, motivated in part by pressures at home and in part by the lure of land and metals abroad.[8] Phoenicians, too, were engaged in colonial activity in the west at this time, although the nature of their colonies appears to have been oriented more toward trade and less concerned than the Greeks were with establishing colonies as independent cities.[9] Thus, in their colonial activity as well as commercial endeavors, Euboeans would have come in contact with Phoenicians eager to establish their own settlements in the western Mediterranean.

Although our archeological sources are fairly meager, scholars have speculated about the nature of Greco-Phoenician commercial and colonial activity.

How much contact, competition, and collaboration took place between the two peoples? David Ridgway proposes a scenario that emphasizes a great deal of cooperation and contact between Euboeans and Phoenicians. He suggests that the smaller-scale Euboean commercial activity met up with a larger, pan-Mediterranean Phoenician system and that the Euboeans inserted themselves into this preexisting Phoenician network.[10] When, in the eighth century, the Euboeans started looking to the west as a new source of metals, Ridgway proposes that it was the Phoenicians who set them in that direction both in search of new metals and for settlement purposes, arguing that the most important commodity that the Euboeans got in the east was information about the west.[11] Although John Boardman is skeptical about assuming that Phoenicia led the Greeks to the west, he too argues for a model of collaboration and coexistence between the Euboeans and Levantines in matters of colonization and trade.[12]

No matter what the exact nature of the relationship between Euboeans and Phoenicians, it is clear that there was contact between these two peoples, especially at several key geographic sites of convergence. The strategic location of the islands of Cyprus, Crete, and Sardinia helps explain their important role in Greco-Phoenician commerce. The trading post of Al Mina, established at the end of the ninth century, may have had Euboean merchants in residence from the beginning, although they formed just a small part of an essentially non-Greek population.[13] Similarly, at the other end of the Mediterranean, the early Greek trading colony of Pithecoussae (ca. 770) had a small Levantine population, and archeological evidence shows that in the mixed community of Pithecoussae, Greeks, Phoenicians, and Italians all lived and worked together.[14] Whatever the nature of its foundation, the archeological evidence for burial rites in this early Euboean colony reveals a city with a significant level of social organization.[15] In addition, the range of ceramic material found suggests a complex network of contact with the outside world, and two remarkable pottery finds bring the world of Homer into this early western colony.[16] First, the so-called Nestor's Cup is inscribed in the alphabet of Eubeoan Chalcis with three lines of verse that allude to the Homeric hero Nestor, famous king of Pylos.[17] Second, a locally painted Late Geometric krater was found bearing a shipwreck scene that evokes the fears of many a Homeric hero returning home from Troy.[18] Together, these finds suggest that the settlement's inhabitants included skilled craftsmen and those familiar with the Homeric poetic tradition in some form or other.[19]

In fact, the Euboeans are implicated in the early production of Homeric epic as much as they are in commercial and colonial developments of the time. In an article that traces the development of Homeric epic as a genre, M. L. West suggests that we look to Euboea and not Asia Minor as the place where epic language and genre took its definitive shape.[20] West identifies several stages in the development of epic: Indo-European praise poetry, early Mycenean epic, late Mycenean and Aeolic epic, and finally Ionian epic. His linguistic analysis shows that the final and formative Ionic phase uses a Central or West Ionic dialect, not, as many have assumed, an Eastern Ionic dialect.[21]

In addition to this linguistic argument, there are signs of a thematic Near Eastern influence on the Homeric poems, and again Euboea is the place where Near Eastern mythological poetry comes in contact with Greek poetry from the tenth to the eighth centuries. The extremely prosperous and progressive status of Euboea at this time, together with its extensive commercial contacts, confirms West's linguistic argument and points to Euboea as the area in which Homeric epic achieved its definitive and normative form. Some have suggested that the wealth of the area would have attracted wandering bards.[22] West hypothesizes that the anonymous king who was celebrated with the massive "heroic" burial at Toumba in Lefkandi might have sought out a bard to commemorate his achievements in song as well.[23] He goes on to suggest that much like Phoenician goldsmiths and other skilled craftsmen, poets educated in the Levant became Hellenized and came to practice their literary skills in Greece, bringing with them themes and images from the east.[24]

Masters of trade, a leading colonial power, and implicated in the production and consumption of epic poetry—these are the Euboeans who live so very far away from the Phaeacians, a distance nevertheless that Phaeacian ships can cover and return in just one day. Alcinous' remark about the extreme geographic distance between Phaeacia and Euboea brings the heterological structure of Odysseus' travel tales to bear on the overseas colonial and trade expeditions of early archaic Greece. In other words, I want to suggest that we now think about the poetic Phaeacians with all their "hermeneutic otherness" (i.e., as neither Phoenician nor Cyclopes) together with the historical Euboeans who traveled and traded, and produced and consumed the *Odyssey*. By this I do not mean to suggest, as others have, that the Phaeacians are the mythic counterparts of the Euboeans in that they offer a kind of idealized portrait of Euboean life.[25] Rather, in light of the prominent role that the Euboeans play in commercial, colonial, and poetic activity in the archaic period, the Janus-like Phaeacians are good for the Euboeans to "think with." In other words, they function as a means of expression, a model of cultural self-scrutiny. They help the Greeks tell themselves a story about themselves.[26]

Certainly our understanding of the ethnographic potential of Phaeacia helps us read the representation of commerce and colonization in the *Odyssey* against the "real" world of contact, competition, and collaboration between Greek and Levantine merchant and colonial powers. While it cannot tell us details of individual trade negotiations between Greek and Phoenician merchants or provide us with a map of colonial settlements, what does emerge from the Phaeacian story is a strong pattern of convergence—of east and west, of Phoenicians and Euboeans, of trade and settlement, of epic and history (or perhaps better, the mythic expression of the past and the lived experience of the present). The layout of Phaeacia, as we have seen, looks somewhat like that of an early Greek colony in the west, and yet Alcinous' palace draws on the wealth of the Near East (both economic and mythic) for its elaborate construction. In this respect, the complexity of the Phaeacian topography reflects the interconnectedness of the commercial and colonial networks in which both Euboeans and Phoenicians participated. It emphasizes the strong ties between east and west, the interdependence of colonization and trade, the well-established contacts between Greece and the Near East. Moreover, it suggests that we stop trying to choose between competing monolithic motivations—between land or trade as the reason for Greek colonization, between Greeks or Phoenicians as the predominant force in colonial and trade networks, and so on.

At the same time, Phaeacia is both famed for its hospitality (exemplified by Alcinous' generous treatment of Odysseus) and rumored to be a place quite hostile to strangers. This ambivalence about the reception of strangers together with the role that hospitality plays in structuring the rules of their reception is linked to the Phaeacians' relationship with their cannibal cousins the Cyclopes and issues of colonial-indigenous contact. In addition, this picture suggests, first, that hybrid communities were common in the archaic period on both sides of the Mediterranean, and second, that relations between Greek colonists and other peoples (whether native occupants or other foreign inhabitants, such as craftsmen or traders) were complicated—sometimes mutually satisfactory and productive, sometimes hostile and threatening.[27] The multicultural communities at Al Mina and Pithecussae offer examples of the kind of world we see refracted (not reflected) through the representation of the Phaeacians in the *Odyssey*.

And so the Phaeacians offer the Euboeans a model to think with—a model of a world of cross-cultural contact, of overseas travel and trade, of movement, change, and innovation. Theirs is an idealized version of that world, to be sure, one in which east and west, trade and settlement converge productively, and where potential colonists are either welcomed into the family or generously showered with gifts and sent on their way. But lurking at the edges of this idealized version, represented by the Phaeacians' heterological relationship with the deceitful Phoenicians and the savage Cyclopes, other models of the New World are to be found—worlds of greedy traders and monstrous cannibals. New World issues combine with traditional mythic themes to create a vision of the present steeped in the past, or a view of the past informed by the present. Taken in all their complexity and ambivalence, the Phaeacians represent both the product and the process of the ethnographic imagination of a world very much involved in overseas travel, trade, and settlement—the world of early archaic Greece.

### Two Shipwrecks

We started our exploration of the brave new worlds of the *Odyssey* with a pair of shipwrecks—with the opening shipwreck of Shakespeare's *Tempest* and a dis-

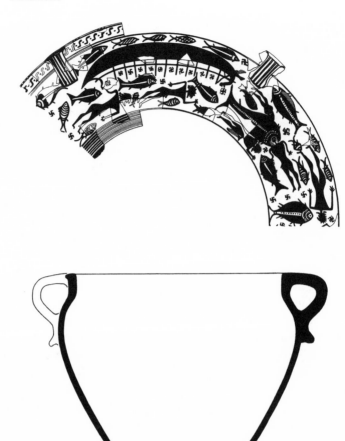

Pithecoussai shipwreck. Late geometric krater. Drawing from *Pithekoussai I*, in *Monumenti Antichi*, serie monographica, vol. 4 (Rome 1993), table 231.

cussion of how this play helps us think about Odysseus'own raft breaking up on the shores of Phaeacia. As in *The Tempest*, the destruction of Odysseus' metapoetic raft creates the opportunity for telling stories while it selects Phaeacia as the site of their production. In concluding this section, then, I want to turn to two more shipwrecks—one painted on a pot found at Pithecoussae and the other marking the end of the Phaeacian story.

As I mentioned earlier, the excavations at Pithecoussae have revealed, among other things, a locally painted Late Geometric krater with a strikingly graphic representation of a shipwreck (see illustration).[28] The front of the bowl is dominated by the image of a capsized ship, a horizontal outrigger with a steering oar, prow, and stern. Surrounding the ship are twenty-four fish with various kinds of decoration and six human figures, all nude. One man seems to be gripping the horn of the prow; another swims under the ship, and the head of a third is entirely engulfed in the mouth of a fish. The ship itself looks Corinthian, the type of vessel probably used by Euboeans in the eighth century, and suggests that the Euboeans may have taken advantage of a *diolkos*, or canal, to the Corinthian Gulf to provide easier access to the west. Such a route would have helped the Euboeans avoid Cape Malea and the very dangers represented on this bowl.[29] It is hard not to read this scene together with similar scenes from epic poetry such as, to take just one example, Odysseus' description of his near-fatal shipwreck in Book 12:

ἡ δ᾽ ἐλελίχθη πᾶσα Διὸς πληγεῖσα κεραυνῷ,
ἐν δὲ θεείου πλῆτο· πέσον δ᾽ ἐκ νηὸς ἑταῖροι.
οἱ δὲ κορώνῃσιν ἴκελοι περὶ νῆα μέλαιναν
κύμασιν ἐμφορέοντο, θεὸς δ᾽ ἀποαίνυτο νόστον.
αὐτὰρ ἐγὼ διὰ νηὸς ἐφοίτων, ὄφρ᾽ ἀπὸ τοίχους
λῦσε κλύδων τρόπιος· τὴν δὲ ψιλὴν φέρε κῦμα.
ἐκ δέ οἱ ἱστὸν ἄραξε ποτὶ τρόπιν· αὐτὰρ ἐπ᾽ αὐτῷ
ἐπίτονος βέβλητο, βοὸς ῥινοῖο τετευχώς.
τῷ ῥ᾽ ἄμφω συνέεργον ὁμοῦ τρόπιν ἠδὲ καὶ ἱστόν,
ἑζόμενος δ᾽ ἐπὶ τοῖς φερόμην ὀλοοῖς ἀνέμοισιν.

And the whole ship was struck by the lightning of Zeus and twirled around and it was filled with sulfur, and my companions were thrown from the ships. Like sea crows they were carried by the waves around the black ship, and the god took away their day of return. But I wandered through the ship to where the high seas had freed the walls from the keel, and the surf bore the bare keel. And it broke the mast toward the keel. But fastened upon it was the backstay of the mast, fashioned of ox hide. With this I lashed together the keel and the mast, and sitting upon them, I was borne by the terrible winds. (*Od.* 12.416–25)

Indeed, some scholars have suggested a direct link between passages like this one from the *Odyssey* and the narrative scene painted on the Pithecoussae krater, although it is unlikely that one directly illustrates the other, and would be difficult to prove.[30] Other scholars reject the notion that the Pithecoussae krater illustrates epic themes, reminding us that the painter may have been memorializing the unfortunate experience of Greek sailors in the western Mediterranean. As John Boardman puts it, "There *are* sharks in the Mediterranean."[31] Still others take a position in between these two extremes. In an article discussing the realia of legendary scenes that appear in Greek art, in particular the archer in Scythian garb often found on Attic Late Archaic vases, Gloria Pinney argues that the scene "belongs neither wholly to history nor to fancy, but is a hybrid creature whose nature and looks partake of both."[32] In much the same way, the shipwreck scene on the Pithecoussae bowl, like that from the *Odyssey*, brings the all too real fears of colonists and merchants sailing treacherous seas together with the famous experiences of epic heroes returning home from war.

It is this latter "hybrid" view that I share in offering this Late Geometric krater as an emblem of the themes of convergence made possible by the sailing (and wrecking) of Euboean ships, both real and imaginary. The Euboeans, "famous for their ships," conducted a thriving trade with the east, successfully settled new territory in the west, composed and listened to epic poetry, and lived and worked in hybrid communities in productive cultural and economic exchange. And in this context, from the ethnographic imagination of poems such as the *Odyssey* emerge another people, equally famous for their nautical expertise: the mythical Phaeacians, who help the Greeks tell a story about themselves to themselves, a story that addresses and accommodates some of the instability and flux of the early archaic period. Their magical ships that "know the thoughts and minds of men as well as the cities and fertile fields of all men" (ἴσασι νοήματα καὶ φρένας ἀνδρῶν, / καὶ πάντων ἴσασι πόλιας καὶ πίονας ἀγροὺς / ἀνθρώπων, 8.559–61) are the key to the richness and productivity of the Phaeacian model. They are the embodiment of the ethnographic imagination: the connection between travel and narrative, the potential for overseas trade and settlement, and all the possibilities of the brave new worlds of early archaic Greece. It is in fact the traveling potential of these magic ships that incurs the anger of Poseidon, god of the sea. So now we turn to our final shipwreck of sorts—the fulfillment of Poseidon's prophecy to the Phaeacians.

At the end of Book 8, right before Odysseus identifies himself and begins the tale of his adventures, Alcinous tells Odysseus that his magic ships will be sure to convey him home safely, and his characterization at this point of his ships as wise and well traveled provides the perfect introduction to the previously anonymous Odysseus, who, as we know from the opening lines of the poem, has also traveled a great deal and seen the minds and cities of men. In other words, the ethnographic power of these ships, waiting to take him home, launches Odysseus' own tale of travel and knowledge.

Once he has promised Odysseus safe passage home, Alcinous recalls his father's prediction that the ability of these ships to convey all men successfully across the sea would some day incur the anger of Poseidon:

φῆ ποτὲ Φαιήκων ἀνδρῶν εὐεργέα νῆα
ἐκ πομπῆς ἀνιοῦσαν ἐν ἠεροειδέι πόντῳ
ῥαίσεσθαι, μέγα δ᾽ ἧμιν ὄρος πόλει ἀμφικαλύψειν.

He said that one day he would strike a well-worked ship of Phaeacian men as it returned from a journey upon the misty sea, and that he would cover over our city with a great mountain. (*Od.* 8.567–69)

The well-built ship of the Phaeacians will one day be destroyed on its return voyage. Mention of the skillful construction (εὐεργέα) of the ship and its imminent destruction reminds us of the metapoetic potential of Odysseus' raft and suggests that again we think about ships and song together here. For this is the passage that introduces Odysseus' own tale of travel and adventure. In spite of this premonition of the end of their sea prowess, Alcinous promises Odysseus safe passage home and asks in return for his story, which, as we know, makes up the whole of the next three books of the poem. Odysseus proceeds to sing the song of his travels, and once he has finished to everyone's satisfaction, Alcinous and Arete prepare to send him home.

Nausithous' prophecy about the destruction of the Phaeacian ship does indeed come true in Book 13 at the end of Odysseus' song once the Phaeacians have successfully delivered Odysseus back home to Ithaca.[33] Poseidon is furious that his own relatives, the Phaeacians, have dishonored him and helped Odysseus return home safely with numberless gifts, more than he would have brought home from Troy. He tells Zeus that (just as Nausithous predicted) he wants to strike the Phaeacian ship as it returns from Ithaca and hide the city under a mountain. Zeus, however, has another idea; he warns against hiding the city under a mountain and suggests instead that Poseidon turn the Phaeacian ship into stone for people to wonder at:

ὦ πέπον, ὡς μὲν ἐμῷ θυμῷ δοκεῖ εἶναι ἄριστα·
ὁππότε κεν δὴ πάντες ἐλαυνομένην προΐδωνται
λαοὶ ἀπὸ πτόλιος, θεῖναι λίθον ἐγγύθι γαίης
νηὶ θοῇ ἴκελον, ἵνα θαυμάζωσιν ἅπαντες
ἄνθρωποι, μηδέ σφιν ὄρος πόλει ἀμφικαλύψαι.

> Dear brother, this is what seems best to my mind: when all the people from the city are watching the ship as it returns, turn it to stone, like a swift ship nearby the shore, so that all men will marvel at it. Do not cover over their city with a mountain. (Od. 13.154–58)

The difference between Poseidon's plan and Zeus' proposal is significant. Whereas Poseidon wanted to destroy the ship and hide the city, Zeus imagines a future for the Phaeacians as a kind of nautical monument—a stone that is like a swift ship—that freezes (or friezes) in a kind of tension of opposites the characteristic speed and mobility of these magical ships.[34] The implausibility of this calcified swift ship will then serve as a source of marvel and wonder for all men. We are reminded of Odysseus' experience at the beginning of Book 7, when he first encounters the walls and harbors of Phaeacia. Marvels, so typical of the ethnographic narrative, thus frame Odysseus' stay at Phaeacia and the stories of his travels.

And so, obeying his brother, Poseidon goes to Scheria to punish the Phaeacians and to put an end to their ability to ferry people across the seas:

βῆ ῥ᾽ ἴμεν ἐς Σχερίην, ὅθι Φαίηκες γεγάασιν.
ἔνθ᾽ ἔμεν· ἡ δὲ μάλα σχεδὸν ἤλυθε ποντοπόρος νηῦς
ῥίμφα διωκομένη· τῆς δὲ σχεδὸν ἦλθ᾽ ἐνοσίχθων,
ὅς μιν λᾶαν θῆκε καὶ ἐρρίζωσεν ἔνερθε
χειρὶ καταπρηνεῖ ἐλάσας· ὁ δὲ νόσφι βεβήκει.

He went to Scheria, where the Phaeacians live, and there he waited. And the seagoing ship came in close, traveling lightly, and the earthshaker approached it and he turned it to stone and rooted in beneath, striking it with a flat hand. And then he went way. (*Od.* 13.160–64)

A wooden ship is turned to stone, and within this passage the strong sense of movement (βῆ ῥ᾽ ἴμεν; ἤλυθε; διωκομένη; ἦλθ᾽) is replaced by an image of rootedness (ἐρρίζωσεν). The ship's capacity for sailing the seas (ποντοπόρος) is once and for all curtailed.

Watching from the city, the Phaeacian people are puzzled to see their ship stop dead in the water, but once Alcinous explains the prophecy, they agree to leave off conveying people across the sea and offer a sacrifice to Poseidon. After this is done, the story shifts in the middle of a line in a remarkable transition—like the ships themselves, as swift as thought—from the Phaeacian men standing around the altar on Scheria to Odysseus awakening from sleep in Ithaca (13.187).

And so, with this shipwreck of sorts, we abruptly leave the fantasy world of Odysseus' travels and the idealized site of their narration to arrive home at the "real" world of Ithaca. The mobility of the Phaeacian ships, along with that of Odysseus and his stories, is curtailed once the ship is turned to stone and rooted in the ground. Odysseus arrived at the island of the Phaeacians on a metapoetic raft whose construction mirrors that of oral poetry and whose cargo capacity and mobility represent issues about the value and authority of song. He leaves the island on a mode of sea transport that participates equally in the intersection of sailing and song: at its moment of destruction, the Phaeacian ship is famous for its ability to travel (ποντοπόρος); it boasts a skillful manner of construction (εὐεργέα); and above all, it knows the minds and cities of men. Just as the breakup of Odysseus' raft selects the Phaeacians as the ideal audience for his travel tales, the calcification of their ship after his return home marks both the end of his travel narrative and its monumentalization as a permanent source of wonder for all men.

The Phaeacians make an offering to appease Poseidon just at the moment when Odysseus awakens, surrounded by his gifts, on the shores of his native Ithaca. And seen from within the poem's ethnographic imagination, the remarkable synchronicity of Poseidon's calcification of the Phaeacian ship and Odysseus' return home signals the obsolescence of the discursive model of the Phaeacians. The utopian Phaeacian vision of overseas exchange and settlement, taken together with the gritty picture of Phoenician piracy and Cyclopean can-

nibalism, has served its purpose in helping imagine the brave new world of archaic Greece. Now, however, after exploring the range of experiences within the
worlds of overseas trade and settlement, Odysseus, with his successful voyage
home, renders the world of the Phaeacians no longer necessary. No longer necessary, that is, to "think with," and so the Phaeacians remain forever cut off from
the rest of the story, far away from Euboea, frozen in an ideal world, a source of
wonder for all who sail by.

And Odysseus is home at last. In returning from the world "over there,"
Odysseus must now shift the focus of his ethnographic gaze onto the world "over
here," to make use of all the profit that he, more than anyone else, was able to
bring home from abroad. Symbolized by the vast piles of cargo that Odysseus
successfully brought home from his travels, the knowledge, insight, and interpretive framework he gained from "thinking with" the Phaeacians must now be
brought to bear on the world he finds at home.[35] What will Ithaca look like after all these years? How will Odysseus' experiences abroad reconfigure his understanding of home? What will the "hermeneutics of the other" have to say
about the self?

## III    Home at Last

# 8

# Odysseus Returned
# and Ithaca Re-founded

The Odysseus of the *Odyssey* justifies himself by his success as
the refounder of his own house; he is ruthless, practical, inven-
tive, self-seeking, and utterly committed to a few close loyalties.
Such a man would surely have found ample play for his talents
in the first great age of Greek entrepreneurial expansion, which
was also the moment of the composition of the *Odyssey*.

James Redfield, "The Economic Man"

---

Home at last. After ten long years of battle at Troy and still ten more at sea,
Odysseus has returned home at last. In his travels he has encountered seductive
nymphs, cannibal monsters, destructive whirlpools, and Golden Age landscapes.
He has gone to Hades and returned, survived the song of the Sirens, and rejected
offers of immortality. He has built a raft and lost it. And after all these travels,
all these experiences, all this suffering, he has now come home; in fact, his travels are precisely what has enabled Odysseus to return home successfully. Like the
Swiss missionary-ethnographer, Jean de Léry, Odysseus has managed a return to
the self—to his Greek self—through his travels among the other. In other words,
he helps forge a new sense of Greek identity out of his experiences among the
peoples and places overseas.

In the first section of this book we looked at the ways in which Odysseus'
raft operates as a vehicle for articulating the poem's ethnographic imagination.
The raft, with its careful construction, its cargo-carrying capacity, and its ability
to travel, serves as an emblem of the inextricable interconnection in the *Odyssey*
of narrative, travel, and trade. It both represents the potential of the ethnographic imagination and transports Odysseus to the site of his New World tales.
The second section then turned its focus to these brave new worlds, and in particular to the land of the Phaeacians. With a landscape that belongs in part to
traditions of the Golden Age and in part to narratives of the New World, Phaeacia offers an ideal site for the ethnographic imagination. In addition, the Phaea-

cians, themselves located discursively somewhere between the Phoenicians and the Cyclopes and opposed to each, articulate a heterological discourse which suggests that we think about the Greeks themselves in these terms.

The logic of the ethnographic narrative explores the world overseas as a way to understand better the world at home. Now, in this last section, it is time to focus on issues of return. In an interesting way, the extended travel tale that Odysseus tells to the Phaeacians prior to arriving back at Ithaca is precisely what enables his return back home. The structure of Odysseus' narrative provides him (and us) with a framework for interpreting his return, and its ethnographic imagination helps formulate a new world for Ithaca and a new role for its king. Familar themes from his encounters among the Phaeacians and the Cyclopes reappear in the second half of the poem to characterize Odysseus' revenge against the suitors and his reunion with Penelope in terms of overseas settlement. In this chapter I focus on the way the relationship between his travels and home recasts Odysseus' return to Ithaca as a kind of colonial foundation. Moreover, Odysseus returned is not the same Odysseus who set out from Ithaca twenty years earlier. As a result of his travels and adventures, Odysseus himself comes to represent a new heroic model for the archaic period. Together with his role as poet, trader, and traveler, Odysseus' position as colonial founder articulates a heroic model that emphasizes change and innovation rather than preserving the status quo. In the conclusion I will return to Odysseus' raft to highlight its reincarnation at the end of the poem in the form of Odysseus' and Penelope's marriage bed. The mobility and overseas potential of the raft is replaced by the rootedness and domesticity of the bed and thus both signals the end of the story and offers a model for the domestication of the ethnographic imagination.

## The New World of Ithaca

As I suggested in chapter 6, Odysseus' travels take him to the new worlds of colonial exploration and settlement. Although he never actually founds a colony in his travels, Odysseus sails far and wide; he discovers new places and meets new peoples, and his encounters with the Phaeacians and the Cyclopes employ prominent motifs and strategies of colonial discourse to imagine the best and the worst models of the colonial encounter. It is not until he returns home to Ithaca, however, that the colonial potential of Odysseus' travels and experience is fully realized. In landing on unfamiliar shores, killing the threatening male suitors who occupy his land, and eventually (re)marrying Penelope, the local queen, he essentially re-founds Ithaca. By drawing so closely from his "colonial" experiences among the Cyclopes and Phaeacians, Odysseus transforms mythic prewar Ithaca and resettles it in the New World of archaic Greece.

When Odysseus finally arrives back "home" at Ithaca in Book 13, it is as if he were landing once again on unfamiliar and unknown shores. In fact, his arrival is prefaced by the kind of ethnographic description that opens some of Odysseus' encounters abroad as well.[1] The poet describes in some detail Ithaca's harbor, ideal for sheltering ships, as well as the cave of the Nymphs, with its shrine full of offerings, as if this island, too, were new territory to Odysseus. In fact, Athena has altered the landscape to become unrecognizable to Odysseus, and in so doing she has transformed it into an "other" land (ἀλλοειδέ, 13.194).[2] In response, Odysseus slaps his thighs in frustration and exclaims:

> ὤ μοι ἐγώ, τέων αὖτε βροτῶν ἐς γαῖαν ἱκάνω:
> ἦ ῥ᾽ οἵ γ᾽ ὑβρισταί τε καὶ ἄγριοι οὐδὲ δίκαιοι,
> ἦε φιλόξεινοι καί σφιν νόος ἐστὶ θεουδής:

> Oh, my, I have come to the land of what sort of men now? Are they savage and wild and unjust, or are they kind to strangers and respectful of the gods? (*Od.* 13.200–203)

In speculating about the kinds of peoples who inhabit this new land—are they civilized or savage?—Odysseus poses the same rhetorical question that he asks of himself upon landing at Phaeacia and among the Cyclopes.[3] Ithaca, too, is a strange new place and represents all the potential benefits and dangers of the New World.

In fact, when Athena, disguised as a young herdsman, describes the Ithacan landscape to a befuddled and frustrated Odysseus, she makes the topography sound very much like a combination of the land of the Cyclopes and the ideal colonial island nearby:

> ἦ τοι μὲν τρηχεῖα καὶ οὐχ ἱππήλατός ἐστιν,
> οὐδὲ λίην λυπρή, ἀτὰρ οὐδ᾽ εὐρεῖα τέτυκται.
> ἐν μὲν γάρ οἱ σῖτος ἀθέσφατος, ἐν δέ τε οἶνος
> γίγνεται· αἰεὶ δ᾽ ὄμβρος ἔχει τεθαλυῖά τ᾽ ἐέρση·
> αἰγίβοτος δ᾽ ἀγαθὴ καὶ βούβοτος· ἔστι μὲν ὕλη
> παντοίη, ἐν δ᾽ ἀρδμοὶ ἐπηετανοὶ παρέασι.

> Indeed it is a rough country and not good for raising horses; nor is it exceedingly worthless although it has not been fashioned a broad land. For there is unlimited grain here, and grapes for wine grow, and there is continous rainfall and copious dew. And it is a good land for raising goats and cattle. There are woods everywhere, and watering places are present year round. (*Od.* 13.242–47)

Athena's mention of the unlimited grain (σῖτος ἀθέσφατος) on Ithaca recalls the wheat and barley (πυροὶ καὶ κριθαί, 9.110) that grow freely in the land of the Cyclopes. The grapes, here watered by rainstorms and copious dew, evoke a similar collocation in Book 9 where the grapes bear full-bodied wine, watered by the storms of Zeus (οἶνον ἐριστάφυλον, καί σφιν Διὸς ὄμβρος ἀέξει, 9.111). At the same time, Athena's description of Ithaca reminds us of the island opposite the land of the Cyclopes. Both are populated by goats and trees, and enjoy plentiful water.[4] The Ithaca that Odysseus encounters at the beginning of Book 13, then, takes on many of the characteristics of the new worlds of his travels—an unfamiliar landscape that holds the promise of either bountiful generosity or hostile dangers.

### Ithaca's Hostile Inhabitants: The Suitors

In fact, Odysseus' arrival at Ithaca mimics his colonial experience among the Cyclopes in more ways than the landscape. In addition, in both locales he confronts the threat posed by the current inhabitants. Although Odysseus does not meet up with literal cannibals in Ithaca, as he did among the Cyclopes and the Laestrygonians, he does face the greedy suitors who are eating him out of house and home, and the poem takes great pains to link the transgressive behavior of the suitors to that of the Cyclops.[5] The Cyclopes are characterized as arrogant men (ἀνδρῶν ὑπερηνορεόντων, 6.5) as well as reckless and lawless (ὑπερφιάλων ἀθεμίστων, 9.106), and all three of these adjectives are regularly used over the course of the poem to represent the suitors as well. In Book 4 Penelope fears that her son has been killed by the reckless suitors (μνηστῆρσιν ὑπεφιάλοισι, 4.790), and in Book 17 Athena contrives that Odysseus should know exactly how lawless (ἀθέμιστοι, 363) these men have been in his absence.[6] In Book 14 Eumaeus sadly explains to the disguised Odysseus the current state of affairs in Ithaca:

> οἵδε δέ τοι ἴσασι, θεοῦ δέ τιν' ἔκλυον αὐδήν,
> κείνου λυγρὸν ὄλεθρον, ὅ τ' οὐκ ἐθέλουσι δικαίως
> μνᾶσθαι οὐδὲ νέεσθαι ἐπὶ σφέτερ', ἀλλὰ ἔκηλοι
> κτήματα δαρδάπτουσιν ὑπέρβιον, οὐδ' ἔπι φειδώ.
> ὅσσαι γὰρ νύκτες τε καὶ ἡμέραι ἐκ Διός εἰσιν,
> οὔ ποθ' ἓν ἱρεύσουσ ἱερήιον, οὐδὲ δύ' οἴω·
> οἶνον δὲ φθινύθουσιν ὑπέρβιον ἐξαφύοντες.

The suitors here know about the terrible destruction of that man; they heard some divine rumor, and they refuse to woo [Penelope] justly or to return to their own homes, but untroubled, they devour his possessions recklessly and there is no holding back. For on as many as are the nights and days from Zeus, they sacrifice not one victim, nor two alone, and they recklessly draw the wine and waste it away. (*Od.* 4.89–95)

The suitors' refusal to obey the rules of justice (δίκη), together with their violent (ὑπέρβιον) actions, locates their behavior outside the bounds of that of civilized men and in league with that of Hesiod's cannibalistic animals for whom violence (βίη) rules in place of justice.[7] Indeed, in their recklessly devouring (δαρδάπ-τουσιν ὑπέρβιον) the possessions of Odysseus, sparing nothing, the suitors' actions recall the all too graphic image of Polyphemus eating two of Odysseus' men raw, like a mountain lion (ὥς τε λέων ὀρεσίτροφος, 9.292). The choice of verb (δαρδάπτουσιν) here evokes images of flesh-eating wild animals, while the reckless and violent (ὑπέρβιον) nature of their behavior strongly recalls the equally transgressive behavior of the Cyclops.[8]

Penelope and Telemachus also use the image of eating to characterize the suitors' monstrous and greedy behavior. Penelope chastises the suitors in a speech to Eurymachus: they dishonor her noble husband by consuming his household (οἶκον ἀτιμάζοντες ἔδουσιν / ἀνδρὸς ἀριστῆος, 21.332–33). Telemachus, too, complains about the suitors' appetite for his own livelihood: they "eat up my household and destroy it" (τοὶ δὲ φθινύθουσιν ἔδοντες οἶκον ἐμόν, 1.250–1 = 16.127–28).[9] The combined force of this imagery takes Ithaca out of the world of civilized men and locates it, in Odysseus' absence, in a primitive landscape of savage cannibals. Our sense of the transgressive nature of the suitors' actions is confirmed by the gruesome terms in which their final feast is described:

οἱ δ' ἤδη γναθμοῖσι γελώων ἀλλοτρίοισιν,
αἱμοφόρυκτα δὲ δὴ κρέα ἤσθιον· ὄσσε δ' ἄρα σφέων
δακρυόφιν πίμπλαντο, γόον δ' ὠΐετο θυμός.

And they laughed with jaws that were not their own, and they ate meat that was sated with blood; their eyes filled with tears and their hearts imagined a lament. (*Od.* 20.347–49)

By this point the suitors have lost all their humanity—they eat raw and bloody meat with the jaws of animals (γναθμοῖσι), jaws that do not belong to them (ἀλλοτρίοισιν). They have crossed over into the primitive world of beasts. In this respect, the suitors' act of consuming the livelihood of Odysseus and his family echoes the tale of the Cyclops' transgressive hunger from Odysseus' travels, and so demands an equal, if not more devastating, act of revenge.

As we have seen in chapter 6, the threat to Odysseus posed by the Cyclops—and so by analogy by the suitors at Ithaca—is cast in colonial terms. Savage, cannibalistic monsters are what the settler, crossing the seas to new lands, can expect to find threatening the colonial project. There is a certain logic, then, to the fact that the colonist's (here Odysseus') tools of revenge against the indigenous cannibal are the very nautical skills and tools that enable him to cross the sea to setttle new lands in the first place. Odysseus' act of violence against Polyphemus in Book 9—piercing his eyeball with a sharp stick and twisting it—depends on his skills at shipmaking. Polyphemus' walking stick, the one that Odysseus uses to blind him, is as big as the mast of a cargo ship (319), and the act of blinding itself is compared to a shipwright drilling a plank (384). The ability to sail is part of what distinguishes the colonist from the native inhabitant, as we learned from the description of the ideal colonial island opposite the Cyclopes in Book 9, and so nautical skill comes to represent the triumph of civilization over nature, that of the colonist over native inhabitants.[10]

This framework, then, explains why parts of a ship's tackle or construction play a key role in Odysseus' revenge against the suitors as well. In preparation for the contest that ostensibly will determine which of the suitors Penelope will marry but in fact initiates their slaughter, Penelope says that she will lay out the axe handles in a row like timbers to hold a ship:

> νῦν γὰρ καταθήσω ἄεθλον,
> τοὺς πελέκεας, τοὺς κεῖνος ἐνὶ μεγάροισιν ἑοῖσιν
> ἵστασχ᾽ ἑξείης, δρυόχους ὥς, δώδεκα πάντας.

For I will now establish a contest, the axes which he used to set up in order in his palace, like a ship's trestle, all twelve of them. (*Od.* 19.572–74)

The very scaffolding of Odysseus' revenge is thus described as a trestle that supports a ship. In addition, right before Odysseus strings the bow and the massacre begins, Philoetus secures the doors with the cable of a ship:

> Σιγῇ δ᾽ ἐξ οἴκοιο Φιλοίτιος ἆλτο θύραζε,
> κλήϊσεν δ᾽ ἄρ᾽ ἔπειτα θύρας ἐϋερκέος αὐλῆς.
> κεῖτο δ᾽ ὑπ᾽ αἰθούσῃ ὅπλον νεὸς ἀμφιελίσσης
> βύβλινον, ᾧ ῥ᾽ ἐπέδησε θύρας, ἐς δ᾽ ἤϊεν αὐτός.

Silently, Philoetus leapt out of the house into the courtyard, and he then closed the doors of the well-made courtyard. A cable from a well-balanced ship, made of papyrus, lay under the portico; with this he fastened the doors and he went in. (*Od.* 21.388–91)[11]

A similar ship's cable (πεῖσμα νεὸς κυανοπρῴοιο) is used to string up the unfaithful serving girls as well (22.465).[12] Thus the very mechanics of Odysseus' revenge against both the Cyclops and the suitors depend on his nautical skill. In both cases the violence that is part of the colonial project is represented as revenge against greedy, transgressive monsters, and in both cases the tools of this violence are nautical. Part of the process of settlement, of the movement from the sea to new land, involves a kind of technology transfer. Tools of the sea are reconfigured as those of colonization, the very means of violence against hostile native inhabitants.

And so, like a colonial founder arriving on unfamiliar shores, Odysseus encounters and must conquer at Ithaca the current inhabitants, here represented as transgressively greedy suitors who devour his household. The poet goes to great lengths to draw analogies between the behavior of the Cyclops and that of the suitors: both devour what they should not; both are excessive and hybristic; and, through the allusions to nautical technology, both receive their respective and appropriate punishments. In the explicitly colonial context of the Cyclops episode, the appearance of cannibals both designates the hostile native inhabitants and legitimates their destruction. Cannibals function rhetorically as a marker of the violence of colonial settlement. Once the *Odyssey* assimilates the suitors' greed to the cannibal behavior of Polyphemus, it projects this colonial framework onto the slaughter of the suitors at Ithaca. By so doing, it recasts the problematic violence of Odysseus' revenge as a positive act of foundation.

Odysseus' slaughter of the suitors is a particularly bloody one, and the poem refuses to let us overlook the extent of this violence or to condone it completely.[13] Odysseus, after all, cuts down an entire generation of young men of Ithaca in cold blood. Penelope's dream of the predatory eagle who swoops down and kills her tame and harmless geese (a dream that itself signals Odysseus' imminent destruction of the suitors) casts Odysseus' wholesale slaughter in seriously questionable light.[14] Once the battle is over, the floor smokes with blood (22.308); Odysseus himself is described as a bloodthirsty lion, covered with gore and battle filth (22.401–6), and the house must be purified of the blood spilt on its floors (22.437ff., 480). After the slaughter, Odysseus orders Telemachus to ask Phemius to strike up a festive dance tune so that any neighbors passing by would think that a wedding was taking place and to prevent them from finding out about the slaughter until he can make a plan. Odysseus' decision to disguise the destruction as a wedding celebration leads quickly and inexorably to his remarriage to Penelope.[15] Moreover, this grim wedding song attempts to disguise the act of brutal violence just committed as something rather more civilized, as the union of man and wife, and in so doing it also helps characterize the reunion of Penelope and Odysseus as a kind of marriage—a colonial marriage.[16]

### A Colonial (Re)Marriage: Odysseus and Penelope

Just as the Cyclops episode prefigures the theme of colonial violence in Odysseus' return, the epithalamial aspects of Odysseus' stay among the Phaeacians, his potential marriage to Nausicaa, set the scene for reading an alternative set of colonial elements at work in characterizing Odysseus' return to Ithaca. Scholars have shown how the possibility of marriage between Nausicaa and Odysseus in Book 6 foreshadows and prefigures the eventual remarriage of Penelope and Odysseus at the end of the poem.[17] The connection between the two episodes is crystallized, finally, in the simile that the poet uses to describe the beautification of Odysseus in Book 23. After sending Telemachus off to arrange for the wedding music, Odysseus retires to the bath, and when he emerges, Athena pours great beauty over him as a skilled goldsmith pours gold over silver:

αὐτὰρ κὰκ κεφαλῆς χεῦεν πολὺ κάλλος Ἀθήνη
μείζονά τ' εἰσιδέειν καὶ πάσσονα· κὰδ δὲ κάρητος
οὔλας ἧκε κόμας, ὑακινθίνῳ ἄνθει ὁμοίας.
ὡς δ' ὅτε τις χρυσὸν περιχεύεται ἀργύρῳ ἀνὴρ
ἴδρις, ὃν Ἥφαιστος δέδαεν καὶ Παλλὰς Ἀθήνη
τέχνην παντοίην—χαρίεντα δὲ ἔργα τελείει—
ὣς μὲν τῷ περίχευε χάριν κεφαλῇ τε καὶ ὤμοις.
ἐκ δ' ἀσαμίνθου βῆ δέμας ἀθανάτοισιν ὁμοῖος.

At once Athena poured much beauty over his head to make him taller
and broader to look upon. She draped curly locks on his head, like the
hyacinth's blossom. As when a skilled craftsman pours gold upon silver, one whom Hephaestus and Pallas Athena have taught every skill
and he accomplishes pleasing work, so Athena poured grace upon his
head and shoulders. And he stepped out of the bath with the body of
the gods. (*Od.* 23.156–63)

This is the same simile used in Book 6 to describe Odysseus as he emerged from
the bath to be admired and courted by Nausicaa; its significant reappearance
here in Book 23 deliberately invokes the possibility of Odysseus' marriage to
Nausicaa to characterize the imminent remarriage of Odysseus to Penelope as itself "colonial."[18] Again, the colonial rhetoric that was laid out explicitly in Odysseus' encounter with Nausicaa—a colonist from overseas is given a local princess
in marriage, together with control of her land—is called into play to describe his
reunion with Penelope as something similar. I have already discussed, in chapter
6, how the wedding theme in Book 6 participates in a larger strategy of colonial
discourse that attempts to naturalize and domesticate the wild forces inherent in
founding a colony just as a husband tames his wife through the institution of
marriage. In Ithaca as well, marriage to Penelope entails control of the land, as
the suitors know all too well, and casting the reunion of Penelope and Odysseus
as a colonial marriage provides a productive, and much less violent, vision of
Odysseus' return to power, one that both complements and counters the wholesale slaughter of the greedy suitors.

In her groundbreaking essay on "reverse-similes" in the *Odyssey,* Helene
Foley suggests that Odysseus' recovery of his marriage and his family are "symbolic of a wider restoration of his kingdom on the same pattern"; marriage is
used "to express a larger range of hierarchical relations between 'strangers.'"[19]
Along these lines, the male-female relationship between Odysseus and Penelope
symbolizes the larger social dynamics of Ithacan society. We can now elaborate
on that formulation by recognizing how the institution of marriage is used in
colonial discourse of the archaic period to represent overseas settlement as a
process of civilization and naturalization. Marriage imagery describes the colonial experience as a peaceful, productive union of the world abroad (the colonist)
and that at home (native populations). In drawing on this colonial rhetorical

strategy to tell Odysseus' story of travel and return, the *Odyssey* suggests a similarly productive and transformative integration of its hero's overseas experiences into his world at home.

### Ithaca Re-founded: From New Worlds and the Golden Age to the Colonial Age

And so in stark contrast to the episode with the Laestrygonians, the colonial themes of cannibalism and marriage that govern Odysseus' antithetical encounters among the Cyclopes and the Phaeacians are combined and finally realized in his return home in a productive way—in the destruction of the greedy and transgressive suitors and his reunion with Penelope. The slaughter of the suitors, prefigured by Odysseus' blinding of the cannibal Polyphemus, acknowledges and attempts to legitimate the violent component of any act of foundation, while the epithalamial overtone to Odysseus and Penelope's reunion, foreshadowed by Odysseus' erotically charged encounter with Nausicaa, attempts to rewrite that violence as a productive and peaceful act of civilization. The combined force of both these colonial strategies serves to recast the problematic aspects of Odysseus' return and revenge in a similarly positive and productive light. By this I do not mean to say that Odysseus literally re-founds Ithaca; rather, the themes and issues of colonial discourse articulate the terms of his return to represent it as a kind of re-foundation.[20] In this way, the *Odyssey* reverses the more typical formulation whereby colonial foundations are represented as the returns, the *nostoi*, of Trojan War heroes.[21] Instead of an explicitly colonial expedition being characterized as the inevitable and rightful return of Greeks to the land they have always inhabited, here Odysseus' fabled return home is recast in a new light—as a colonial foundation with all the potential for and promise of a new city.[22]

In other words, Odysseus metaphorically re-founds Ithaca, and the fertile connections between this re-foundation and scenes from his encounters at Phaeacia and in the land of the Cyclopes imbue this new foundation with some of the productive qualities of the New World and the Golden Age. The opening description of Ithaca's landscape reminded us of the colonial potential of the Cyclopes' land and island. The account of Laertes' orchard given in Book 24, however, paints a slightly different picture of Ithaca's post-foundation landscape, one that recalls the Golden Age orchard of Alcinous as suggestive of the productivity of the colonial landscape in actual practice.

Even after the slaughter of the suitors and the reunion with his wife, Odysseus' status as re-founder of his home is not yet fully achieved. He must still consolidate his new foundation—ward off possible retaliation—and part of the way he achieves this is expressed through his control of the landscape. He goes to visit his father, Laertes, who has moved from the palace to live on a farm outside the city. As proof of his identity, Odysseus lists all the trees in the orchard (ὄρχατος) that Laertes planted for him when he was a child:

εἰ δ' ἄγε τοι καὶ δένδρε' εὐκτιμένην κατ' ἀλωὴν
εἴπω, ἅ μοί ποτ' ἔδωκας, ἐγὼ δ' ᾔτεόν σε ἕκαστα
παιδνὸς ἐών, κατὰ κῆπον ἐπισπόμενος· διὰ δ' αὐτῶν
ἱκνεύμεσθα, σὺ δ' ὠνόμασας καὶ ἔειπες ἕκαστα.
ὄγχνας μοι δῶκας τρισκαίδεκα καὶ δέκα μηλέας,
συκέας τεσσαράκοντ'· ὄρχους δέ μοι ὧδ' ὀνόμηνας
δώσειν πεντήκοντα, διατρύγιος δὲ ἕκαστος
ἦν· ἔνθα δ' ἀνὰ σταφυλαὶ παντοῖαι ἔασιν,
ὁππότε δὴ Διὸς ὧραι ἐπιβρίσειαν ὕπερθεν.

Come and I will tell you about the trees in the well laid out orchard, which you gave me once, and I used to ask you about each one when I was a child, following you throughout the garden. We walked among them, and you named and told me about each one. You gave me thirteen pear trees and ten apple trees, and forty fig trees, and you named the fifty rows of vines you would give me, and each one was never-failing. And there were all sorts of grapes upon them whenever the seasons of Zeus weighed them down from above. (*Od.* 24.336–44)

On the one hand, this scene of father-son recognition enacts the long-delayed but inevitable transfer of power and assets from the father to the son. Odysseus itemizes the family's holdings, emphasizing the peaceful nature of this transfer of power by his reiteration of the verb "to give" (δῶκας; δώσειν). While the counting and naming that form the heart of this scene reveals Odysseus' true identity to his father, they also provide an inventory of his inheritance which announces him as ready to reclaim it after his lengthy absence. But at the same time, this scene is imbued with colonial overtones that characterize this traditional father-son transfer of power as something different, something much more transformative.

Odysseus offers to list the trees planted in the well laid out (εὐκτιμένην) orchard. His choice of adjective here is one often used to describe a city that has been well founded; in fact, it is the same adjective used in Book 9 to describe the colonial potential of the island opposite the Cyclopes (νῆσον εὐκτιμένην).[23] The colonial tone of this passage is further established by Odysseus' repeated mention of naming (ὠνόμασας; ὀνόμηνας), an act that belongs to the colonial founder. Finally, the elaborate list of trees—pears, apples, and figs—together with the mention of grape clusters is a sign of a productive landscape, one that reminds us of the orchard of Alcinous on the island of the Phaeacians:

ἔκτοσθεν δ' αὐλῆς μέγας ὄρχατος ἄγχι θυράων
τετράγυος· περὶ δ' ἕρκος ἐλήλαται ἀμφοτέρωθεν.

ἔνθα δὲ δένδρεα μακρὰ πεφύκασι τηλεθόωντα,
ὄγχναι καὶ ῥοιαὶ καὶ μηλέαι ἀγλαόκαρποι
συκέαι τε γλυκεραὶ καὶ ἐλαῖαι τηλεθόωσαι.
τάων οὔ ποτε καρπὸς ἀπόλλυται οὐδ᾽ ἀπολείπει
χείματος οὐδὲ θέρευς, ἐπετήσιος· ἀλλὰ μάλ᾽ αἰεὶ
Ζεφυρίη πνείουσα τὰ μὲν φύει, ἄλλα δὲ πέσσει.
ὄγχνη ἐπ᾽ ὄγχνῃ γηράσκει, μῆλον δ᾽ ἐπὶ μήλῳ,
αὐτὰρ ἐπὶ σταφυλῇ σταφυλή, σῦκον δ᾽ ἐπὶ σύκῳ.

Outside the courtyard there was a great orchard, near the gates, four
measures of land, and a fence was driven all around it. There great blossoming trees are growing, pears and pomegranate and glorious-fruited
apple trees and sweet figs and blossoming olive trees. Never does the
fruit of these trees rot nor does it ever run out, neither in winter nor
summer, but is year-long; and the ever-blowing West Wind starts some
growing and ripens others. Pear grows upon pear, apple upon apple,
grape upon grape, and fig upon fig. (*Od.* 7.112–21)

Both orchards include a number of different kinds of fruit trees together with
vineyards, and in each the fruit is plentiful and unceasing. In his speech to his father, Odysseus thus invokes the Golden Age image of Alcinous' ever fruitful and
productive orchard and plants it here in Ithaca. Alcinous' garden was, as we saw,
paradigmatic of the productivity and potential of a successful, well-established
colonial settlement. By invoking this image at the moment when he reveals himself as Odysseus to his father, he shows himself to be not just his father's son,
prepared to inherit and preserve his patrimony, but also Ithaca's colonial founder,
ready and able to resettle his patrimony in a new world.

There is, of course, an important difference here between the orchards of
Alcinous and Laertes, one that marks a key distinction between the idealized image of the Golden Age and the real experience of the colonial era, and that is the
presence of work in Ithaca.[24] Whereas in Alcinous' orchard the fruit appears to
bloom and prosper on its own, in Laertes' garden there has been need of work.
Indeed, when Odysseus comes upon his father, he finds him alone in the well laid
out orchard (ἐυκτιμένῃ ἐν ἀλωῇ, 24.226), digging around a plant (λιστρεύοντα
φυτόν, 24.227), and Odysseus praises Laertes for the care of his orchard:

ὦ γέρον, οὐκ ἀδαημονίη σ᾽ ἔχει ἀμφιπολεύειν
ὄρχατον, ἀλλ᾽ εὖ τοι κομιδὴ ἔχει, οὐδέ τι πάμπαν,
οὐ φυτόν, οὐ συκῆ, οὐκ ἄμπελος, οὐ μὲν ἐλαίη,
οὐκ ὄγχνη, οὐ πρασιή τοι ἄνευ κομιδῆς κατὰ κῆπον.

Old man, you have no lack of experience in tending your orchard, but
it is well cared for. There is no plant, no fig, no grape, no olive, no pear,
no bed of leeks without care throughout the garden. (*Od.* 24.244–47)

Thus it has been hard work and care that has caused this orchard to flourish, and in this respect it locates the re-foundation of Ithaca in the age of colonization, not the Golden Age, although it appears to be nearly as fruitful (πολυκάρπου ἀλωῆς, 24.221).[25]

In other words, the scene between Laertes and Odysseus helps establish the ways in which colonial discourse draws on both the New World and the Golden Age to imagine the colonial landscape, all the while emphasizing the very important differences between the potential, the ideal, and the actualized colonial experience. When Odysseus first arrives on Ithaca, it looks like the Cyclopes' primitive landscape—in other words, it has the potential to make a good colonial site. After he has "re-founded" it, however, it takes on some of the characteristics of Alcinous' ideal colonial foundation—a productive and ever fertile landscape. And finally, through his reunion with this father, Odysseus reclaims his patrimony and establishes it as an archaic colonial site marked by agricultural labor. Thus Odysseus' re-foundation transforms Ithaca's landscape from a potential or ideal colonial site, as articulated through his experiences in his travels, to a fully realized one suitable for the real world of archaic Greece. Ithaca's postcolonial landscape, as represented by Laertes' garden, is productive and fertile, but this productivity is achieved through hard work and human toil rather than by magic or the intervention of the gods.

## Teiresias' Prophecy: From Land to Sea

A productive colonial experience can be characterized as one that has successfully made the transition from sailing to agriculture. In this respect, our reading of the colonial themes governing Odysseus' return and his reunion with Laertes is confirmed by Teiresias' prophecy of Odysseus' final journey. For like a colonial expedition, Odysseus' final journey will be one that moves from the sea to the land, one that represents the transition from travel and discovery of new territory to its settlement and domestication.

When Odysseus meets Teiresias in the Underworld, the famed prophet gives him the information he needs to arrive home safely. He also offers the prophecy of yet another journey: once Odysseus has successfully killed the suitors in his halls, he must take up a well-made oar (εὐῆρες ἐρετμόν, 11.121) and travel until he meets people who do not know the sea (οὐ ἴσασι θάλασσαν, 11.122) or red-prowed ships (νέας φοινικοπαρῄους, 11.124) or broad oars (εὐήρε᾽ ἐρετμά, 11.125). When he meets another traveler who mistakes his oar for a winnowing fan (ὁππότε κεν δή τοι ξυμβλήμενος ἄλλος ὁδίτης / φήῃ ἀθηρηλοιγὸν ἔχειν ἀνὰ φαιδίμῳ ὤμῳ, 11.127–28), he must plant the oar in the ground and offer sacrifices to the gods, especially Poseidon. Once he does this, a harmless death will come to him away from the sea (ἐξ ἁλός, 11.1.34), and his people will prosper.[26]

As so often with Greek oracular discourse, there is more than one way to read this prophecy: either the tale tells of the conversion from the sea to the land (the oar becomes a winnowing fan), or it represents the expansion of the sea into the land (the oar is taken to a people unfamiliar with it and inaugurates a religious celebration of the sea).[27] Either way, it captures the relationship between the sea and the land that is so fundamental to the *Odyssey*, and so here I think we can have it both ways at once.[28] On one level, in bringing the sea to the land, Teiresias' prophecy offers the necessary closure to the Odysseus story; it reconciles the poem's two primary antagonists and restores the proper sense of order to the Homeric world.[29] After all, "those who do not know the sea or ships" are, in fact, the Cyclopes of Book 9, and with this allusion, the passage brings us back to the scene of the Odysseus' original transgression against the son of Poseidon. Polyphemus learns all too quickly about ships once Odysseus brings the mast of his cargo ship to bear upon his eye, and as a result, Odysseus must now make a propitious offering to the god Poseidon, acting as a kind of religious envoy, bringing the cult of Poseidon and tools of the sea to other peoples who are unaware of him and his powers. This expansionist reading takes the sea to those who do not know it. A tale of travel and encounter, it celebrates both the raw elemental power of the sea (Poseidon) and the sophisticated tools of civilization that have enabled mankind to tame, if not conquer, it.

At the same time, however—and this is where the prophecy confirms the colonial themes of Odysseus' return—Teiresias predicts the transformation of Odysseus' nautical experiences into those of the land. When Odysseus plants his oar in the ground, he evokes the burial of Elpenor, a sailor who no longer has need of his oar, and the action, like the calcification of the Phaeacian ship, signifies the oar's obsolescence.[30] Reminiscent of the Yukon traveler who never wants to shovel another bit of snow, Odysseus' actions mark the end of his overseas travels and signal a future life of agriculture and plentitude. He will die a peaceful death as a "settled king" in his old age, far from the sea, rather than that of "an unlucky hero or wanderer."[31] As Charles Segal has observed, Teiresias' prophecy forms part of a much larger pattern of movement or escape from the sea that is at work in the *Odyssey*.[32] Two similes compare Odysseus and Penelope to shipwrecked sailors, thereby describing Odysseus' return to Ithaca as a kind of rescue from the dangers of the sea: the sight of welcome land to the waterlogged sailor.[33] Similarly, right before Odysseus is to be transported home by the Phaeacians, his keenness to leave is compared to a farmer's eagerness for dinner after a long day of plowing the fields.[34] Odysseus' first action after realizing that he has returned to Ithaca is to kiss the grain-giving earth.[35] And, in Book 19, Odysseus greets Penelope by comparing her to a king whose fertile fields yield barley and wheat and whose trees are heavy with fruit.[36] In other words, images of the land and its produce form a recurrent motif in the second half of the *Odyssey*, replacing the poem's fascination with travel and the sea with the potential and promise of the earth.

Within this larger context, then, Teiresias' prophecy offers an emblem of the colonial experience, charting its movement from the sea to the land, from the tools of sailing to those of agriculture, just as new colonists must abandon their sailing skills once they have established a settlement and take up agricultural tasks in order that the new colony prosper.[37] The colonial experience does, after all, entail a shift from the experience of sailing to one of agriculture, a transition that is captured by the emphasis on the land and its topography that is found in some colonial tales.[38] No matter what the original motivation for settlement, in order for a colony to make the successful transition from initial settlement to established city, its people must plant, grow, and harvest their own food.[39] I noted earlier that Odysseus' nautical tools are converted into the instruments of his revenge against the suitors and suggested that this "technology transfer" was emblematic of the colonial process. Now we can refine this observation a bit. While the initial conversion of nautical tools into instruments of revenge reflects the violence that often accompanies the first phase of colonial settlement (a ship's cable helps strangle traitorous serving girls; a ship's trestle enables Odysseus' slaughter of the suitors), the subsequent transformation of nautical technology into the tools necessary to work the land and maintain the colony represents the agricultural nature of most early Greek colonies (an oar becomes a winnowing fan).

And so Teiresias' prophecy pushes the colonial imagery that governs Odysseus' return beyond the boundaries of the poem to imagine a future for Odysseus and for Greece in the New World.[40] Odysseus has rid the country of its savage inhabitants, and by marrying the local queen, he brings a civilized structure to the land. And so, in his return to his native Ithaca, the wily and much-traveled Odysseus comes to represent important aspects of the colonial founder familiar to his archaic Greek audience.[41] As Peter Rose has observed, "Odysseus' heroic characteristics, his psychological profile, and his cultural role evoke the energetic and aggressive elements in the late eighth-century Greek society—elements that were the force behind the extraordinary burst of colonization into the western Mediterranean, northern Aegean, and Black seas."[42] Odysseus' return is not a return to the same world he left behind; his is not a story of conservation. Rather, Odysseus draws on his experiences in the New World, his encounters with cannibal monsters and welcoming princesses, to bring part of that world back home, to go beyond the restoration of his kingdom as it was—to give it a new start in a new age. It is the ethnographic imagination embodied in Odysseus' travels that makes this transformation possible, that enables the re-foundation of Ithaca. This same imaginative power transforms the Greek notion of heroism as well to conform to the changed circumstances of a new age; it establishes Odysseus as a new heroic model for the archaic period.

### Odysseus: Culture Hero for a New Age

In his travels, Odysseus encounters new worlds and new peoples, some welcoming and generous, others hostile and dangerous, and at every encounter he stops to wonder what kinds of people he will meet. Are they pious and just, or are they unjust and violent? Part of what distinguishes Odysseus from other mythic travelers in the Greek tradition is both this curiosity about the new worlds he visits and his narrative skill at transforming his experiences overseas into elaborate and elegant song. In this respect, Odysseus not only experiences the New World, but also is the one who interprets those experiences and brings them back to those at home. As we have seen, Odysseus' role as traveling poet acknowledges the contingency and mobility of poetic truth; it signals the elusive truth values of the ethnographic narrative as well. His is a narrative about the other—about cannibals, Golden Age landscapes, and women who turn men into swine. Moreover, like those of more traditional ethnographers, Odysseus' stories find meaning for the Greek self in this world of strangeness and alterity. The *Odyssey* imagines a place for Greeks overseas, it speculates about new means of exchange and value, and above all, it celebrates the power and potential of narrative to articulate these new ways of life in a world of upheaval and change.

Odysseus' role as re-founder of his native Ithaca is thus part of the bigger picture in which he represents a new kind of hero for a culture in transition. Many scholars have remarked on the paradigmatic status of Odysseus as epic hero. [43] His travels—the knowledge he gains, the risks he runs, the losses he endures—and his successful return home have come to represent, as one critic put it, "a return to humanity in the broadest sense."[44] This archetypal man, however, as Simon Goldhill has pointed out, is not Everyman; he has a distinct set of qualities—qualities that have made his return possible.[45] Odysseus, for example, is no Achilles; his fame depends less on his martial escapades and physical prowess than on his cleverness and skill. [46] When he finally identifies himself to Alcinous at the beginning of Book 9, Odysseus boasts that he excels all men in trickery (δόλοι, 9.19–20), not force. Above all he is *polutropos*—a man of many ways—and the proliferation of resonances in this epithet is emblematic of the multiplicity inherent in Odysseus' nature.[47] He has traveled a great deal; there are many turns and twists to his mind. His legendary survival skills are due in large part to his willingness to adapt and endure, even to suffer anonymity if necessary. Unlike Achilles or Ajax—literal casualties of the Trojan War and its aftermath—Odysseus survives, and the *Odyssey* tells the story of his survival.[48]

In this respect, Odysseus represents a new kind of Greek epic hero—a trickster, a man of *metis*, a man of many-ness—and scholars have remarked on the ways in which the *Odyssey* appears to compete with or respond to the *Iliad* with an epic vision of its own.[49] But the dimensions of Odysseus' role as new epic hero extend beyond issues of literary genre and characterization and into the changing and innovative world of archaic Greece.[50] In representing the spirit of the colonial age, as well as developments in trade and in the production and circulation of poetry, Odysseus is a new hero for a new age—the archaic period— and the story of his many adventures and ultimate survival offers a new heroic model for a culture similarly riding the wave of innovation and change.[51] Instead of a hero who stands and fights to the death to defend his established way of life, Odysseus represents the potential of travel—both its opportunities and its risks. He helps open up the world across the sea to those Greeks at home. As colonist he negotiates a place for Greeks in the New World, and as trader he establishes networks of profitable contact and exchange. Finally, as poet Odysseus brings these foreign experiences home, and through his tales, he helps the Greeks imagine a New World at home in the Old World.

# Conclusion: From Raft to Bed

οὕτω τοι τόδε σῆμα πιφαύσκομαι· οὐδέ τι οἶδα,
ἤ μοι ἔτ᾽ ἔμπεδον ἐστι, γύναι, λέχος, ἦέ τις ἤδη
ἀνδρῶν ἄλλοσε θῆκε, ταμὼν ὕπο πυθμέν᾽ ἐλαίης.

In this way, I reveal this sign, but I do not know, woman, if my bed is still secure, or whether some man has already moved it elsewhere, cutting down the olive tree at its stump.

*Odyssey*, Book 23

---

Odysseus' successful return home and his re-foundation of Ithaca mark the conclusion of his travels, and, as a result, the end of his movement as hero of the *Odyssey*. In the previous chapter, we have seen how his shift from a life on the move at sea to a more sedentary existence at home is prefigured by the transformation of his nautical tackle first into tools of revenge against the suitors and then into tools of agriculture, emblematic of a settled, colonial life. Now, in this conclusion, I want to look at a parallel phenomenon: the reconfiguration of Odysseus' mobile raft into his famous marriage bed, rooted in the ground. Once he has successfully arrived home, Odysseus' sailing days, symbolic of the complicated nature of his identity as poet, merchant, and traveler, as well as of the mobility of his song, are left behind; instead, the focus of the narrative turns to his reintegration into life at Ithaca both in political terms, as king, and in personal terms, as husband and father. Whereas a detailed account of the making of Odysseus' raft introduces his story and his role as narrator in Book 5, now the description of his bed's construction in Book 23 gives us a signal that the story of his travels is coming to an end. The account both confirms his complex identity as a new cultural hero of the archaic age and, perhaps more important, offers a second model for rooting Odysseus' ethnographic experiences abroad in his life at home.

## The Marriage Bed: Constructing Odysseus' Identity

After the slaughter of the suitors and the purification of Odysseus' house, the scene is finally set for the reunion of Penelope and Odysseus. Both Penelope's nurse and her son urge her to acknowledge her long-lost husband's return and to welcome him back into their home and lives, but Penelope remains aloof and skeptical. Odysseus himself is willing to let his wife take her time, to allow her to discover her own signs of his identity. He remains patient and calm, that is, until she asks the nurse, Eurycleia, to move their marriage bed outside for him. At this point, Odysseus speaks out in anger, revealing at once both the secret of their bed and his own true identity. There is a special feature of this bed, which Odysseus made himself—it is rooted in the ground and cannot be moved—and as proof of his proprietary knowledge of this bed, Odysseus describes the manner of its construction:

θάμνος ἔφυ τανύφυλλος ἐλαίης ἔρκεος ἐντός,
ἀκμηνὸς θαλέθων· πάχετος δ᾽ ἦν ἠΰτε κίων.
τῷ δ᾽ ἐγὼ ἀμφιβαλὼν θάλαμον δέμον, ὄφρ᾽ ἐτέλεσσα,
πυκνῇσιν λιθάδεσσι, καὶ εὖ καθύπερθεν ἔρεψα,
κολλητὰς δ᾽ ἐπέθηκα θύρας, πυκινῶς ἀραρυίας.
καὶ τότ᾽ ἔπειτ᾽ ἀπέκοψα κόμην τανυφύλλου ἐλαίης,
κορμὸν δ᾽ ἐκ ῥίζης προταμὼν ἀμφέξεσα χαλκῷ
εὖ καὶ ἐπισταμένως, καὶ ἐπὶ στάθμην ἴθυνα,
ἑρμῖν᾽ ἀσκήσας, τέτρηνα δὲ πάντα τερέτρῳ.
ἐκ δὲ τοῦ ἀρχόμενος λέχος ἔξεον, ὄφρ᾽ ἐτέλεσσα,
δαιδάλλων χρυσῷ τε καὶ ἀργύρῳ ἠδ᾽ ἐλέφαντι·
ἐν δ᾽ ἐτάνυσσ᾽ ἱμάντα βοὸς φοίνικι φαεινόν.
οὕτω τοι τόδε σῆμα πιφαύσκομαι· οὐδέ τι οἶδα,
ἤ μοι ἔτ᾽ ἔμπεδόν ἐστι, γύναι, λέχος, ἦέ τις ἤδη
ἀνδρῶν ἄλλοσε θῆκε, ταμὼν ὕπο πυθμέν᾽ ἐλαίης.

A long-leafed olive tree grew outside the courtyard, flourishing, and it was like a column in thickness. And I built our bedroom around it until I finished it with closely set stones, and I roofed it well from above. I placed overlapping doors, fitted closely. And then I cut away the foliage from the long-leafed olive, and I trimmed the trunk from the roots, planing it with bronze well and skillfully, and I made it straight to a chalk line, fashioning bedposts, and I drilled them all with an awl. Beginning with this I worked until I finished it, decorating it with gold and silver and ivory. And I stretched the hide of an ox, shining with purple, across it. In this way, I reveal this sign, but I do not know, woman, if my bed is still secure, or whether some man has already moved it elsewhere, cutting down the olive tree at its stump. (*Od.* 23.190–204)

With this bravura account of how he built their marriage bed, Odysseus thus reveals himself as his wife's husband, the only other person who knew of the bed's unique qualities, and the scene is set for his reunion with Penelope and the long-delayed reintegration of their home. Upon closer inspection, however, something more is at work in this speech as well.

Odysseus' description dwells on the details of the bed's construction. In fashioning their bed around a live olive tree, Odysseus employed the same wood-working skills that helped him build the raft to leave Calypso's island. Odysseus explains how he trimmed the tree trunk with the bronze (χαλκῷ; he did it skillfully (εὖ καὶ ἐπισταμένως), made it straight to a chalk line (ἐπὶ στάθμην ἴθυνα), and bored holes into the bedposts with an auger (τέτρηνα δὲ πάντα τερέτρῳ). In so doing, he recalls a similar process that is repeated later (although told earlier) when he built his raft:

εἴκοσι δ᾽ ἔκβαλε πάντα, πελέκκησεν δ᾽ ἄρα χαλκῷ,
ξέσσε δ᾽ ἐπισταμένως καὶ ἐπὶ στάθμην ἴθυνεν.
τόφρα δ᾽ ἔνεικε τέρετρα Καλυψώ, δῖα θεάων·
τέτρηνεν δ᾽ ἄρα πάντα καὶ ἥρμοσεν ἀλλήλοισι,
γόμφοισιν δ᾽ ἄρα τήν γε καὶ ἁρμονίῃσιν ἄρασσεν.

He threw down twenty [trees] in all and trimmed them with his bronze axe; he planed them expertly, and made them straight to a chalk line. Then Calypso, the shining goddess, brought him an auger. He drilled them all and fitted them to one another, and with pegs and cords he hammered it together. (*Od.* 5.244–48)

Both the vocabulary and the skills are the same, and by reiterating the process of its construction, Odysseus both rescues and reconstructs his raft, the one that broke up prior to his arrival among the Phaeacians. But this time, instead of floating free on the open seas, the product of Odysseus' handiwork is rooted permanently in the ground. We will return to the manner of the bed's construction and its connection to the metapoetic aspects of Odysseus' raft, but first I want to focus on the significance of invoking the raft at this point in the narrative. What are the connections between Odysseus' raft and his marriage bed?

Clearly, the most distinctive aspect of this bed is its immobility. Scholars have remarked on the ways in which it functions as a figure for the institution of marriage—for its stability and for the fidelity of Penelope.[1] Froma Zeitlin notes that the fixed position of the bed in the house signals the permanence of marriage, while the secrecy about its unique manner of construction reflects the intimacy of man and wife.[2] Marilyn Katz argues that the "narrative of the bed and its construction, then, is a complex figuration for the moment in the poem when the marriage of Penelope and Odysseus is reconstituted."[3] The building of the bed-chamber around the bed which in turn is constructed around the olive tree emphasizes the privacy and sense of enclosed space shared exclusively by man and wife which marks the institution of marriage. In addition, the construction of the bed on a living tree reenacts the acculturation of nature that lies at the very heart of Greek marriage ideology: the taming of the wild natural element by the tools of civilization.[4]

But in addition to its role in symbolizing the stability of Penelope and Odysseus' marriage, this bed and the account of its construction recapitulate the complexity of Odysseus' identity.[5] Certainly, the narrative presents Odysseus as an artisan, and above all, it serves its purpose in reconstructing his identity as Penelope's husband.[6] But not only does the scene reinforce Odysseus' former role as Penelope's husband; it also reiterates aspects of his new identity as cultural hero of a new age. In a way typical of the complicated narrative movement of the *Odyssey*, Odysseus' account of building the marriage bed before he left for Troy provides a consolidation or reification of the skills that stem from his subsequent travels and experiences overseas.

First of all, as others have pointed out, through his account of the bed's origin, Odysseus identifies himself not in personal terms (I am your husband) but rather in terms of construction: I, and no one else, built this bed (τὸ δ' ἐγὼ κάμον οὐδέ τις ἄλλος, 23.189).[7] But more important, Odysseus alludes to the skill (ἐπισταμένως) with which he blinded the Cyclops (potential colonist), built the raft that enabled him to return home (sailor-poet), and strung the bow (archer-poet) that killed the suitors and restored his marriage. Thus, the experiences of the traveling Odysseus converge with those of the husband returned. The passage both provides a brief reprise of Odysseus' overseas adventures and begins to suggest a way to integrate those travel skills with his identity at home.

Second, the olive tree and the bed's elaborate metal decoration reinforce the analogies between Phaeacia and Ithaca that we explored in the previous chapter. Odysseus built his bedroom around a long-leaved olive tree (θάμνος ... τανύφυλλος ἐλαίης) that grows inside the courtyard, a tree with a very thick trunk, recalling the olive under which Odysseus made yet another bed, this one much less permanent, upon arriving on the shores of Scheria.[8] The bed's manner of decoration (δαιδάλλων χρυσῷ τε καὶ ἀργύρῳ ἠδ' ἐλέφαντι) evokes Phaeacia as well, in particular Alcinous' palace, a structure similarly adorned with precious metals (7.86–90) and resonant with the potential of the metals trade.[9] In this way, Odysseus' experiences in Phaeacia are given a place at the heart of his identity at home; both the rich lifestyle and the promise of trade, embodied in his Phaeacian experience, are here built into the centerpiece of his Ithacan life.

Finally, in stretching thongs of rawhide across the bed, Odysseus reenacts the stringing of the bow, his slaughter of the suitors, and the moment of his revelation as Odysseus to the suitors (21.407, 409). Thus Odysseus' recovery of his bed signals much more than the fidelity of his wife and the sanctity of his marriage; in addition, it embodies the skills and experiences that have brought him back to Ithaca. It makes a place for those skills; it roots them in his life at home.

In addition to revealing the long-lost Odysseus as Penelope's authentic husband, the manner of the bed's construction evokes Odysseus' raft with all its ethnographic associations and adds new dimensions to Odysseus' identity at this point in the poem. It integrates the qualities and insights gained from his travels into the Greek experience at home.

### From Raft to Bed: The End of the Story

At the same time, the construction of Odysseus and Penelope's marriage bed, as described in Book 23, offers an emblem of the story of the *Odyssey*, a story that was once mobile, like Odysseus' raft, but which now, in coming to a close, has taken root. The account of the construction of Odysseus' raft, in Book 5, highlights the woodworking techniques of a good fit (ἁρμονία): sanding the planks and fitting the boards together tightly to keep out the water. In addition, the passage underscores the construction process through the repetition of words for "making" (ποιέω) and an emphasis on the knowledge and craftsmanship involved. These are the very same skills required of an oral poet. I have already discussed the ways in which the raft-making passage works metaphorically to help establish Odysseus as the narrator of his own travels. This is a metapoetic raft, its construction echoing the process of making poetry and its cargo-carrying capacity representing issues of poetic value. But in particular, it is the raft's ability to sail, to take Odysseus away from the hidden island of Calypso and onto the open seas, that is significant here. Odysseus' raft gives him the opportunity and voice to sing his own song, and its very mobility prefigures the nature of the Odyssean narrative to follow—a song of travel, a song that travels.

And so, in Book 23, when we encounter another woodworking scene, it evokes Odysseus' construction of his raft with all its metapoetic possibilities. But this time Odysseus is building an immovable bed (ἔμπεδον . . . λέχος, 23.203) rather than a mobile raft. The wreck of Odysseus' raft, the tool of his escape from Calypso's island and the symbol of his narrative powers, has now been rescued and reconstructed precisely to end the story. But instead of a symbol of the flexibility and mobility of the story in progress, this bed, fixed in the ground, offers an image of a tale that is finished, put to rest, like Odysseus himself.

In my discussion of Odysseus' encounter with the Sirens in Book 12, I explored the ways in which the episode addresses the tension in the *Odyssey* between two narrative ideals: the ordered, Iliadic narrative of the past, celebrated by the Sirens, on the one hand, and Odysseus' wandering, ever mobile song of the future, on the other. The island of the Sirens, filled with the rotting corpses of those who succumbed to their song, offers a stark contrast to the figure of Odysseus, whose raft embodies the connection between movement, travel, and song. The tension between these two images of poetic narrative is perhaps best captured by the figure of Odysseus himself, unmoved, tied securely to the mast

of his ship in motion (ὄφρα ἔμπεδον αὐτόθι μίμνων ὀρθὸν ἐν ἱστοπέδῃ, 12.161).
The fixity of Odysseus' position is counterposed by the ability of his ship, with
all its metapoetic connotations, to move with impunity past the threat posed by
the Sirens. Now, here in Book 23, once Odysseus has returned home, the image
of Odysseus, himself steadfast, tied to the mast of his ship, is reconfigured and
relocated onto his marriage bed. The power of the Sirens scene stems from the
tension between mobility and fixity—between Odysseus' steadfast resolve to
hear the song of the Sirens and the mobility of his ship as it sails by their island
filled with rotting corpses. Here, while Odysseus remains fixed in place, tied to
the mast, his ship continues to travel, and mobility wins out, thus guaranteeing
and symbolizing the enduring power of his song.

With the marriage bed, however, this tension between mobility and fixity is
resolved in favor of stability, but here it is the stability and longevity that come
from being productively planted in the ground rather than the stultification of
being marooned in the past.[10] Now, the raft itself, with all its metaphorical associations, is finally grounded; like Odysseus at the mast, like the ship of the
Phaeacians after their last mission of transport, it is fixed in place. Its mast has
grown into a tree trunk, signaling to us that Odysseus' story, the story of his travels, is near completion. Accordingly, in contrast to the flexibility and mobility of
the narratives of his adventures told earlier in the poem, the account of his travels that Odysseus tells Penelope after their reunion is told in chronological order, without any detours or flashbacks, that is, in an order that conforms with
his tales to Alcinous (23.310–43). The marriage bed of Penelope and Odysseus
has been there all along, rooted in the center of their bedroom; but it remains
unseen and unheard of by the audience, covered with spiderwebs, until the final
moments of the tale.[11] Now it is revealed, just as Odysseus reveals himself, at
the end of the poem, in order to suggest that the poem is coming to an end.[12] Of
course, neither Odysseus' story nor his travels, as Teiresias' prophecy makes
clear, are actually over at this point. Odysseus still needs to make his journey to
propitiate Poseidon before he will die a peaceful death "far from the sea."
Nevertheless, the image of the bed offers the suggestion of closure at this point
in the narrative in spite of the imminent continuation of Odysseus' travels and
song. Throughout the poem, part of what makes Odysseus' story so compelling
is the tension between travel and home; so here, too, the inevitability of future
travel and song is provocatively juxtaposed to images of rootedness and closure.
The mobile raft has been transformed into a permanently stationary bed, and the
story of Odysseus, like Odysseus himself, has found its home.

Odysseus, culture hero of a brave new world, travels beyond the boundaries
of conventional Greek experience and returns home to his lovely and faithful
bride, whose own creative powers of delay have protected the integrity of home
in his absence. Odysseus' experience—both his dangerous and instructive travel
abroad and his successful return home to a like-minded marriage—offers the
Greeks of the early archaic period a model for the successful and productive in-

tegration of the world abroad, with all its dangers and its opportunities, back home. As Odysseus' raft, the vehicle for his travels abroad and the emblem of their narration, is finally transformed into his marriage bed, the symbol of the steadfast identity of home, Odysseus the wanderer is domesticated, and the ethnographic imagination of archaic Greece takes root in the New World.

# Notes

## Introduction

1. Clifford 1989.177. For additional (cross-cultural) examples and discussion of the association of travel and knowledge, see Helms 1988.7–19, 66–80.

2. Hdt. 3.139: "When Cambyses, son of Cyrus, marched upon Egypt, many other Greeks arrived in Egypt as well; some, as is fitting, for trading (κατ᾽ ἐμπορίην), others for war (στρατευόμενοι), and some as spectators of this country (αὐτῆς τῆς χώρης θεηταί)."

3. The Pre-Socratic philosopher Parmenides, of course, also comes to mind in the context of connecting conceptions of travel and knowledge. See Havelock 1958 and Mourelatos 1970.16–25 for an interesting discussion of Parmenides' use of the journey motif from the *Odyssey*, emphasizing travel as a source of learning and drawing on the image of the "route" of inquiry.

4. See Redfield 1985.98. Homer's *Odyssey* is just one example of a culture's appropriation of this myth as a means of self-examination. Cf. Hartog 1996.13 and note 10 for further examples.

5. Clifford 1992.108.

6. See Wolff 1993 for a useful discussion of the ways in which practitioners of contemporary cultural criticism (in particular postcolonialism, postmodernism, and poststructuralism) have turned to images of travel to represent their own work: "In all three cases, it is easy to see why notions of mobility, fluidity, provisionality and process have been preferable to alternative notions of stasis and fixity. In cultural criticism in the late twentieth century we have had to realize that only ideologies and vested interests 'fix' meaning, and it is the job of cultural critics to destabilize those meanings." The primary focus of her essay is on the ways in which these travel metaphors are gendered and the implications of this choice of "male-oriented" metaphor for cultural criticism.

7. Jameson 1984.89.

8. Purcell 1990; Morris 2000.257–61.

9. See Wallinga 1993.33–65 on shipping in the eighth century.

10. See Morris 2000.259–60. Morris acknowledges the hypothetical nature of this argument, given our lack of information about Dark Age settlement practices, but argues that if these hypotheses are well grounded, "the eighth century saw diametrically opposed processes: on the one hand, an exploding sense of *space*, as the whole Mediterranean became (some of) the Greeks' backyard; and on the other, a contracting sense of *place*, as the countryside filled up, mobility declined, and boundaries hardened."

11. Morris 2000.260; he refers to Harvey 1989.240. See also Harvey 1989.239, where he argues that spatial and temporal practices are always implicated in social and cultural contexts, and as a result, major shifts in the experience of space and time will inevitably entail a substantial disruption of systems of representation as well.

12. Hartog 1996.

13. Hartog 1996.15–16.

14. Hartog 1996.12–14.

15. Hartog 1996.12: "L'objectif, ici, n'est pas de dessiner une carte de cette culture antique, grande et lourde machine synoptique déployée sous les yeux du lecteur, où les changements se marquent par un lent ou, au contraire, brusque resserrement des courbes de niveaux, mais seulement de choisir quelques voyageurs et de les suivre un temps."

16. Hartog 1996.29–34.

17. Hartog. 1996.34: "Anthropologie poétique, l'*Odyssée* est aux fondements de la vision que les Grecs ont eue d'eux-mémes et des autres. Elle a fourni, non pas abstraitement, mais à travers un récit d'aventures, un cadre, un paradigme de trés longue durée, certes repris, retravaillé, complété, revisité, et critiqué, pour voir et dire le monde, pour le parcourir et le représenter, pour l'⟨⟨habiter⟩⟩ et en faire un monde ⟨⟨humain⟩⟩, c'est-à-dire grec."

18. See Loraux 1993.3–7 for a helpful discussion of the importance of working across the great divide of myth and history in classical scholarship.

19. These kinds of questions have been taken up by some recent work on the material culture side, especially with respect to the role of the east in Greek identity formation. Whitley 1994 addresses the complexity of responses on the part of early archaic Greece to the Orient and orientalizing art. Foxhall 1998 explores attitudes toward faraway places and goods, looking at how foreign goods help an individual link the self to broader sets of values and ideologies. Shanks 1999 focuses on the art and architecture of Corinth and the relationship between mobility, trade, political identity formation, and the dynamics between east and west. Morris 2000.195–256 looks at burial practices and commercial contacts with the east in the early archaic period and concludes that a redefinition of temporal relations with heroes of the past (shifts in burial practices) is stimulated by a reconfiguration of spatial relations with the east (renewal of Phoenician commerce).

20. To complete the analogy between ethnography and literature, see James Clifford's introduction to Clifford/Marcus 1986.4 on the literariness of ethnography: "Literary processes—metaphor, figuration, narrative—affect the ways cultural phenomena are registered, from the first jotted 'observations,' to the completed book, to the ways these configurations 'make sense' in determined acts of reading." See also the essays collected in Geertz 1988.

21. Geertz 1973.6.

22. Geertz 1973.7.

23. I realize that in making such a claim, I am open to all the risks and complications of doing ethnography. See Comaroff and Comaroff 1992.6–10 for a discussion of the perennial epistemological issues surrounding ethnography. Ethnographers have alternately been accused of serving the cause of imperialism, of either fetishizing cultural difference or erasing it, and of trusting in the naive empiricism of participant observation. Yet a strength of ethnography may lie precisely in this weakness, a more explicit mani-

festation of a problem common to all modern epistemologies: the imperfection of knowledge, the impossibility of the true and absolute. Ethnography is a culturally specific mode of understanding historically situated contexts. In it we tell of the unfamiliar to confront the limits of our own ways of knowledge. Such critiques will always remain partial since they are embedded in modes of thought and practice of which we are not fully conscious. But they do provide a way to decode those signs that disguise themselves as universal or natural—and even more important, a way to engage with those who live in different worlds.

24. For a sampling of some of this ethnographic soul-searching, see the essays collected in Clifford and Marcus 1986; Geertz 1988, esp. bibliography cited 131; Rosaldo 1989; Comaroff and Comaroff 1992.3–48.

25. Rabinow 1977.5. In characterizing the nature of his work as such, Rabinow is here using Ricoeur's definition of hermeneutics; see Ricouer 1969.20.

26. De Certeau 1988. 213. I will discuss this text and de Certeau's reading of it in more detail in chapter 4.

27. See the sources cited in note 19. For a critique of the role of the eyewitness authority in ethnography, what he calls a "rejection of visualism," see Clifford in Clifford/Marcus 1986.11–13; see also Geertz 1988.73–101.

28. Cf. Clifford in Clifford/Marcus 1986.2–3: "Ethnography is actively situated *between* powerful systems of meaning. It poses its questions at the boundaries of civilizations, cultures, classes, races, and genders. Ethnography decodes and recodes, telling the grounds of collective order and diversity, inclusion and exclusion. It describes processes of innovation and structuration, and is itself part of these processes."

29. Cf. Morris 2000.257: "The *Odyssey*, one of the foundations of Greek literature, can even be called the first ethnography."

30. Hartog 1996.25 argues that it is precisely Odysseus' delayed return that creates the space for the poem's anthropological orientation: "C'est dans l'espace ouvert par ce retard (dont joue l'aéde) que va s'inscrire l'expérience de l'autre et que vont se déployer, dans le mouvement d'un récit, les grands partages de l'anthropologie grecque." See Frame 1978 for the convergence in Greek of the notions of knowledge (*noos*) and return (*nostos*).

31. See Morris 2000.195–256 for a compatible argument about the interconnection between contemporary Greek experiences with the east and relationships with the Mycenean past.

32. Redfield 1985.101. He goes on to say: "Our interest in cultural systems may then be interpreted as a search for the sources of cultural coherence, of control. We are interested in *nomoi* because we experience *anomie*. Ethnography, from this point of view, is an effort intellectually to rescue ouselves from our own history, and the ethnographer is never more modern than when he leaves this modern scene to immerse himself in another culture."

33. For a brief discussion of the awareness of the mutual implication of colonialism and ethnography, see Clifford in Clifford/Marcus 1986.8–9 with bibliography cited there and Rosaldo 1989.30–34.

34. On the historicity of the poems, see, for example, Morris 1986b; 1997; Raaflaub 1997. For an example of a more strictly historical approach to the *Odyssey* and questions of ethnicity (not ethnography), see Malkin 1998.

35. E.g., Kirk 1985; Morris 1986b; 1997; Tandy 1997.8–13; Raaflaub 1997.625; Thalmann 1998. Those who argue for a seventh-century date include Crielaard 1995; Osborne 1996.156–60. Malkin 1998 argues for a ninth-century date.

36. For a helpful discussion of the relationship between the composition and performance of oral poetry and the fact of a unified Homeric text inherited from the ancient world, see Nagy 1996a.29–63. He suggests (140–42) that we think of a gradual process of "textualization" of the poems rather than posit the intervention of writing as a factor in the production of a definitive text. See also Nagy 1990.53.

37. For the sake of convenience, however, I will use the name "Homer" to refer to the author or authors of the *Iliad* and the *Odyssey*.

38. Oral poetry provides its audience—and by audience I mean both immediate (those at any given performance) and cultural (the larger society to which both singer and audience belong)—with a narrative that makes sense of their world. The very technical conventions of oral poetic composition/performance dictate its continued relevance and flexibility. For more on issues of oral poetics, see Lord 1960; Finnegan 1977; Morris 1986b.

39. See Morris 1986b for a more detailed argument why Homeric society must be derived from the real world in which Homer and his audience lived. See Tandy 1997.2–5 for a brief overview of some of these key changes and developments that marked the eighth century. See also Snodgrass 1980; Morris 1986b.122–23; 1997.545–48. Raaflaub 1997.646–47 connects the transitional and unstable nature of life at the end of the eighth century with some of the inconsistencies in the portrayal of Homeric society in the poems.

40. Obviously, the poem incorporates a range of time frames and experiences from the Mycenean period to the archaic period. Rather, I mean to say that the poem speaks to an archaic audience; it is part of their world.

41. Cf. *Od.* 19.203 and Hesiod *Th.* 27–28.

42. Cf. Morris 1997.539: "Material culture and poetic culture were two ways in which people in eighth-century Greece constructed the social world within which they moved. Both were important arenas in which people fashioned images of what they wanted their world to be, and challenged competing constructions which they did not like. Reducing either to a passive reflection of the other is simplistic." I take issue, however, with Morris's argument for the idealizing, aristocratic emphasis of the Homeric poems. In rejecting the argument that Homer is a mirror (albeit a distorted one) of material culture, he insists that "the epic was not some kind of bad history. It was a poetic creation, what *some* eighth-century Greeks thought the heroic world *ought* to have been like" (Morris 1997.558). Instead I would argue that a poetic text such as the *Odyssey* stands both as a ratification of the ideals of a community (or parts of one) and as a forum for the articulation of responses or challenges to shared dilemmas and thus an instrument of change. See also Morris 1986b.

43. Thalmann 1998.1.

44. It should go without saying that the "historicizing" reading of the *Odyssey* that I offer here is only a partial one, one that is primarily interested in the poem's fascination with matters of travel, trade, and overseas contact. These, obviously, are not the only issues at stake, and I hope that my efforts here will complement other kinds of interpretive approaches—more literary, materialist, or feminist, just to name a few—rather than compete with them.

Chapter 1

1. This nautical metaphor extends beyond language to the very frame of the poem as well. *Omeros* opens with a programmatic passage in which Philoctete explains to the tourists how he cuts down the laurier-cannelles to make canoes. His prayer for strength here recalls the typical Homeric appeal to the Muses and launches Walcott's poetic endeavor. The c/raft metaphor then reappears near the very end of *Omeros* when Walcott says that he has finished his poem: "my craft slips the chain of its anchor . . . " (323). The theme of cutting down trees to build a ship at the beginning of an epic poem also recalls the story of the building of the *Argo*, the first ship, and its role at the center of another epic tradition, the *Argonautica*. Taplin 1992.1–2 uses this same passage from *Omeros* in the introductory chapter to his book on the *Iliad*. He, too, invokes the metaphor of the sea and sailing to capture the Homeric experience: "To hear or read the *Iliad* is to embark on a voyage, whether undertaken for pleasure, exercise, experience, or whatever mixture of motives. I see it as my role to chart, to map the coast, trace currents, document weather patterns, take soundings."

2. For further examples, see Dougherty 1997.

3. Relevant passages from Hesiod, Ibycus, and Pindar will be discussed later in this chapter. See also Pindar P.10.51–54; P.11.39–40; N.3.26–28; and Péron's (1974) discussion of maritime imagery in Pindar. See also the beginning of Bacchyl. 16. See Bowie 1998.9–10 for an interesting discussion of the way in which a Phoenician merchant ship (crafted with an eye to beauty and size) operates in Heliodorus as an image of a literary work of art.

4. See Nagy 1982.66 and especially Rosen 1990.99–113 for discussions of the metapoetic nature of this passage. While I agree with Rosen's reading of the Nautilia as a programmatic statement about poetry, we disagree about how to interpret it. Rosen argues that Hesiod sets up the metaphor of sailing for poetry to designate the heroic poetry of Homer; by contrast, his is a song of the earth, and the appropriate metaphor for Hesiodic poetry is farming rather than sailing. As will become clear in this chapter, I argue that Hesiod's use of the metaphorical system of sailing and poetry in the *Works and Days* goes back to Homer and that Hesiod consciously adopts the language of sailing to locate himself within this tradition.

5. Rosen 1990.101n9 argues that the phrase πολυφλοίσβοιο θαλάσσης has distinct associations with the *Iliad*, where it appears six times.

6. West 1978.319. Even though he does not suggest a metapoetic reading of this passage, West cites the following examples of *sophia* designating poetic skill: Hesiod Fr. 306; Thgn. 19; Solon 13.52; Ibyc. 282.23; among others. West also cites passages in which *sophia* refers to other kinds of professional skills as well, such as those of a carpenter (*Il.* 15.412); the horseback rider (Alcm. 2.6; Anac. 417.2); the assayer (Thgn. 120); and the helmsman (Archil. 211).

7. Cf. Thgn. 876 on the poet who has the measure of *sophia* (μέτρον ἔχων σοφίης). See West 1978.318 for further examples of *metra* used in this way; also Rosen 1990.101.

8. Nagy 1982.66; Thalmann 1984.152–53; Rosen 1990.100 The sophist Alcidamas took this passage as a reference to the famous contest between Homer and Hesiod. See West 1978.319.

9. Walcott 1990.291.

10. The verb ἐπιβαίνω means "to set foot upon" (intrans.) or "to cause to set foot upon" (trans.) and is used to represent the act of mounting horses, chariots, and beds as well as ships. It is the explicit seafaring context of the lines that follow that encourages me to emphasize the nautical potential of the term and to translate the transitive use of the verb here a bit loosely in an effort to capture the flavor of the metaphor: "they first launched my sweet song" instead of the more literal "they first caused me to embark upon my sweet song." For examples of ἐπιβαίνω in Homer meaning to board a ship, see *Il.* 8.197, 512; *Od.* 4.708; 5.177; 9.101; 13.319. The verb is also used to mean to debark from a ship onto land: *Od.* 4.521; 5.399; 7.196; 9.83; 11.167, 482; 12.282.

11. As Rosen 1990.112n46 observes, the interpretation of Hesiod's Nautilia as metapoetic is confirmed by allusions to Hesiod along these lines by two later poets of antiquity; cf. Callimachus Fr. 178 Pfeiffer, and Propertius 3.3.13–24.

12. As, for example, in Clytamnestra's Beacon speech in Aesch. *Ag.* 281–316. Some of the catalogue entries contain brief narrative excursus, and several of them do, however, contribute to the sense of sea travel. Tlepolemus, for example, the leader of the Rhodian contingent, had earlier settled the island of Rhodes after he sailed across the sea from Argos (653–70). Philoctetes, however, has been abandoned on the island of Lemnos, at midpoint of the journey from Greece to Troy (716–28). And the mention of Protesilaus marks the end of the journey; his name means "first jumper," and we learn that he was killed while jumping ashore from his ship. His death marks the end of the sea journey together with the beginning of the war (695–702).

13. See Kirk's (1985.183–84) commentary on the *Iliad* for this point.

14. For a discussion of the textual issues presented by this poem, see Barron 1969.

15. Barron 1969.133–34 notes the similarities between the opening of the third triad of the Ibycus poem and both the Iliadic Catalogue of Ships and the Nautilia section of Hesiod's *Works and Days*. He concludes that these poetic allusions have the effect of highlighting the poet's intention of appropriating the immortality of epic poetry to praise the beauty of Polycrates. He does not, however, comment on the significance of the nautical language that forms the substance of these literary allusions.

16. Notice that while the Iliadic poet claims that no mortal poet could list all the men at Troy, but offers to catalogue the ships, here Ibycus dares not even attempt to enumerate the ships. Barron 1969.133–34 notes that the τὰ ἔκαστα of Ibycus picks up the προπάσας from the Iliadic passage. The fact that Ibycus alludes to the Catalogue of Ships, with its focus on the astonishing number of Greeks who sailed to Troy, helps defend the reading of ὅ[σσος ἀρι]θμὸς at line 27 (instead of Menelaus). Cf. Barron 1969.129.

17. Cf. Rosen 1990.103n16, who suggests that the adjective πολυγόμφος might refer to "the style of heroic poetry, i.e., 'much-nailed' = 'monumental,' 'manifold.'" I will argue that the association of πολυγόμφος with epic poetry is more closely linked to the similarities in modes of production of both ships and songs.

18. Marco Polo, Bk. I, chap. xviii, trans. H. Yule (3rd ed. [London 1903], 1:108), cited in Casson 1994.11–12. Casson includes a photo of a modern sewn boat at Madras, showing exactly this same technique.

19. Hornell 1946.192–93, 234–37; Morrison and Williams 1968.50; Casson 1971.9–10; Casson 1994.11–12.

20. Scholia ad Aesch. *Supp.* 134–35: λινορραφὴς δόμος δορός· ἡ ναῦς, παρόσον τρυπῶντες τὰς ναῦς σπάρτοις αὐτὰς συνέρραπτον. καὶ τὸ παρ᾽ Ὁμήρωι νῆας ἀκειόμενον τὸ συρράπτοντα δηλοῖ."

21. *Aen.* 6.413–14.

22. Pacuvius 277–78 Warmington (apud Festus 508): Nec ulla subscus cohibet co-magem alvei/sed suta lino et sparteis serilibus.

23. Morrison and Williams 1968.50. See Wallinga 1993.33–65 on shipping in the eighth century. For visual representations of early Greek ships, see Kirk 1949; Ahlberg 1971; Gray 1974; Popham 1987. Kirk 1949.144–53 discusses the popularity of ship scenes in Geometric pottery and suggests that ships captured the imagination of painters as subject matter especially in a time of travel and discovery. It is interesting to speculate about the parallel fascination with ships and their construction in the work of both literary and visual artists at this time.

24. Casson 1971.201–19.

25. Casson 1994.32 includes a sketch of this mortise and tenon technique.

26. See Casson 1971.217–19 for a discussion of the construction of Odysseus' raft or ship. Casson argues that what Odysseus builds in Book 5 is not a raft, as we typically understand that term, but rather a ship. This, he claims, is the only way to make sense of Homer's account of its construction. The vessel is referred to by the poet as a raft in the sense that it was put together in an improvisatory manner rather than to designate its design. For this reason, I will continue to refer to Odysseus' vessel as a raft, all the while keeping in mind the specific details of its manner of construction.

27. *Od.* 9. 384–86. Cf. Euripides' version of this simile in his *Cyclops* 460–61.

28. From ῥάπτω + ἀοιδή. For this etymology of *rhapsode*, see Schmitt 1967. 300–301; Durante 1976.177–79; Nagy 1979.298; 1990.28; 1996b.61–64; Ford 1988. Herington 1985.167–76 collects the ancient evidence for this term. The same image is at the root of the term *proemium*, a prelude or preliminary song, deriving οἶμος from the verb "to sew."

29. Kirk 1962.97, 318–19; Wolf 1963.71–76.

30. Nagy 1996b.67–69.

31. See Nagy 1996b.64–66 for his argument about the relationship between the weaving and stitching metaphors. He suggests that the stitcher is the specialist, the one who stitches together the cloth that has already been woven by others into a work of skill and expertise. I am persuaded by his arguments against Scheid and Svenbro 1994.120, who argue that the sewing metaphor does not go back to Homer. See Ford 1988 for a discussion of why the stitching (versus weaving) metaphor is confined to epic poetry.

32. The image of poet as skilled craftsmen is perhaps captured best by the passage in Book 18 of the *Iliad* that describes the making of Achilles' shield. In fact, the polu-daedalic skill of the shield is also attributed to ships. See Morris 1992.42–43: εὐδαίδαλον νέα (Simonides Dith. 17; cf. *Il.* 5.60–64); πολυδαίδαλος ἱστός (Hesiod *WD* 64).

33. See Pausanias 9.11.4: "For when he [Daedalus] was fleeing from Crete he made small sailing vessels for himself and his son Icarus and he devised sails for the ships, which had not yet been discovered, so that he might, making use of the favorable wind, outstrip the oared fleet of Minos. But they say that Icarus' ship overturned since he was a less skilled helmsman." Cf. Morris 1992.193–94.

34. The importance of skill and craftsmanship for shipbuilding is perhaps best captured in the genealogy of one of the many Phaeacians endowed with nautical names: Seagirt, son of Many-Ships, son of Shipbuilder (Ἀμφίαλος, υἱὸς Πολυνήου Τεκτονίδαο, *Od.* 8.114).

35. Aesch. *Persians* 392–97.

36. Hdt. 8.88 (τὸ ἐπίσημον); 8.92 (τὸ σημήιον).

37. *Od.* 11.125. Cf. *Od.* 23.272; 13.86; Hes. *WD* 628 and West's (1978) note *ad loc.* Examples of ἔπεα πτερόεντα include *Il.* 1.201; 3.155; 4.69; 5.242; *Od.* 1.122; 2.269; 4.25; etc. See Hart 1988.89–93 on connections between flight and sea travel in the Greek imagination.

38. Martin 1989.30–37.

39. On sewing and weaving as poetic metaphors, see Schmitt 1967.298–300; Scheid and Svenbro 1994.111–55; Nagy 1996b.62–74.

40. Sail: *Od.* 5.318; 6.269; clothes: *Od.* 4.245; 6.153.

41. Mast: *Il.* 1.434; 480; 23.852; 878; *Od.* 2.424; 4.578; 5.254; 9.77; 11.3; 12.409; 15.496; loom: *Il.* 6.491 = *Od.* 1.357 = 21.351; 13.107.

42. See Hainsworth 1988.257 (at line 5.33) for a discussion of the etymology of σχεδίη. See also Wallinga 1993.36–37. Herodotus, at 7.36, describes the bridge that Xerxes' men built across the Hellespont, explaining that it is made of papyrus cables and logs cut the width of a floating raft (σχεδίη).

43. There is a massive bibliography on the techniques and nature of the oral composition of Homeric poetry. Some of the major contributions include Lord 1960; 1995; Parry 1971; Martin 1989; Nagy 1996b.

44. See Dougherty 1991a for a more detailed discussion of the Phemius passage along these lines.

45. The significance of this nautical frame is confirmed by the fact that Odysseus' song is also enclosed within two accounts of the prophecy that Poseidon would destroy the Phaeacians' ships. In addition, storms and shipwrecks punctuate the beginning of his song to the Phaeacians (his voyage from Calypso's island at 5.291–332, 366–76) and the end (the storm that marooned him on Ogygia at 12.403–46).

46. *Od.* 5.141–42. In this respect, Odysseus' lack of poetic voice while marooned on Calypso's island foreshadows the dangers posed to Odysseus' song by the Sirens in Book 12. We will pick up this theme again in Chapter 3.

47. We recall Odysseus' famous lament once the storm tears up his raft (5.306–12) that it would have been better to have died at Troy rather than at sea. Death at sea is anonymous, whereas if he had died fighting at Troy, he would have been the subject of much song.

48. Some may object to the associative nature of my argument thus far—making ships is like stitching and weaving; stitching and weaving are like songmaking; making ships is like making songs; therefore, Odysseus' raft is a metapoetic vehicle able to carry a cargo of songs. While this approach may lack the conclusive force of a more logical method of argumentation, it does help identify important connections between thematic elements of the poem. The next two chapters, then, explore some of the implications of these associations both for the literary exposition of the poem and for a richer understanding of the "world of the *Odyssey*." Taken as a unit, then, this first section will, I hope, provide a persuasive argument for the significance of thinking about ships and song together in the *Odyssey*.

Chapter 2

1. See Stanford's commentary (1959) on this passage: "The comparison implies a surprisingly large girth for Odysseus' boat."

2. See West 1978.326.

3. Even though the poetry of Pindar is not contemporaneous with that of Homer and Hesiod and does not, for this reason, reflect the identical social and economic situation, Pindar's more explicit use of economic imagery can help us appreciate what underlies a similar if more oblique use of this same imagery in Homer and Hesiod.

4. Casson 1971.159–60. Cf. Athen. 1.28c for mention of Carian φορτηγοὺς ἀκάτους.

5. See P.2.67–68, where Pindar characterizes his song as Phoenician cargo.

6. See Gernet 1981.73–111 on *agalma* and value in archaic Greece; for a statue/ *agalma* as source of talismanic power, see Faraone 1992; Kurke 1993.

7. See Kurke 1991, esp. 85–107, for a discussion of Pindar in light of contested paradigms of exchange. See also Steiner 1994.91–99 on *agalma* as metaphor in the poetics of Pindar and Theognis.

8. Like Prospero, who at the end of *The Tempest* calls on the audience to fill his sails with gentle breath "or else my project fails" (V.i), Pindar here invokes an image of ships with full billowing sails to capture the success of both Themistius' athletic victory and his own poetic celebration of it. See Péron 1974 for further examples of the metapoetic use of ship imagery in Pindar.

9. The cargo boat's ability to travel, especially in comparison with the statue, fixed on its base, underlies this choice of image as well. I will take up the mobile aspect of the ship metaphor in chapter 3.

10. See Svenbro 1976.173–212; Gentili 1988.155–76; Kurke 1991.225–39; von Reden 1995b for discussions of how economic imagery operates within archaic lyric and elegiac poetry.

11. Von Reden 1995a.58–74; 1995b.38–41 also discusses how expressions of economic value, derived from gift and commodity exchange systems, help conceptualize poetic value in the *Odyssey*. Her discussion is quite compatible with mine; her focus is on the ways in which economic value represent the moral or truth value of poetry. I look more at the different ways in which economic value is constructed and how these competing notions of economic value are transferred to the poetic arena, e.g., developments in the production, consumption, and circulation of song.

12. See Sahlins 1972.185–230 for his discussion of "the sociology of primitive exchange"; his typology of reciprocities is laid out on 191–96. Cf. Donlan 1981–82 and von Reden 1995a for discussions of Homeric reciprocity in light of Sahlins's framework.

13. For further discussions, drawing on a broad range of anthropological evidence, of the ways in which economic systems such as trade are embedded in larger cultural systems, see Helms 1988 and the essays collected in Appadurai 1986 and Parry and Bloch 1989.

14. Once again, in taking some time to discuss these economic issues briefly here, I do not mean to reify problematic historical categories, such as those of gift exchange and trade. Rather, I aim to do just the opposite, that is, starting from the poem itself, to read it as a literary text to see what it can tell us about different modes of exchange, and to explore the nature of their contested status both in the the literary world of the *Odyssey* and in the historical world in which the poem operates.

15. For general studies of economics in Homeric and archaic Greece, see Benveniste 1973; Finley 1979; Mele 1979; Snodgrass 1980; Donlan 1981–82, 1997; Cartledge 1983; Morris 1986a, 1986b; Redfield 1986; van Wees 1992; Tandy 1997. On ritualized gift exchange in particular, see Lajvi-Strauss 1969; Sahlins 1972.149–84; Finley 1979; Gregory 1982; Herman 1987; Mauss 1990; van Wees 1992.

16. Herman 1987.78. As this discussion will show, I argue that gift exchange is but one of several exchange systems at work in the world of the *Odyssey.*

17. For further evidence of the importance of reciprocity to gift exchange, see *Od.* 1.318 and 24.285.

18. Finley 1979.61–62.

19. Herman 1987.80.

20. Van Wees 1992.208–10 discusses piracy in the Homeric world (he calls it "freebooting").

21. Cf. *Od.* 9.252–55.

22. For further examples of trade in Homer, see Donlan 1997.651–54.

23. See *Od.* 13.256–86; 14.288–300 for additional appearances of Phoenician traders. See Winter 1995 for a discussion of the negative construction of Phoenicians as greedy traders in the *Odyssey.* I take up the role of the Phoenicians in further detail in chapter 5.

24. Cf. 15.421. It is not clear whether they intended to sell her into slavery as well; we never learn what the Phoenicians had in mind for this woman, since she dies aboard ship.

25. See Benveniste 1973.105–6 for a discussion of the association of the verb ἀλ-φάνω and its cognates with exchange value and profit. He defines ἀλφή as the exchange value, particularly of slaves for sale; the verb ἀλφάνω means to get a price or to make a profit.

26. Eumaeus' account, although fictional, does correspond to the archeological evidence for early Greek trade. For discussions of the scope and mechanics of Greek trade, especially its relationship to politics, see Hasebroek 1933; Bravo 1977; Mele 1979 and Cartledge's (1983) critique; Crielaard 1993; 1995.224–31; Tandy 1997.59–83; Foxhall 1998.

27. Finley 1979.67–68 argues that exchange value in the *Odyssey* was conventional and customary; cf. van Wees 1992.241 for a critique of that view. See Sahlins 1972.185–227, especially 187, for a discussion of the fact that exchange in traditional economies is less oriented toward production of commodities and more geared toward the redistribution of goods. The most influential and elaborated discussion of the notion of commodities, of course, appears in Volume 1, Part 1 of Marx's *Capital;* for relevant excerpts, see McLellan 1977.421–45. In dealing with the economy of the Homeric poems, however, I have found anthropological perspectives that focus on the nature of exchange in premonetary societies more helpful for framing the theoretical issues at stake in the *Odyssey.* See, for example, the essays collected in Appadurai 1986, especially the editor's introduction, for this approach to the circulation of commodities in a social perspective, as well as those collected in Parry and Bloch 1989.

28. See chapter 5 for a more detailed discussion of this passage and the importance of the metal trade with the Near East in the world of the *Odyssey.*

29. See also *Od.* 3.299–302.

30. While it is less common than their participation in gift exchange networks, heroes do engage in the practice of trade from time to time in the Homeric world. In the *Iliad*, for example, the Lemnians trade with the Achaeans at Troy, and Achilles and other Greek leaders participate in the slave trade. At *Il.* 7.467–75, the Achaeans trade bronze, iron, oxen, and slaves for Lemnian wine. For further examples of the slave trade, see also *Il.* 21.40–41; 23.746–47; 24.751–53. Cf. Donlan 1997.652–53.

31. Expeditions to Egypt for profit: *Od.* 3.300–303; 14.245–86. Egypt as source of wealth: *Od.* 3.301; 4.125–32. See also Hdt. 4.152 for the potential of the market in Egypt. On trade with Egypt in the *Odyssey*, see Morris 1997.613.

32. See, for example, the passage from Aelian quoted at the beginning of this chapter. There are some interesting parallels in language between Nestor's characterization of Menelaus' trip to Egypt and other more explicit trade expeditions. At *Od.* 3.301–2 Nestor says that Menelaus gathered much gold and livelihood: πολὺν βίοτον καὶ χρυσὸν ἀγείρων. Cf. 14.285–86, Odysseus' tale to Eumaeus about how he also gathered (ἄγειρα / χρήματ') many goods from Egypt, and 15.446, the Phoenicians from Eumaeus' tale whose ship was full of goods (νηῦς πλείη βιότοιο). In addition, Menelaus' trip took him overseas to foreign peoples (ἀλλοθρόους ἀνθρώπους, 3.302). Cf. 1.183 (Mentes' trade expedition) and 15.453 (slave trade), where trade partners are foreign-speaking peoples.

33. For the gifts that Menelaus received from the king of Egypt, see *Od.* 4.125–35; from Phoenicia, 4.615–19. The issues of profit and gift exchange are equally well assimilated to each other at the beginning of Book 15 (80–85), when Menelaus offers to take Telemachus on a tour of the cities of men guaranteed to produce valuable gifts.

34. See Redfield 1986.31, who discusses a vocabulary of trade here; but see Benveniste 1973.113–20, who argues that there is no specific vocabulary for commerce in Indo-European languages. Instead, to represent commercial activity, Greek, like other Indo-European languages, draws on words with no specific reference to buying and selling.

35. Van Wees 1992.242–44 argues that this passage does not express any criticism either of heroes who trade or of anyone who seeks profit. Malkin 1998.89 agrees that there is no "general derogation of trade" in the poem, although at the same time he suggests that there is a "conflict of values" here. It seems to me very difficult to deny any criticism of trade expressed in this passage. Instead of trying to smooth out the discrepancies in the poem to arrive at a consistent picture of trade in the Homeric world, I am interested in preserving the areas of contention (e.g., the Mentes and the Euryalus passages) to see what they can tell us. A "conflict of values" is exactly what is going on here and elsewhere in the poem: one set of values denigrates trade for its love of profit; another celebrates its potential. Both are present in the world of the *Odyssey*. In this respect, my discussion here of the tension between the institutions of trade and gift exchange overlaps with that of those scholars who are interested in issues of class at work in the world of the *Odyssey*. See, for example, Rose 1992 and Thalmann 1998.

36. See *Od.* 9.1–11 on the important role of poet at feasts and celebrations. Cf. Segal 1994.113–41 on the relationship between the bard and his audience.

37. See Svenbro 1976.16–35 for this notion of the relationship between poet and Muse. Cf. von Reden 1995b.37 for a discussion of the gift exchange framework governing the relationship between Muse and poet.

38. See *Od.* 8.43–45, where Alcinous says that the god gave Demodocus the gift of

pleasing song. See also 1.338, where Phemius' job is to charm his audience, and 17.514–20, where Eumaeus compares Odysseus to a poet "whose stories would charm the dear heart within you." The Sirens are obviously the embodiment of the association between poetry and charm or beguilement. Cf. Scully 1981; Walsh 1984.14–15.

39. Demodocus, literally "received by the people," is etymologized as "honored by the people" at Od. 8.472: Δημόδοκον λαοῖσι τετιμένον.

40. Od. 1.351–52.

41. Svenbro 1976.17.

42. See von Reden 1995b.34–37 on the nature of what she calls the "récit-contrat" between the poet and his community.

43. See Od. 17 514–20, where Eumaeus compares Odysseus to a poet, and 21.403–9 for the simile of poet used to describe Odysseus as he strings the bow in preparation for killing the suitors. On Odysseus as poet, see Moulton 1977.145–53; Suzuki 1989.70–73; Goldhill 1991.66; Rose 1992.112–19; Segal 1994.85–109; Doherty 1995.89.

44. In this respect I disagree with Svenbro 1976.193–212, who sees no notion of poetry as commodity at work in Homer. He opposes the figure of Demodocus, as poet of the Muses in Homer, to the choral poet who sells his skill and whose poem is the ultimate product. Svenbro's analysis, however, fails to take Odysseus into account as poet in the Odyssey. Gentili 1988.155–56 (and note 2) also fails to acknowledge Odysseus' role as a mobile poet in this poem when he connects the notion of a poet whose profession takes him from place to place with a later period and contrasts it with the picture of Demodocus in the Odyssey. Von Reden 1995b.34 identifies three different kinds of récit-contrats or poetic relationships in the Odyssey: "Bards, like Phemius and Demodocus, belonging to an oikos, sing tales about the heroes of Troy to a feasting audience; Odysseus as wandering storyteller brings news about Odysseus to people who wish to know; and he tells stories which are both stories of Troy and news about Odysseus to an audience who are both a feasting community and people who wish to know about Odysseus."

45. When Odysseus tells stories to Eumaeus and Penelope, even though he knows they are acquainted, his disguise characterizes their relationship as that of strangers.

46. Od. 15.419, 421. See also 13.327, where Odysseus uses this same verb in accusing the disguised Athena of deceiving him with a story about his arrival at Ithaca.

47. Cf. Segal 1994.149 for a different interpretation of this passage. He argues that Alcinous here invokes the image of the beggar, rather than the trader, to characterize the poet. Segal's disucssion of this passage forms part of a larger discussion of the way in which the Odyssey explores the anomaly of the bard's social position by placing his activity between the heroic exchange of gifts and the dependency of the beggar.

48. See Cozzo 1988, esp. 13–35, and Roisman 1990 for discussions of the semantic range of kerdos.

49. In fact, Books 7 and 8 offer an extended meditation on the range and rationale of the system of xenia. First of all, the similarity between the status of a suppliant and that of an unknown guest is established. Odysseus arrives adopting the role of suppliant, but is quickly raised up and treated as a guest since Zeus looks out for both (Od. 7.159–66; 8.26–29). The rationale for treating both guests and suppliants is the same—either might be a god in disguise—and is raised explicitly by Alcinous in a speech to his fellow leaders asking them to welcome Odysseus and to offer sacrifices for him (Od. 7.186–206).

50. Alcinous' reception of Odysseus includes reference to two other aristocratic modes of circulating goods as well: marriage (7.314) and athletic contests (8.100ff.).

51. *Od.* 11.330–32.

52. Although he was invited, Odysseus refused to stay among the Phaeacians; he graciously refuses Alcinous' offer of Nausicaa as his bride.

53. Our sense that Odysseus has traded his song for goods is confirmed by Alcinous' remarks at the beginning of Book 13 (1–15). He encourages the leaders of the Phaeacians to go home and bring Odysseus more gifts since they enjoyed his song. Doherty 1995.65–66 makes a similar claim about this scene; she argues that Odysseus manipulates the curiosity of his audience (Alcinous and Arete) to his own profit.

54. These are the same qualities that Arete praises in Odysseus directly in her response at 11.336–41.

55. At 14.459–60 the poet explains that Odysseus is testing Eumaeus with this story to see if he will give him a cloak.

56. Notice that Eumaeus also invokes his obligation to take care of suppliants—yet another long-standing social mechanism that would provide a reason for giving Odysseus a cloak which stands outside a trade relationship. Cf. von Reden 1995a.71–74 and 1995b.39–40 for a discussion of this scene along similar lines.

57. Furthermore, as the episode with Eumaeus shows, there is room for conflict between cultural structures of commoditization and individual attempts to bring a sense of value to one's own experience of the world. Like the man who refuses to sell his house for a million dollars and forces the skyscraper to be built around it, Eumaeus refuses to conceptualize narrative as a kind of commodity open for exchange. Instead, he insists on excluding narrative from that sphere and keeping it within the noncommodified realms of gift exchange. See Kopytoff 1986.76 for the skyscraper example and further discussion of this issue.

58. We will return to the idealized world of the Phaeacians, especially with respect to modes of exchange, in chapter 5.

59. Moerman 1975.158–59, cited in Helms 1988.68. See Helms 1988.66–130 for an interesting discussion of the many motivations for long-range travel, focusing in particular on the overlap between the quests for profit and knowledge.


Chapter 3

1. Pind. N.5.1–3; the passage is cited in chapter 2.

2. Although Theognis' image here is not strictly one of sailing—he includes mention of wings and an allusion to Bellerophon as well—the force of the metaphor clearly intends to emphasize the great distances that Theognis' poetry will travel, the broad range of audiences that will hear his praise. Gentili 1988.163 discusses both Pindar's Nemean 5 and this Theognis passage along these lines. See also Goldhill 1991.109–11; von Reden 1995a.43–44.

3. We recall that the *Odyssey* includes poets among a list of itinerant craftsmen (14.383–86).

4. *Od.* 11.364–66.

5. This debate often takes as its point of departure the prologue of Hesiod's *Theogony*, where the Muses claim to know how to speak the truth when they want and how to lie as well (*Th.* 27–28). For discussions of the role of truth and lies with respect to poetic discourse, see Adkins 1972; Pratt 1993; Detienne 1996.

6. See, for example, Goldhill 1991.37–56: "In Eumaeus' house, then, we see not merely Odysseus telling a false tale to protect his disguise and to test Eumaeus' fidelity, but a series of exchanges that revolve around wandering, deception, misplaced faith; a series of conversations, set in the context of reciprocal rituals of guest-friendship, that both veil and reveal the two speakers in a complex network of truths and fictions, fidelity and belief" (42). Murnaghan 1987.148–75 discusses the ways in which the themes of disguise and recognition are connected with poetic issues of representation, imitation, and narrative authority. Cf. Rose 1992.112–19; Segal 1994.177–83.

7. See Cole 1983.27; he also observes that *alethea* is never used as a predicate of divine speech. See also Pratt 1993.22.

8. Other examples of *alethea* used as the object of verbs of speech in the *Odyssey* include 3.247; 7.297; 11.507; 13.254; 16.61, 226; 17.15, 122; 18.342; 21.212; 22.420.

9. In many ways, Proteus, the "truthful old man of the sea," is a figure who is emblematic of the *Odyssey*'s collocation of overseas travel, narrative, and truth. His daughter Eidothea tells Menelaus in Book 4 that he should ask her father if he wants to learn how to get home again, for Proteus "knows the depths of the seas" (4.385–86.) Proteus' source of knowledge is the sea, and in the story that follows, he will tell Menelaus both the route of his return, his *nostos*, and knowledge of events that have happened in his absence. Proteus embodies the poem's fascination with the connections between travel and knowledge; his story maps out Menelaus' successful return home while it recounts the problematic voyages of his brother and of Odysseus.

10. *Od.* 1.280–86. Notice too the close association between sailing and stories in this passage. Athena tells Telemachus to rig the finest ship to set sail in order that he may hear about his father and others who have sailed. Sailing and stories operate in close relationship with each other, and the stories told in the *Odyssey* are primarily travel tales. Even when Odysseus' own travels have ended and he has returned safely to Ithaca, the stories do not stop. A significant part of the second half of the poem as well is composed of the travel tales Odysseus tells Eumaeus and Penelope. For other examples of Telemachus sailing in search of songs about his father, see also *Od.* 2.212–23, 359–60, 363; 3.13–16, 79–95; 4.316–27.

11. See Helms 1988.66–80 for examples from many different cultures of travel as a way to learn and tell about the world.

12. *Od.* 8.572–76. These are, of course, the same questions that Odysseus himself poses in anticipation of his visit to those who live in the land of the Phaeacians (*Od.* 6.119–21) and of the Cyclops (*Od.* 9.172–76).

13. For the importance of eyewitness accounts in ethnographic writing, see, for example, Pratt 1986; Geertz 1988.1–24.

14. Of course, Odysseus' travels are not adventure or exploratory travels in the literal sense since his is a journey home from Troy. Nevertheless, what makes the *Odyssey* such an engaging tale is the tension between the hero's desire to return home and both his curiosity about new peoples and places (e.g., his wish to explore the Cyclopes' land) and his motivation to come home with a full cargo.

15. *Od.* 13.256–86.

16. As I will argue, I prefer not to think of this speech as a lie, and thus dismiss it from discussion, but rather include it in my analysis of all the travel narratives in the *Odyssey* and the question of narrative truth.

17. *Od.* 19.215–19.

18. It is interesting to note that the verb τεκταίνομαι is used in the *Iliad* to designate both the building of ships (5.62) and the construction of clever plans (10.19).

19. Cf. *Od.* 3.138 for the same collocation of οὐ κατὰ κόσμον and μαψιδίως used there to describe the disorderly Achaeans as they gather for an assembly after the sack of Troy.

20. *Od.* 3.71–74, cited in chapter 2.

21. For further discussion of the notion of singing *kata kosmon* and its relationship to questions of narrative truth, see Adkins 1972; Walsh 1984.13–19. Walsh's sense of the way that *kosmos* designates order includes the shape of the poem, its order, and its appropriateness. In addition, Walsh reads λίην γὰρ κατὰ κόσμον as slightly critical and contrasts Odysseus' use of κατὰ κόσμον here with his later request that Demodocus sing a song κατὰ μοῖραν (8.496), a phrase that Walsh interprets to designate a less comprehensive and more selective principle of song-making: Odysseus is requesting a song about himself.

22. Demodocus' songs are indeed comprehensive. Odysseus remarks that he sang the story of the Achaeans very well, including what they did and experienced and suffered (8.490).

23. Stories of the Trojan War heroes are also what Alcinous requests from Odysseus after the break in his story to the king's court at Phaeacia. See *Od.* 11.370–72. In characterizing Demodocus' song as fixed and stable, I do not mean to suggest that it is literally unchanged from one rendition to the next as if it were written down. Rather my argument is that his audience appreciates and rewards a familiar and predictable song tradition instead of one that offers something new and different on each occasion.

24. See Murnaghan 1987.171–72 for a discussion of the contrast between Demodocus and Odysseus as poets who represent two different kinds of claims to narrative truth. Demodocus' songs are accurate because they come from the Muses, while Odysseus' songs represent a human version that cannot be counted on to be true in the same way. Murnaghan argues that the *Odyssey*'s depiction of a manipulative hero as a storyteller points to the potential for deceit in narrative. See also Walsh 1984.13–21. While I agree that Odysseus and Demodocus help articulate two competing notions of poetic truth, I would argue that the Odyssean notion emphasizes the mobility and flexibility of narrative rather than its potential for deception.

25. We might say that this "Odyssean" model of narrative in the *Odyssey* is consistent with the qualities of *metis*, with which Odysseus is clearly allied through both Athena's patronage and his own *metis/outis* pun in Book 9. Cf. Detienne and Vernant 1978 for the best discussion of the semantic range of *metis* in Greek culture. They show that *metis* is associated with qualities of swiftness, mobility, a world of movement, multiplicity, and ambiguity; *metis* operates in shifting terrain; it occupies a range of time frames. Cf. Pucci 1987.243–45 on the connections between Odyssean notions of poetic truth and the concept of *metis*.

26. Pucci 1996.196–98. My argument here has been very much influenced by Pucci's intertextual reading of the Sirens episode; see Pucci 1996.191–96; 1987.209–14.

27. For general discussions of the "lying tales" of the *Odyssey*, see Trahman 1952; Walcott 1977; Haft 1984; Emlyn-Jones 1986. For discussions of these "lying tales" within the context of poetic truth and narrative, see Murnaghan 1987.166–69; Goldhill 1991.36–56; Pratt 1993.85–94; Segal 1994.164–83.

28. *Od.* 13.256–86.

29. *Od.* 14.192–359.

30. *Od.* 17.419–44.

31. *Od.* 19.172–202, 270–307.

32. *Od.* 24.303–14. For the association between Alybas and ἀλάομαι, see Stanford's commentary (1959) on 24.304–5.

33. *Od.* 13.291–99. Before Odysseus begins the tale, the narrator comments that Odysseus held back truth from this story to Athena (13.254–55).

34. The entire passage is quoted as the epigraph to this chapter.

35. Vidal-Naquet 1986.19: "Odysseus's travels have nothing to do with geography, and there is more geographical truth in the 'untrue' stories he tells Eumaeus and Penelope (14.191–359; 19.164–202) than in all the stories in Alcinous's palace."

36. See Vidal-Naquet 1986 for a fuller discussion of some of the key aspects of the human condition absent from Odysseus' stories to the Phaeacians: agriculture, sacrifice, and so on.

37. Another way of looking at what I am presenting here as contrasting models of poetic truth is in light of work done by human geographers (e.g., Harvey 1989), to say that these two models are rooted in competing conceptions of place and space. One celebrates the potential of the foreign and the far away, the other the familiarity and stability of the world at home. For examples of ways in which shifting notions of place affect broader social categories in the ancient world, see Foxhall 1998, who discusses the significance of the consumption of foreign products in archaic Greece as a way for the individual to link himself or herself to larger, more global sets of values and ideologies. See also Morris 2000.257–306 for a reevaluation of issues of time and space and their ultimate impact on the formulation of democratic ideology in Athens.

38. Quint 1993.249. See also Nohrnberg 1976.9–11; Parker 1979.42–43.

39. Also at work in this opposition between the epic voyage and the romance-adventure in the Renaissance are ideological tensions over trade. Quint discusses two different narrative strategies to overcome these tensions: the assimilation of the trade expedition into the voyage of discovery and the epic genre, or the association of trade with the romance-adventure and the love of riches. Even in antiquity, Odysseus and others were famous for their monetary motives. Quint connects this tendency to view the voyage of Odysseus as a trading expedition with the association of the *Odyssey* with the genre of romance. See Quint 1993.257–67.

40. Walcott, 1990.291.

Chapter 4

1. The following lines, for example, from Odysseus' story to Eumaeus are near or exact repetitions of lines from his earlier adventures: 14.301–4 = 12.403–6; 14.305–9 = 12.415–19. In addition, Odysseus' account to Eumaeus of his attack on the Egyptians

(14.257–75) is very similar to the story of the attack made by him and his men on the Ciconians (9.39–59). Similarly, some lines from Odysseus' story to Penelope in Book 19 are familiar: the description of Thrinacia at 19.273–76 reminds us of 12.127ff. and 12.261; the storm at 19.278ff. combines two earlier storms and shipwrecks (12.402–50; 5.313ff.).

2. Malkin 1998.16–20 raises objections to using New World analogies in the context of Greek studies on the grounds that the differences between "the Greek and the Spanish situations are too significant" to be helpful. The objections he raises, however, focus narrowly on differences between Greek and Spanish religion and on their respective points of departure for the New World. What Malkin misses are the important ways in which European settlement of the New World more generally construed—especially the simultaneous proliferation of literary production and overseas exploration and settlement—can shed helpful light on the early archaic period in Greece. In particular, I am interested in how both cultures looked to familiar mythic and literary traditions to conceptualize and represent contemporary overseas contact and colonization—both the ways in which poets looked to mythic traditions to elevate contemporary mercantile expeditions and strategies for using contemporary experience overseas to help reinterpret traditional mythic tales of travel.

3. While it may be the case that the *Odyssey* establishes a New World discourse that continues to wield literary influence 2,500 years later, my primary goal here is not to argue for direct literary influence by the *Odyssey* upon *The Tempest*. Rather, my aims are methodological. Given the similarities both in plot structure and in historical context between the two works, I maintain that recent historically grounded interpretations of *The Tempest* can guide our reading of the *Odyssey* in useful and productive ways.

4. See Langbaum 1987.125–27 for a discussion and bibliography on the sources of *The Tempest*.

5. See Langbaum 1987.125–39 for a more thorough discussion of these and other historical sources of the play. Cf. Quint 1998.75–101 for a discussion of the ways in which Montaigne's essay itself uses his examination of Brazilian culture to describe a society all too similar to that of Montaigne's France.

6. The passage is from Sylvester Jourdain, *A Discovery of the Barmudas* (1610), quoted in Langbaum 1987.133–35. Shakespeare was connected with leaders of the Virginia Company, which sponsored the colonial expedition to Jamestown.

7. See, for example, Greenblatt 1970; Orgel 1984; Barker and Hulme 1985; Brown 1985; Willis 1989. Even those who do not follow these more New Historicist readings of *The Tempest*, but who favor readings that focus more on Prospero as artist, acknowledge the allusions to recent historical events. See Orgel 1987.5–18 for a brief overview of some of the major interpretive issues raised by the play.

8. It cannot be overemphasized that the *Odyssey*, like *The Tempest*, is a work of poetic creativity and imagination, and in showing how this poetic creativity is grounded in real historical events, we must not deny the poem its primary status as poetry. Far too often, in the absence of other more objective contemporary historical sources for the early archaic period, the *Odyssey* is invoked as clear, unproblematic evidence of life in early Greece.

9. Compare *The Tempest* I.i, where Ferdinand and Miranda first meet ("M: I might call him divine; F: If you be maid or no?") with the passage in *Odyssey* 6 when Odysseus

and Nausicaa meet. At 6.149–50, Odysseus addresses Nausicaa, "I beg you, queen, are you a goddess or a mortal?" And at 6.243–4, once Odysseus has bathed, Nausicaa remarks about him, "Now he is like the gods who hold broad heaven."

10. Even though Odysseus turns down Alcinous' offer of Nausicaa's hand, the thematic significance remains. I discuss this theme in more detail in chapter 6.

11. The resettlement of Phaeacia: *Od.* 6.7–10. For more on the colonial aspect of the Phaeacians, see chapter 6. The theme of fraternal strife often appears in archaic Greek colonial contexts as well as a way to represent the internal conflict at home that prompts overseas settlement. For a discussion of fraternal conflict in Greek colonial traditions, see Dougherty 1993.16–18.

12. For example, see the German broadsheet from 1505 cited in Honour 1975.12: "No one owns anything but all things are in common. And the men have as wives those that please them, be they mothers, sisters or friends; therein they make no difference. They also fight with each other. They also eat each other, even those who are slain, and hang the flesh of them in smoke. They live one hundred and fifty years. And have no government." See Quint 1998.75 for a discussion of this rhetorical technique in Montaigne's "Essay on the Cannibals."

13. I will discuss the metallic splendor of Alcinous' palace further in chapter 5.

14. Edwards 1993.47.

15. Edwards 1993.47: "Such a complete ellipsis of a verb's subject is uncharacteristic of Homer, and distracts attention from the activity itself to its result."

16. Hesiod links economic self-sufficiency to the absence of ships and the need for overseas trade elsewhere in the *Works and Days* as well; see *WD* 45, 634.

17. Cf. Hes. Fr. 204.109f. See West's (1978) commentary on *WD* 236–37, where he observes that later poets extend this association of ships with the fall from the Golden Age into the notion of man's trespassing on the sea as impiety: Lucretius 5.1006; Virgil *Ecl.* 4.31–32; Ovid *Met.* 1.128–29; Seneca *Med.* 301ff., 326ff.

18. I will discuss the Phaeacians and their nautical skill further in the next chapter.

19. As I noted earlier, Odysseus' arrival on the island of Phaeacia and his initial encounter with and possible marriage to Nausicaa belong to a familiar narrative of colonial settlement told as marriage between foreign man and native woman. I develop this theme further in chapter 6.

20. See de Certeau 1988.209–43. Again, my primary motive here is methodological—that is, to use de Certeau's analysis of the structure of Léry's text to reveal a similar structure underlying the *Odyssey*'s account of Odysseus' travels.

21. De Certeau 1988.218–26. Chapter references are to the text of Léry's account edited by Paul Gaffarel (1880).

22. De Certeau 1988.218–19. He quotes Léry: "This American land where, as I shall be deducing, everything that is seen, whether in the customs of its inhabitants, the shapes of its animals, or in general in what the earth produces, is *dissimilar* in respect to what we have in Europe, Asia, and Africa, might well in our eyes be called a *new* world" (de Certeau's italics).

23. De Certeau 1988.219: "A part of the world which appeared to be entirely other is brought back to the same by a displacement that throws uncanniness out of skew in order to turn it into an exteriority behind which an interiority, the unique definition of man, can be recognized."

24. Cf. de Certeau 1988.221: "The initial dangerous and skeptical bipolarity (truth is over here while error is over there) is replaced by a circular schema built over a triangle with three guide points: first of all, *Geneva*, the point of departure and return, of the two terms of the initial relation that the story leaves intact and even reinforces by placing it out of the field, as beginning and ending but not the object of the story; then this strange *nature* and this exemplary *humanity* (however sinful it may be) into which the alterity of the New World is divided, thus reclassified into an exotic universe and an ethical utopia, according to the order that Léry's writing introduces."

25. Cf. de Certeau 1988.221: "This work is indeed a *hermeneutics of the other*. Onto the shores of the New World it transports the Christian exegetical apparatus which, born of a necessary relation with Jewish alterity, has been applied in turn to the biblical tradition, to Greco-Latin antiquity, and to many more foreign totalities. On one more occasion it draws effects of meaning from its relation with the other. Ethnology will become a form of exegesis that has not ceased providing the modern West with what it needs in order to articulate its identity through a relation with the past or the future, with foreigners or with nature."

26. For a discussion of the connection between Odysseus' return journey (νόστος) and the knowledge he acquires (νόος) embedded in the etymological relationship between these two Greek words, see Frame 1978.

27. We recognize this rhetorical strategy of description in terms of privatives, typical of New World accounts of a state of nature, from our earlier discussion of *The Tempest*.

28. Hesiod *WD* 276–80 identifies the absence of eating one's own as the difference between humans and animals.

29. Cf. de Lauretis 1984.103–57 for a feminist critique of this prominent narrative pattern which engenders the mythic hero as male and the obstacles to his journey and his story as female.

30. We notice that in the *Odyssey* this opposition is made by the contrast between two different cultures, whereas in Léry's account of the Tupinamba, it was two competing aspects of the same culture. In a subsequent chapter we will explore the specific connection and complementarity of the Cyclopes and Phaeacians within the structure of the *Odyssey*, especially with respect to overseas settlement.

31. In addition, of course, any attempt to impose an arbitrary order or explanatory scheme on a work of literature runs the risk of highlighting some elements of the narrative and downplaying others. These attempts to find and articulate the basic structure of a narrative are useful only insofar as they replicate or help elucidate our more subjective experience of reading the narrative. For a very different structural analysis of Odysseus' adventure tales, see Most 1989. His analysis, which he derives from J. D. Miles, emphasizes good and bad hosts and is designed to encourage the Phaeacians to send Odysseus home. The problem with this analysis, in my opinion, is that the structure highlights minor episodes (Thrinacia, Aeolus) and overlooks the major ones (Cyclopes, Phaeacians).

32. There are two other sets of oppositions at work in the poem that operate a bit differently, and I will discuss them in the following chapters. The opposition between the Phaeacians and the Phoenicians (chapter 5), for example, extends from the world of Odysseus' travels to that of the second half of the poem. Yet another opposition between the Phaeacians and the historical Euboeans (chapter 7) extends even further, outside the confines of the poem and into the world of the audience.

33. Book 9 begins, of course with the two short episodes with the Ciconians and the Lotus-Eaters, but Odysseus' encounter with the Cyclops is the main focus of this book.

## Chapter 5

1. The notion of wonder and marvel is an important component of ethnographic discourse. For a discussion of the way in which marvels operate in an ethnographic context in Herodotus, see Hartog 1988.230-37. See Greenblatt 1991.1-25 for a discussion of the theme more generally in New World discourse.

2. On the double nature of the land of Scheria, see Vidal-Naquet 1986.26-30; Reece 1993.101; Segal 1994.12-25; Ahl and Roisman 1996.97.

3. Some scholars have tried to reconcile these conflicting reports to present a coherent, internally consistent picture of the Phaeacians. See, for example, Rose 1969; Most 1989; and Reece 1993.107-16 for a review of scholarship along these lines. Reece himself argues (118-21) that the ambiguity of the Phaeacians' behavior toward Odysseus stems from its origins as a combination of a folklore tradition of the castaway sailor and the king's daughter and a foreshadowing of Odysseus' arrival at Ithaca. In this way, the Phaeacian episode connects thematically with Odysseus' previous adventures as well as anticipating his arrival at Ithaca.

4. Segal 1994.14 (first published in *Arion* in 1962): "On Scheria, the Phaeacian island, Odysseus experiences the waning of the imaginary and the return of reality, that is, the demands of life in a human setting of city and family. In the process of making this transition, he reviews his past and thereby reintegrates the two areas of his life experience (psychologically, the conscious and subconsious dimensions of his being). More broadly, he also shapes an implicit definition of what it means to be human in this world of abrupt change and multiple identities."

5. See Garvie 1994.181 for this literary analysis.

6. There is some debate about how to interpret Hesiod's myth of ages. For the chronological progression approach, see West 1978 and 1997.312; for a structuralist interpretation that does not see the notion of decline in the myth, see Vernant 1983.

7. WD 112-13; cf. West 1978.178, where he argues that Hesiod does not imagine that the races are made of the different metals: "They are more symbolic. Gold is the metal of the gods, not only rare and precious but spotless and incorruptible." Further symbolic associations with gold, he shows, include moral sincerity (Theog. 449ff., Call. Fr. 75.30) and ingenuousness (Plato *Phdr.* 235e; Menander D. 675).

8. WD 126; cf. Vernant 1983.9.

9. WD 116-19. Cf. Forbes 1971.155-58 on early gold technology.

10. Vernant 1983.11

11. WD 134-37.

12. Bronze Age and weapons of war: WD 145-46; 150-54. Ares is bronze. Iron Age and tools of agriculture: WD 176-78. Cf. Vernant 1983.12-16 on the symbolic associations of bronze with the powers possessed by the defensive arms of the warrior; for his discussion of the themes of work and fertility in Hesiod's Iron Age, see 8-20. Cf. Snodgrass 1980 on the technology and economy of ironworking in the Mediterranean.

13. West 1997.312-19. He observes (312): "The use of metal symbolism is most

likely to have originated in the Near East, where the technologies of metal-working were most highly developed." See also his earlier commentary to the *Works and Days* (1978.172–77).

14. This tradition is paraphrased in *Bahman Yast* 1.2–5; an alternate version, reported in *Bahman Yast* 2.14–22, has seven branches of seven different metals representing seven ages. See West 1978.174–75 and 1997.313 for the bibliography.

15. Daniel 2:31ff. See West 1978.175 and 1997.313 for further discussion of this and other traditions that may have influenced Hesiod. West himself (1997.318–19) suggests that Mesopotamia is the most likely place of origin for this myth and for its subsequent dissemination to the Greeks: "It seems necessary to postulate a common source, dating from the earlier first millennium (not before the archaeological Iron Age) and located somewhere in the Near East. A Phoenician source would be imaginable in itself, but could hardly account for the spread of the myth to Iran and India. It is natural to think of Mesopotamia, in view of its outstanding importance as a centre of cultural diffusion; but Urartu to the north also has a potential claim that should not be overlooked." See also Burkert 1992.5–7.

16. *Od.* 7.84–85. See Garvie 1994.180 for the unusualness of the repeated simile here and its reference to the scene with Telemachus in Sparta: "The simile surely recalls that earlier occaison on which Telemachus too arrived at a splendid royal palace, and, like his father, stood in wonder at its appearance." In other ways as well, Telemachus' encounter with Menelaus' palace foreshadows Odysseus' visit to the palace of Alcinous on the island of Scheria. The arrival of both Telemachus and Odysseus is located within a marriage context. In Sparta, the household of Menelaus and Helen is celebrating the marriages of their son and daughter; in Phaeacia, the imminent marriage of Nausicaa runs through Odysseus' entire stay. In both cases it is the female member of the royal couple who takes charge of welcoming the guest from Ithaca; in both places the guest is welcomed with song, especially songs about Odysseus. And finally, in both Sparta and Phaeacia, we find extreme wealth and a convergence of commerce and gift exchange.

17. Hephaestus makes the houses of the gods (*Il.* 1.608 = 20.12); he is also responsible, in part at least, for Alcinous' palace (he made the magic guard dogs), and so Telemachus' comparison of Menelaus' palace to that of Zeus further establishes the link between the extravagant homes of both Alcinous and Menelaus.

18. *Od.* 4.78–85.

19. There are some interesting similarities between the figures of Odysseus and Menelaus. Menelaus is the second-to-last Greek to return home from Troy; he traveled extensively, and he got lots of goods from exotic places. He even explains, in a line (4.267–68) that evokes our introduction to Odysseus in Book 1, that he has learned about men and their cities from his travels. Although no one would confuse Menelaus' intellectual powers with those of Odysseus, he does claim a similar knowledge of people and cities that stems from his travels. At 4.104ff. Menelaus compares his grief with that of Odysseus. And in this respect, Telemachus' meeting with Menelaus prepares him for his reunion with his father later in the poem.

20. Cf. 4.90–91, where Menelaus laments that his brother was killed while he was traveling and collecting a great deal of goods: πολὺν βίοτον συναγείρων. This passage calls to mind the one describing the Phoenician traders in Eumaeus' story in Book 14.

21. Merry and Ridell.1886 at lines 6.263ff.: "The topography finds a remarkable il-

lustration in the Phoenician city of Tyre, which was built originally on an island just off the coast, and was afterwards connected with the mainland by a causeway and subsequent accretions of sand. This causeway formed a narrow εἰσίθμη (ἴθμα, ἰέναι) to the town, and on either side of it lay a harbor, the north or Sidonian harbor, and the south or Egyptian." Cf. Harden 1962.25–30, who describes the typical location of a Phoenician settlement in terms that are quite similar to the settlement of Phaeacia: at a spring, with suitably sheltered anchorage, in a rocky limestone area where stones could be quarried.

22. Lorimer.1950.97. See also her more general assessment of the potential for Near Eastern influence on the scenes from the *Odyssey* (429): "It is natural that Oriental modes of decoration, of which some knowledge and much rumour must have been current in the eighth century, should have left their traces in the *Odyssey*."

23. Webster 1958.32.

24. Faraone 1987. See also Braun 1982.13, who claims that although archaic Greek houses could not have afforded the kind of metalwork that appears regularly in Homer, "Homer's dreams of wealth from the orient are based in fact." See also West 1997.412–15, who sees Gilgamesh motifs in the Phaeacian episode.

25. Thuc. 1.25.4 and 3.70.4; cf. Hellanicus *FGrH* 4 F77; Callim. Fr. 12 Pfeiffer; Ap. Rhod. 4.1209ff.; Diodorus 4.72; Tibullus 1.3.3. Garvie 1994.147 remarks on the similarities between Phaeacia and Old Smyrna or other eighth-century colonies such as Corcyra or Syracuse. Malkin 1998.74 and 111 argues that in antiquity, Phaeacia was unambiguously identified with Corcyra, although he also asserts that he himself believes that Phaeacia is a mythical place. His subsequent argument, however, seems to depend on the identification of Scheria and Corcyra.

26. Segal 1994.12–64; Ahl and Roisman 1996.47–48; Malkin 1998.111–12.

27. In this respect I follow Vidal-Naquet 1986.19n29, who argues that "Homeric wonders, like all wonders, bear some relation to the realities of their time." Along these lines, see also Garvie 1994.178: "The description [of Alcinous' palace] may owe something to distant memory of Minoan luxury, especially of the Palace at Cnossus, something also to oriental influence, but it also depends heavily on fantasy." In focusing here on the Near Easternness of Phaeacia, I do not mean to rule out any allusions to early Greek colonial sites. We will look at this connection further in the next chapter.

28. The archeological evidence is by no means definitive and continues to be subject to debate and reevaluation. I make no claims here to represent this ongoing scholarly debate in all its complexity and details; rather, I aim for a sensible and accurate overview.

29. For more detailed discussions of early Greek and Near Eastern contact and trade, see Moscati 1968; Coldstream 1969; 1977; 1982; 1998; Muhly 1970; Frankenstein 1979; Boardman 1980; 1999; Riis 1982; Morris 1992; 1997; Burkert 1992; Kopcke 1992; Snodgrass 1994; Popham 1994; Winter 1995.249–55; Hoffman 1997.

30. Morris 1992.101–49. See also Burkert 1992.11; Winter 1995.253; Giardino 1995; Muhly 1998; and Coldstream 1998.356 for the significance of the metal trade in particular for establishing commercial and cultural contacts between Greece and Phoenicia. See Tandy 1997.72–75 for evidence of the metal trade in Homer. For Morris, Greco-Phoenician trade contacts go all the way back to the Bronze Age. She argues (1992.103–5, with bibliography) that remains from two Bronze Age shipwrecks off Cape Gelidonya and Ulu Burun suggest a circle of trade connecting Egypt, the Levant, and the Aegean. One ship's cargo of bronze and copper ingots, metal scrap, and tools provides

tangible evidence of an early trade in metals. The contents of the other reveals traffic in much more lucrative cargo as well: gold, ivory, amber, and jars of exotic unguents.

31. Morris 2000.209.

32. Although there is some debate about whether trade along these lines continued without a break after 1200 B.C.E., from the early ninth century on, there certainly is evidence of Phoenician presence in the Mediterranean, especially in Euboea, Athens, Crete, Cyprus, and the Dodecanese. Although Greeks traded with Egypt in the Bronze Age, there is no evidence for a resumption of direct trade with Egypt until the seventh century. See Coldstream 1989.91; 1998.356. It is perhaps the nature of the commodities traded—food rather than metals—that accounts for the later development of Greek trade relations with Egypt compared with the rest of the Levant.

33. Popham, Sackett, and Themelis 1980; 1996. See also Coldstream 1982; Morris 1992.139–41; Thomas and Conant 1999.91–102; Morris 2000.218–38.

34. Coldstream. 1977.70–71.

35. See Morris 1992.150–94 for a detailed discussion of the evidence for contact and commerce between the Greeks and the east on Crete. A Phoenician bowl dating to 900 B.C.E. was found in Knossos, and bronze, gold, ivory, and amber goods of Levantine workmanship were discovered in the Idaian cave. Cf. Boardman 1967; Burkert 1992.11n3; Morris 1992.154 n18; Hoffman 1997.191–245.

36. Cf. Moscati 1968.8–29; Frankenstein 1979; Coldstream 1982; Morris 1992.125–49; Burkert 1992.11–12; Kopcke 1992. Phoenicia colonized Kition in Cyprus in the mid-ninth century, and the traditional date for Carthage's foundation is ca. 814 B.C.E. (Timaeus *FGrH* 566 F 60), even though archeologists continue to debate this date. Cf. Winter 1995.254 and bibliography cited in note 50 on the date of Carthage. Phoenicia also established colonies in Sicily, Sardinia, and Spain at this time, although the nature of Phoenician colonization is still much debated. See Crielaard 1992–93; Boardman 1999.268–69 for the different Greek and Phoenician colonial patterns.

37. Archeological evidence for Greeks in the Near East before the eighth century is thin; nevertheless, it seems probable that some Greeks were trading and living in the Levant at this time. See Braun 1982.9–11; Burkert 1992.11–12; Kopcke 1992; Morris 1992; Coldstream 1992; 1998. For a more cautious approach, see Snodgrass 1994. The date of a Greek presence at Al Mina and the nature of the Greeks' role there continues to be debated. Although it was previously believed that Greeks were present at Al Mina as early as its foundation in 825 B.C.E., a reevaluation of the evidence by Kearsley (1995) has led some to the conclusion that Greek participation at Al Mina started no earlier than 750. The still unresolved debate hangs on the dating of pendent semicircle *skyphoi*; cf. Kearsley 1989. Those who argue for an earlier Greek presence at Al Mina include Boardman 1990.169–90; Popham and Lemos 1992; Popham 1994. Those who question that early date include Graham 1986.51–65; Snodgrass 1994.

38. Coldstream 1998.353–55.

39. Snodgrass 1971.335–36; Ridgway 1992.25–29. Cf. Markoe 1992 for a discussion of Greek and Phoenician search for metals in Italy.

40. Burkert 1992.21–25 suggests that the migration of craftsmen from the east to Greece corresponds with Assyrian campaigns before 800 and again after 700 B.C.E. Morris 1992.101–24 dates this contact back to the Bronze Age and suggests that from 1500 to 1200 B.C.E. was the most significant phase of Aegean relations with the Near East in terms

of both intellectual and social exchange as well as trade between the Aegean, Hittite, Egyptian, and Mesopotamian empires. She argues that the world of the itinerant Homeric *demiourgoi* should be the model for understanding early Greek orientalizing culture. See also Coldstream 1969; 1982 for a more cautious assessment, see Hoffman 1997.153–245.

41. See Coldstream 1993 for a discussion of intermarriage between Greeks and native populations at the frontiers of the early Greek world.

42. Quint 1993.250–51.

43. Quint 1993.262. See also Pagden 1993.18–21 for a similar discussion of the ways in which Columbus assimilated the commercial value of gold with its more metaphorical sense in Christianity; Columbus claimed that he had found the legendary mines of King Solomon.

44. Shakespeare locates Prospero's island in the Bermudas, as we observed in chapter 4.

45. See Morris 2000.208–18 for an interesting discussion of the different cultural ideologies associated with bronze and iron in the eleventh century B.C.E. As a result of the break in Greek trade with the east from 1025 to 950, access to bronze, gold, and other fine metals was limited, and central Greeks began to use iron instead in their burials. Drawing on this archeological evidence together with Hesiod's myth of metals/ages, Morris concludes that bronze is the metal associated with the past and with the east, while iron is associated with the present and with a sense of locality.

46. See Winter 1995.255–58, where she lays out what she calls the "facts" of this trope. She emphasizes that the historical identity of the Phoenicians adds weight and substance to their imagery but warns us that we must realize that these images are created as part of a Greek, not Phoenician, reality. Earlier scholars assumed a historical reality for the Phoenicians in their debates over the date of the poem and the role of Phoenicians in Greece; see, for example, Muhly 1970. Cf. Kopcke 1992.107 for the ways in which the poetic power of Homer continues to influence the historical study of Greco-Phoenician contact. Cf. Mele 1979.87–91 on Phoenician trade in Homer.

47. Winter 1995.258–62. She argues that the *Odyssey* does not directly reflect the time period in which it was composed; rather, following Vance (1973), she sees epic (like hero cult and athletic games) as a product of cultural processes associated with early state formation in which heroic action and archaizing values are glorified and treated rhetorically in order to make room for new institutions and values.

48. Winter 1995.261.

49. Winter 1995.261: "On the one hand, they represent the 'different and foreign' of the traditional enemy, and we must read them in terms of alterity; on the other hand, they represent a projection of the social and economic present, the becoming 'self,' and we must read them with all of the ambivalence and discomfort, denial even, that contemporary Greeks must have felt about the changes their society was presently undergoing."

50. Cf. Winter 1995.257, where she does see "Odysseus as centered between extremes," but not in her analysis of the Phoenician trope.

51. My analysis comes to many conclusions compatible with those of Winter; the difference has more to do with how the poetics of the *Odyssey* works—more specifically, how the ethnographic imagination operates; I see the principle of triangulation rather than simple opposition at work here.

52. At *Od.*5.333–34, Odysseus encounters Leucothea; she guides him to Phaeacia at 5.344–45.

53. *Od.* 6.163. See Bowie 1998 for an interesting essay that unpacks the rich and sophisticated complexity of Phoenix/Phoenician imagery in the text of Heliodorus, together with its invocation of the *Odyssey*.

54. *Od.* 4.611–19. See also *Il.* 23.740–47, where Achilles offers a Phoenician-made bowl as a prize in the funeral games for Patrocles.

55. *Od.* 13.10.

56. Phoenician women weave: *Il.* 6.289–90; Phaeacian women: *Od.* 7.108–11.

57. Phoenicians: *Od.* 15.415; Phaeacians: *Od.* 7.39; 8.191, 369. In addition, one of the Phaeacians is named Ναυσικλειτὸς Δύμας (*Od.* 6.22).

58. The one exception comes at *Od.* 4.611–19, where Menelaus gives Telemachus a finely worked silver and gold bowl that had been given to him by Phaedimus, king of the Sidonians.

59. *Od.* 13.271–86.

60. *Od.* 14.285–300.

61. *Od.* 15.403–84. An interesting point that helps support Winter's argument about the constructed, rather than historically accurate, representation of the Phoenicians in the *Odyssey* is that each of the three times that Phoenicians are mentioned in the second half of the poem (the source of the negative image), it is as part of an embedded tale rather than the larger Homeric narrative.

62. Their ships are black (νηὶ μελαίνῃ 15.416; they cleave the sea (νῆος ποντοπόροιο), 14.295; they are hollow (νηὶ γλαφυρῇ), 13.283; 15.456; (κοίλῃ νηὶ), 15.420, 457; swift (ὠκύαλος νηῦς), 15. 473.

63. Cf. *Od.* 8.5, where we see that the agora is built beside the ships.

64. In an attempt to capture the wordplay in Greek, I have transliterated these names exactly (with the exception of Alcinous) and given a translation, when appropriate, for each name in parentheses.

65. *Od.* 6.9–10; 7.34; 13.65, 96. Cf. Ahl and Roisman 1996.99 for the ingenious suggestion that the name Alcinous, "strong in mind," contains a wordplay on Alcinaus, "strong in ships."

66. Cf. Rosen 1990.103–4n9, who argues that the Phaeacians are not real traders.

67. *Od.* 11.363–66.

68. Said 1978, reprinted with an afterword in 1995.

69. Winter 1995.263.

70. West 1988.119. For the second etymology she cites Hesychius s.v. ἀλφησταί and Aesch. *Th.* 770. See also Garvie 1994.83 for these two etymological possibilities.

71. *Od.* 13.291–95.

72. Winter 1995.256–57 argues that, while Odysseus shares some qualities with the Phoenicians, especially those of guile and artifice, unlike that of the Phoenicians, Odysseus' behavior never violates social codes. While she is right that Odysseus is not portrayed as unrelentingly greedy and tricky as are the Phoenicians, she underestimates the extent to which he (more than any other hero) is like them: he is most profit-making; he does live by trickery rather than by force; he does travel the seas and bring home lots of goods.

73. *Od.* 11.355–59, cited in chapter 2.

74. The Greek word for trader is ἔμπορος, literally, one who "sails on the ship of an-

other." See Finkelstein 1935 on the terminology of trade. This, in fact, is the life Odysseus describes as his own to Eumaeus in Book 14.285–300, when he claims that he is a Cretan man shipwrecked on Ithaca. Among his many adventures, he stayed in Egypt for seven years gathering a great deal of goods and also joined a Phoenician trader in a trip to Libya in the hopes of gathering cargo.

75. Redfield 1983.234.

76. For discussions of this passage as evidence for the ancient metal trade, see Tandy 1997.63–64; Malkin 1998.72–73. Morris (1992.119 and note 79) suggests an etymology for Temeses from the Semitic word for "foundry." She notes the imaginary nature of the Taphians, but sees the passage as indicative of a plausible merchant journey, moving metal cargo east or west across the Mediterranean.

77. *Od.* 3.71–74. Edwards 1979.30–31, 37 notes that the *Etymologicum Magnum* s.v. "Taphioi" includes pirates who traveled with Cadmus.

78. Apparently they excel in slave trade; see 14.452: Eumaeus bought Mesaulius from Taphians.

79. Of Phaeacians: 5.386; of Taphians: here and 1.419.

80. Winter 1995.268n43. She mentions that the term "bright iron" is associated with Greece in the catalogue of trade goods brought into Tyre (Ezekiel 27:19) and hypothesizes that the Taphians thus might represent a synthesis of first-millennium Mediterranean trade, representing the importance of Cyprus to Mediterranean commerce, Greek iron being traded for Cypriot copper.

81. *Od.* 13.256–86.

82. Cf. *Od.* 13.71 and 120 where the same adjective is used in the same line position to describe the Phaeacians who convey Odysseus home.

83. The Phaeacians are famous for conveying men: *Od.* 8.31–33.


Chapter 6


1. Clay 1983.125–32; Mondi 1983.25–28; Vidal-Naquet 1986.27; Segal 1994.30–33, 202–15; Ahl and Roisman 1996.101–2.

2. Segal 1994.32–3 observes that both similes used to describe the blinding of Polyphemus are drawn from the world of technology: shipbuilding (9.383–88) and metalworking (9.391–94). See also Rose 1992.138. The use of the metalworking simile in this respect is interesting, too, in light of the significance of the metal trade to the construction of the Phaeacians, as we saw in the previous chapter. Here, it would seem that the Cyclopes are as ignorant of metalworking as they are of shipbuilding, two defining characteristics of the Phaeacians. Or perhaps Homer is making a veiled allusion to the Hesiodic tradition (*Th.* 139–46, 501–6) that portrays the Cyclopes as famous metalworkers. On the relationship between Hesiod's Cyclopes and those in *Odyssey* 9, see Mondi 1983; Ahl and Roisman 1996.115–18.

3. Cf. *Od.* 5.225, where the raft of Odysseus is said to be as big as the hull of a broad cargo ship. It is interesting here that the simile specifies a cargo ship, given the Cyclopes' lack of commercial activity and Odysseus' associations with trade in the poem.

4. Cf. *Od.* 5, where Odysseus uses just this technique to build his raft.

5. Segal 1994.31.

6. See Edwards 1993.47–48 and my discussion in chapter 4.

7. Vidal-Naquet 1986.28–29 observes that the social institutions of Pylos, Sparta, and Ithaca are found on Scheria as well; cf. Segal 1994.30–33.

8. Ahl and Roisman 1996.102 note the similarities between Polyphemus' courtyard here and that of the precinct of Poseidon at Phaeacia.

9. Cf. Mondi 1983.25–28. Cf. Podlecki 1961.127–29 and Reece 1993.123–43 for discussions of the theme of hospitality in *Odyssey* 9. Segal 1994.202 connects the theme of hospitality to the differing manifestations of the proximity to the gods experienced by the Cyclopes and the Phaeacians: "Taken together, the Phaeacians and the Cyclopes embody the two poles of a privileged closeness to the gods."

10. See Vidal-Naquet 1986.27; Clay 1983.127–32 and 1980.263, esp. note 10, where she makes this observation, noting that that the island nearby the Cyclopes is occupied by goats, an animal that is both wild and civilized. Kirk 1970.162–71 discusses the theme of nature and culture in *Odyssey* 9.

11. In addition, both the Phaeacians and the Cyclopes suffer as a result of their interactions with Odysseus, and in both cases Poseidon is involved. The Phaeacians are forever cut off from their seafaring past when Poseidon freezes their ship as a rock. Polyphemus is blinded by Odysseus and then calls on Poseidon for revenge. Furthermore, Polyphemus' act of throwing the rock at Odysseus' departing ship at the end of Book 9 anticipates Poseidon's act of calicifying the ship of the Phaeacians in Book 13.

12. *Od.* 6.273–85 (Nausicaa); 7.16–17 (Athena); 8.443–45 (Arete). The ambivalence shown by the Phaeacians toward their guests is reflected in their landscape. After Odysseus loses his raft and is casting about for a place to land on the island of the Phaeacians, at first he remarks that this is a land without harbors (5.404); this initial impression of inaccessibility, however, is countered by his discovery of the gentle river mouth (5.441) that leads him safely to shore.

13. For this point, see Detienne 1981; Vidal-Naquet 1986; cf. Calame 1977, who argues for the ternary structure of *Odyssey* 9.

14. For a historical overview of the archaic Greek colonization movement, see Bérard 1957; 1960; Graham 1964; 1982; Boardman 1980; 1999.

15. For discussions of the Euboean role in colonizing the west, see Boardman 1980.161–89; Ridgway 1990; 1992.11–42; 2000; Crielaard 1992–93; 1993; Tandy 1997.76–78; Malkin 1998.74–87.

16. Ridgway 1992.20–26; 2000.5–6.

17. For the debate over the motivations behind the archaic colonial movement, see Gwynn 1918; Blakeway 1933; Snodgrass 1980; Graham 1982; Ridgway 1990; 1992; Tandy 1997.4; 75–76.

18. For more on the contact between Greek colonists and native populations, see the essays collected in Descoeudres 1990; Ridgway 2000. For two different kinds of discussions of the issues arising from colonial-indigenous contact and conflict, see Dougherty 1993 and Malkin 1998.

19. See Malkin 1998, who argues that *nostoi* legends are particularly useful in articulating ethnic identity. See also Bérard 1957.323–83; Fabre 1981.149–214.

20. Strabo 6.1.15.

21. Strabo 6.1.12.

22. Thuc. 2.68; cf. Strabo 7.7.7.

23. For others who read the *Odyssey* within early Greek colonial discourse, see Hall 1989.49–50; Dench 1995.36–38. Finley 1978.61–63 notes that the poem reflects curiosity about the west in an age of colonization. Crielaard 1995.236–39 argues for the *Odyssey*'s awareness of colonization. Rose 1992.134–40 discusses the ways in which the nature/culture themes of the *Odyssey* participate in colonial ideology. Malkin 1998.21, by contrast, argues that the *Odyssey* has nothing to do with colonial ideology since the poem does not directly describe a colonial foundation. Instead, its interests are with the travel and exploration that predate the colonial movement; thus, for Malkin, the *Odyssey* is a precolonial text.

24. In the previous chapter, I argued for an etymology of this adjective that connects it with the word for commercial gain, suggesting that this helped characterize the Phaeacian antipathy to trade that forms the basis for the opposition between them and the Phoenicians in the poem: the Phaeacians live far from profit-hungry men. Now, within the framework of an opposition between the very civilized, hospitable Phaeacians and their cannibalistic cousins, I want to activate the etymology that translates the phrase as "men who eat bread." Again, both meanings of the word make sense in a context of Phaeacian duality.

25. This passage is almost always cited as evidence for the practice of founding a colony in archaic Greece and the role of the founder or *oikist*. See Graham 1964.29; Malkin 1987.138; Dougherty 1993.23.

26. Garvie 1994.83–84; Crielaard 1995.236–39.

27. Vidal-Naquet 1986.26.

28. In fact, we might say that Book 9 is a mini-colonial book. Both of the shorter episodes that precede Odysseus' encounter with the Cyclops can also be seen within the conventions of colonial discourse. The raid on the Ciconians is reminiscent of the kind of force often necessary for colonial settlement. The episode with the Lotus-Eaters represents the threat that colonists will go native—not want to return to Greece or stay Greek.

29. See Clay 1980 for the intriguing suggestion that this is the island from which the Phaeacians colonized Scheria. She argues that χηρεύει means "to be widowed" and must indicate not the absence of any previous settlement but the fact that previous settlers have abandoned the site.

30. *Od.* 9.146–48. See Malkin 1987.27–28; "surprised oikist" is his term. See also Dougherty 1993.18, where I argue that this colonial motif displaces the responsibility for colonization away from the colonists themselves and onto Apollo, the "patron saint" of colonization.

31. On the marriage theme in *Odyssey* 6, see Hague 1983.136–38; Winkler 1990.178–80; Austin 1991.235–43; Segal 1994.23.

32. See Dougherty 1993.61–80, where this argument is made in much more detail.

33. Sappho Fr. 105a and c L–P. See also Catullus 1.22–24 and 62.39–58 for additional examples in Latin poetry that seem clearly to derive from Greek tradition; see Hague 1983.135–38 for further discussion and examples.

34. See Dougherty 1993.63–64 for this imagery in Greek colonial traditions. See Kolodny 1975 and Parker 1987.140–46 for discussions of feminized representations of the New World in Renaissance and later American traditions.

35. Plut. *Mor.* 140e–f. Of course, this partnership is rarely an equal one, as Plutarch notes at *Mor.* 139d. Part of what the rhetoric of acculturation does is to establish the terms

of this relationship between husband and wife. The imagery equates the bride here with the land to be cultivated and gives the husband the tools of acculturation. He is the one with the plough; he has the power and control. See Dubois 1988.39–85; Henderson 1991.134–36, 166–69 for the use of plowing imagery to represent sexual activity.

36. Aeneas at *Aen.* 1.94–96 echoes Odysseus at *Od.* 5.306–7.

37. Of course, Aeneas does not actually found the city of Rome itself within the scope of the *Aeneid*, but the rhetoric of the poem characterizes his marriage with Lavinia as symbolic of the eventual founding of Rome.

38. See Zeitlin 1986.143 for a discussion of the inseparability of the erotic from notions of coercive power within the institution and the ideology of Greek marriage.

39. See Carson 1982 for an insightful discussion of the marriage imagery in this ode.

40. See Dougherty 1993.136–56 for a fuller discussion of Pythian 9 along these lines.

41. *Od.* 6.161–69.

42. Cf. *Od.* 6.119–21.

43. Hulme 1986.86. In this book (esp. 13–87), Hulme carefully distinguishes the social practice of eating humans, or anthropophagy, from the discourse of cannibalism, which he locates historically within the gold mining industry of the Caribbean and the introduction of slave trading by Columbus. Although the word "cannibal" (linked as it is linguistically to "Carib") certainly dates to Columbus's expeditions, I would argue that the discourse of cannibalism as Hulme defines it predates European New World colonization. For a more succinct presentation of his argument, see Hulme 1992.

44. In addition, cannibal narratives reveal an equally prevalent concern with a regression to a primitive state—the state of eating raw flesh. A great deal of recent scholarship from many periods, ancient and modern, has addressed this topic. See, for example, Arens 1979; Pagden 1982; Clark and Motto 1984; Rawson 1984; Hulme 1986; 1992; Obeyesekere 1992; Rigby 1992; Coplan 1993; Smith 1995.

45. For a discussion of how "cannibalism can be defined within the structure of Greek thinking," see Detienne 1981. On this topic see also Burkert 1983. Rawson 1984 offers a general discussion of the literary appearances of cannibalism including Greek literature.

46. E.g., *Il.* 5.782; 7.256; 11.454, 479; 15.592; 16.157; 22.67.

47. Hera: *Il.* 4.34–36; Achilles: *Il.* 22.345–48; Hecuba: *Il.* 24.212–14.

48. Rawson (1984.1165–67) has argued that Hecuba's wish to eat Achilles' liver is a mark of her identity as a barbarian queen. Cf. Redfield 1975.192–99; Griffin 1980.19–21; Rawson 1984.1164–65 for discussion of "vicarious cannibalism," or the tendency to displace the behavior onto dogs and animals of prey, a pattern that marks the wishes of Achilles and Hecuba as all the more savage.

49. Detienne 1981.218: "The animal world knows neither justice nor injustice; and it is this fundamental ignorance which the Greeks regarded as the essential distinction between animals and mankind. Separated from men, who live under the rule of *dike*, within legally-defined relations, animals are condemned to eat each other. The kingdom of cannibalism begins at the frontier where justice ends." The description of cannibalism in Hesiod's passage corresponds to Odysseus' initial division of men at 9.175–76: men who are wild and not just.

50. This same theme is developed in the context of Athenian fifth-century imperial-

ism in Euripides' version of the Polyphemus tale in his satyr play *Cyclops*. See Dougherty 1999 for a discussion of this play along these lines.

51. Detienne 1981.219 argues that cannibalism is located within clusters of images that Greeks constructed about themselves and outsiders. This system proclaims the eating of raw flesh to be a form of bestiality clearly rejected by the Greek city; it sets cannibalism on the margins of its history, in a previous age or on geographical edges or both. Cf. Vidal-Naquet 1986.21, who notes that the mythical aspects of the episode are conflated with a quasi-ethnographic desciption of pastoral peoples with an overt, realistic reference to colonization; he suggests that the non-human is a way to express that which is savage among humans.

52. Thuc. 6.1–5.

53. See Dougherty 1993.40–41 for further bibliography and discussion of the violence of colonization.

54. Crielaard 1992–93.239–42.

55. What I am calling "the discourse of cannibalism" here is just one of several ways in which Greek colonial narratives attempt to address and expiate the violence inherent in overseas settlement. See also Dougherty 1993 for additional strategies along these lines. This material, if read correctly, provides strong testimony against the claim made by Malkin 1998.229 that colonial violence was rarely perceived as sacrilege: "We are told, time and again, of expulsions, annexations of native territories, and even the subjugation of natives as serfs. Hardly ever do we find implicit or explicit apologies or the idea that the act of possession in and of itself was hubristic." See also 233, where he argues, in a somewhat contradictory fashion, that "awareness of violence in relation to natives is highly exceptional in the world of Greek colonization."

56. See Rose 1992.137–38 for a similar reading of Odysseus' blinding of Polyphemus: "In the adventure that most obviously pits nature against culture, the encounter with the Cyclopes, Odysseus emerges most concretely as the aggressive colonist." He goes on to discuss the way in which the sufferings that Odysseus endures as a result of his violence against Polyphemus acknowledge some aspects of colonial guilt or misgivings: "It is thus not accidental that Odysseus' crime against Polyphemus is repeatedly cited (e.g., 1.68–75, 13.341–3) as the reason for Odysseus' sufferings. As with the descendants of Cain, a gain in technology bears the stain of a crime against the status quo. It is as if the poet has internalized the opprobrium associated with colonizers, who, like Hesiod's father, 'fleeing bitter poverty,' imposed their mastery on the sea and the simpler cultures living on its periphery, by either butchering them or driving them inland."

57. Reece 1993.126 points out that the theme of hospitality as part of the Cyclops story is Homer's innovation; it appears in none of the more than two hundred other versions of this folktale. At 131–43 Reece documents the ways in which the Polyphemus scene deviates from the customary Homeric hospitality scene.

58. This "*Outis* trick" belongs to the tradition of including intellectual trickery within colonial discourse. In this respect, intellectual prowess replaces physical might as the way to gain territory from native inhabitants. See Dougherty 1993.53. For other examples, see Virgil *Aen.* 1.367–68 (Dido's trick to gain the territory of Byrsa) and Scheid and Svenbro's discussion (1985.328–42) and Plut. *Mor.* 293f–294c; 296d–e.

59. See Rose 1992.134–40 for a similar argument.

60. *Od.* 10.80–132.

61. See Heubeck 1989.49–50 for a collection of the verbal parallels that emphasize the similarities between the Laestrygonians and the Cyclopes.

62. At *Od.* 10.120, we learn that the Laestrygonians are not like men but like Giants; cf. 7.56–59 for the relationship between the Phaeacians and the Giants and 7.205–6 for their shared closeness to the gods.

Chapter 7

1. See Geertz 1973.448 for this notion of a story that a culture tells itself about itself.

2. We recall that the Phaeacians have settled in Scheria, "far from profit-hungry men" (ἑκὰς ἀνδρῶν ἀλφηστάων, *Od.* 6.8), i.e., the Phoenicians, and in so doing, they have put a great distance between themselves and their cannibalistic cousins, the Cyclopes. In other words, both sets of oppositions are marked by a geographic distance as well.

3. For reports on the archeological material, see Popham et al. 1980; 1982a and b; 1986; 1990; 1996; for a general overview of "the Euboeans at home," see Ridgway 1992.11–20; for the importance of Lefkandi, see Boardman 1999.272; Thomas and Conant 1999.85–114.

4. Popham et al. 1980.7–8; 362–63; 1982a.171; 1982b.247. Antonaccio 1995 provides a helpful overview and interpretation of the archeological evidence at Lefkandi, focusing on the burial at Toumba.

5. Popham 1987. The pyxis was found as part of a deposit of broken pottery included in the refill of a shaft grave that had apparently destroyed an earlier tomb.

6. Apollod. *Epit.* 6.7–8 and Ap. Rhod. 1.134–38. Cf. *Od.* 8.111–19 for the catalogue of Phaeacian names. Both Ναύβολος and Κλυτόνηος appear in the Phaeacian catalogue.

7. See Ridgway 1992.21–30 for a helpful review of "the Euboeans abroad," and Boardman 1999.270–75 for a review of Greek contact with the east.

8. Ridgway 2000.180. For the role of mining and metallurgy in exploring and settling the western Mediterannean from the fourteenth to the eighth centuries B.C.E., see Giardino 1995.

9. See Crielaard 1992–93 for a discussion of the difference between Greek and Phoenician models of colonial expansion. He argues that the Phoenicians were looking to establish a network of coastal settlements for the acquisition of trade goods and food. The Euboeans did in fact conquer territory, and their colonial settlements, intended for independent survival, replicated the fairly simple structure of the Greek homeland. See Boardman 1999.268–69 on the different patterns of movement and settlement for Greeks and Phoenicians in the eighth century. For more on Greeks and Phoenicians in the west, see Frankenstein 1979; Coldstream 1982; 1994; Markoe 1992; Ridgway 1992; 1994; 2000; Aubet 1993.

10. Ridgway 1992.13. He argues that at the end of the ninth century, the peoples living in the Levant in general enjoyed a more sophisticated culture than Greece, especially in the areas of metalworking and seafaring.

11. Ridgway 1992.25–29; 2000.183. He argues that the Phoenicians were already mining in Sardinia at the end of the ninth century, and Euboeans followed them westward when their need for additional sources of raw metals increased. See also Snodgrass

1971.335–36 for the increased need for metals. Ridgway 1992.83 also makes the intriguing observation that the topography of the Euboean colony of Pithecoussae was itself reminiscent of the kinds of sites on which the Phoenicians liked to build cities.

12. Boardman 1999.273: "All the evidence suggests that in our period they got on well with each other, sometimes in matters of positive collaboration, and living side by side." And at 275–76 Boardman argues that, with respect to Greek and Phoenician settlement in the west, "Who first?" is a meaningless question. Crielaard 1995.231 also agrees that there was cooperation between the Phoenicians and the Greeks in the west, as does Tandy 1997.71. Winter 1995.254–55 argues for some degree of competition operative in the Mediterranean sea trade in the archaic period. See also Markoe 1992 for a discussion of the "symbiotic" relationship between Greeks and Phoenicians in central Italy from the late eighth to the early seventh centuries.

13. If not at the moment of its foundation, there do seem to have been Euboeans participating at Al Mina by the second half of the eighth century. For more on the complicated question of the date of Euboean participation at Al Mina, see the bibliography cited in chapter 5, note 35.

14. Ancient sources for founding of Pithecoussae: Str. 5.4.9; Livy 8.22.5–6. For archeological reports, see Buchner and Ridgway 1993. For a brief and very helpful overview, with more specific bibliographic references, of the Pithecoussae site, see Ridgway 1992.31–120. On the Levantine presence at Pithecoussae, see Boardman 1990.182; 1999.276; Ridgway 1992.111–18; 2000.183–85.

15. See Ridgway 1992.67–77 on the social organization of Pithecoussae.

16. On the pottery finds, see Ridgway 1992.54–67. Ridgway (1988 and 1992.60–65) characterizes the settlement at Pithecussae as a stable domicile and safe port of call for merchants, metalworkers, artisans, and craftsmen.

17. For a discussion of Nestor's Cup, found in the tomb of a twelve-year-old boy, see Ridgway 1992.55–57 and 116, where he argues that Nestor's Cup may have belonged to a non-Greek family. Cf. Malkin 1998.156–60, who argues that Nestor's Cup belonged to a Greek rather than Levantine family, and Thomas and Conant 1999.110–11. The inscription reads: "Nestor had a fine drinking cup, but anyone who drinks from this cup will soon be struck with desire for fair-crowned Aphrodite." See Faraone 1996 for the text and a translation as well as for a discussion of the magical implications of the inscription.

18. On the shipwreck krater, see Ridgway 1988 and 1992.57–60 and further discussion in this chapter.

19. Powell 1991.163–67 argues that Nestor's Cup shows that Euboeans in the west knew their Homer very well. What the exact relationship is between the Homeric poems and the narrative scenes painted on these pots is, of course, a difficult question. While both the painted representations and the Homeric passages show a fondness for the same stories and characters, this does not mean that one must be derived from the other. More likely, both painter and poet work within the rich mythological tradition of the period. See Snodgrass 1998.12 for a skeptical view of the relationship between Homer and the painter at this time: "The assumption that any of these earliest figure-scenes can be read as pictures of episodes already known, to the artist and to us, from the *Iliad* and the *Odyssey* seems to me (to use no harsher word) an optimistic one."

20. M. L. West 1988. For criticism of West's linguistic analysis, see Chadwick 1990, and Wyatt 1992 with West's 1992 reply. Cf. Ruijgh 1995.47–50 for a different explana-

tion for the Euboean elements in Homeric language. He suggests that Homer frequented Euboea for epic recitals, invited by a king familiar with East Ionic poetry. Scholars who accept West's argument include Powell 1991.232 and Winter 1995.261–62.

21. M. L. West 1988.166. He lists three linguistic features that point to Euboea: the use of π instead of κ in ποῦ, πῶς, πότε, and so on; the occasional absence of compensatory lengthening following the loss of postconsonantal *wau* (ἐνάτη for εἰνάτη); and "Attic" correption. Ruigjh 1995.48 argues that Euboean Ionians could not have directly borrowed the epic tradition from poets of the Aeolic phase.

22. Powell 1991.231 argues that the Euboeans were an ideal audience for the Homeric poems, especially the *Odyssey*: "The *Odyssey* is tailor-made for Euboians of c. 800 B.C., a time when the far West was just being entered, where everything was yet mysterious and strange."

23. M. L. West 1988.166–67. Cf. Antonaccio 1995.13–15 for a discussion of the use of the burial building at Lefkandi.

24. M. L. West 1988.170–71.

25. Crielaard 1995; Ruijgh 1995.48: "In effect, the legendary island of the Phaeacians seems to be, up to a certain degree, the counterpart to the Euboea of the real world" (my translation). I want to be clear about what the Phaeacian story does and does not tell us. It is important to recognize not just the narrative similarities but also the elaborate oppositional structure of the Phaeacian tale and to bring that to bear on its relationship with the Euboeans.

26. In focusing here on the potential relationship between the mythical Phaeacians and the historical Euboeans in the poem, I do not mean to overlook the poem's Panhellenic status to suggest that what we have here is the equivalent of a Euboean epic. Instead, in trying to make sense of the significant role of the Phaeacians, I am interested in untangling just one of the poems' many threads linking poem and audience.

27. See Coldstream 1993 on hybrid communities at the frontiers of the Greek world.

28. See Ridgway 1988.98. In this article on the krater, Ridgway includes a detailed description of the shipwreck image.

29. Morrison and Williams 1968.34 argue that the style of ship is closer to Corinthian than Attic representations; cf. Popham 1981 on possible cooperation between Euboea and Corinth.

30. Webster 1958.170.

31. Boardman 1980.166.

32. Pinney 1983.127–46, cited in support by Ridgway 1988.97. See also Snodgrass 1998. At 35–36 he discusses this issue with respect to an Attic Geometric *oinochoe* decorated with a similar shipwreck scene, concluding that it, too, is not a direct illustration of the *Odyssey* passage but rather reflects a view that is both contemporary and heroizing.

33. It is interesting to note here the similarities between the prophecy of Poseidon's destruction of the Phaeacians' ship (because they help Odysseus) and the prediction that Odysseus will blind Polyphemus, which leads immediately to Polyphemus' attempt to destroy Odysseus' ship with a rock and ultimately to Poseidon's curse upon Odysseus and his ships—just one more way in which the stories of the Phaeacians and Polyphemus are interconnected.

34. Cf. Vernant 1983.313 and note 34 for a similar observation about the tension between the "aerial mobility of the *psuché* and the immobility of the funerary stele." He

refs to the *Iliad* passage (17.434ff.) where Achilles' horses, as swift as the wind, suddenly become as still as death, just like a funerary stele. Cf. Hoekstra 1992.174 for the theory that this story provides an *aition* for the rock opposite Corcyra, the island often identified in antiquity as Phaeacia.

35. I am thinking in part of David Ridgway's claim that the most important cargo that the Euboeans brought home from the east was knowledge of the west.

## Chapter 8

1. Ithaca: 13.96–112; cf. Cyclopes: 9.105–41; Aeolus: 10.1–12; Laestrygonians: 10.80–99.

2. See 13.325–26, where Odysseus asks himself, upon failing to recognize Ithaca, what other land he has come to (ἀλλά τιν' ἄλλην / γαῖαν ἀναστρέφομαι·). See also 13.191 and 397, where Athena makes Odysseus himself an unknown stranger (ἄγνωστον) at Ithaca.

3. Cf. *Od.* 6.119–21 and 9.174–76. This significant collocation of passages thus further reinforces the colonial nature of Odysseus' arrival at Ithaca.

4. Goats: 9.118; trees: 9.118; water: 9.133. In addition, the cave of the Nymphs (13.102–5) evokes the cave of Polyphemus (9.182–86); Athena safeguards Odysseus' possessions in the cave by stopping it with a rock (13.70–71), much as Polyphemus did at 9.240–43.

5. See Saïd 1977; Edwards 1993.51 on the parallels between the suitors and the Cyclops.

6. Other examples include ὑπερφίαλος: *Od.* 1.134, 227; 2.310; 11.116; 13.373; 14.27; 15.12, 315, 376; 16.271; 17.481; 18.71, 167; 20.12; ὑπερηνορέοντες: *Od.* 2.266, 324; 4.766; 17.482, 581; 18.111.

7. Hesiod *WD* 276–80. See also *Od.* 18.275, where the suitors are without δίκη.

8. See also *Od.* 16.315 for the use of this verb and adverb to describe the suitors. In the *Iliad*, the verb is used only of wild animals. See *Il.* 11.479: ὠμοφάγοι μιν θῶες ἐν οὔρεσι δαρδάπτουσιν. The suitors' appetite and behavior are also characterized in terms of ὕβρις. See *Od.* 1.227, 368; 3.206–7; 4.321, 627; 15.329; 16.86, 410; 17.169, 565, 581, 588; 20.370.

9. For additional examples of eating imagery used in this way, see *Od.* 1.160, 374–77; 2.203, 237; 4.318; 11.116; 13.396, 419, 428; 14.377; 15.12–13; 17.378.

10. *Od.* 9.125–30.

11. See Fernández-Galiano 1992.197–98 for a discussion of this nautical tool made of papyrus and its possible connections with Phoenicia or Egypt.

12. See Fernández-Galiano 1992.301–2 for this nautical term; it is almost always used for mooring a ship.

13. Cf. Nagler 1990 for a discussion of the problematic violence of Odysseus' revenge.

14. *Od.* 19.535.53.

15. The sequence of actions is clear and deliberate: the plans to disguise the slaughter as a wedding lead directly to the simile describing the beautification of Odysseus, the bed scene, the shipwreck simile, and, finally, the reunion of Penelope and Odysseus.

16. See Pucci 1987.91 on the significance of the suitors' death disguised as marriage: "On the one hand, it is devised simply to deflect the attention of people outside, who, hearing the merry music, will think Penelope has finally decided to marry one of the suitors. On the other hand, this sham also functions as the musical accompaniment to Odysseus' courtship of his wife and their new marriage; for it is indeed a new erotic scene and an exchange of witty clues (in which Penelope outdoes her husband) that finally establishes the recognition." Pucci also remarks on the undertone of lament that accompanies the wedding tune; περιστεναχίζετο is used at 23.146, suggesting a tone of lament amidst the resounding sound.

17. Austin 1991.237: "The marriage toward which the whole poem moves is now split into two, with some aspects distributed to the Nausicaa episode and others reserved for Penelope's reunion with Odysseus. The ceremonies begin with Nausicaa's vision, which opens Book 6, when Athena fills her young mind with romantic notions, but they are not concluded until Odysseus and Penelope retire in Book 23, and some will say not until the end of Book 24." See also Katz 1991.166–70; Zeitlin 1996.41.

18. *Od.* 6.229–35.

19. Foley 1984.71.

20. Cf. Redfield 1983.222, cited as the epigram for this chapter, for the notion of Odysseus as "re-founder" of his house.

21. In this respect, I disagree with Malkin 1998.4, 14, 119, who argues that Odysseus is a hero of proto-colonization rather than colonization (although see 210, where he does refer to Odysseus as a hero of colonization). Malkin argues that unlike other *nostoi* who never returned and are therefore heroes of colonization, since Odysseus does return home, he cannot be a colonial hero. This strikes me as a difficult argument to maintain, especially in light of the explicit colonial themes at work in the poem, and stems, I think, from a misreading of the ways in which themes of return and colonial discourse operate in this work of literature.

22. Often a colonial foundation will be figured as a kind of return (this is obviously part of the rationale behind the appropriation of figures from *nostoi* legends as colonial founders), and so the *Odyssey* inverts this convention to represent Odysseus' return as a kind of re-foundation. For a particularly interesting example of a colonial foundation figured as return, see the fragment from Aeschylus' lost play *Aetnaeae* (Fr. 6 Radt), which was written in celebration of Hieron's foundation of the city of Aetna. The fragment includes an etymology of the name of a local cult to mean "those who have returned" in Greek. For the passage and further discussion, see Dougherty 1991b.

23. *Od.* 9.130. Cf. Casevitz 1985 on the vocabulary of colonization.

24. Redfield 1983.232 compares the gardens of Alcinous and Laertes, highlighting the fact that Laertes' grows by work and Alcinous' by magic. He reads this theme as indicative of the ethical basis of Greek colonization here, "which from the beginning involved the agricultural exploitation of the *chora*, most often by Greek smallholders, and was thus in contrast to Phoenician colonization, which until the fifth century was a matter of outposts and emporia, focused on the search for metals."

25. See also *Od.* 24.207 for the labor Laertes expended to reclaim this house in the country: ἐπεὶ μάλα πόλλ᾽ ἐμόγησεν. At 24.222–25, Dolius and his sons are gathering stones to make a retaining wall for the orchard.

26. *Od.* 11.119–37. For the translation of the ambiguous phrase ἐξ ἁλὸς as "away

from the sea," see Hansen 1977.42–48 and Heubeck 1989.86. Hansen 1977.37 comments on the narrative potential of the ambiguity of this phrase and observes that modern Greek versions of the tale always imply an uneventful death away from the sea.

27. Cf. Hansen 1977 and 1990, who reads the prophecy together with the modern Greek (and other) folklore tradition of sailors and fishermen who forsake the life of the sea as well as other versions of the "sailor and his oar" tale. One modern Greek story says that Saint Elias was a seaman who hated the sea and who thus resolved to go where no one knew about ships or the sea. He put an oar on his shoulder and set out on land, asking the people he met along the way what it was that he was carrying. When, finally at the top of a mountain, someone replied, "a stick," he decided to stay there. Another version features the prophet Elias, a fisherman who became afraid of the sea because of his experience of terrible weather and storms. He put an oar on his shoulder and took to the hills. As soon as he met three people who mistook his oar for a stick, he decided to stay there. He planted the oar in the ground, and that is why all his chapels are built on hilltops. The basic theme of the tale emerges in an account from Alaska as well. A weary Yukon resident longed to "tie a snow shovel to the hood of my car and drive south until nobody had the faintest idea what the damn thing was." For another version of this tale, see Dorson 1964.38–39. For other discussions of Teiresias' prophecy, see Peradotto 1985; Pucci 1987.148–50; Ballabriga 1989; Segal 1994.187–94; Malkin 1998.120–26.

28. See Hansen 1990.260: "All the tellings of the story show a strong structural opposition between sea and land: whatever one realm signifies, the other signifies the opposite."

29. See Heubeck 1989.85 "The significant point is that the lines have an important function in the context of the present poem; the poet must say something about the propitiation of the angry god, since without the god's goodwill the reign of peace in Ithaca, the τέλος of both action and poem, could not be established on a firm basis; hence the ceremonies of expiation outside the sea-god's own domain."

30. Segal 1994.189–90 points out the parallels between the Phaeacians' sacrifice to Poseidon once their ship has been frozen and their sailing activities curtailed and Odysseus' sacrifice mentioned in the prophecy.

31. Segal 1994.189.

32. Segal 1994.189–90.

33. *Od.* 5.398–99 and 23.233–40.

34. *Od.* 13.31–35.

35. *Od.* 13.354. Cf. Vidal-Naquet 1986.18.

36. *Od.* 19.106–14.

37. In addition, the very narrative shape of the tale that tells the sailor to go somewhere until he sees or experiences something is very similar to that of Delphic oracles, especially those that advise the potential colonist to travel until he sees something particular (a wooden dog, a cow sitting down) and then to settle that spot. In both cases, the selection of the site is determined by a combination of randomness and care, by divine authority supplemented by human powers of interpretation. See Dougherty 1993.45–60 for further examples.

38. Cf. Diod. 8.17.1 re: Croton; Pind. Pyth. 9.7–9; 57 re: Cyrene.

39. Along these lines, Teiresias' command that Odysseus plant his oar in the ground

resonates with echoes of the rituals of harvest festivals at which harvest shovels are planted in the presence of Demeter. See Harrison 1904.246.

40. Another part of what is interesting about Teiresias' prophecy to Odysseus, his prediction of another journey, is its permanent status as prophecy. Framed only in imperatives and the future tense, this final adventure is never actually narrated as part of the poem itself; it is never told in the straight past or present tense. Rather, this aspect of Odysseus' story and his travels always remains beyond the boundaries of the story, as if its key feature is its unfinishedness. If the journey were undertaken and its story told, Odysseus' status as traveler and narrator would be finished, and this can never happen. The end of the story is within sight—he will die a peaceful death away from the sea—but it has not happened yet, and as long as Odysseus sails the seas, there will always be another story. See Pucci 1987.149 for a similar reading of this prophecy.

41. Moreover, in an interesting way, the many aspects of Odysseus' composite heroic profile converge at the moment of his return and re-foundation. His act of revenge against the suitors is made possible through his expertise with the tools of sailing. He is transformed into a poet at the very moment when he strings the bow to kill the suitors.

42. Rose 1992.120. Cf. 120–21, where Rose observes that the composite character of Odysseus contains the disparate elements of Greek society involved in colonization: those without land, poorer relations and bastard sons of the ruling elite, full-time traders.

43. See Goldhill 1991.2: "In *andra*, then, there is to be recognized a paradigmatic and normative representation of what it is to be a man in society, an announcement that the narrative to come will explore the terms in which an adult male's place is to be determined."

44. Segal 1994.37. See also Vidal-Naquet 1986.19: "The *Odyssey* as a whole is in one sense the story of Odysseus' return to normality, of his deliberate acceptance of the human condition"; and Clay 1983.132: "He [Odysseus] finally embodies the best possibilities of the human in its precarious position between god and beast."

45. Goldhill 1991.2.

46. See Clay 1983.96–112.

47. On *polutropos* and notions of multiplicty, see Finley 1978.30–35; Detienne and Vernant 1978.39–43; Clay 1983.29–34; Pucci 1987; Goldhill 1991.3–4.

48. Cf. Pucci 1987.45–49, who notes that one of the distinctions between Achilles and Odysseus as Homeric heroes has to do with their different uses of the verb τλάομαι: Achilles dares; Odysseus endures. See also Finley 1978.35–36. Redfield 1983.221–22 notes that as Odysseus moves from Troy to Ithaca, he moves toward the world of the audience; he survives because of his own kind of heroism. Moreover, his talents—ruthlessness, practicality, inventiveness, and so on—are good ones for an age of entrepreneurial expansion.

49. On Odysseus as new hero, see Clay 1983.34–132; Pucci 1987.44–49; Goldhill 1991.1–5. Dimock 1962 discusses the problematic nature of Odysseus' heroic identity. For the competition between Odysseus and Achilles as a contest between cleverness and force, see Nagy 1979.42–58. See also Clay 1983.102–12; Suzuki 1989.57–59.

50. See Redfield 1983, Rose 1992, and Thalmann 1998 for examples of other scholars who have attempted to historicize the epic character of Odysseus.

51. Cf. Redfield 1983.224, where he discusses the *Odyssey* as a document drama-
tizing the progressive economic ethic of late eighth-century Greece.


## Conclusion

1. Cf. Clarke 1967.78; Murnaghan 1987.140–41; Katz 1991.179–82; Zeitlin 1996.

2. Zeitlin 1996.24–26; she also discusses the ways in which the poem connects the
bed's lack of mobility with Penelope's fidelity.

3. Katz.1991.182. She draws on Starobinski 1975.350 here.

4. Katz 1991.180: "An additional feature of its fabrication is that the bed was constructed through an acculturation of what is otherwise an object in nature." See also Vidal-
Naquet 1986 on the nature-culture theme here.

5. See Zeitlin 1996.24–27 for a discussion of the apparent imbalance between the
bed as symbol of Odysseus' identity and Penelope's fidelity. See also Pucci 1987.93.

6. See Zeitlin 1996.22–23. Katz 1991.178 argues that the scene emphasizes the constructed aspects of identity in addition to the issue of Penelope's fidelity; she emphasizes
the ways in which the passage links Odysseus' identity with his construction of the bed.

7. Starobinski 1975.349–51; Zeitlin 1996.42; Katz 1991.178.

8. There it was a double tree (δοιοὺς . . . θάμνους. 5.476), and Odysseus made a bed
for himself with the many leaves that had fallen on the ground (φύλλων . . . πολλή, 5.483).
On the significance of the olive tree, as the tree of Athena, in the poem, see Schein
1970.75–76; Vidal-Naquet 1986.20; Segal 1994.47.

9. Zeitlin 1996.32–42 discusses the bed and its allusions to episodes in Phaeacia, especially parallels between Hephaestus and Odysseus and the significance of the Ares/
Aphrodite song for Odysseus and Penelope's reunion.

10. See Zeitlin 1996.29–31 on the significance of ἔμπεδος. She shows that it is primarily a masculine trait in the *Odyssey*, signifying physical valor and mental resolve, most
often used of Odysseus, although Penelope, too, has powers of endurance. The theme of
steadfastness (ἔμπεδος) appears as a kind of leit motif in the poem; it reflects the nature
of Odysseus' heroism; it is part of what he and Penelope share, and it forms half of the
fixity/mobility dichotomy that drives the plot and informs the poetics of the poem.

11. At *Od.* 16.34–35, Telemachus expresses his hope that his mother has not yet
agreed to marry one of the suitors and that her bed with his father remains bereft of sleep-
ers, covered over by spiderwebs.

12. I do not mean to suggest here that the poem does actually end at this point in
Book 23, as some have, rather that the image of the bed here signals closure whereas the
image of the raft in Book 5 represented the launch of Odysseus' travels and tale.

# Bibliography

Adkins, A. W. H. 1972. "Truth, KOSMOS, and ARETH in the Homeric Poems." *Classical Quarterly* 22.5–18.

Ahl, F., and H. Roisman. 1996. *The Odyssey Re-formed*. Ithaca.

Ahlberg, G. 1971. *Fighting on Land and Sea in Greek Geometric Art*. Stockholm.

Antonaccio, C. 1995. "Lefkandi and Homer." In *Homer's World: Fiction, Tradition, Reality*, ed. O. Anderson and M. Dickie, 5–27. Bergen.

Appadurai, A., ed. 1986. *The Social Life of Things: Commodities in Cultural Perspective*. Cambridge.

Arens, W. 1979. *The Man-Eating Myth: Anthropology and Anthropophagy*. New York.

Aubet, M. E. 1993. *The Phoenicians and the West*. Trans. Mary Turton. Cambridge.

Austin, M. M. 1970. *Greece and Egypt in the Archaic Age*. (Proceedings of the Cambridge Philological Society Supplement 2) Cambridge.

Austin, M. M., and P. Vidal-Naquet. 1977. *Economic and Social History of Ancient Greece*. Trans. and rev. M. M. Austin. Berkeley.

Austin, N. 1981. "Odysseus Polytropos: Man of Many Minds." *Arche* 81.40–52.

———. 1991. "The Wedding Text in Homer's *Odyssey*." *Arion*, 3rd ser., 1.2.227–43.

Ballabriga, A. 1989. "La prophétie de Tirésias." *Métis* 4.291–304.

Barker, F., and P. Hulme. 1985. "Nymphs and Reapers Heavily Vanish: The Discursive Con-texts of *The Tempest*." In *Alternative Shakespeares*, ed. J. Drakakis, 191–205. London.

Barron, J. P. 1969. "Ibycus. To Polycrates." *Bulletin of the Institute of Classical Studies* 16.119–49.

Benveniste, E. 1973. *Indo-European Language and Society*. Trans. Elizabeth Palmer. Coral Gables, Fla.

Bérard, J. 1957. *La colonisation grecque de l'Italie et de la Sicile dans l'antiquité: histoire et la légende*. Paris.

———. 1960. *L'expansion et la colonisation grecques*. Paris.

Bickerman, E. J. 1952. "Origines Gentium." *Classical Philology* 47.65–81.

Blakeway, A. 1933. "Prolegomena to the Study of Greek Commerce with Italy, Sicily, and France in the Eighth and Seventh Centuries B.C." *Annual of the British School at Athens* 33.170–208.

Boardman, J. 1967. "The Khaniale Tekke Tombs II." *Annual of the British School at Athens* 62.57–75.

———. 1980. *The Greeks Overseas*. London.

————. 1990. "Al Mina and History." *Oxford Journal of Archeology* 9.2.169–90.

————. 1999. *The Greeks Overseas*. 4th ed. with epilogue. London.

Bowie, E. 1998. "Phoenician Games in Heliodorus' Aithiopika." In *Studies in Heliodorus*, ed. R. Hunter, 1–18. Cambridge.

Braun, T. F. G. R. 1982. "The Greeks in the Near East." In *The Cambridge Ancient History*, 1–31. 2nd ed. Vol. 3.3. Cambridge.

Bravo, B. 1977. "Remarques sur les assises sociales, les formes d'organisation et la terminologie du commerce maritime grec à l'epoque archaïque." *Dialogues d'histoire ancienne* 3.1–59.

Brown, P. 1985. "This Thing of Darkness I Acknowledge Mine." In *Political Shakespeare: New Essays in Cultural Materialism*, ed. J. Dollimore and A. Sinfield, 48–71. Ithaca.

Buchner, G. 1966. "Pithekoussai: Oldest Greek Colony in the West." *Expedition* 8 (Summer) 4–12.

Buchner, G., and D. Ridgway, eds. 1993. *Pithekoussai I*. Rome.

Burkert, W. 1983. *Homo Necans. The Anthropology of Ancient Greek Sacrificial Ritual and Myth*. Trans. Peter Bing. Berkeley.

————. 1992. *The Orientalizing Revolution: Near Eastern Influence on Greek Culture in the Early Archaic Age*. Trans. Margaret E. Pinder and Walter Burkert. Cambridge, Mass.

Calame, C. 1977. "L'univers cyclopéen de L'Odyssée entre le carré et l'hexagone logiques." *Ziva Antika* 28.2.315–22.

Carson, A. 1982. "Wedding at Noon in Pindar's Ninth Pythian." *Greek, Roman, and Byzantine Studies* 23.121–28.

Cartledge, P. 1983. "'Trade and Politics' Revisited: Archaic Greece." In Garnsey et al. 1983, 1–15.

Casevitz, M. 1985. *Le vocabulaire de la colonisation en Grèce ancien*. Paris.

Casson, L. 1971. *Ships and Seamanship in the Ancient World*. Princeton.

————. 1994 *Ships and Seafaring in Ancient Times*. London.

Chadwick, J. 1990. "The Descent of the Greek Epic." *Journal of Hellenic Studies* 110.174–77.

Clark, J. R., and L. Motto. 1984. "The Progress of Cannibalism in Satire." *Midwest Quarterly* 25.174–86.

Clarke, H. W. 1967. *The Art of the Odyssey*. Englewood Cliffs, N.J.

Clay, J. 1980. "Goat Island: OD. 9.116–141." *Classical Philology* 74.262–64.

✓ ————. 1983. *The Wrath of Athena: Gods and Men in the Odyssey*. Princeton.

Clifford, J. 1988. *The Predicament of Culture: Twentieth-Century Ethnography, Literature, and Art*. Cambridge, Mass.

✓ ————. 1989. "Notes on Travel and Theory." *Inscriptions* 5.177–88.

————. 1992. "Traveling Cultures." In *Cultural Studies*, ed. L. Grossberg et al., 96–116. London.

Clifford, J., and G. Marcus, eds. 1986. *Writing Culture: The Poetics and Politics of Ethnography*. Berkeley.

Coldstream, N. 1969. "Phoenicians in Ialysos." *Bulletin of the Institute of Classical Studies* 16.1–8.

————. 1977. *Geometric Greece*. New York.

————. 1982. "Greeks and Phoenicians in the Aegean." In Niemeyer 1982, 261–75.

————. 1989. "Early Greek Visitors to Cyprus and the Eastern Mediterranean." In *Proceedings of the Seventh British Museum Classical Colloquium: Cyprus and the East Mediterranean in the Iron Age*, ed. V. Tatton-Brown, 90–96. London.

————. 1993. "Mixed Marriages at the Frontiers of the Early Greek World." *Oxford Journal of Archaeology* 12.1.89–107.

————. 1994. "Prospectors and Pioneers: Pithekoussai, Kyme and Central Italy." In Tsetskhladze and De Angelis 1994.47–59.

————. 1998. "The First Exchanges between Euboeans and Phoenicians: Who Took the Initiative?" In *Mediterranean Peoples in Transition*, ed. S. Gitin, A. Mazar, and E. Stern, 353–60. Jerusalem.

Cole, T. 1983. "Archaic Truth." *Quaderni Urbinati di Cultura Classica* 13.7–28.

Comaroff, J., and J. Comaroff, eds. 1992. *Ethnography and the Historical Imagination*. Boulder.

Coplan, D. B. 1993. "History Is Eaten Whole: Consuming Tropes in Sesotho Auriture." *History and Theory* 32.4.80–104.

Cozzo, A. 1988. *Kerdos: semantica, ideologie e società nella Grecia antica*. Rome.

Crielaard, J.-P. 1992–93. "How the West Was Won: Euboeans vs. Phoenicians." *Hamburger Beiträge zur Archäologie* 19/20.235–60.

————. 1993. "The Social Organization of Euboean Trade with the Eastern Mediterranean during the 10th to 8th Centuries B.C." *Pharos* 1.139–46.

————. 1995. "Homer, History, and Archeology." In *Homeric Questions*, ed. J.-P. Crielaard, 201–88. Amsterdam.

Curtin, P. D. 1984. *Cross-cultural Trade in World History*. Cambridge.

Davies, M., ed. 1992. *Poetarum Melicorum Graecorum Fragmenta*. Vol. 1. Oxford.

Day, J. 1989. "Rituals in Stone: Early Greek Grave Epigrams and Monuments." *Journal of Hellenic Studies* 109.16–28.

De Certeau, M. 1988. *The Writing of History*. Trans. Tom Conley. New York.

De Jong, I. 1992. "The Subjective Style of Odysseus." *Classical Quarterly* 42.1–11.

De Lauretis, T. 1984. *Alice Doesn't: Feminism, Semiotics, Cinema*. Bloomington, Ind.

Dench, E. 1995. *From Barbarians to New Men: Greek, Roman, and Modern Perceptions of Peoples of the Central Apennines*. Oxford.

Desborough, V. R. 1972. *The Greek Dark Ages*. New York.

Descoeudres, J.-P., ed. 1990. *Greek Colonists and Native Populations: Proceedings of the First Australian Congress of Classical Archaeology Held in Honour of Emeritus Professor A. D. Trendall, Sydney, 9–14 July 1985*. Oxford.

Detienne, M. 1981. "Between Beasts and Gods." In *Myth, Religion, and Society*, ed. R. L. Gordon and R. G. A. Buxton, 215–28. Cambridge.

————. 1996. *The Masters of Truth in Archaic Greece*. Trans. Janet Lloyd. New York.

————, ed. 1992. *Les savoirs de l'écriture: en Grèce ancienne*. Lille.

Detienne, M., and J.-P. Vernant. 1978. *Cunning Intelligence in Greek Culture and Society*. Trans. Janet Lloyd. Englewood Cliffs, N.J.

✓Dimock, G. 1962. "The Name of Odysseus." In *Homer: A Collection of Essays*, ed. G. Steiner and R. Fagles, 106–21. Englewood Cliffs, N.J.

Dion, R. 1977. *Aspects politiques de la géographie antique*. Paris.

Doherty, L. 1995. *Siren Songs: Gender, Audiences, and Narrators in the Odyssey*. Ann Arbor.

Donlan, W. 1981. "Scale, Value, and Function in the Homeric Economy." *American Journal of Ancient History* 6.2.101–17.

———. 1981–82. "Reciprocities in Homer." *Classical World* 75.137–74.

———. 1989. "The Unequal Exchange Between Glaucus and Diomedes in Light of the Homeric Gift Economy." *Phoenix* 43.1–15.

———. 1997. "The Homeric Economy. " In Morris and Powell 1997, 649–67.

Dorson, R. 1964. *Buying the Wind: Regional Folklore in the United States*. Chicago.

Dougherty, C. 1991a. "Phemius' Last Stand: The Impact of Occasion on Tradition in the *Odyssey*." *Oral Tradition* 6.1.93–103.

———. 1991b. "Linguistic Colonialism in Aeschylus' *Aetnaeae*." *Greek, Roman, and Byzantine Studies* 32.2.119–32.

———. 1993. *The Poetics of Colonization: From City to Text in Archaic Greece*. New York.

———. 1997. "Homer after Omeros: Reading a H/Omeric Text." In *The Poetics of Derek Walcott: Intercultural Perspectives*. Special edition of *South Atlantic Quarterly*, ed. G. Davis, 96. 335–57.

———. 1999. "The Double Vision of Euripides' *Cyclops*: An Ethnographic *Odyssey* on the Satyr Stage." *Comparative Drama* 33.3.313–38.

Dougherty, C., and L. Kurke, eds. 1993. *Cultural Poetics in Archaic Greece: Cult, Performance, Politics*. Cambridge.

Dubois, P. 1988. *Sowing the Body: Psychoanalysis and Ancient Representations of Women*. Chicago.

Durante, M. 1976. *Sulla preistoria della tradizione poetica greca*. Vol. 2. *Risultanze della comparazione indoeuropea*. Incunabula Graeca 64. Rome

Edwards, A. 1993. "Homer's Ethical Geography: Country and City in the *Odyssey*." *Transactions of the American Philological Association* 123.27–77.

Edwards, R. 1979. *Kadmos the Phoenician: A Study in Greek Legends and the Mycenaean Age*. Amsterdam.

Emlyn-Jones, C. 1986. "True and Lying Tales in the *Odyssey*." *Greece and Rome* 33.1–10.

Fabre, P. 1981. *Les grecs et la connaissance de l'occident*. Lille.

Faraone, C. 1987. "Hephaestus the Magician and Near Eastern Parallels for Alcinous' Watchdogs." *Greek, Roman, and Byzantine Studies* 28.257–80.

———. 1992. *Talismans and Trojan Horses: Guardian Statues in Ancient Greek Myth and Ritual*. New York.

———. 1996. "Taking the 'Nestor's Cup Inscripton' Seriously: Erotic Magic and Conditional Curses in the Earliest Inscribed Hexameters." *Classical Antiquity* 15.77–112.

Fenik, B. 1974. *Studies in the Odyssey*. Wiesbaden.

Fernández-Galiano, M. 1992. See Heubeck et al. 1988–92.

Finkelstein, M. I. (= Finley, M. I.) 1935. "Ἔμπορος, Ναύκληρος, and Κάπηλος: A Prolegomena to the study of Athenian Trade." *Classical Philology* 30.320–36.

Finley, J. 1978. *Homer's Odyssey*. Cambridge, Mass.

Finley, M. I. 1979. *The World of Odysseus*. Rev. ed. Harmondsworth.

Finnegan, R. 1977. *Oral Poetry: Its Nature, Significance, and Social Context*. Cambridge.

Fisher, N., and H. van Wees, eds. 1998. *Archaic Greece: New Approaches and New Evidence*. London.

Foley, H. 1984. "'Reverse Similes' and Sex Roles in the Odyssey." In *Women in the Ancient World*, ed. J. Peradotto and J. P. Sullivan, 59–78. Albany.

Forbes, R. J. 1971. *Studies in Ancient Technology.* Vol. 8. Leiden.

Ford, A. 1988 "The Classical Definition of ΡΑΨΩΙΔΙΑ." *Classsical Philology* 83.300–7.

Foxhall, L. 1998. "Cargoes of the Heart's Desire: The Character of Trade in the Archaic Mediterranean World." In Fisher and van Wees 1998, 295–309.

Frame, D. 1978. *The Myth of Return in Early Greek Epic.* New Haven.

Frankenstein, S. 1979. "The Phoenicians in the Far West: A Function of Neo-Assyrian Imperialism." In *Power and Propaganda: A Symposium on Ancient Empires*, ed. M. T. Larsen, 263–94. Copenhagen.

Frazer, A. D. 1929. "Scheria and the Phaeacians." *Transactions of the American Philological Association* 60.155–78.

Gaffarel, P., ed. 1880. *Jean de Léry: histoire d'un voyage faict en la terre du Brésil.* Paris.

Garnsey, P., et al., eds. 1983. *Trade in the Ancient Economy.* Berkeley.

Garvie, A. F., ed. 1994. *Homer. Odyssey Books VI–VIII.* Cambridge.

Geertz, C. 1973. *The Interpretation of Cultures.* New York.

———. 1988. *Works and Lives: The Anthropologist as Author.* Stanford.

Gentili, B. 1988. *Poetry and Its Public in Ancient Greece.* Trans. Thomas Cole. Baltimore.

Gernet, L. 1981. *The Anthropology of Ancient Greece.* Trans. John Hamilton and Blaise Nagy. Baltimore.

Giardino, C. 1995. *The West Mediterranean between the 14th and 8th centuries B.C.: Mining and Metallurgical Spheres.* BAR International Series 612. Oxford.

Glenn, J. 1971. "The Polyphemus Folktale and Homer's Kyklopeia." *Transactions of the American Philological Association* 102.133–81.

Goldhill, S. 1991. *The Poet's Voice.* Cambridge.

Gordon, M. 1991. "Good Boys and Dead Girls." In *Good Boys and Dead Girls and Other Essays*, 1–23. New York.

Graham, A. J. 1964. *Colony and Mother City in Ancient Greece.* New York.

———. 1982. "The Colonial Expansion of Greece." In *The Cambridge Ancient History*, 2nd ed. Vol. 3.3, 83–162. Cambridge.

———. 1986. "The Historical Interpretation of Al Mina." *Dialogues d'histoire ancienne* 12.51–65.

Gray, D. 1953. "Metalworking in Homer." *Journal of Hellenic Studies* 73.1–15.

———. 1974. "Seewesen." In *Archaeologica Homerica* I, G. Gottingen.

Greenblatt, S. 1970. "Learning to Curse: Aspects of Linguistic Colonialism in the 16th Century." In *First Images of America: The Impact of the New World on the Old*, ed. F. Chiapelli, 561–80. Berkeley.

———. 1991. *Marvelous Possessions: The Wonder of the New World.* Chicago.

Gregory, C. A. 1982. *Gifts and Commodities.* London.

Griffin, J. 1980. *Homer on Life and Death.* Oxford.

Gwynn, A. 1918. "The Character of Greek Colonization." *Journal of Hellenic Studies* 38.88–123.

Hägg, R., ed. 1983. *The Greek Renaissance of the Eighth Century B.C.: Tradition and Innovation.* Stockholm.

Haft, A. 1984. "Odysseus, Idomeneus, and Meriones: The Cretan Lies of Odyssey 13–19." *Classical Journal* 79.289–306.

Hague, R. 1983. "Ancient Greek Wedding Songs: The Tradition of Praise." *Journal of Folklore Research* 20.131–43.

Hainsworth, J. B. 1988. See Heubeck et al. 1988–92.

Hall, E. 1989. *Inventing the Barbarian: Greek Self-Definition through Tragedy*. Oxford.

Hall, J. 1997. *Ethnic Identity in Greek Antiquity*. Cambridge.

Hansen, W. 1977. "Odysseus' Last Journey." *Quaderni Urbinati di Cultura Classica* 24.27–48.

———. 1990. "Odysseus and the Oar: A Folklore Approach." In *Approaches to Greek Myth*, ed. L. Edmunds, 241–72. Baltimore.

Harden, D. 1962. *The Phoenicians*. New York.

Harrison, J. 1904. "Mystica Vannus Iacchi." *Journal of Hellenic Studies* 24.241–54.

Hart, C. 1988. *Images of Flight*. Berkeley.

Hartog, F. 1988. *The Mirror of Herodotus*. Trans. Janet Lloyd. Berkeley.

✓ ———. 1996. *Mémoire d'Ulysse: récits sur la frontière en Grèce ancienne*. Paris.

Harvey, D. 1989. *The Condition of Postmodernity*. Cambridge, Mass.

Hasebroek, J. 1933. *Trade and Politics in Ancient Greece*. Trans. L. M. Fraser and D. C. MacGregor. London.

Havelock, E. 1958. "Parmenides and Odysseus." *Harvard Studies in Classical Philology* 63.133–43.

———. 1982. *The Literate Revolution in Greece and Its Cultural Consequences*. Princeton.

Healy, J. F. 1978. *Mining and Metallurgy in the Greek and Roman World*. London.

✓ Helms, M. 1988. *Ulysses' Sail: An Ethnographic Odyssey of Power, Knowledge, and Geographical Distance*. Princeton.

Henderson, J. 1991. *The Maculate Muse*. New York.

Herman, G. 1987. *Ritualized Friendship and the Greek City*. Cambridge.

Herington, C. J. 1985. *Poetry into Drama: Early Tragedy and the Greek Poetic Tradition*. Berkeley.

Heubeck, A. 1989. See Heubeck et al. 1988–92.

Heubeck, A., S. West, J. Hainsworth, J. Russo, M. Fernandez-Galiano, A. Hoekstra, eds. 1988–92. *A Commentary on Homer's Odyssey*. 3 vols. Oxford.

Hoekstra, A. 1992. See Heubeck et al. 1988–92.

Hoffman, G. 1997. *Imports and Immigrants: Near Eastern Contacts with Iron Age Crete*. Ann Arbor.

Honour, H. 1975. *The New Golden Land: European Images of America from the Discoveries to the Present Time*. New York.

Hooker, J. T., ed. 1990. *Reading the Past*. Berkeley.

Hornell, J. 1946. *Water Transport*. Cambridge.

Hulme, P. 1986. *Colonial Encounters*. London.

———. 1992. "Making No Bones: A Response to Myra Jehlen." *Critical Inquiry*. 20.179–86.

Jameson, F. 1984. "Postmodernism, or the Cultural Logic of Late Capitalism." *New Left Review* 146.53–92.

Jeffery, L. H. 1961. *The Local Scripts of Archaic Greece*. Oxford.

———. 1976. *Archaic Greece: The City States, c. 700–500 B.C.* New York.

Jeffery, L. H. and A. Morpurgo Davis. 1970. "Poinikastas." *Kadmos* 9.118–54.

Johnston, A. 1983. "The Extent and Use of Literacy: The Archeological Evidence." In Hägg 1983, 63–68.

Katz, M. 1991. *Penelope's Renown: Meaning and Indeterminacy in the Odyssey.* Princeton.

Kearsley, R. A. 1989. *The Pendent Semi-circle Skyphos. Bulletin of the Institute of Classical Studies* Supplement 44.

———. 1995. "The Greek Geometric Wares from Al Mina Levels 10–8 and Associated Pottery." *Mediterranean Archaeology* 8.7–81.

Kirk, G. S. 1949. "Ships on Geometric Vases." *Annual of the British School at Athens* 44.93–153

———. 1962. *The Songs of Homer.* Cambridge.

———. 1970. *Myth: Its Meaning and Functions in Ancient and Other Cultures.* Cambridge.

———, ed. 1985. *The Iliad: A Commentary.* Vol. 1. Books 1–4. Cambridge.

Knorringa, H. 1926. *Emporos: Data on Trade and Traders in Greek Literature from Homer to Aristotle.* Amsterdam.

Kolodny, A. 1975. *The Lay of the Land: Metaphor as Experience and History in American Life and Letters.* Chapel Hill.

Kopcke, G. 1992. "What Role for Phoenicians?" In Kopcke and Tokumaru 1992, 103–13.

Kopcke, G., and I. Tokumaru, eds. 1992. *Greece between East and West: Papers of the Meetings at the Institute of Fine Arts, New York University, March 15–16, 1990.* Mainz.

Kopytoff, I. 1986. "The Cultural Biography of Things: Commoditization as Process." In Appadurai 1986, 64–91.

Kurke, L. 1991. *The Traffic in Praise: Pindar and the Poetics of Social Economy.* Ithaca.

———. 1993. "The Economy of Kudos." In Dougherty and Kurke 1993, 131–63.

Langbaum, R., ed. 1987. *The Tempest.* Signet Classic Shakespeare. New York.

Lawrence, K. 1994. *Penelope Voyages: Women and Travel in the British Literary Tradition.* Ithaca.

Levin, H. 1969. *The Myth of the Golden Age in the Renaissance.* Bloomington, Ind.

Lévi-Strauss, C. 1969. *The Elementary Structures of Kinship.* Boston.

Lombardo, M. 1992. "Marchands, transactions économiques, écriture." In Detienne 1992, 159–87.

Loraux, N. 1993. *The Children of Athena.* Trans. Caroline Levine. Princeton.

Lord, A. B. 1960. *The Singer of Tales.* Cambridge, Mass.

———. 1995. *The Singer Resumes the Tale.* Ed. M. L. Lord. Ithaca.

Lorimer, H. L. 1950. *Homer and the Monuments.* London

Malkin, I. 1987. *Religion and Colonization in Ancient Greece.* Leiden.

———. 1998. *The Returns of Odysseus: Colonization and Ethnicity.* Berkeley.

Markoe, G. 1992. "In Pursuit of Metal: Phoenicians and Greeks in Italy." In Kopcke and Tokumaru 1992, 61–84.

Martin, C. G. 1990. "Orientalism and the Ethnographer: Saïd, Herodotus, and the Discourse of Alterity." *Criticism* 32.511–29.

Martin, R. 1989. *The Language of Heroes: Speech and Performance in the Iliad.* Ithaca.

Mason, P. 1986. "Imaginary Worlds, Counterfact, and Artefact." In *Myth and the Imaginary in the New World,* ed. E. Magaña and P. Mason, 43–71. Amsterdam.

Mauss, M. 1990. *The Gift*. Trans. W. D. Halls. New York. Originally published in French, 1950.

McLellan, D., ed. 1977. *Karl Marx: Selected Writings*. Oxford.

Mele, A. 1979. *Il commercio greco arcaico: Prexis ed Emporie*. Naples.

Merkelbach, R., and M. L. West, eds. 1967. *Fragmenta Hesiodea*. Oxford.

Merry, W. W., and J. Riddell, eds. 1886. *Homer's Odyssey*. Oxford.

Moerman, M. 1975. "Chiangkham's Trade in the 'Old Days.'" In *Change and Persistence in Thai Society*, ed. G. W. Skiner and A. T. Kirsch, 151–71. Ithaca.

Mondi, R. 1983. "The Homeric Cyclopes: Folktale, Tradition, and Theme." *Transactions of the American Philological Association* 113.17–38.

Morris, I. 1986a. "Gift and Commodity in Archaic Greece." *Man* 21.1–17.

———. 1986b. "The Use and Abuse of Homer." *Classical Antiquity* 5.81–129.

✓ ———. 1997. "Homer and the Iron Age." In Morris and Powell 1997, 534–59.

✓ ———. 2000. *Archaeology as Cultural History*. Malden, Mass.

✓ Morris, I., and B. Powell, eds. 1997. *A New Companion to Homer*. Leiden.

✓ Morris, S. 1992. *Daidalos and the Origins of Greek Art*. Princeton.

✓ ———. 1997. "Homer and the Near East." In Morris and Powell 1997, 599–623.

Morrison, J. S., and R. T. Williams. 1968. *Greek Oared Ships, 900–322 B.C.* Cambridge.

Moscati, S. 1968. *The World of the Phoenicians*. Trans. A. Hamilton. New York.

Most, G. 1989. "Structure and Function of Odysseus' Apologoi." *Transactions of the American Philological Association* 119.15–30.

Moulton, C. 1977. *Similes in the Homeric Poems*. Göttingen.

Mourelatos, A. 1970. *The Route of Parmenides*. New Haven.

Muhly, J. 1970. "Homer and the Phoenicians." *Berytus* 19.19–64.

———. 1998. "Copper, Tin, Silver, and Iron: The Search for Metallic Ores as an Incentive for Foreign Expansion." In *Mediterranean Peoples in Transition*, ed. S. Gitin, A. Mazar, and E. Stern, 314–29. Jerusalem.

Murakawa, K. 1957. "Demiurgos." *Historia* 6.385–415.

Murnaghan, S. 1987. *Disguise and Recognition in the Odyssey*. Princeton.

Nagler, M. 1974. *Spontaneity and Tradition: A Study in the Oral Art of Homer*. Berkeley.

———. 1990. "Odysseus: The Proem and the Problem." *Classical Antiquity* 9.2.335–56.

Nagy, G. 1979. *The Best of the Achaeans: Concepts of the Hero in Archaic Greek Poetry*. Baltimore.

———. 1982. "Hesiod." In *Ancient Writers*, ed. T. J. Luce, 43–73. New York.

———. 1990. *Pindar's Homer: The Lyric Possession of an Epic Past*. Baltimore.

———. 1996a. *Homeric Questions*. Austin, Tex.

———. 1996b. *Poetry as Performance: Homer and Beyond*. Cambridge.

Niemeyer, H. G., von, ed. 1982. *Phönizier im Westen*. Mainz.

Nohrnberg, J. 1976. *The Analogy of the Faerie Queene*. Princeton.

Obeyesekere, G. 1992. "'British Cannibals': Contemplation of an Event in the Death and Resurrection of James Cook, Explorer" *Critical Inquiry* 18.630–54.

Orgel, S. 1984. "Prospero's Wife." *Representations* 8.1–13.

———, ed. 1987. *The Tempest*. World's Classics. Oxford.

Ormerod, H. 1924. *Piracy in the Ancient World*. Liverpool.

Osborne, R. 1993. "À la grecque: A Review of W. Burkert, *The Orientalizing Revolution:*

*Near Eastern Influence on Greek Culture in the Early Archaic Age* (1992), and S. P. Morris, *Daidalos and the Origins of Greek Art* (1992)." *Journal of Mediterranean Archeology* 6.2. 231–37.

———. 1996. *Greece in the Making, 1200–479 B.C.* London.

O'Sullivan, J. 1990. "Nature and Culture in Odyssey 9." *Symbolae Osloenses* 65.7–17.

Pagden. A. 1982. "Cannibalismo e contagio: sull'importanza dell'anthropofagia nell'Europa preindustriale." *Quaderni Storici* 50.533–50.

———. 1993. *European Encounters with the New World from Renaissance to Romanticism.* New Haven.

Page, D. 1955. *The Homeric Odyssey.* Oxford.

Papadopoulos, J. 1997. "The Phantom Euboeans." *Journal of Mediterranean Archeology* 10.191–219.

Parker, P. 1979. *Inescapable Romance.* Princeton.

———. 1987. *Literary Fat Ladies: Rhetoric, Gender, Property.* London.

Parry, J., and M. Bloch. 1989. *Money and the Morality of Exchange.* Cambridge.

Parry, M. 1971. *The Making of Homeric Verse: The Collected Papers of Milman Parry.* Ed. A. Parry. Oxford.

Peradotto, J., 1985. "Prophecy Degree Zero: Tiresias and the End of the *Odyssey*." In *Oralità, letteratura, discorso: atti del convegno internazionale*, ed. B. Gentili and G. Paoioni, 429–55. Rome.

———. 1990. *Man in the Middle Voice: Name and Narration in the Odyssey.* Princeton.

Péron, J. 1974. *Les images maritimes de Pindare.* Paris.

Pfeiffer, R., ed. 1949. *Callimachus.* Vol. 1. Oxford.

Pinney, G. 1983. "Achilles Lord of Scythia." In *Ancient Greek Art and Iconography*, ed. W. G. Moon, 127–46. Madison.

Podlecki, A. J. 1961. "Guest-Gifts and Nobodies in Odyssey 9." *Phoenix* 15.125–33.

Popham, M. 1981. "Why Euboea?" *Annuario della Scuola Archeologica di Atene* 59.237–39.

———.1987. "An Early Euboean Ship." *Oxford Journal of Archeology* 6.3.353–59.

———. 1994. "Precolonisation: Early Greek Contact with the East." In Tsetskhladze and De Angelis 1994, 11–34.

Popham, M., and I. Lemos. 1992. Review of Kearsley 1989. *Gnomon* 64.152–55.

Popham. M., P. G. Calligas, L. H. Sackett, eds. 1990. *Lefkandi II: The Protogeometric Building at Toumba.* London.

Popham, M., L. H. Sackett, and P. G. Themelis, eds. 1980. *Lefkandi I: The Iron Age.* London.

Popham, M., E. Touloupa, and L. H. Sackett. 1982a. "The Hero of Lefkandi." *Antiquity* 46.169–74.

———. 1982b. "Further Excavation of the Toumba Cemetary at Lefkandi, 1981." *Annual of the British School at Athens* 77.213–48.

———. 1986. "Further Excavation of the Toumba Cemetary, 1984 and 1986." *Archaeological Reports* 35.117–29.

Popham, M., et al. 1996. *Lefkandi III: The Toumba Cemetery: The Excavations of 1981, 1984, 1986, and 1992–94.* Athens.

Powell, B. 1991. *Homer and the Origin of the Greek Alphabet.* Cambridge.

Pratt, L. 1993. *Lying and Poetry from Homer to Pindar.* Ann Arbor.

Pratt, M. 1986. "Fieldwork in Common Places." In *Writing Culture: The Poetics and Politics of Ethnography*, ed. J. Clifford and G. Marcus, 27–50. Berkeley.

Pucci, P. 1987. *Odysseus Polutropos*. Ithaca.

———. 1996. "The Song of the Sirens." In Schein 1996, 191–99.

Purcell, N. 1990. "Mobility and the Polis." In *The Greek City: From Homer to Alexander*, ed. O. Murray and S. Price, 29–58. Oxford.

Quint, D. 1993. *Epic and Empire*. Princeton.

———. 1998. *Montaigne and the Quality of Mercy: Ethical and Political Themes in the Essais*. Princeton.

Raaflaub, K. 1997. "Homeric Society." In Morris and Powell 1997, 624–48.

Rabinow, P. 1977. *Reflections on Fieldwork in Morocco*. Berkeley.

Rawson, C. J. 1984. "Narrative and the Proscribed Act: Homer, Euripides, and the Literature of Cannibalism." In *Literary Theory and Criticism*, ed. J. P. Strelka, 1159–87. Bern.

Reden, S. von. 1995a. *Exchange in Ancient Greece*. London.

———. 1995b. "Deceptive Readings: Poetry and Its Value Reconsidered." *Classical Quarterly* 45.30–50.

Redfield, J. 1975. *Nature and Culture in the Iliad*. Chicago.

———. 1983. "The Economic Man." In *Approaches to Homer*, ed. C. A. Rubino and C. Shelmerdine, 218–47. Austin, Tex.

———. 1985. "Herodotus the Tourist." *Classical Philology* 80.2.97–118.

———. 1986. "The Development of the Market in Archaic Greece." In *The Market in History*, ed. L. Anderson and A. J. H. Latham, 29–58. London.

Reece, S. 1993. *The Stranger's Welcome*. Ann Arbor.

Ricoeur, P. 1969. *Le conflit des interpretations*. Paris.

Ridgway, D. 1988. "The Pithekoussai Shipwreck." In *Studies in Honour of T. B. L. Webster*, ed. J. H. Betts, J. T. Hooker, and J. R. Green, 2.97–107. Bristol.

———. 1990. "The First Western Greeks and Their Neighbours, 1935–1985." In Descouedres 1990, 61–72.

———. 1992. *The First Western Greeks*. Cambridge.

———. 1994. "Phoenicians and Greeks in the West: A View from Pithekoussai." In Tsetskhladze and De Angelis 1994, 35–46.

———. 2000. "The First Western Greeks Revisited." In *Ancient Italy in All Its Mediterranean Setting: Studies in Honour of Ellen MacNamara*, ed. M. Pearce et al., 179–91. London.

Rigby, N. 1992. "Sober Cannibals and Drunken Christians: Colonial Encounters of the Cannibal Kind." *Journal of Commonwealth Literature* 27.171–82.

Riis, J. R. 1982. "Griechen in Phönizien." In Niemeyer 1982, 237–60.

Roisman, H. 1990. "*Kerdion* in the *Iliad*: Profit and Trickiness." *Transactions of the American Philological Association* 120.23–35.

Rosaldo, R. 1989. *Culture and Truth: The Remaking of Social Analysis*. Boston.

Rose, G. 1969. "The Unfriendly Phaeacians." *Transactions of the American Philological Association* 100.387–406.

Rose, P. 1992. *Sons of the Gods, Children of Earth*. Ithaca.

Rosen, R. 1990. "Poetry and Sailing in Hesiod's Works and Days." *Classical Antiquity* 9.1.99–113.

Runciman, W. G. 1982. "Origins of States: The Case of Archaic Greece." *Journal of Comparative Study of Society and History* 24.351–77.

Ruijgh, C. J. 1995. "D'Homère aux origines proto-mycéniennes de la tradition épique." In *Homeric Questions*, ed. J.-P. Crielaard, 1–96. Amsterdam.

Sahlins, M. 1972. *Stone Age Economics*. Chicago.

Said, E. 1978. *Orientalism*. New York.

Saïd, S. 1977. "Les crimes des prétendants." *Cahiers de l'École Normale Superieure* 9–49.

Scheid, J., and J. Svenbro. 1985. "La ruse d'Élissa et la fondation de Carthage." *Annales: Économie, Sociétés, Civilisations* 40.2.328–42.

———. 1994. *The Craft of Zeus*. Trans. Carol Volk. Cambridge, Mass.

Schein, S. 1970. "Odysseus and Polyphemus in the Odyssey." *Greek, Roman, and Byzantine Studies* 11.73–83.

———, ed. 1996. *Reading the Odyssey*. Princeton.

Schmandt-Besserat, D. 1989. "Two Precursors of Writing: Plain and Complex Tokens." In Senner 1989, 27–41.

Schmitt, R. 1967. *Dichtung und Dichtersprache in indogermanischer Zeit*. Wiesbaden.

Scully, S. 1981. "The Bard as Custodian of Homeric Society: *Odyssey* 3.263–72." *Journal of Hellenic Studies* 8.67–83.

———. 1990. *Homer and the Sacred City: Myth and Poetics*. Ithaca.

Segal, C. 1994. *Singers, Heroes, and Gods in the Odyssey*. Ithaca.

Senner, W., ed. 1989. *The Origins of Writing*. Lincoln, Neb.

Serres, M. 1982. *Hermes: Literature, Science, Philosophy*. Baltimore.

Shanks, M. 1999. *Art and the Early Greek State: An Interpretive Archeology*. Cambridge.

Shewan, A. 1919. "The Scheria of the Odyssey." *Classical Quarterly* 13.4–11, 57–67.

Smith, J. 1995. "People Eaters." *Granta* 52.69–84.

Smith, O. L., ed. 1976. *Scholia Graeca in Aeschylum quae Extant Omnia*. Part 1. Leipzig

Snodgrass, A. 1971. *The Dark Age of Greece*. Edinburgh.

———. 1974. "An Historical Homeric Society?" *Journal of Hellenic Studies* 94.114–25.

———. 1980. *Archaic Greece: The Age of Experiment*. Berkeley.

———. 1994. "The Growth and Standing of the Early Western Colonies." In Tsetskhladze and De Angelis 1994, 1–10.

———. 1998. *Homer and the Artists: Text and Picture in Early Greek Art*. Cambridge.

Stanford, W. B., ed. 1959. *The Odyssey of Homer*. 2 vols. 2nd ed. London.

Starobinski, J. 1975. "Inside and Outside." *Hudson Review* 28.333–51.

Starr, C. G. 1977. *The Economic and Social Growth of Early Greece, 800–500 B.C.* New York.

Steiner, D. 1993. "Pindar's 'Oggetti Parlanti.'" *Harvard Studies in Classical Philology* 95.159–80.

———. 1994. *The Tyrant's Writ: Myths and Images of Writing in Ancient Greece*. Princeton.

Street, B. 1984. *Literacy in Theory and Practice*. Cambridge.

Suzuki, M. 1989. *The Metamorphoses of Helen: Authority, Difference, and the Epic*. Ithaca.

Svenbro, J. 1976. *La parole et le marbre: aux origines de la poétique grecque*. Lund.

Tandy, D. 1997. *Warriors into Traders: The Power of the Market in Early Greece*. Berkeley.

Taplin, O. 1992. *Homeric Soundings: The Shaping of the Iliad*. Oxford.

Thalmann, W. 1984. *Conventions of Form and Thought in Early Greek Epic Poetry*. Baltimore.

———. 1998. *The Swineherd and the Bow*. Ithaca.

Thomas, C., and C. Conant. 1999. *Citadel to City-State: The Transformation of Greece, 1200–700 B.C.E.* Bloomington, Ind.

Thomas, N. 1991. *Entangled Objects: Exchange, Material Culture, and Colonialism in the Pacific*. Cambridge, Mass.

Thomas, R. 1989. *Oral Tradition and Written Record in Classical Athens*. Cambridge.

———. 1992. *Literacy and Orality in Ancient Greece*. Cambridge.

Todorov, T. 1977. *The Poetics of Prose*. Trans. Richard Howard. Ithaca.

Trahman, C. 1952. "Odysseus' Lies." *Phoenix* 6.31–43.

Tsetskhladze, G. R., and De Angelis, F., eds. 1994. *The Archaeology of Greek Colonisation*. Oxford.

Turner, V. 1974. *Dramas, Fields, and Metaphors*. Ithaca.

Vance, E. 1973. "Signs of the City: Medieval Poetry as Detour." *New Literary History* 4.557–74.

Vernant, J.-P. 1983. "Hesiod's Myth of the Races: An Essay in Structural Analysis." In *Myth and Thought among the Greeks*, 3–72. London.

Vidal-Naquet, P. 1986. "Land and Sacrifice in the Odyssey." In *The Black Hunter*, 15–38. Baltimore.

Walcott, D. 1990. *Omeros*. New York.

Walcott, P. 1977. "Odysseus and the Art of Lying." *Ancient Society* 8.1–19.

Wallinga, H. T. 1993. *Ships and Sea-Power Before the Great Persian War*. Leiden.

Walsh, G. B. 1984. *The Varieties of Enchantment: Early Greek Views of the Nature of Poetry*. Chapel Hill.

Webster, T. B. L. 1958. *From Mycenae to Homer*. New York.

Wees, H. van. 1992. *Status Warriors: War, Violence, and Society in Homer and History*. Amsterdam.

West, M. L. 1988. "The Rise of the Greek Epic." *Journal of Hellenic Studies* 108.151–72.

———. 1992. "The Descent of the Greek Epic: A Reply." *Journal of Hellenic Studies* 112.173–75.

———. 1997. *The East Face of Helicon: West Asiatic Elements in Greek Poetry and Myth*. Oxford.

———, ed. 1978. *Hesiod: Works and Days*. Oxford.

West, S., 1988. See Heubeck et al. 1988–92.

Whitley, J. 1994. "Protoattic Pottery: A Contextual Approach." In *Classical Greece: Ancient Histories and Modern Archaeologies*, ed. I. Morris, 51–70. Cambridge.

Whittaker, C. R. 1974. "The Western Phoenicians: Colonisation and Assimilation." *Proceedings of Cambridge Philological Society* 20.58–79.

Willis, D. 1989. "Shakespeare's *Tempest* and the Discourse of Colonialism." *Studies in English Literature* 29.277–89.

Winkler, J. 1990. *Constraints of Desire: The Anthropology of Sex and Gender in Ancient Greece*. New York.

Winter, I. 1995. "Homer's Phoenicians: History, Ethnography, or Literary Trope?" In *The Ages of Homer*, ed. J. P. Carter and S. P. Morris, 247–71. Austin, Tex.

Wolf, F. A. 1963. *Prolegomena ad Homerum*. Hildesheim.

Wolff, J. 1993. "On the Road Again: Metaphors of Travel in Cultural Criticism." *Cultural Studies* 7.2.224–39.

Wyatt, W. 1992. "Homer's Linguistic Forebears." *Journal of Hellenic Studies* 112.167–73.

Zeitlin, F. I. 1986. "Configurations of Rape in Greek Myth." In *Rape*, ed. S. Tomaselli and R. Porter, 122–51. Oxford.

———. 1996. "Figuring Fidelity in Homer's Odyssey." In *Playing the Other*, 19–52. Chicago.

Zimansky, P. 1993. "Scholars, Sailors, and Peddlers of Influence at Civilization's Edge: A review of W. Burkert, *The Orientalizing Revolution: Near Eastern Influence on Greek Culture in the Early Archaic Age* (1992), and S. P. Morris, *Daidalos and the Origins of Greek Art* (1992)." *Journal of Mediterranean Archeology* 6.2.239–45.

# Index

## DATE DUE